British Sociability in the
Long Eighteenth Century

Studies in the Eighteenth Century
2398-9904

This major series from Boydell & Brewer, published in association with the British Society for Eighteenth Century Studies, aims to bring into fruitful dialogue the different disciplines involved in all aspects of the study of the long eighteenth century (c.1660–1820). It publishes innovative volumes, singly or co-authored, on any topic in history, science, music, literature and the visual arts in any area of the world in the long eighteenth century and particularly encourages proposals that explore links among the disciplines, and which aim to develop new cross-disciplinary fields of enquiry.

Series editors: Ros Ballaster, University of Oxford, UK; Matthew Grenby, Newcastle University, UK; Robert D. Hume, Penn State University, USA; Mark Knights, University of Warwick, UK; Renaud Morieux, University of Cambridge, UK

Previously published:

Material Enlightenment: Women Writers and the Science of Mind, 1770–1830, Joanna Wharton, 2018

Celebrity Culture and the Myth of Oceania in Britain, 1770–1823, Ruth Scobie, 2019

British Sociability in the Long Eighteenth Century

Challenging the Anglo-French Connection

Edited by
Valérie Capdeville and Alain Kerhervé

THE BOYDELL PRESS

© Contributors 2019

All Rights Reserved. Except as permitted under current legislation no part of this work may be photocopied, stored in a retrieval system, published, performed in public, adapted, broadcast, transmitted, recorded or reproduced in any form or by any means, without the prior permission of the copyright owner

First published 2019
Paperback edition 2024
The Boydell Press, Woodbridge

ISBN 978 1 78327 359 1 (Hardback)
ISBN 978 1 83765 128 3 (Paperback)

The Boydell Press is an imprint of Boydell & Brewer Ltd
PO Box 9, Woodbridge, Suffolk IP12 3DF, UK
and of Boydell & Brewer Inc.
668 Mt Hope Avenue, Rochester, NY 14620–2731, USA
website: www.boydellandbrewer.com

A CIP catalogue record for this book is available
from the British Library

The publisher has no responsibility for the continued existence or accuracy of URLs for external or third-party internet websites referred to in this book, and does not guarantee that any content on such websites is, or will remain, accurate or appropriate

Contents

List of illustrations	vii
List of contributors	ix
Foreword by Michèle Cohen	xiii
Acknowledgements	xvi
Introduction *Valérie Capdeville and Alain Kerhervé*	1

Part 1 Emergence of new political and social practices — 5

1. 'Restoration' England and the history of sociability
   Brian Cowan — 7

2. Mapping sociability on Restoration townscapes
   Marie-Madeleine Martinet — 25

3. Club sociability and the emergence of new 'sociable' practices
   Valérie Capdeville — 45

4. The tea-table, women and gossip in early eighteenth-century Britain
   Markman Ellis — 69

Part 2 Competing models of sociability — 89

5. 'Amateurs' vs connoisseurs in French and English academies of painting
   Elisabeth Martichou — 91

6. Masonic connections and rivalries between France and Britain
   Pierre-Yves Beaurepaire — 109

7. Competing models of sociability: Smollett's repossession of an ailing British body
   Annick Cossic-Péricarpin — 127

8 A theory of British epistolary sociability?
Alain Kerhervé   145

9 Gender and the practices of polite sociability in late eighteenth-century Edinburgh
Jane Rendall   163

Part 3 **Paradoxes of British sociability**   183

10 In company and out: the public/private selves of Johnson and Boswell
Allan Ingram   185

11 Friendship and unsociable sociability in eighteenth-century literature
Emrys Jones   199

12 The anti-social convivialist: toasting and resistance to sociability
Ian Newman   219

13 Sociability and the Glorious Revolution: a dubious connection in Burke's philosophy
Norbert Col   237

14 Respectability vs political agency: a dilemma for British radical societies
Rémy Duthille   251

Conclusion
Valérie Capdeville   271

Bibliography   275

Index   295

Illustrations

Figure 1. Genealogy of the Russell family and map of associated London place names (from Georgian Cities http://www.18thc.cities.paris-sorbonne.fr) — 30

Figure 2. A strip map by John Ogilby, *Britannia* (1675) — 33

Figure 3. Frontispiece of John Ogilby's *Britannia* (1675) — 34

Figure 4. *Gresham College*, by George Vertue (1740) — 35

Figure 5. *Byrsa Londinensis, vulgo The Royall Exchange of London* (1644), by Wenceslaus Hollar (1607–77). (Royal Collection Trust / © Her Majesty Queen Elizabeth II, 2018) — 36

Figure 6. Sutton Nicholls, *The Monument to the Great Fire of London, 1671–76* (c. 1754). (Courtesy of the Lewis Walpole Library, Yale University) — 38

Figure 7. Robert Hooke, *Picture Box* (1694) — 41

Figure 8. *Members of the Society of Dilettanti*, by William Say (printmaker, 1812–16), after Joshua Reynolds (1777–78). (Courtesy of the Lewis Walpole Library, Yale University) — 65

Figure 9. *The Tea-Table*, c. 1710. (Courtesy of the Lewis Walpole Library, Yale University) — 83

The editors, contributors and publisher are grateful to all the institutions and persons listed for permission to reproduce the materials in which they hold copyright. Every effort has been made to trace the copyright holders; apologies are offered for any omission, and the publisher will be pleased to add any necessary acknowledgement in subsequent editions.

The publishers and editors acknowledge the
generous financial support of
the Université de Bretagne Occidentale

Notes on contributors

Pierre-Yves Beaurepaire is Professor of Early Modern History at the University of Côte d'Azur (France) and an honorary fellow of the Institut Universitaire de France. He chaired the 'Centre de la Méditerranée moderne et contemporaine'. His research concerns the history of the Enlightenment in France and Europe, freemasonry, sociability and networks in the eighteenth century. He is the author of fifteen books, among which are *Le Mythe de l'Europe française. Diplomatie, culture et sociabilités au temps des Lumières* (Paris, 2007) ; *Echec au roi. Irrespect, contestations et révoltes dans la France des Lumières* (Paris, 2015). He recently edited *La Communication en Europe de l'âge classique au siècle des Lumières* (Paris, 2014); *Religious Interactions in Europe and the Mediterranean World: Coexistence and Dialogue from Twelfth to the Twentieth Centuries* (London, 2017) with Katsumi Fukasawa and Benjamin Kaplan; *Moving Scenes: The Circulation of Music and Theatre in Europe, 1700–1815* (Oxford, 2018) with Philippe Bourdin and Charlotta Wolff.

Valérie Capdeville is a Senior Lecturer in British History and Civilisation at the University of Paris 13 (France). She has specialised in the social and cultural history of British clubs and sociability in the eighteenth century. She is the author of *L'Age d'or des clubs londoniens (1730–1784)* (Paris, 2008) and she co-edited *La Sociabilité en France et en Grande-Bretagne au siècle des Lumières*, vol. 3. *Les Espaces de sociabilité* (Paris, 2014) with Eric Francalanza. She is currently working on the exportation of the British club model to the American colonies (1720–70). She is the co-founder of the GIS Sociabilités/Sociability in the Long Eighteenth Century (an international Research Interest Group) and the President of its Scientific Council.

Michèle Cohen is Emeritus Professor in Humanities at Richmond American International University in London. She works on education, gender and national character. She is the author of *Fashioning Masculinity: National Identity and Language in the Eighteenth Century* (Abingdon,

1996) and co-edited *English masculinities 1660–1800* (London, 1999) with Tim Hitchcock. More recently, she has been focusing on the education of both sexes, and has published several articles on the role of conversation in the education of males and females in social and domestic spaces. Her current project is a book on the education and fashioning of the Lady and the Gentleman in eighteenth-century England.

Norbert Col is Professor of British History and Literature at the University of Southern Brittany, Lorient (France). He has specialised in the history of ideas, mostly around Edmund Burke and Jonathan Swift. He is the author of *À la Recherche du conservatisme britannique: Historiographie, britannicité, modernité (XVIIe–XVIIIe siècles)* (Rennes, 2007) and co-edited *La Sociabilité en France et en Grande-Bretagne au siècle des Lumières*, vol. 4 : *Utopie, individu et société : la sociabilité en question* (Paris, 2015) with Allan Ingram.

Annick Cossic-Péricarpin is Professor of English at the University of Western Brittany, Brest (France). She is the author of *Bath au XVIIIe siècle: les fastes d'une cité palladienne* (Rennes, 2000) and of an annotated edition of *The New Bath Guide by Christopher Anstey* (Oxford, 2010). She also co-edited *Spas in Britain and in France in the Eighteenth and Nineteenth Centuries* (Newcastle, 2006) and is the series editor of 'Transversales' (Paris), for which she co-edited three volumes of *La Sociabilité en France et en Grande-Bretagne au siècle des Lumières* (vol. 1, 2012; vol. 2, 2013; vol. 5, 2016). She is the co-founder and Director of the GIS Sociabilités/Sociability in the Long Eighteenth Century (an international Research Interest Group).

Brian Cowan is an Associate Professor at McGill University (Montreal) and holds the Canada Research Chair in Early Modern British History. He studies the social and cultural history of ideas in early modern Britain and Europe. He is the author of *The Social Life of Coffee: The Emergence of the British Coffeehouse* (New Haven, CT, 2005) and of *The State Trial of Doctor Henry Sacheverell* (Chichester, 2012). He is currently working on the politics of celebrity in Britain (1650–1800).

Rémy Duthille is a Senior Lecturer in British Civilisation at the University of Bordeaux Montaigne (France). He works on political discourse in Britain in the late eighteenth century (especially Richard Price). His current research concerns political sociability, with a special focus on political drinking and toasting. He is the author of *Le Discours radical en Grande-Bretagne, 1768–1789* (Oxford, 2017) and the co-editor of 'Sociabilité et convivialité en Europe et en Amérique du Nord, XVIIe–XVIIIe siècles', *Lumières* 21 (2013) with Jean Mondot and Cécile Révauger.

Markman Ellis is Professor of Eighteenth-Century Studies at Queen Mary University of London. He is the author of *The Politics of Sensibility* (Cambridge, 1996), *The History of Gothic Fiction* (Edinburgh, 2000) and *The Coffee-House: a Cultural History* (London, 2004). He edited *Eighteenth-Century Coffee House Culture* (London, 2006) and *Tea and the Tea-Table in Eighteenth-Century England* (London, 2010). He recently co-authored *Empire of Tea* (London, 2014) and is now working on the sociability of science and literature in mid-eighteenth century London.

Allan Ingram is Emeritus Professor of English at the University of Northumbria. He has specialised in eighteenth-century literature and medicine, worked on Boswell and Johnson, and on topics such as melancholy, insanity and depression. He is the author of *The Madhouse of Language: Writing and Reading Madness in the Eighteenth Century* (Abingdon, 1992) and co-authored *Cultural Constructions of Madness in Eighteenth-Century Writing* (Basingstoke, 2005). He has published an edition of Jonathan Swift's *Gulliver's Travels* (Calgary, 2012). He also co-edited the four-volume *Depression and Melancholy, 1660–1800* (London, 2012) with Leigh Wetherhall-Dickson, and *La Sociabilité en France et en Grande-Bretagne au siècle des Lumières*, vol. 4 : 'Utopie, individu et société : la sociabilité en question' (Paris, 2015) with Norbert Col.

Emrys D. Jones is Lecturer in Eighteenth-Century Literature and Culture at King's College London. He completed his Ph.D. at the University of Cambridge, his thesis examining representations of friendship in eighteenth-century political discourse. This research gave rise to his first monograph, *Friendship and Allegiance in Eighteenth-Century Literature* (Basingstoke, 2013). He is co-editor of the journal *Literature and History*. He also co-edited *Intimacy and Celebrity in Eighteenth-Century Literature: Public Interiors* (Basingstoke, 2018) with Victoria Joule.

Alain Kerhervé is Professor of British studies at the University of Western Brittany, Brest (France) and the current Director of research unit HCTI (Héritages et Constructions dans le Texte et l'Image). He has specialised in the theory and practice of letter-writing in eighteenth-century England. He is the author of *Polite Letters: The Correspondence of Mary Delany (1700–1788) and Francis North, Lord Guilford (1704–1790)* (Newcastle, 2009), of *The Ladies Complete Letter-Writer (1763)* (Newcastle) and of *Memoirs of the Court of George III. Volume 2. Mary Delany (1700–1788) and the Court of George III* (London, 2015), and co-edited *La Sociabilité en France et en Grande-Bretagne au Siècle des Lumières : l'émergence d'un nouveau modèle de société*, vol. 5. *Sociabilités et esthétique de la marge* (Paris, 2016) with Annick Cossic. He is the co-founder of the GIS Sociabilités/Sociability in the Long Eighteenth Century.

Elisabeth Martichou is a Senior Lecturer in British Civilisation at the University of Paris 13 (France). She has specialised in art history and more particularly in art theory in eighteenth-century England. She has published several articles on Joshua Reynolds and on artistic sociability, including 'Le peintre-gentleman : un modèle de sociabilité et ses variations dans l'Angleterre du dix-huitième siècle', in *Artistes, savants et amateurs: Art et Sociabilité au XVIIIe siècle (1715–1815)*, ed. Jessica L. Fripp, Amandine Gorse, Nathalie Manceau and Nina Struckmeyer (Paris, 2016), pp. 29–37.

Marie-Madeleine Martinet is an Honorary Professor at Sorbonne-Université (France) and the Director of research group 'Cultures, Sociétés et Technologies de l'Information'. She has specialised in historical visual culture, the aesthetics of landscape and space in English culture, and e-media. She has published several books: *Art et nature en Grande-Bretagne au XVIIIe siècle* (Paris, 1980); *Le Voyage d'Italie dans les littératures européennes* (Paris, 1996) and worked extensively on digital imaging and aesthetic virtual models, which recently led to the creation of the *Georgian Cities* website (http://www.18thc-cities.paris-sorbonne.fr, 2014).

Ian Newman is an Assistant Professor at the University of Notre Dame (Indiana, USA). He works at the intersections of literature, song, politics and urban space across the eighteenth and nineteenth centuries in Britain and Ireland. He is co-editor with Oskar Cox Jensen and David Kennerley of *Charles Dibdin and Late Georgian Culture* (Oxford, 2018). He is also the author of *The Romantic Tavern: Literature and Conviviality in the Age of Revolution* (Cambridge, 2019).

Jane Rendall is an Honorary Fellow of the History Department and the Centre for Eighteenth Century Studies at the University of York. She has worked on the history of the Scottish Enlightenment and currently researches women's activities and writing in late eighteenth- and early nineteenth-century Britain, especially Scotland. She is the author of *The Origins of Modern Feminism: Women in Britain, France, and the United States, 1780–1860* (Basingstoke, 1985) and other works. She has co-edited various volumes on women's history and gender politics, including *Gender, War and Politics: Transatlantic Perspectives, 1775–1830* (Basingstoke, 2010) and, most recently, *The New Biographical Dictionary of Scottish Women* (Edinburgh, 2018).

Foreword
Michèle Cohen

ENCOUNTERING the concept of sociability was for me a kind of magical portal into history. I had been working on 'conversation in the eighteenth century', originally to understand why French conversation was such an important feature of eighteenth-century gentlemen and ladies' education. When reading the *Spectator* and L. E. Klein's Ph.D. thesis 'The Rise of "Politeness" in England, 1660–1715', I realised that conversation was not just talk but was the ultimate expression of a set of practices performed within a specific and crucial context, sociability. In its most essential meaning, it refers to the ability of people who are not necessarily related by blood or alliance to relate to each other in society. While the term sociability is mostly used by historians, it is now virtually taken for granted, due to the pervasiveness of social media. Thinking about the similarities and differences between sociability in the eighteenth and the twenty-first centuries, I was struck by what these can tell us about human interaction.

What struck me most about sociability, when I first began to study it, was its aim to be an 'ideological space' where social equality could be practised despite other inequalities.[1] Sociability in the eighteenth century had to be tempered by politeness and the requirement to observe rules of *bienséance* – tact, civility and putting the needs of the group before one's own. In our own time, modern social media too provide a virtually infinite space for people to communicate, regardless of race, class or religion, as long as the technology is available. In theory, social media allow sharing and the conquering of difference and selfishness. In practice, as they develop, issues about observing propriety in the face of 'trolling'[2] behaviour have come to the fore. These contradictions and how the people involved negotiate them

---

[1] Daniel Gordon *Citizens without Sovereignty: Equality and Sociability in French Thought, 1670–1789* (Princeton, 1994), 7.
[2] Internet slang defined as 'Unleashing one or more cynical or sarcastic remarks on an innocent by-stander, because it's the internet and, hey, you can.' https://www.lifewire.com/what-is-internet-trolling-3485891.

are central to all forms of sociability in any age, and they are a central focus of this book.

This collection of essays is not an attempt to bring together a variety of harmonious views on sociability. Rather, while it 'aims to investigate the origins and evolutions of sociability in Britain in the long eighteenth century', as stated by the editors in their introduction, it argues that 'a British model of sociability progressively took shape from the Restoration period and developed throughout the eighteenth century, defining itself thanks to exchanges and tensions with France and *expressing itself through paradoxes that both reflected and constructed the national character*'.[3]

What also makes the volume unique and unusual is that it arises from a group of French and British scholars, with whom I have been working for a number of years, arguing that there is a 'British sociability'. We want to extricate sociability from its position as metonymically French and demonstrate that there is a British sociability – a project initiated by Roy Porter's ground-breaking and influential *Enlightenment: Britain and the Creation of the Modern World.*[4]

The first question that came to mind was how the sum of the chapters grouped together in this collection demonstrates what it was that made sociability in Britain distinctively British. More than comparing British and French practices of sociability, which might have been instructive but perhaps less stimulating or original, they focus, rather, on how British sociability's very practices fit into the broader culture, while at the same time serving as analytical tools throwing light on aspects of that culture unavailable in more conventional analyses. One example is the chapter on tea. Is there anything more British than tea? Tea and its social practices can be an analytical tool to help understand the specifically British gendered practices of sociability: in Britain, the public sphere was marked 'masculine', and both the coffeehouse and the tavern, its main sites of sociability, were predominantly homosocial. By contrast, tea was marked 'feminine', although the company was 'mixed', as highlighted in visual representations of the tea table. The chapter also brilliantly links the material culture of 'the polite equipment' of the tea table to the key role of women in patterns and practices of consumption. The sociability around tea, as different from the coffeehouse and the tavern, delineates one crucial aspect of the British contours of sociability: for it was at the tea table that women's 'intellectual sociability', as Roger Chartier called it, could take place: as one of Mrs Delany's letters illustrates, 'I am just

---

[3] My emphasis.
[4] Roy Porter, *Enlightenment Britain and the Creation of the Modern World'* (London, 2000).

come from the tea-table, where we [a number of ladies] have had a warm dispute occasioned by Mme de Sévigné's *Letters*.'[5]

One of the most instructive aspects of the book is that it shows that sociability changed over time and thus highlights not only that it was a living practice but that it was protean without losing its core values, so that apparently contradictory practices could co-exist without being antithetical.

Thus, while Addison's ideal sociability was defined by politeness, heterosexual conversation and exchange of opinion similar to French salons, sociability as it developed in Britain over the course of the century included a conviviality whose spiritual home was the homosocial tavern and coffeehouse. This distances it not just from the 'dinners' of Parisian salons but also from the Addisonian model, because its emphasis was less on the exchange of rational opinion than on warm-hearted good humour. At the same time, even though convivial practices developed distinctive characteristics in the later part of the century, this does not in my view challenge the Addisonian model of sociability. Rather, the ability of sociability was precisely to retain essential features even as its performance required contradictory forms of expression. Demonstrating this ability is one of the main achievements of this collection of essays.

Take, for example, sociability's core feature of collectivity: it is manifested in the foundation of the London Corresponding Society, a plebeian society composed of artisans, 'even if its forms of sociability were enmeshed in contradictions of several kinds'; in the early formation of clubs as part of the realisation that 'meeting spaces' for free discussion and debate might be 'a useful instrument to influence public opinion'; in the Society of Dilettanti, all of whose members had already shared one of the most important male educational institutions of the British eighteenth century, the Grand Tour; in sociability networks' connections to urban spaces; in the multiple roles of women in Edinburgh's expansion of its associational worlds in the early nineteenth century; and in the Britishness of the epistolary manual, a guide to the sociable 'art of living in society'.

The essays in *British Sociability in the Long Eighteenth Century* explore one of the most significant conceptualisations of civil society in the eighteenth century and provide a thoughtful and multifaceted investigation of its failures as well as successes. In this sense, it is a volume for today's concerns too.

---

[5] Roger Chartier, 'Loisir et sociabilité: lire à haute voix dans l'Europe moderne', *Littératures classiques* 12 (1990), 131. Mrs Pendarves (later Mrs Delany) to Mrs Dewes, 17 December 1740, *The Autobiography and Correspondence of Mary Granville, Mrs Delany*, 1st series, vol. 2 (1862), 135.

Acknowledgements

We should first like to thank our respective research laboratories HCTI (Heritage and Construction in Text and Image) and PLEIADE (Multi-disciplinary Research Centre for Literature, Languages, Humanities and Social Sciences), which have both strongly supported this project and enhanced our fruitful collaboration. This book started life as a set of international workshops and conference held in 2014–15, co-organised by the University of Western Brittany (UBO Brest) and the University of Paris 13, which brought together a group of British, North American and French scholars working on British sociability in the long eighteenth century. This project not only stimulated scholarly exchanges between researchers from various disciplinary fields but it also strengthened institutional collaboration while promoting an intellectual and convivial sociability within our expanding network. Special thanks are due to Professor Annick Cossic (UBO), who has been the instigating and steering force of our collective venture since 2009. We should also like to thank Professor Mark Knights, a keynote speaker at one of our workshops in 2014 and an active member of our research network since, for encouraging us to publish in this new series dedicated to eighteenth-century studies. We are also thankful to Professor Michèle Cohen for accepting to write the foreword of this volume and for her precious, insightful advice from the beginning of the book project. We should, of course, like to thank Mari Shullaw, Commissioning Editor of the 'Eighteenth Century Studies and Modern History' series at Boydell & Brewer, for her constant enthusiasm and support throughout the project. Finally, we are particularly thankful to the contributors of this volume for keeping to a tight schedule and making our task much easier, but above all for making this study an original and rich insight into British sociability in the long eighteenth century.

Introduction
Valérie Capdeville and Alain Kervé

IN ENGLISH, the primary definition of sociability dates back to the fifteenth century, when it designated 'the character or quality of being sociable, friendly disposition or intercourse' (*Oxford English Dictionary*). In France, the word *sociabilité* was first used in 1665, and was later defined in the *Dictionnaire de l'Académie française* in 1798 as 'l'aptitude de l'espèce humaine à vivre en société' and 'l'aptitude de l'individu à fréquenter agréablement ses semblables'.[1] From the seventeenth century, the theories of natural rights and social contract included the essential issue of people's propensity to join into society. While in *The Leviathan* (1651) Thomas Hobbes pointed out a number of limits to man's sociability in a state of nature: man's selfishness, man's cunning and intellectual strength, man's quarrelsome nature, in *An Essay Concerning the True Original Extent and End of Civil Government*, John Locke justified man's willingness to 'join in society with others' by his desire for self-preservation.[2] In 1711, Joseph Addison offered a more precise, refined definition of a model of sociability:

> Man is said to be a Sociable Animal, and, as an Instance of it, we may observe, that we take all Occasions and Pretences of forming ourselves into those little Nocturnal Assemblies, which are commonly known by the name of Clubs. When a Sett of Men find themselves agree in any Particular, tho' never so trivial, they establish themselves into a kind of Fraternity, and meet once or twice a Week, upon the Account of such a Fantastick Resemblance. ... When Men are thus knit together, by Love of Society, not a Spirit of Faction, and do not meet to censure or annoy those that are absent, but to enjoy one another: When they are thus combined for their own Improvement, or for the Good of others, or at least to relax themselves from the Business of the Day, by an innocent and

---

[1] *Dictionnaire de l'Académie françoise* (1798), fifth edition (Paris, 1798), 577.
[2] John Locke, *An Essay Concerning the True Original Extent and End of Civil Government* (1690), chap. IX, 'Of the Ends of Political Society and Government'.

chearful Conversation, there may be something very useful in these little Institutions and Establishments.³

Addison's stance helped the German sociologist Georg Simmel to define a somewhat artificial model of sociability in which the individual renounces his own 'personal features' to experience the pleasure of collective interaction as a goal in itself.⁴ Simmel's theories informed research into sociability throughout most of the twentieth century. They were afterwards further complemented by Habermas's widely discussed theories of the public and private spheres, which also helped to differentiate several modes of sociability.

New approaches to the evolution of social bonds and social networks have been proposed since the start of the twenty-first century. They offer new, more complex visions of a British sociability based on networks and London social institutions⁵ and also more marginal, peripheral examples.⁶ A large place has been allotted to studies of literary sociability, laying the emphasis on the role of conversation and of literary exchanges and networks from early modern times to the Romantic period.⁷

Additionally, a major contribution to the study of sociability was the multi-volume publication *La Sociabilité en France et en Grande-Bretagne au Siècle des Lumières* (Paris, 2012–17). The main purpose of this series of six volumes was to establish links, to highlight differences and to identify possible influences on both sides of the Channel: while the French Enlightenment generated new practices of sociability,⁸ the British model was developing a character of its own. This collective work, to which several authors in the present volume contributed, has allowed the exploration of a number of social practices, via a comparative approach, through the therapeutic and aesthetic aspects of social interaction and the common

---

3   *Spectator*, no. 9 (10 March 1711).
4   See Ileana Baird, *Social Networks in the Long Eighteenth Century: Clubs, Literary Salons* (Newcastle-upon-Tyne, 2014), 2.
5   Baird, *Social Networks in the Long Eighteenth Century*.
6   Scott Breuninger and David Burrow, *Sociability and Cosmopolitanism: Social Bonds on the Fringes of the Enlightenment* (London, 2012, 2015).
7   Gillian Russell and Clara Tuite, *Romantic Sociability: Social Networks and Literary Culture in Britain, 1770–1840* (Cambridge, 2006); Jon Mee, *Conversable Worlds: Literature, Contention, and Community 1762–1830* (Oxford, 2011); Amy Prendergast, *Literary Salons Across Britain and Ireland in the Long Eighteenth Century* (Basingstoke, 2015); Paul Trolander, *Literary Sociability in Early Modern England: The Epistolary Record* (Lanham, 2014).
8   See, for instance, Patrick Coleman, *Anger, Gratitude, and the Enlightenment Writer* (New York, 2011), Ch. 1: 'Anger, Gratitude, and Enlightenment Sociability', 1–32.

and specific features of spaces of sociability in France and in Britain; and the investigation of ideas of a crisis of sociability, marginal expressions of sociability and forms of resistance to sociability.

Sociability is both a value and a social practice, yet it is not universal. The ability to live in society, as well as the degree of sociability of an individual, seems to depend on his culture and on the character of his nation. According to the eighteenth-century Scottish anthropologist and historian William Robertson, 'the dispositions and manners of men are formed by their situation, and arise from the state of society in which they live'.[9] The same principle was re-assessed by contemporary French historian Michel Morineau, who posited that the ability to live in society was an ability to live in '*one* given society', judging that individual as well as collective sociability depended on the character of that particular society.[10]

In a major contribution to the historiography of French thought in the Enlightenment period, Daniel Gordon argues that by mid-century a 'politics of sociability' was trying to replace traditional conceptions of political power with manners, politeness becoming the new discipline.[11] Indeed, polite sociability became the symbol of civilisation and, as Dena Goodman claims, French men of letters or thinkers 'forged the commonplace that France was the most civilized because it was the most sociable and most polite of nations'. As a consequence, French culture was represented as 'the leading edge of civilization'.[12]

The French model of sociability was built thanks to the idealisation of the Parisian salon and the privileged role it granted to women.[13] Contrary to what happened in England, woman occupied a choice position in the French public sphere: she was considered as indispensable to the refinement of manners, to politeness and sociability. The French salon was a form of sociability that allowed the mixed conversation of the sexes and

[9] William Robertson, *The History of the Discovery and Settlement of America* [1777] (New York, 1857), 131.
[10] 'L'aptitude à vivre en société [...] est aptitude à vivre dans *une* société déterminée. De sorte que la sociabilité individuelle et collective est informée et investie, en chaque occurrence, par les caractères de cette société', Michel Morineau, 'La Douceur d'être inclus', in *Sociabilité, pouvoirs et société. Actes du colloque de Rouen, 24–26 nov. 1983*, ed. Françoise Thélamon (Rouen, 1987), 30.
[11] Daniel L. Gordon, 'The Idea of Sociability in Pre-Revolutionary France' (Ph.D. dissertation, University of Chicago, 1990), 72–3; *Citizens Without Sovereignty: Equality and Sociability in French Thought, 1670–1789* (Princeton, 1994).
[12] Dena Goodman, *The Republic of Letters: A Cultural History of the French Enlightenment* (Ithaca, NY, 1996), 4.
[13] See Antoine Lilti, *Le Monde des salons, sociabilité et mondanité à Paris au XVIIIe siècle* (Paris, 2005).

in which woman reigned: 'The French Enlightenment was grounded in a female-centred mixed-gender sociability that gendered French culture, the Enlightenment and civilization as feminine.'[14]

Therefore, the present volume aims to investigate the origins and evolutions of sociability in Britain in the long eighteenth century by challenging the hegemony of the French model of sociability and establishing the ways and means by which a form of national sociability evolved in the British Isles in the long eighteenth century.[15] It examines a number of new primary sources in order to further analyse British sociability as it developed over the long eighteenth century. They include a number of public documents on the working of such institutions as the London Academy or the Masonic lodges, conduct manuals and letter-writers, maps, paintings, essays (on politics and aesthetics), travel accounts, medical treatises, newspapers and literary sources (poems, satires) as well as private archival material. Moreover, although the global approach is historical and, in several places, historiographical, it includes many other disciplinary fields, such as geography, lexicography, epistolography… It also raises a number of epistemological issues, since it questions the use of certain sources and analytical tools to further elaborate on the notion of sociability. A British model of sociability progressively took shape from the Restoration period and developed throughout the eighteenth century, defining itself thanks to exchanges and tensions with France and expressing itself through paradoxes that both reflected and constructed the national character.

---

[14] Goodman, *The Republic of Letters*, 6.
[15] Through the example of the London club, Valérie Capdeville demonstrates that this exclusive homosocial institution had a prominent role in the questioning of a French-inspired model of sociability and in the shaping of a 'home-made' sociability that mirrored the characteristics and paradoxes of the English character. See Capdeville, 'London clubs or the invention of a home-made sociability', in *La Sociabilité en France et en Grande-Bretagne au siècle des Lumières: L'émergence d'un nouveau modèle de société*. Tome 3: *Les Espaces de sociabilité*, ed. Valérie Capdeville and Eric Francalanza (Paris, 2014), 75–100.

Part 1
Emergence of new political and social practices

THE FIRST section, entitled '**Emergence of new political and social practices**', traces the foundations of British sociability to identify when and due to what factors a different kind of sociability emerged in different parts of Britain. Several key examples provide a vivid picture of a burgeoning social life increasingly organised around distinctive social institutions and driven by new social norms and behaviours.

Tracing the origins of sociability back to the Restoration provides a starting point for defining the nature of sociability, and the historiographical approach chosen by **Brian Cowan** in the opening chapter helps one to understand the connection between the history of sociability and politics. Arguing that the history of post-Restoration sociabilities must be a social history of politics, the author shows that the development of many new social spaces (coffeehouses, clubs, theatres, pleasure gardens, etc.) was integrally related to the political divisions that helped to contribute to the development of political parties, the most important political innovation of the Restoration era.

The establishment of a new and distinctly modern regime of British sociability was also determined by spatial factors. This aspect is emphasised in the second chapter, which identifies discrepancies as well as coordination between the urban environment and social structure. Supported by some new cartographic and geopositioning methods, **Marie-Madeleine Martinet**'s objective is to highlight the correspondence between urban design and social functions, with buildings designed for specific traditional activities. At the same time, the spatial turn adopted by this analysis reveals various emerging networks of hidden economic and scientific sociability.

In fact, the formation of social networks and the shaping of British practices of sociability were very much stimulated by the emergence and development of these new social institutions. **Valérie Capdeville** argues in chapter 3 that the first gentlemen's clubs, which multiplied in London from the Restoration years into the reign of Queen Anne, answered new 'sociable' aspirations in post-Restoration Britain. The success of club sociability and the development of its polite and exclusive character not only depended on the emergence of an 'alternative political nation' but also on the rise of a commercial society and an urban culture that were specifically British. The author also demonstrates the ambiguous function of club sociability in the fashioning of the British gentleman, arguing that the London club can be considered a key instrument of both self and social construction for its members, thereby emphasising the importance of social performance and gender identification.

Tea drinking was strongly associated with female sociability, not only through the performance of tea serving, but also through related practices of conversation, reading polite literature and the culture of visiting. As such, the idea of the tea-table and its associated social event was constructed in culture as a location of feminised manners, even when the company gathered there was heterosocial, a major distinction from the coffeehouse or the club, which were homosocial spaces. **Markman Ellis**'s chapter 4 closes this first section and analyses the tea-table as an item of furniture, a social event and an idea about sociability, in the context of a significant increase, in the first four decades of the eighteenth century, of both tea consumption and discourses on tea.

Chapter 1
'Restoration' England and the history of sociability

Brian Cowan

THE RESTORATION has always held a somewhat awkward place in the broader narrative of English history. On the one hand, it has been seen as the endpoint to a turbulent Stuart century riven by civil wars and revolutionary regime changes. William of Orange's invasion by invitation and the Glorious Revolution that gave him the crowns to England, Scotland and Ireland is remarkable, in this perspective, only because the constitutional settlement which it provoked happened to endure for much longer than that of the previous Stuart regimes. Because of the significance accorded here to the Glorious Revolution, this perspective has mainly been adopted by political historians, particularly those with Whiggish sympathies. Its most famous articulation may be found in Thomas Babington Macaulay's *History of England from the Accession of James II* (1848), but it remains alive and well in the work of contemporary historians such as Steven Pincus and Tim Harris.[1]

On the other hand, the Restoration era is sometimes understood not as the ending but, rather, as the beginning of a new era: the *soi disant* 'long eighteenth century'. Here, the Restoration era inaugurates the construction of a distinctly English old regime, one which managed to survive the age of the French revolution and persisted until at least the passing of the First Reform Act of 1832, and perhaps even longer than that. While the most vociferous promulgator of this argument for a long eighteenth-century English old regime has been Jonathan Clark, for whom the pillars of eighteenth-century society were the monarchy, the established church and the aristocracy, he has found unlikely fellow travellers amongst a host of

---

[1] Thomas Babington Macaulay, *History of England from the Accession of James II*, 5 vols. (London, 1848); Steven Pincus, *1688: The First Modern Revolution* (New Haven, 2009); Tim Harris, *Restoration: Charles II and His Kingdoms* (London, 2005) and *Revolution: The Great Crisis of the British Monarchy, 1685–1720* (London, 2007).

cultural and social historians who may disagree with Clark's argument for Anglican monarcho-aristocratic hegemony but who nevertheless see lines of continuity from the restoration of the Stuarts in 1660 until at least the long reign of George III.[2] Historians such as Clark and Roy Porter disagreed deeply about the nature of English society in the long eighteenth century, but they agreed that the period began not in 1700, or even 1688–89, but decades earlier, with the Restoration in 1660.[3]

For historians of sociability, the Restoration is most commonly fit into the long eighteenth century paradigm. Very few social or cultural histories of eighteenth-century England begin in 1700: they prefer to begin their story forty years earlier, with the Restoration. The same is true (perhaps even more so) for literary historians, for whom the Restoration is the first chapter in a long eighteenth century that ends with the age of Romanticism and Revolution.[4] Why should this be? What is it about the later decades of the seventeenth century that make them seem to 'fit' better with the succeeding eighteenth century than with the 1600s in which they are chronologically located? Did the political counter-revolution that ended England's short-lived republican experiment have any lasting effect on the configuration of social life that would persist for the next century and a half or longer? This chapter addresses and queries this peculiar historiographic conjuncture and the questions it raises.

The Restoration was indeed an important watershed moment in the history of English sociability, but the significance of the Restoration era lies less in the new social formations of the period than in the new political tensions created by the restoration of monarchical government and a re-established Church of England after two decades in which neither had existed. The

---

[2] J. C. D. Clark, *English Society, 1660–1832: Religion, Ideology and Politics During the Ancien Régime* (Cambridge, 2000).

[3] Roy Porter, *The Creation of the Modern World: The Untold Story of the British Enlightenment* (New York, 2000), esp. 24–33; Roy Porter, *English Society in the Eighteenth Century*, second edition (Harmondsworth, 1990). For Porter's engagement with Clark's works, see his 'English Society in the Eighteenth Century Revisited', in *British Politics and Society from Walpole to Pitt 1742–1789* (Basingstoke, 1990), 29–52 and 'Georgian Britain: An Ancien Régime', *British Journal for Eighteenth-Century Studies* 15 (1992), 141–44. See also Joanna Innes, 'Jonathan Clark, Social History and England's "Ancien Régime"', *Past & Present* 115 (1987), 165–200.

[4] This is a traditional periodisation of English literary history that begins in the later Victorian era, if not earlier. See, e.g., Leslie Stephen's 1903 Ford Lectures: *English Literature and Society in the Eighteenth Century* (London, 1904) and Alexandre Beljame, *Le Public et les hommes de lettres en Angleterre au dix-huitième siècle, 1660–1744* (Paris, 1881).

Restoration failure to resolve the pre-existing religious and political conflicts left by the preceding decades of civil war and revolution created a new set of social tensions, and restraints on conflict, as the memory of the violent and unstable interregnum decades would remain difficult to erase. The decades after 1660 set the template for an uneasy coexistence between rival political and religious world-views that would be characteristic of the social life of England's long eighteenth century.

If one integrates political history into the history of sociability, then the Restoration era can be understood as truly distinctive. In recent decades, historians of the Tudor–Stuart era have articulated an innovative social history of politics that is also (and equally) a new political history of English society.[5] Despite their growing appreciation of the importance of the 'fiscal-military' state for English society, eighteenth-century historians have not articulated an equivalent socio-political history for the post-Restoration era.[6] The transformative role of the state, the many competing visions of how to order the state, and the various interests who conspired to control or guide the power of the state, all helped to change the nature of sociability from 1660 onwards.

The most important political innovation of the Restoration era was the political party. The divisions between Whigs and Tories that began with the Exclusion Bill debates of the late 1670s would lead to the primary ideological contest of the long eighteenth century.[7] The Restoration origins of party politics can therefore shed light on the some of the key structures

---

[5] Key works here include: Paul Griffiths, Adam Fox and Steve Hindle, eds., *The Experience of Authority in Early Modern England* (New York, 1996); Steve Hindle, *The State and Social Change in Early Modern England c. 1550–1640* (Basingstoke, 2000); and Michael Braddick, *State Formation in Early Modern England, c. 1550–1700* (Cambridge, 2000).

[6] John Brewer, *The Sinews of Power: War, Money and the English State, 1688–1783* (New York, 1989); Lawrence Stone, ed., *An Imperial State at War: Britain from 1689 to 1815* (London, 1994); important contributions have been made by historians such as Julian Hoppit, 'The Nation, the State, and the Industrial Revolution', *Journal of British Studies* 50, no. 2 (2011), 307–31, Hoppit, *Britain's Political Economies: Parliament and Economic Life, 1660–1800* (Cambridge, 2017) and Joanna Innes, *Inferior Politics: Social Problems and Social Policies in Eighteenth-Century Britain* (Oxford, 2009), but they have not had the same transformative impact on the history of the eighteenth century that the works of Tudor–Stuart social historians of politics have achieved.

[7] The Namierite vision of eighteenth-century politics as essentially interest based has now been almost thoroughly discredited. See Brian Cowan, 'Geoffrey Holmes and the Public Sphere: Augustan Historiography from Post-Namierite to the Post-Habermasian', *Parliamentary History* 28, no. 1 (2009), 166–78.

of sociability in the succeeding century. The development of many new social spaces (such as coffeehouses, clubs and dissenting conventicles) was integrally related to the political divisions that helped to contribute to the development of political parties; the political culture of partisanship also shaped sociable interactions in many of the characteristic public and private venues of the long eighteenth century, from theatres and pleasure gardens to country houses and their drawing rooms and tea-tables. The establishment of a new, and distinctly modern, regime of English sociability was a paradoxical result of the restoration of those two pillars of the traditional old regime, the monarchy and the established church.

Social history and the Restoration

Arguments for the innovative nature of post-Restoration sociability have mainly associated these supposed changes with claims for broader transformations in the social and/or cultural order experienced in the later seventeenth century. Three paradigms stand out as perhaps the most prominent arguments for the novelty of post-Restoration social relations. They are not necessarily distinct, and indeed are often presented as part of a general package of transformations that made the later seventeenth century a more modern society than the preceding Tudor–Stuart era.[8] Nevertheless, it is useful to unpack them each in turn. They include arguments for a long eighteenth-century consumer revolution and an associated urban renaissance; the rise of the bourgeois public sphere; and the emergence of a new culture of politeness.

The 1980s saw the publication of two key works that helped to articulate a new understanding of post-Restoration society (and sociability): the enormously influential collection of essays by John Brewer, Neil McKendrick and J. H. Plumb, *The Birth of a Consumer Society* (1982) and Peter Borsay's *The English Urban Renaissance* (1989). Both books crystallised arguments that had developed over the preceding decade.[9] Together, the

---

[8] See especially, John Brewer, *The Pleasures of the Imagination: English Culture in the Eighteenth Century* (London, 1997), which may be understood as a synthesis of the more specialised historiographies discussed in this section.

[9] John Brewer, Neil McKendrick and J. H. Plumb, eds., *The Birth of a Consumer Society: The Commercialization of Eighteenth-Century England* (London, 1982); Peter Borsay, *The English Urban Renaissance: Culture and Society in the Provincial Town 1660–1770* (Oxford, 1989) and Borsay, 'The English Urban Renaissance: The Development of Provincial Urban Culture, c. 1680–c. 1760', *Social History* 5 (1977), 581–603.

books presented a vision of post-Restoration society that was progressive, commercially oriented, increasingly urban dwelling and energised by a vibrant and expanding middle class. It was a perspective summarised by William Blackstone's characterisation of the English as 'a polite and commercial people' that was adopted by Paul Langford as the title for his contribution to the new Oxford History of England.[10]

The consumer revolution and the urban renaissance went hand in hand: the growth of towns was a sign of a flourishing economy in which an increasing variety and quantity of goods and services were offered for sale, and much of the changing character of urban life was related to these growing consumer options. While Borsay's work was devoted to studying the remarkable efflorescence of English urban culture in cities outside of London such as Bath, Birmingham, Bristol, Exeter, Liverpool, Manchester, Newcastle, Norwich, Preston, Shrewsbury, Tunbridge Wells and York, the cosmopolitan example of the metropolis (as well as other Enlightenment metropolises such as Paris and Rome) deeply influenced the cultural horizons of these provincial cities. London 'fully participated in the Urban Renaissance and in many respects led it'. In contrast to the supposedly inward focus of Tudor–Stuart urban life, the towns of England's post-Restoration urban renaissance 'looked outwards towards London and the continent'.[11]

They were also marked by the emergence of new, or more plentiful, commercial options for spending. A key aspect of the urban renaissance was the efflorescence of commercialised leisure possibilities as well as shopping venues. Towns throughout England saw the construction of new theatres; concert halls; pleasure gardens; spas, pump rooms and assembly halls; bookshops and libraries; as well as coffeehouses and other commercial eating and drinking spots such as chop houses and taverns. All of these developments are undoubtedly an important characteristic of post-Restoration urban life, but do they really constitute a decisive break with the past?

---

[10] William Blackstone, *Commentaries on the Laws of England*, 4 vols. (London, 1765–69), vol. 3, 326; Paul Langford, *A Polite and Commercial People: England 1727–1783* (Oxford, 1989).

[11] Borsay, *English Urban Renaissance*, x, 286 (quotes). On pre-Restoration English urban culture, see the many works of Robert Tittler, such as: *The Reformation and the Towns in England: Politics and Political Culture, c. 1540–1640* (Oxford, 1998); *Townspeople and Nation: English Urban Experiences, 1540–1640* (Stanford, 2002); and *The Face of the City: Civic Portraiture and Civic Identity in Early Modern England* (Manchester, 2013).

More recent histories of seventeenth-century consumer culture suggest that they do not. Instead, they have tended to emphasise the continuities between the earlier and the later seventeenth century. The theatres of Restoration London may indeed have been even less popular and less commercialised than those of the pre-civil war era, due to the monopolies held by the King's and the Duke's Companies and the higher prices that they charged for admission; in any case, the development of commercial theatre in provincial towns beyond London was a process that began well before the Restoration. Although the playhouses of London were shut down after 1649, theatrical culture and commercialised entertainment persisted through the puritanical 1650s.[12] Shopping and consumerism were hardly invented in 1660 and certainly were not new practices brought over to England by the restored Stuart court, as works by Joan Thirsk and Linda Levy Peck (amongst others) have demonstrated. The old shibboleth that the civil wars and interregnum regimes were so disruptive as to put a hold on English commercial development has now been discredited.[13] The spa culture and commercialised leisure industry in towns such as Bath and Tunbridge Wells predated the Restoration, even if they continued to develop further in succeeding years.[14] Coffee was known, if not commonly consumed, in early seventeenth-century England and coffeehouses were introduced and began to flourish in the 1650s, well before the Restoration.[15] Even before the invention of the coffeehouse in the mid-seventeenth century, commercialised drinking and sociability had already flourished for centuries in the

---

[12] Jessica Muns, 'Theatrical Culture 1: Politics and Theatre', in *The Cambridge Companion to English Literature 1650–1740* (Cambridge, 1998), 87; Siobhan Keenan, 'Provincial playing places and performances in early modern England, 1559–1625' (Ph.D. thesis, University of Warwick, 1999); Bernard Capp, *England's Culture Wars: Puritan Reformation and its Enemies in the Interregnum, 1649–1660* (Oxford, 2012).

[13] Joan Thirsk, *Economic Policy and Projects: The Development of a Consumer Society in Early Modern England* (Oxford, 1978); Linda Levy Peck, *Consuming Splendour: Society and Culture in Seventeenth-Century England* (Cambridge, 2005); Derek Hirst, 'Locating the 1650s in England's Seventeenth Century', *History* 81 (1996), 359–83. See also Jane Whittle and Elizabeth Griffiths, *Consumption and Gender in the Early Seventeenth-Century Household* (Oxford, 2012) and J. F. Merritt, *The Social World of Early Modern Westminster: Abbey, Court and Community, 1525–1640* (Manchester, 2005).

[14] Amanda E. Herbert, *Female Alliances: Gender, Identity, and Friendship in Early Modern Britain* (New Haven, 2014), 117–41; Annick Cossic and Patrick Galliou, eds., *Spas in Britain and in France in the Eighteenth and Nineteenth Centuries* (Cambridge, 2006).

[15] Brian Cowan, *The Social Life of Coffee: The Emergence of the British Coffeehouse* (New Haven, 2005).

form of alehouses, inns and taverns, and these establishments had played a key role in shaping the social template for the more modern coffeehouse.[16]

This is not to deny that commercialisation and consumerism were more pronounced and further developed in the later seventeenth century, for they certainly were. Undoubtedly, there were more shops, more goods on offer and more ways to learn about, desire and purchase things for sale in the reign of Charles II than there had been during his father's and grandfather's rule.[17] There were some innovations: the sale of books and pictures by auction was introduced in the 1670s, and some spas began to develop into commercial pleasure gardens.[18] But the difference was more a matter of scale than of quality; the later seventeenth century simply continued developments whose origins we can locate in the preceding era. The urban renaissance and the concomitant birth of a consumer society were *longue durée* processes and both began well before the Restoration.

Another claim for the distinctiveness of post-Restoration sociability has developed out of the substantial historiography that has followed from Jürgen Habermas's now famous thesis that late seventeenth-century Britain witnessed the 'structural transformation of the bourgeois public sphere'.[19] For Habermas, the post-Restoration period, especially in the wake of the Glorious Revolution, witnessed a transformation in the role and the status of 'the public' as a source of social and political legitimacy. The claim for the rise of a new form of public sphere in the later seventeenth century has been particularly influential because of the way in which it deliberately conflated changes in public sociability (especially through the emergence of coffeehouses, salons and dining clubs) and changing valuations of the idea of the public, and especially public opinion. Transformations in social practice and social imagination took place in tandem and created the conditions for the rise of a modern public.

---

[16] Mark Hailwood, *Alehouses and Good Fellowship in Early Modern England* (London, 2014); Beat Kümin and B. Ann Tlusty, eds., *The World of the Tavern: Public Houses in Early Modern Europe* (Aldershot, 1996).

[17] Lorna Weatherill, *Consumer Behaviour and Material Culture in Britain, 1660–1760* (London, 1996); Carole Shammas, *The Pre-Industrial Consumer in England and America* (Oxford, 1990).

[18] Brian Cowan, 'Arenas of Connoisseurship: Auctioning Art in Later Stuart England', in *Art Markets in Europe, 1400–1800*, ed. Michael North and David Ormrod (Farnham, 1998), 153–65; Warwick Wroth, *The London Pleasure Gardens of the Eighteenth Century* (New York, 1896); Penelope J. Corfield, *Vauxhall: Sex and Entertainment: London's Pioneering Urban Pleasure Garden* (London, 2012).

[19] Jürgen Habermas, *The Structural Transformation of the Public Sphere: An Inquiry into a Category of Bourgeois Society*, Thomas Burger, trans. (Cambridge, MA, 1989).

Of course, the Habermasian thesis has never been accepted wholesale. Qualifications, modifications and reservations abound with regard to many aspects of Habermas's public sphere theory. Various scholars have taken issue with his chronology; his Marxist categories of historical analysis; the relative importance of the practical and normative elements of the public sphere; and the distinctiveness of the public sphere from the state, another political sphere that was also in formation throughout the early modern era.[20] After all of these revisions to the Habermas thesis, it is by no means clear that Restoration England can easily be identified as the birthplace of the bourgeois public sphere.[21]

When historians do speak of the Restoration as the key moment in the emergence of a public sphere, they most commonly look to two key developments: the birth of the coffeehouse and the explosion of print culture, and especially news culture, in the later seventeenth century.[22] But neither was new to Restoration England: it is true that both coffeehouses and newspapers became much more prevalent after 1660, but this efflorescence of news mongering can hardly be attributed to the return of the Stuart monarchy. Indeed, the post-Restoration regimes observed the growth of news and coffee culture with great trepidation. Pre-publication censorship was revived by parliamentary statute in 1662 and was allowed to lapse only due to the political crisis caused by the exclusion debates in 1679. Charles II famously tried to suppress the English coffeehouses by royal proclamation in 1675, and failed to achieve this only due to legal and practical reservations; nevertheless, further attempts to suppress or restrain coffeehouse sociability remained on the agenda for the rest of his reign and were continued by James II as well.[23]

Of equal importance is the continuing anxiety with regard to the legitimacy of public opinion as the basis for political persuasion. Later Stuart England still viewed the 'public' as a potentially dangerous, demotic and unstable force in politics. While the practical necessity of appealing to public opinion was increasingly recognised even by high-flying Tories

---

[20] Dena Goodman, *The Republic of Letters: A Cultural History of the French Enlightenment* (Baton Rouge, 1994); Tim Blanning, *The Culture of Power and the Power of Culture: Old Regime Europe 1660–1789* (Oxford, 2000).
[21] Paul Yachnin and Bronwen Wilson, eds., *Making Publics in Early Modern Europe* (London, 2008).
[22] Steven Pincus, '"Coffee Does Politicians Create": Coffeehouses and Restoration Political Culture', *Journal of Modern History* 67, no. 4 (1995), 807–34; Mark Knights, *Representation and Misrepresentation in Later Stuart Britain: Partisanship and Political Culture* (Oxford, 2005).
[23] Cowan, *The Social Life of Coffee*.

such as Roger L'Estrange, who combined the roles of chief censor and chief propagandist for the Caroline regime, the desirability of doing so was much less often recognised.[24] This ambivalence with regard to the legitimacy of public opinion was famously summed up by L'Estrange's declaration that "'tis the press that has made 'em mad, and the press must set 'em right again."[25] Post-Restoration public opinion was still largely opposed to letting public opinion guide politics. It would take a very long time before opinion would be accepted as a legitimate voice of the people that should be heeded by heads of state.

What was new about Restoration sociability?

When compared to the early seventeenth century that preceded it and the eighteenth century that followed, the social history of the Restoration era no longer looks so distinctive. If one were to look for key moments in which society or 'the social' was re-envisioned, recent scholarship suggests that we would be better advised to examine the humanist moment of the long sixteenth century, or else perhaps the late eighteenth-century and early nineteenth-century age of revolutions and reforms, rather than the mid-seventeenth century. Phil Withington's work on the language of early modern social description, particularly in printed works, identifies the 1570s as a key point of departure for the development of a variegated but decidedly humanist-influenced social imaginary. Latinate words such as 'society' and 'company' began to figure more prominently in the titles of printed works at least, whereas Anglo-Saxon terms such as 'fellowship' began to fall out of favour. This is particularly important for the history of sociability, for Withington has identified the later sixteenth century as the moment when a long-term process began in which the English social vocabulary began to develop in two distinct directions. He imagines the development in terms of a broadening spectrum:

> At one end of the associational spectrum, 'society' and especially 'company' described sociability of the most informal and transient kind: those everyday interactions through which lives are constituted. At the other end of the spectrum, 'society' was used to denote idealized notions and

---

[24] Anne Dunan-Page and Beth Lynch, eds., *Roger L'Estrange and the Making of Restoration Culture* (Aldershot, 2008).
[25] *Observator* no. 1 (13 April 1681).

theories of association: in particular, 'commonwealth,' but also constructions like 'Christian society,' 'humane society,' and 'civil society'.[26]

One major implication of Withington's work is that the concept of sociability that has played such an important role in histories of the long eighteenth century had its origins in the English reception of renaissance humanist notions of the individual as a socially shaped being. In this view, Desiderius Erasmus and Sir Thomas Smith deserve recognition as some of the founding fathers, as it were, of sociability theory rather than the usual, more modern, suspects such as Georg Simmel and Norbert Elias.[27]

On the other hand, if one looks past the later Stuart era and looks forward to the latter years of the long eighteenth century, we find yet another watershed moment for the history of the social imaginary in the decades surrounding the revolutionary 1790s. It was at this moment that the modern language of class began to replace the more traditional discourses of social orders and 'sorts'.[28] Other forms of social description took on new forms or were elaborated upon with greater energy in the later eighteenth century: it was the later Georgian era that saw concepts such as 'fashion' or 'celebrity' take on their modern resonances.[29] It was also a key moment in the refiguring of the language of politics: words such as 'reform', 'radical', 'democracy' and 'socialism' either emerged or took on new resonance in the political imagination of the age.[30] In terms of the practices of sociability,

---

[26] Phil Withington, *Society in Early Modern England: The Vernacular Origins of Some Powerful Ideas* (Cambridge, 2010), 114. See also Withington, 'Company and Sociability in Early Modern England', *Social History* 32, no. 3 (2007), 291–307.

[27] Compare, for example, Brian Cowan, 'Public Spaces, Knowledge and Sociability', in *The Oxford Handbook of the History of Consumption*, ed. Frank Trentmann (Oxford, 2012), 251–66.

[28] Key works in this rich historiography include: E. P. Thompson, *The Making of the English Working Class* (London, 1963); Gareth Stedman Jones, *Languages of Class: Studies in English Working Class History 1832–1982* (Cambridge, 1983); Dror Wahrman, *Imagining the Middle Class: The Political Representation of Class in Britain, c. 1780–1840* (Cambridge, 1995); and Penelope Corfield, ed., *Language, History and Class* (Oxford, 1995).

[29] Hannah Greig, *The Beau Monde* (Oxford, 2013); Stella Tillyard, 'Celebrity in Eighteenth-Century London', *History Today* (June 2005), 20–27; Antoine Lilti, *Figures Publiques: L'Invention de la Célébrité 1750–1850* (Paris, 2014); and Brian Cowan, 'News, Biography, and Eighteenth-Century Celebrity', in *Oxford Handbooks Online*, ed. Thomas Keymer, general ed. Colin Burrow (Oxford, 7 September 2016), doi: 10.1093/oxfordhb/9780199935338.013.132.

[30] Arthur Burns and Joanna Innes, eds., *Rethinking the Age of Reform: Britain 1780–1850* (Cambridge, 2003); J. C. D. Clark, 'Religion and the Origins of Radicalism in Nineteenth-Century Britain', in *English Radicalism, 1550–1850*, ed. Glenn Burgess

the romantic age also saw the development of a much more developed system of commercialised leisure and entertainment that facilitated social interaction on a scale that would have been impossible to imagine in the Restoration era. Assembly rooms such as Carlisle House or the Pantheon, the commercial theatres at Covent Garden, Drury Lane and Haymarket, masquerades, dinners and other forms of entertainment flourished in the later Georgian era. The scandal press of the day also publicised social interactions and controversies with an intensity and a degree of regularity that was unknown to the later Stuart decades.[31]

The social spaces and practices that comprised the Restoration public sphere were not particularly novel, nor was the imaginative role of 'the public' in political discourse. As with the urban renaissance and the consumer revolution, the Restoration public sphere differed from the early Stuart public sphere only in terms of quantities, rather than qualities. There were more spaces for public sociability; there were more newspapers and pamphlets, which were published more often; there were more readers; and the savviest politicians of the day became more aware that these venues for public debate were not going to go away. But these facts of late seventeenth-century social life are better understood as continuations of already existing processes rather than as evidence of a distinct break with the past.

Did the Restoration initiate a new culture of politeness that would eventually become hegemonic in the eighteenth century? The concept of 'politeness' and the use of the word 'polite' as a means of describing sociable manners and cultural mores certainly did become much more prominent after the Restoration.[32] This appears to reflect a more generalised process of increasing French influence over English elite discourse that took place in the age of Louis XIV and his Stuart royal clients; the culture of Francophilia in later Stuart England is an important topic that remains understudied and

---

and Matthew Festenstein (Cambridge, 2011), 241–84; Joanna Innes and Mark Philp, eds., *Re-Imagining Democracy in the Age of Revolutions: America, France, Britain, Ireland 1750–1850* (Oxford, 2013).

[31] Gillian Russell, *Women, Sociability and Theatre in Georgian London* (Cambridge, 2007); Gillian Russell and Clara Tuite, eds., *Romantic Sociability: Social Networks and Literary Culture in Britain, 1770–1840* (Cambridge, 2002); Julia Swindells and David Francis Taylor, eds., *The Oxford Handbook of the Georgian Theatre 1737–1832* (Oxford, 2014).

[32] Lawrence Klein, *Shaftesbury and the Culture of Politeness: Moral Discourse and Cultural Politics in Early Eighteenth-Century England* (Cambridge, 1994), 3; see also Klein, 'Politeness and the Interpretation of the British Eighteenth Century', *Historical Journal* 45, no. 4 (Dec., 2002), 869–98.

poorly understood, especially when compared with the more familiar phenomenon of Francophobia.[33] French courtesy manuals often employed a discourse of *honnêteté*, *politesse* and *civilité* that was translated into English with terms such as gentility, politeness and civility, and the terms became a common mode of social description for proper genteel conduct.[34] The transformation of a French discourse of social description into an English one was an important new development in English elite sociability, but it was also not entirely novel. The later Stuart and eighteenth-century culture of politeness developed out of, and elaborated upon, an Italianate late renaissance discourse of civility and courtesy that influenced English concepts of elite manners from the Tudor era through the seventeenth century.[35] The reasons for, and the precise nature of, this transformation remain somewhat unclear, but it will never be fully understood if the Restoration is habitually understood as the *terminus a quo*, or year zero, for the history of polite sociability.

Of course, the culture of politeness was never hegemonic, and this was particularly so in the later seventeenth century. While Klein's case for the progress of politeness in post-Restoration culture sees 'politeness' as the result of a slow cultural retreat from prominence by the court and the church and the concomitant rise of the urbane cultures of London's genteel Town and its commercial City, this schema fits poorly with the picture of a renewed and active court under Charles II and a perhaps even more

---

[33] On Francophobia, see Steven Pincus, 'From Butter Boxes to Wooden Shoes: The Shift in English Popular Sentiment from Anti-Dutch to Anti-French in the 1670s', *Historical Journal* 38 (1995), 333–61; Linda Colley, *Britons: Forging the Nation, 1707–1837* (New Haven, 1992). On francophilia in the eighteenth century, see Gerald Newman, *The Rise of English Nationalism: A Cultural History 1740–1830* (New York, 1987); Robin Eagles, *Francophilia in English Society, 1748–1815* (Basingstoke, 2000). Later Stuart francophilia is a topic that requires further study; for an introduction to the complexities of this issue, see Lawrence E. Klein, 'The Figure of France: The Politics of Sociability in England, 1660–1715', *Yale French Studies* 92 (1997), 30–45.

[34] Michèle Cohen, *Fashioning Masculinity: National Identity and Language in the Eighteenth Century* (London, 1996); Daniel Gordon, *Citizens Without Sovereignty: Equality and Sociability in French Thought, 1670–1789* (Princeton, 1994); Elizabeth C. Goldsmith, *Exclusive Conversations: The Art of Interaction in Seventeenth-Century France* (Philadelphia, 1988).

[35] Markku Peltonen, *The Duel in Early Modern England: Civility, Politeness and Honour* (Cambridge, 2003), 149–50; Jennifer Richards, *Rhetoric and Courtliness in Early Modern Literature* (Cambridge, 2003); John Leon Lievsay, *Stefano Guazzo and the English Renaissance 1575–1675* (Chapel Hill, 1961); John L. Lievsay, *The Englishman's Italian Books 1550–1700* (Philadelphia, 1969); J. R. Hale, *England and the Italian Renaissance: The Growth of Interest in Its History and Art* (London, 1954).

assertive re-established Church of England. The replacement of the court and church with urbane and commercial codes of civility may have been on the wish list of some later Stuart Whigs such as John Locke and his erstwhile protégé the third Earl of Shaftesbury, but it was by no means clear that this vision would prevail even well after the Glorious Revolution. Tory, and even some Jacobite, visions of politeness also require more attention than they have yet received.[36] The Jacobite court in exile in France and Italy developed a distinctive form of courtly politeness that has only recently received serious historical attention.[37]

It is worth pondering the paradoxical juxtaposition of politeness and libertinism in Restoration culture: although seemingly at odds, both polite manners and libertine impropriety have been identified as hallmarks of the age. Both have been understood in some ways as reactions to the revolutionary 1640s and 1650s. Some leading intellectuals of the later Stuart era, such as John Dryden and the third Earl of Shaftesbury, could endorse both politeness and libertinism at various moments.[38] Anna Bryson has argued cogently that libertinism was 'just as much an aspect of the development of "civil society" as the "official" code of civility itself. It was parasitic on the development of the official code, in that its motive was essentially transgressive, but paradoxically it fulfilled some of the same strategic ends of the official code, above all in defining social identity and effecting social exclusion.'[39] One could make a similar argument with regard to the efflorescence of the 'libertine' genre of pornographic writing that began in the seventeenth century and played a prominent role in the literary world of the eighteenth century.[40] The progress of politeness and libertinism went hand in hand.

---

[36] Markku Peltonen, 'Politeness and Whiggism, 1688–1732', *Historical Journal* 48, no. 2 (June 2005), 391–414.

[37] Edward Corp, *A Court in Exile: The Stuarts in France, 1689–1718* (Cambridge, 2004); Corp, *The Stuarts in Italy 1719–1766: A Royal Court in Permanent Exile* (Cambridge, 2011); and Corp, ed., *The Stuart Court in Rome: The Legacy of Exile* (Aldershot, 2003).

[38] Brian Cowan, 'Reasonable Ecstasies: Shaftesbury and the Languages of Libertinism', *Journal of British Studies* 37 (1998), 111–38; James Grantham Turner, *Libertines and Radicals in Early Modern London: Sexuality, Politics and Literary Culture, 1630–1685* (Cambridge, 2002).

[39] Anna Bryson, *From Courtesy to Civility: Changing Codes of Conduct in Early Modern England* (Oxford, 1998), 268.

[40] Sarah Toulalan, *Imagining Sex: Pornography and Bodies in Seventeenth-Century England* (Oxford, 2007); David Foxon, *Libertine Literature in England 1660–1745* (London, 1964); Bradford Mudge, *The Whore's Story: Women, Pornography, and the British Novel, 1684–1830* (New York, 2000); Lynn Hunt, ed., *The Invention of*

When the place of the Restoration era in social histories of the long eighteenth century is put under scrutiny, it appears less distinctive than it does when considered as part of a larger argument about the *soi disant* long eighteenth century. The restoration of the monarchy did not inaugurate a consumer revolution, an urban renaissance, a new public sphere or even the culture of politeness. To assume that it did is to attribute far too much social-cultural importance and causal force to one political event, or at best a short-term conjuncture of events. The grand-scale structural transformations in sociability that are often located in the long eighteenth century cannot be attributed to a relatively short-term and not particularly long-lasting regime change. To be fair, of course, no historian associated with these major arguments has done so. Instead, many historians tend to use the Restoration, and even more so the concept of a 'post-Restoration' era, as a convenient shorthand for a period in which they see the changes they wish to identify as important as becoming *predominant* from the later seventeenth century onwards. Earlier examples of precocious developments that later proliferated and became normalised (such as the introduction of coffee and coffeehouses in pre-Restoration England) do not obviate the usefulness of such concepts. Nevertheless, the continuities between the Restoration era and the eighteenth century have been largely overstated in these historiographies, whereas the connections between the beginning and the end of the seventeenth century have tended to be understated.

Political history and the Restoration

The political history of the later Stuart period has been dominated by the question of party and partisanship.[41] Was the Restoration of the monarchy popular? Was the political debate over the possibility of excluding the Duke of York from the throne the moment that forged two distinct political parties? To what extent did the pro-exclusionist Whigs or their Tory opponents represent the opinion of the majority or, rather, that of a disgruntled minority? Were the political divisions of the period motivated by profound

---

Pornography: 1500–1800: Obscenity and the Origins of Modernity (New York, 1993); and Robert Darnton, *The Forbidden Best-Sellers of Pre-Revolutionary France* (New York, 1995).

[41] For overviews, see Tim Harris, *Politics Under the Later Stuarts: Party Conflict in a Divided Society, 1660–1715* (London, 1993); Gary S. De Krey, *Restoration and Revolution in Britain* (Houndmills, 2007); George Southcombe and Grant Tapsell, *Restoration Politics, Religion, and Culture: Britain and Ireland, 1660–1714* (Houndmills, 2010).

differences in ideology or were they the reflections of long-standing conflicts of interest? These debates continue to animate the history of Restoration politics and they have yielded a number of important insights that can be useful to historians of sociability as well.

Recent work on Restoration politics has yielded two recognitions that are particularly useful: there is now a general acknowledgement of the centrality of religion as a source of political conflict, and of the importance played by the continuing memory of the violence of the civil wars as both an animating and a moderating force in that conflict.[42]

The problem of religious dissent divided both Restoration politics and society from the moment that it became clear that the return of the Stuarts would also be accompanied by a restoration of Anglican uniformity under an Episcopal Church settlement. The congeries of legislation from the 1660s known as the 'Clarendon Code' created a clear distinction between now orthodox Anglican conformists and those Protestant dissenters who were barred by law from the peaceful expression of their faith. From here on out, the complex and often shifting lines of Protestant religious belief that marked the first half of the seventeenth century were now fixed into a harder and stronger division between the established church and dissent. Even the repeal of much of this legislation after the Glorious Revolution through the 1689 Toleration Act could not undo these divisions, and the conflicts between Whigs and Tories well into the eighteenth century can be seen in large part as a continuing contest between proponents of the established church and those who were sympathetic to protestant dissent.[43]

Perhaps this division has not been taken as seriously as it should by historians of sociability because both sides continued to emphasise the desirability of reconciliation and ultimate comprehension of all Protestants within a unitary church, even if that dream became more and more remote as the decades passed. Even after the failure of the 1689 Comprehension Bill, the language of a Protestant front united in the face of Popish and

---

[42] Mark Goldie, Tim Harris and Paul Seaward, eds., *The Politics of Religion in Restoration England* (Oxford, 1990); Matthew Neufield, *The Civil Wars after 1660: Public Remembering in Late Stuart England* (Woodbridge, 2013). On the broader context, see Brian Cowan, 'The Long Revolution Revisited', review of Tyacke, Nicholas, ed., *The English Revolution c.1590–1720: Politics, Religion and Communities*. H-Albion, H-Net Reviews. July, 2015: http://www.h-net.org/reviews/showrev.php?id=42073.

[43] William Gibson and Robert G. Ingram, eds., *Religious Identities in Britain, 1660–1832* (Aldershot, 2005); Grant Tapsell, ed., *The Later Stuart Church, 1660–1714* (Manchester, 2012); and John Marshall, *John Locke, Toleration and Early Enlightenment Culture: Religious Toleration and Arguments for Religious Toleration in Early Modern and Early Enlightenment Europe* (Cambridge, 2006).

absolutist challengers remained strong, but it did not obviate the deep cultural divide between the church and its dissenters. True Tory believers in the sole legitimacy and the singular orthodoxy of the established Church of England did not give up hope of forcing dissenters to become reconciled to the church through the reintroduction of persecution: this provided the animus behind the vociferous 'high church' movement of the first few decades of the eighteenth century.[44]

If the creation of a division between orthodoxy and dissent kept the social divisions of the day animated, the memories of just how bad those divisions could be for all concerned created an opposite pull towards moderation. While moderation tended to be understood in the decades after the Glorious Revolution as a sort of shorthand code for Whig politics, especially with regard to religious matters, the fear of further civil unrest, possibly resulting in yet another civil war or revolution, gave both Whigs and Tories a powerful incentive towards accepting compromise and reining in extremist elements within both parties.[45] Despite the supposed Tory abhorrence of moderation, it took a Tory victory at the general election of 1710 and the establishment of a Tory ministry headed by Robert Harley to bring a truly 'moderate' administration to power in the last years of Queen Anne's reign.[46]

It was this paradoxical combination of a restored monarchy and a re-established church along with the persistence of long-standing political and religious animosities animating party political conflict in the later seventeenth and early eighteenth centuries that created a unique environment for the development of English sociability after the Restoration. Party politics was obviously a source of great anxiety in later Stuart England, and the divisions engendered by the deep partisanship of the age threatened on many occasions to provoke a return to the violence of civil wars

---

[44] Brent S. Sirota, *The Christian Monitors: The Church of England and the Age of Benevolence, 1680–1730* (New Haven, 2014); G. V. Bennett, *The Tory Crisis in Church and State 1688–1730: The Career of Francis Atterbury Bishop of Rochester* (Oxford, 1975).

[45] On moderation, see Ethan Shagan, *The Rule of Moderation: Violence, Religion and the Politics of Restraint in Early Modern England* (Cambridge, 2011); on the early eighteenth-century use of 'moderation' rhetoric, see Brian Cowan, 'Daniel Defoe's *Review* and the Transformations of the English Periodical', *Huntington Library Quarterly* 77, no. 1 (Spring 2014), 79–110.

[46] J. A. Downie, *Robert Harley and the Press: Propaganda and Public Opinion in the Age of Swift and Defoe* (Cambridge, 1979); Brian W. Hill, *Robert Harley: Speaker, Secretary of State and Premier Minister* (New Haven, 1988), and Geoffrey Holmes, *British Politics in the Age of Anne*, revised edition (London, 1987).

or revolutions, but it also provided the context in which many of the key institutions of sociability were forged and modernised.[47]

The coffeehouse offers perhaps the best example. English coffeehouses were from their inception associated with political sedition and dangerously promiscuous political discourse, and yet it did not take long before many Restoration coffeehouses became centres for Tory political organising and opposition to Whig politics. While simultaneously denouncing Whiggish talk in the kingdom's coffeehouses, Sir Roger L'Estrange saw no problem with using Sam's Coffeehouse in London as the base for his own Tory propaganda efforts.[48] By Queen Anne's reign, Whig propagandists such as Joseph Addison and Richard Steele were working hard to construct an ideal of the coffeehouse as a venue for polite sociability that was purged of partisanship, and was hence safe for moderation in both politics and social life.[49] Whereas the Restoration-era coffeehouse had a serious legitimation problem, in the wake of the partisan debates of the later Stuarts and the civilising impulses that these conflicts engendered, it could be experienced by Hanoverian Britons as a space for tranquil and serene sociability.[50] Much the same could be said of the other institutions of post-Restoration sociability, including the theatres, pleasure gardens, clubs, taverns, and the country houses of the gentry, although much more research needs to be done on these topics before any solid conclusions may be made.

Here we find ourselves brought back to the central question posed by J. H. Plumb in his influential Ford lectures of 1965 on the origins of 'political stability' in late seventeenth- and early eighteenth-century England. Plumb credited Sir Robert Walpole and his ability to construct and maintain a 'Whig oligarchy' in the aftermath of the destruction of the Tory party in George I's reign with the establishment of the relatively stable politics of the Hanoverian state.[51] This view has come under increasing scrutiny in

[47] Knights, *Representation and Misrepresentation in Later Stuart Britain*; Knights, *The Devil in Disguise: Deception, Delusion, and Fanaticism in the Early English Enlightenment* (Oxford, 2011).
[48] Peter Hinds, *'The Horrid Popish Plot': Roger L'Estrange and the Circulation of Political Discourse in Late Seventeenth-Century London* (London, 2010).
[49] Brian Cowan, 'Mr. Spectator and the Coffeehouse Public Sphere', *Eighteenth-Century Studies* 37, no. 3 (2004), 345–66.
[50] Lawrence Klein, 'Coffeehouse Civility, 1660–1714: An Aspect of Post-Courtly Culture in England', *Huntington Library Quarterly* 59, no. 1 (1996), 30–52; Brian Cowan, 'Publicity and Privacy in the History of the British Coffeehouse', *History Compass* 5, no. 4 (July 2007), 1180–1213.
[51] J. H. Plumb, *The Origins of Political Stability, England 1675–1725* (Boston, 1967). For developments of this argument, see J. V. Beckett, 'Introduction: Stability in Politics and Society, 1680–1750', in *Britain in the First Age of Party 1680–1750: Essays*

recent decades and few eighteenth-century historians now give Walpole so much credit for astute political management, or indeed see Hanoverian Britain as quite so stable as Plumb did.[52] One part of the answer to the problem of political stability in post-Restoration England may lie in the history of sociability. While the Restoration did not inaugurate a decidedly new world of sociability, the religious and political dilemmas posed by the Restoration helped to shape the ways in which sociable practices and sociable ideals would develop in the later seventeenth and early eighteenth centuries. Perhaps it was the very real threat of political instability and the fear of a renewed outbreak of chaotic violence, or perhaps even a new civil war, that encouraged contemporaries to search for a sociable solution to these problems. Political historians have much to contribute to the history of post-Restoration sociability.

Presented to Geoffrey Holmes (London, 1987), 1–18; and Geoffrey Holmes, 'The Achievement of Stability: The Social Context of Politics from the 1680s to the Age of Walpole', in *Politics, Religion, and Society in England, 1679–1742* (London, 1986), 249–80.

[52] Linda Colley, *In Defiance of Oligarchy: The Tory Party 1714–1760* (Cambridge, 1982); Paul Monod, *Jacobitism and the English People 1688–1788* (Cambridge, 1989); Kathleen Wilson, *Politics, Culture and Imperialism in England, 1715–1785* (Cambridge, 1995).

Chapter 2
Mapping sociability on Restoration townscapes
Marie-Madeleine Martinet

THE PRESENT interest in the 'spatial turn' might lead us to consider Restoration sociability in the light of the spatial qualities associated with different types of early modern social practices; moreover, recent approaches involving digital imagery might be invoked. Several issues are involved. How did the layout of urban space interact with social structures and with practices of sociability? With respect to representation, how did images of urban places embody that period's view of relations between or within social groups? How did methodologies of visualising social relations evolve at that time? How does science add a new perception of social spaces, both by creating new patterns of sociability and by providing new spatial concepts which can be applied to the visualisation of sociability? How do present-day methods of digital visualisation and spatial representation shed new light on social practices and networks of the past – from 'maps' to the present-day notion of 'mapping'?

The Restoration is known as a period of urban change. The rebuilding of London after the Great Fire was a moment of tension between the several plans proposed for it and the resulting layout.[1] As is well known, each of the options corresponded to a distinct view of urban life, such as Wren's ceremonial plan with grand avenues leading to monuments, Hooke's scientific grid, or the preservation of the existing layout based on properties and the integration of new architecture into the existing urban environment. Thus, plan and reality interact, both at the moment of rebuilding and, retrospectively, in the public imagination, where real buildings are consciously or half-consciously seen against more or less imaginary projects. Urban renewal may be seen at the scale of urban design – architecture in context

---

[1] It was very well pictured in the 2016 exhibition 'Creation from Catastrophe: How Architecture Rebuilds Communities' at The Architecture Gallery, RIBA, London, January–April 2016.

– which in turn raises the question of the interaction between urban design and society.

The society of the period may itself be viewed in different ways, combining partly inherited appearances of the social structure with new patterns of sociability arising from economic and scientific changes, sometimes clearly visible and sometimes partly guessed only in outline. This is another form of interplay between image and reality.

As usual, both discrepancies and coordination may be traced between the urban environment and social structures. Restoration architecture is well known for proclaiming both renewal and traditional appearance based on classical styles. In a changing society is this a deliberate screen or a mark of awkward tension? The urban environment partly corresponded to social functions, with buildings for specific traditional activities; but many of the newly important activities were carried on in informal networks. For example, it is well known that the Lord Mayor, the incarnation of the City's growing power, although an ancient institution, had no official residence until the eighteenth century; and that the new insurance companies, for instance, had no building of their own, meeting in the coffeehouses which eventually gave them their names, Lloyd's being the most famous. Thus we are led to consider that one urban design form may have several social functions: an obvious one and a secondary one; and we shall later see that some ceremonial buildings had scientific uses. We can thus trace two different, superimposed patterns: that of social roles with corresponding architectural presence, and the network of hidden economic and scientific sociability. We should also consider both our retrospective reconstruction of such differences and the way in which they were felt, if at all, at the time.

Finally, we have to bear in mind the multiplicity of present-day approaches on which such representation studies depend when attempting to reconstruct a view of the Restoration. Studying images of sociability and social spaces, as part of representation studies, raises several issues: how do the conceptual and technical tools available to present-day historians, including mapping technologies, mediate our research on the social spaces of the past, bringing out new patterns in Restoration society linked to the urban renewal? How did representational conventions and practices in past times, especially the traditional framing and structuring of townscape paintings, deal with tensions between the image of social space and the image of social relations? How did inherited representational practices interact with science, which, as a newly institutionalised activity, was redefining the perception of the universe and of human society within it?

Cartography and sociability networks

Studying sociability networks in urban spaces can be viewed at different levels and from several approaches. One of them is cartographic: it implies making a cartography of sociability networks, questioning whether social interaction was correlated to spatial coordinates, and we should take into account the gap between mental images of urban space then and now – the geometrical view of space as a homogeneous grid was still in its early stages of formation. This in turn raises a question of perception: how was the space/social interaction perceived at the time, and how do we model it now using present-day approaches? In recent research, present-day mapping techniques have been applied to studies of Restoration society; they can offer a new approach to the representation of social bonds and interactions, and, using new visualisation techniques, either confirm earlier studies by historians of urban culture or bring out hitherto unsuspected social patterns.

Present-day cartography and Restoration society
We should first review examples of work by researchers adapting present-day cartographic methods to studies of urban social development from Elizabethan times to the Victorian era, marking the Restoration as the moment when expansion becomes a 'real-estate activity'.[2] Using the options offered by digital cartography, both urban-planning tools and thematic population-mapping tools, present-day researchers have turned to S. R. Rasmussen's famous books on urban history.[3] These studies are now translated into the medium of digital maps with geopositioning, and accompanied by quotations. Rassmussen showed that measuring practices produced a homogeneous planning system corresponding to the social structure, the 'one family-per-house' system. The Austrian architect and theorist Franz Sdoutz has recently translated such research into digital maps as part of his website 'mediaarchitecture' in the section of architectural theory, a line of enquiry started in the 2006–7 website and updated in mid-2015.[4] The typology of London urban motifs is explored via aerial

---

[2] Cynthia Wall, *The Literary and Cultural Spaces of Restoration* (Cambridge,1998).
[3] Steen Eiler Rasmussen's work on London dates from the 1930s, with revised versions and new work in the 1970s and 1980s. His more general books from the 1950s formed a basis for his later work. His works include *London, the Unique City* (1937), *Towns and Buildings* (1951), *Experiencing Architecture* (1959).
[4] http://www.mediaarchitecture.at/architekturtheorie/unique_city/2011_google_urbanism_en.shtml (accessed June 2018).

views supported by diagrams of measured units and geopositioning references; thematic maps with time animation; historical maps; texts with the typology of urban spaces, including comments by Sdoutz and embedded quotations by Rasmussen, with links to the theoretical chapters of the website to provide context. The new tools emphasise the multiple approaches which converge in such studies, from digital cartography to theories of urban form, and the insights into the social structure that they can give us.

Historians have also produced population mappings such as the 'Locating London Past' website (2011),[5] which incorporate datasets such as plague deaths, Old Bailey court records, population statistics and archaeological finds, allowing the user to plot the data against maps, including Rocque's 1746 map of London and present-day maps. The steps by which the project was formed – first creating georeferenced maps, starting from historical maps (done by archaeologists), then linking place names in the datasets to the maps (done by archivists and historians), and generating population statistics – suggests the multiplicity of coordinated approaches necessary for such a project and, more importantly, the order in which each group has to act: the archaeologists and cartographers to create the framework, then the historians to fill in the datasets. The account of the methodology emphasises both the spatial focus and the correlates of the database resources. The need of a tutorial to use the project also suggests that a fresh approach will give the best results and that users should adapt to such new methods. The two maps used, the eighteenth-century one and the present-day one, underline the historical perspective. The spatial approach to population and sociability data draws attention to the new methodologies.

This approach results in new forms of information visualisation, such as plotting seventeenth- and eighteenth-century addresses on a London map in a way which suggests the locations of the various sociability groups and makes them apparent. For instance, networks can be plotted for coffeehouses, new places of sociability at the time. We know that in the economic or scientific field such new, informal places of sociability were of great importance for the development of activities which were not yet institutionalised and had no official buildings of their own. The original

---

[5] http://www.locatinglondon.org/, set up by teams from the University of Hertfordshire, the Institute of Historical Research of the University of London, the University of Sheffield and the Museum of London Department of Archaeology, is discussed by web editors. Web editors specialising in urban history and architecture review it, suggesting that users should first study the tutorial videos (http://londonist.com/2011/12/locating-londons-past-mapping-17th-and-18th-century-london.php and https://vimeo.com/album/1770693 [accessed June 2018]).

layout of Adam Dant's map,[6] with a coffee pot serving as an outline of the coffeehouse area, is a case in point, as is the method of zooming in to read details about each coffeehouse, revealing the importance of such apparently insignificant institutions as you change the scale.

Such multiple spatial representations of sociability make us aware of the multiplicity of points of view, and throw into relief the interaction between real urban spaces and the multiple diagrammatic visual models of sociability.

Social bonds and topographical layout

The Restoration was an intermediary period in which social bonds and topographical layout still partly corresponded. The landowners who developed areas of London still resided on their estates, which were thus both a spatial area and a sociability environment, grouping landlords and dependents, as is shown by a study of the Russell estates in London in the Restoration period; we can create visuals to show this superimposition, as well as the move away from it which occurred later. We can look at an interactive map of the estates, plotting the successive generations of the Russell family (Dukes of Bedford) on the plan of the area (Figure 1).

The map traces the development of the estates by throwing into relief the names of allied families which were given to new streets. In this way history (the Bedford family genealogy and alliances) is projected onto space (the growth of the estate). When we walk about the area nowadays, we actually follow the time sequence of the Russell generations. The southern Bloomsbury part of the estate, corresponding to the earlier generations, was developed around Southampton House (acquired by marriage – hence Southampton Street), which was inhabited by the Russells. The area corresponds to a sociability network: the landlord's house, and around it the estate with the developers and tenants, as in the first Russell estates around Covent Garden, which was built near Bedford House in the seventeenth century. The northern part of the estate, built by later generations in the course of the eighteenth century, became an estate development largely inhabited by lawyers and other professions who needed buildings in the classical style to show their status; but the Russells themselves moved to then more fashionable areas in the West End.

---

[6] http://spitalfieldslife.com/2014/01/21/adam-dants-map-of-the-coffee-houses/ (accessed June 2018). More comments on http://googlemapsmania.blogspot.fr/2014/01/mapping-londons-17th-century-coffee.html (accessed June 2018).

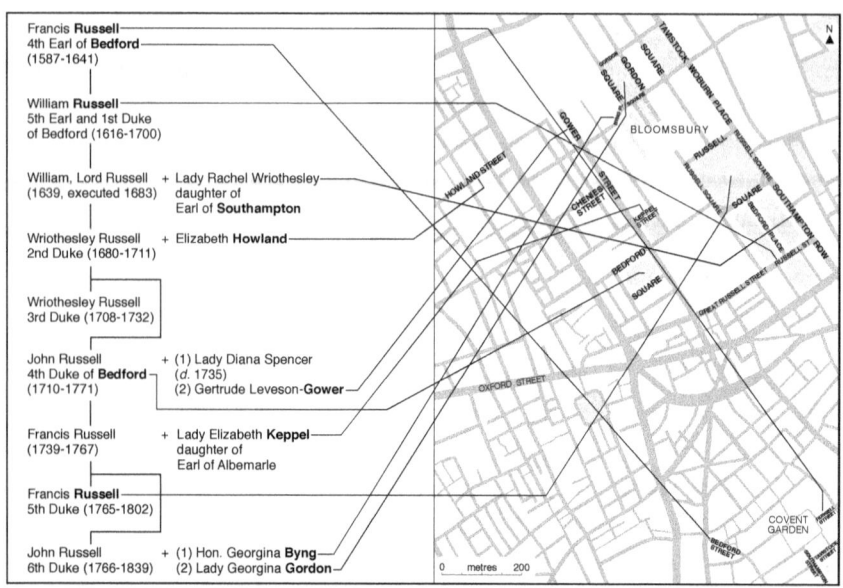

Country estates of the Russell family: **Bedford**, Bedfordshire; **Woburn**, Bedfordshire; **Chenies**, Buckinghamshire; **Tavistock**, Devon

The first generations of the Russell family (top of the genealogical table) developed the Southern parts of the estate (bottom of the map), and conversely the later generations (bottom of the table) developed the Northern parts (top of the map)

Figure 1. Genealogy of the Russell family and map of associated London place names
Source: *Georgian Cities* http://www.18thc-cities.paris-sorbonne.fr/spip.php?article194 (accessed June 2018).

We can thus use current 'information visualisation' techniques to reveal patterns in the social evolution of the time which were both in keeping with the urban renewal and contradictory to it.

Social space and urban design

We also need to take into account the spatial context and the different approaches to the conceptualisation of urban space: the links with the country beyond the city,[7] the texts which reveal how spaces were classified – texts on parks and shops as public spaces distinct from private places[8] – and the use of architecture as a political statement.[9] Such multiple perceptions of social spaces have been highlighted in the 'urban history' approach

---

[7] See Elizabeth McKellar, *The Birth of Modern London* (Manchester, 1999).
[8] Cynthia Wall, *The Literary and Cultural Spaces of Restoration* (Cambridge, 1998).
[9] Christine Stevenson, *The City and the King: Architecture and Politics in Restoration* (London, 2013).

to Restoration London research from the 1990s onwards, as part of a wider movement articulating 'spatial humanities', as they are now known, with architectural studies, social history and literary-representation approaches. We can transfer these approaches to research into the visual representations of urban scenes, where such superimposed cross-currents will also be revealed in the sociability networks of the time if we look at the structuring of images both as images of urban spaces and as images of society. We need to take into account artists' historical practices in the composition of pictures – the framing of townscapes, the use of depth cues to mark distances, the height of the point of view, the lines of sight and the relative positioning of figures in the urban setting – and see how they were used to project a view of society and its tensions.

Public spaces and processions

Events such as ceremonies which include processions testify to the dual perception of urban space as a spatial frame and as a network of social patterns created by the movements of people. Processions represent a hierarchical order, with the various groups of participants in sequence.

For images of celebrations, two visual structures are superimposed: the social hierarchy embodied by the procession is mapped onto the topography of the city. Engravings of triumphal entries contain both a recognisable townscape as a background and a full view of the procession. Those two elements are combined in an unrealistic way, even if the technique seems to be realistic: the procession is depicted in its entirety, in winding sequence so as to show the complete order of the participants, and is placed within the frame of a single picture showing one restricted London landmark visible at a glance – a layout which would not correspond to reality, where the procession would progress in a fairly straight line along the streets, with only one part of it visible to a static observer at any one instant, the rest being out of view behind the more distant houses.

Showing a winding procession is an old convention, a way of showing all the participants; see, for example, the cavalcade of the Magi by Gozzoli at the Medici Palace in Florence (fifteenth century), moving along the paths of a hilly countryside viewed slightly from above. But such a representational mode poses problems when the procession is supposed to take place in a townscape of narrow streets, since the whole procession is visible, whether immediately opposite the observer (which is normal) or more distant at the rear and the front of the sequence – the latter being groups that should realistically be partly or totally hidden by the houses. The alternative option of depicting the whole procession in a long frieze, focusing only on the characters, is not used because it would mean sacrificing the architectural background, omitting a realistic view of the chosen area as taken in by an observer. Processions were directed so as to pass from one significant landmark to another, and the change of place was itself significant, but the new visual practices implied a homogeneous space, rather than a simultaneous setting, as a way of glorifying the new, regular, classical architecture of London, with each place forming a coherent geometrical motif. The desire to combine a view of social hierarchy with a townscape celebrating urban renewal leads to such a dual solution. Sociability patterns would imply both a common purpose for the participants, with the celebration of a national event or of a monarch acting as a social bond, and the distinction between the different recognisable social groups taking part as established bodies each fulfilling a separate role – army, guilds, for instance, each having their own sociability practices. Images of celebrations followed visual codes expressing such social structures, with the help of visual structures.

The artists adapt the view of the city to the requirements of the representation of society in different ways, from minor spatial distortions to full, entirely symbolic views giving precedence to the procession over the surroundings.

An example is the entry of Charles II into the City of London:[10] in engravings, the street has been broadened to show the procession, as is usual practice in the townscapes of the period, where the narrow streets of the time were frequently depicted as wide avenues; but here this is exaggerated to the point that the street looks like a square. In the view of Charles II's coronation by Dirck Stoop (Museum of London), the same pattern can be observed. In order to show the full cavalcade the houses have been suppressed and only the triumphal arches are seen; the arches, each with a symbolic meaning, had been a feature of royal entries for decades, and they, more than buildings, represent the city. The arches give rhythm to the groups in the procession, emphasising the social structure represented by the order of the cavalcade.[11] We find the same practice again for the coronation of William III:[12] in a 1689 Dutch engraving the procession is

---

[10] *King Charles II's triumphal Entry into the City of London at his Restoration.* Engraving, 1660.

[11] https://www.magnoliabox.com/search?type=product&q=cavalcade (accessed March 2019).

[12] *Alle de bijsondere en particuliere Ceremonien, geschied in en omtrent de Krooning WILLIAM de III. en MARIA de II. KONING en KONINGINNE Van Groot Brittanien, Vrankrijk en Yrlandt, Op den 11 Aprl, 1689. Oude Stijl.* | Romijn de Hooghe fecit.

meandering and the view of London shows the significant monuments only: the Tower, the usual point of departure.

On the significance of arches, we should look at Hogarth's illustrations (1725–26) to *Hudibras* (1663–1664–1678) for the scene with Temple Bar (Plate 11, *Burning the Rumps at Temple Barr*):[13] it shows Temple Bar as restored in the days of Hogarth, not in its pre-Restoration dilapidated state, at the time of the poem; Temple Bar is the limit between the City and Westminster, and it is here presented as a sign of conflict between those two social worlds, whereas in the celebration scenes it was seen as a victorious passage.

Focusing on the path followed by passers-by was actually also part of the scientific approach to urban and rural space, at least as much as the map-making coordinates view evoked above. In Ogilby's *Britannia* (1675), which is actually a representation of the routes followed by travellers, the map looked like a scrolled itinerary (Figure 2).[14]

The frontispiece of the book also shows several perceptions of space, one by geometrical instruments (right-hand lower corner) and one by direct

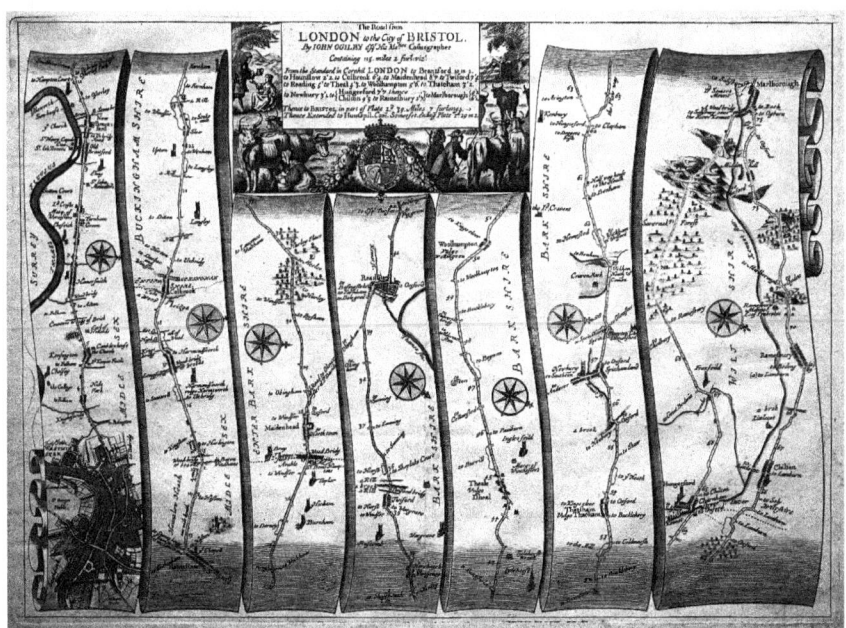

Figure 2. A strip map by John Ogilby from *Britannia Atlas* (1675), showing the route from London to Bristol.

---

[13] http://www.william-hogarth.com/hogarth/14730_e.php (accessed June 2018).
[14] John Ogilby, *Britannia* (London, 1675).

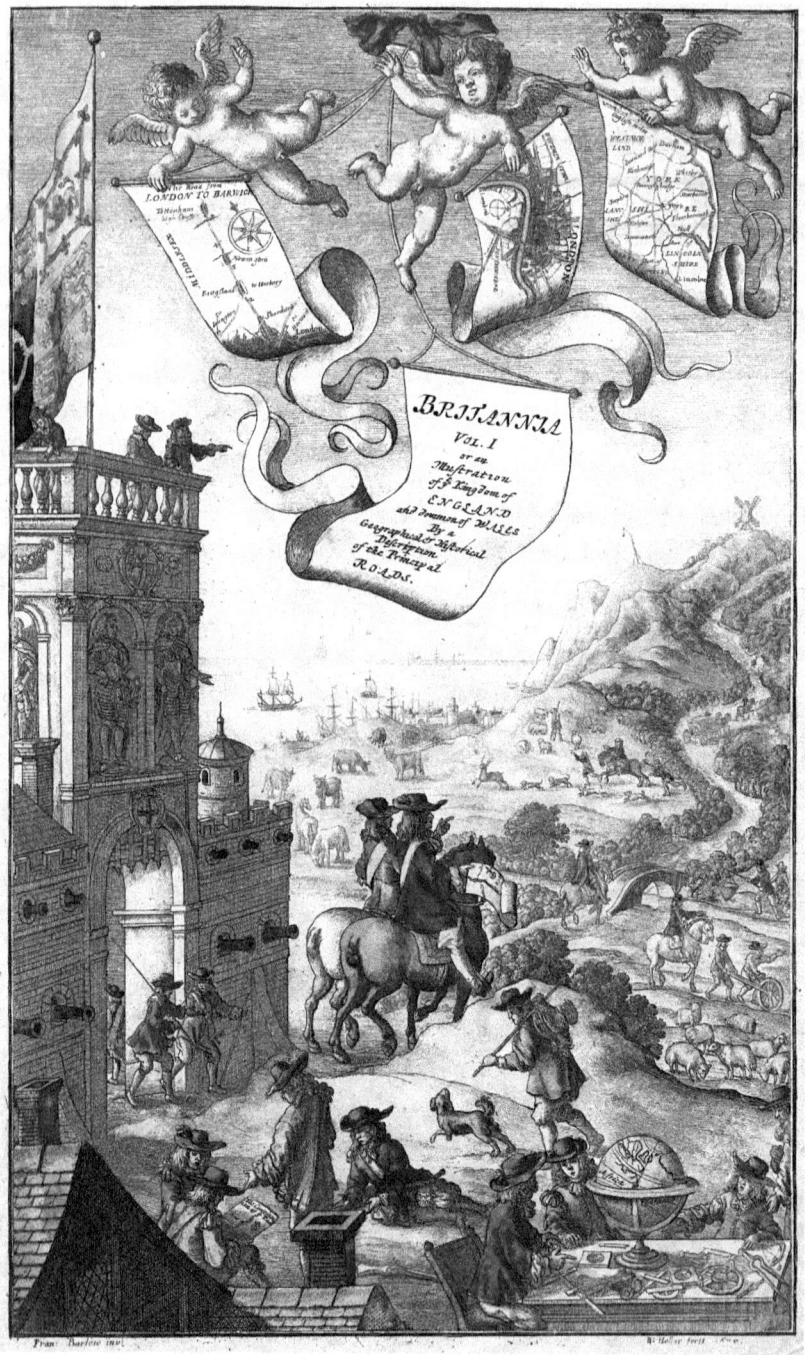

Figure 3. Frontispiece of John Ogilby's *Britannia* (1675). Drawn by Francis Barlow, engraved by Wenzel Hollar.

measurement with a 'waywiser' – both by groups of people, the waywiser with one rolling the instrument and the other one counting (Figure 3).

They are contradictory or complementary views, one emphasising the surroundings and one emphasising the route taken by travellers, giving us a clue to the tensions implicit in the engravings of the processions. These two map-making practices correspond to a different type of sociability, that of the cooperating scientific groups attempting to develop representations of space: those who have an abstract geometrical approach and those who work by field studies.

Meeting places for social groups and professions

The representation of social space may be that of long-established sites of professional gathering, part of the old associational culture of guilds and livery companies, as well as of new types of sociability. Two well-known architectural motifs, the quadrangle and the street, correspond to two models of sociability. Numerous views of pre-existing institutions – scientific or financial – dating from periods before the Restoration, such as Gresham College or the Exchange, show them in the traditional layout of the quadrangle, the meeting place inherited both from the university colleges and from the medieval trade exchanges. These courtyards, rather than the buildings, are seen as the normal places for sociability; in addition,

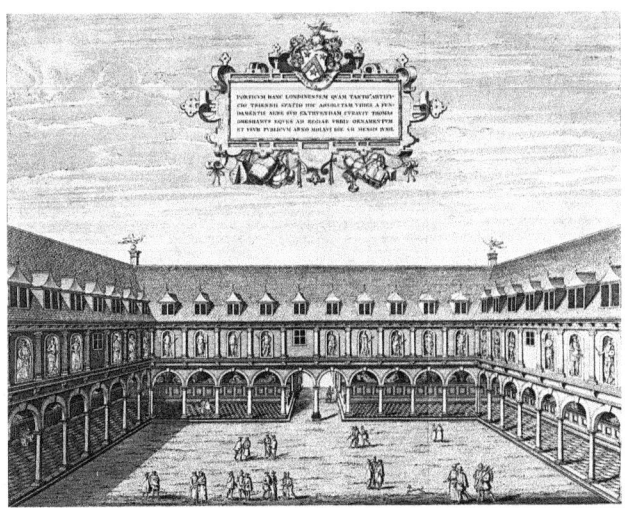

Figure 4. Gresham College from John Ward's *The Lives of the Professors of Gresham College* (1740). Engraved by George Vertue.

for the draughtsmen, they have the advantage of being visible from the outside in aerial view. A later view of Gresham College by George Vertue for John Ward's *The Lives of the Professors of Gresham College* (1740) shows this aerial view, emphasising the quadrangle shape (Figure 4).

An earlier view of the Royal Exchange by Pieter Van Der Aa also shows the same design, with the arches of the galleries – the significant meeting places – well outlined (Figure 5).

The square space as a place of sociability also underlies views such as that of the Restoration 'frost fairs' which were held on the frozen Thames in winter, where the area dedicated to the fair between the banks and the bridges is shown in frontal perspective and shaped like a quadrangle.

Thus, what appear as voids on maps, such as courtyards, were the significant meeting points: marks of sociability. In a plan of the houses destroyed in the Great Fire, the courtyards are clearly marked, and so are the large quadrangles such as the Royal Exchange: *An Exact Surveigh of the Streets Lanes and Churches Contained Within the Ruines of the City of London* (1666). This precedes Nolli's map of Rome (1748) in recent research

Figure 5. *Byrsa Londinensis, vulgo The Royall Exchange of London* (1644). Engraved by Wenceslaus Hollar.

on the interpretation of historical cartography now seen as a remarkable model of social/spatial interaction based on the inclusion of solid/void areas.[15]

The social function of meeting places thus dictates the presentation of the architectural layout: the implicit presence of sociability networks influences the perception of architecture and townscape, where 'negative' shapes (empty spaces) interact with solid or 'positive' shapes – an interpretation that would be emphasised by twentieth-century urban theorists.[16]

Buildings: utilitarian and commemorative
In the perception of social space, with the rise of professional attitudes we should take into account the rise of purpose-built structures. These were a well-known feature of the time and ranged from the Sheldonian theatre in Oxford, housing ceremonies, to dockyards and hospitals. If we look at utilitarian buildings meant for a particular social group, such as the Chelsea Hospital for old soldiers, one of the characteristic buildings of the Restoration, we see that it was a subject for experiments in visual representation: Thomas Malton uses it to demonstrate his new perspective system in his 1775 treatise.[17] Such buildings, where regular classical façades in straight lines covered a sequence of functional areas (the chapel and the hall and the residences) provided a good example for a demonstration of skilful spatial layout.[18]

If we now look at commemorative buildings, and primarily the Monument built after the Great Fire (1671–76), the most famous engraving (by Sutton Nicholls, 1753) shows it as centrepiece of a square space shown frontally, but later engravings (late eighteenth century) emphasise the sequence of spaces towards the church, the bridge and the Thames, and the movement of people (Figure 6).[19]

The Monument has a dual function: a heritage function, commemorating the Great Fire, and a scientific one: for Hooke and Wren, it served as the location for a telescope, which was placed inside; they conducted 'height'

[15] http://nolli.uoregon.edu/cartography.asp (accessed June 2018).
[16] Notably Bruno Zevi, *Saper Vedere la Città*, Turin, Einaudi, 1960, in which he sees the capacity to remember the shape of empty places – the *piazze* – as the test of an observer's sensitivity to cityscape (p. 6).
[17] Thomas Malton, *A Compleat Treatise on Perspective, in Theory and Practice* (London, 1775).
[18] http://www.18thc-cities.paris-sorbonne.fr/spip.php?article225 (accessed June 2018).
[19] *A View of the Monument erected in Memory of the dreadfull Fire in the Year 1666*, 1741.

Figure 6. Robert Hooke, *The Monument to the Great Fire of London, 1671–76*. Engraved by Sutton Nicholls (c. 1753).

experiments from the balcony. Scientific perception was superimposed on urban images. This affected sociability, since scientific networks extended social links, and such places were thus loci of sociability in two ways – as civic monuments and as meeting points for scientific experiments; the rise of science allows for urban places to have this dual reading according to sociability groups.[20]

We can thus decipher multiple sociability patterns if we analyse the structure of images in terms of seventeenth-century constituent visual conventions: framing of views, depiction of figures, aerial views, angles of view with frontal or oblique perspective. These options offered to draughtsmen according to the artistic practices of the time were used in a manner which reveals the perception of changing sociability patterns and, in many cases, of tensions or multiple readings.

Beyond the human scale: images of the very small and the very large, and their influence on the representation of society

When discussing visual conventions in a changing intellectual context, different sets of such conventions actually emerge, corresponding to distinct approaches; more particularly in the Restoration period, the rise of scientific representational practices introduced new modes of vision or 'information visualisation', as we call it now, and we have to ask how far they interacted with images of society. Perhaps reciprocally: were scientific diagrams used in the description of sociability networks in the same way as mathematical concepts started to be used to study society?[21] And vice versa, were concepts from the philosophical or historical field used to identify the newly discovered scientific phenomena? Studying in what respects images of society interacted with the new modes of scientific representation raises a question of scale, with the invention of optical instruments (the telescope and the microscope) providing images of objects of much larger or smaller size than the human scale, creating a challenge to terminology and conceptualisation which affected all spheres of thought as well as public attitudes.

The microscopic scale: from society to science

As an example of such transfer, Hooke invented the word 'cell' in biology for his study of a slice of cork viewed with a microscope, by analogy with

---

[20] See Matthew F. Walker, 'The limits of collaboration: Robert Hooke, Christopher Wren and the designing of the monument to the great fire of London', *Notes and Records of the Royal Society of London* (2011) 65: 121–43. http://rsnr.royalsocietypublishing.org/content/65/2/121 (accessed June 2018).

[21] 'Political arithmetic' was then a new field of study, quantifying social data such as population statistics, or the value of land, in the work of William Petty and Charles Davenant for instance – see, for instance, Ted McCormick, *William Petty and the Ambitions of Political Arithmetic* (Oxford, 2009).

monks' cells: with a change of scale, a type of social organisation, that of the monastery, provided a model for a new scientific concept (*Micrographia*, 1665).[22] It is worth noting that monasteries no longer existed in Hooke's England; when we discuss perceptions of social bonds, we should note how models of sociability relate to time: they may be meant as still uncertain interpretations of emerging phenomena, turned towards the future; or, on the contrary they may be based on obsolete or foreign forms of sociability, more fixed and stable. Also, such metaphors are dependent on the degree of precision of the tools used: we now know that the 'cell' analogy was dependent on the quality of the instrument. As the *Oxford English Dictionary* stresses, the reason for the use of the term was that the cell was seen as empty with a low-resolution microscope, so that it looked like a frame rather than a content of social organisation; we revert to the notion of empty spaces. It was for the definition of such empty spaces that Hooke had to resort to the social field to find a new term. We should note that he was interested in grid-like modes of representation in the social field as well, his plan for the rebuilding of London after the Great Fire being of such a type, as opposed to the other famous centralised projects.[23]

The spatial layout may be seen as a 'cognitive node', to be compared with other plans for the rebuilding of London related to other 'cognitive nodes': the interaction between scientific and social representation affects cognitive modes more generally.[24]

Moreover, since such forms of conceptualisation are dependent on the instruments used to mediate perception, the metaphorical transfers are valid for a given scale and a given resolution of the instrument. The question of scale in vision is one that also preoccupied Hooke: he was among the first to have projected a portable *camera obscura*; earlier models were whole rooms in which the observer sat, whereas the portable *camera*, by becoming smaller, allows scientists to carry on their observations in the vaster, outside world, thus ranging from the small to the large – meant to draw the 'picture of anything', as an illustrated account explains (Figure 7).

From the Restoration onward, we should be prepared to look for analogies to human society at different scales: scientific notions had become available, highlighting the differences of scale at which it was now possible

---

[22] https://royalsociety.org/collections/micrographia/ (accessed June 2018).
[23] Wren's in particular, according to the notorious debate.
[24] See Pascal Brioist, 'Hooke et Pepys. Deux espaces-vécus du Londres du XVIIe siècle', in *Images et imaginaires de la ville à l'époque moderne*, ed. Claude Petitfrère, (Tours, 1998), 15–34, http://books.openedition.org/pufr/2001 (accessed June 2018).

Figure 7. Robert Hooke, *Picture Box*, 1694. From Robert Hooke, 'An Instrument of Use to take the Draught, or Picture of any Thing. Communicated by Dr. Hook [sic] to the Royal Society Dec. 19., 1694', in William Derham, *Philosophical Experiments and Observations of the late eminent Dr. Hooke* (London, 1726), 295.

to make observations using the new optical instruments.[25] As we have seen above with regard to the origin of the term 'cell', they were soon to interact with metaphors in scientific language and in everyday language describing social phenomena.

The global scale: from science to society
If, for the newly discovered diminutive scientific objects of the 1660s, terms describing a type of sociability are a source of modelling, the reverse process operates for the research activities of the time at the scale of the universe. In the 1680s the scientific exploration of vast geographical phenomena – the winds – was in turn to influence modes of sociability: networks of scientists had to expand beyond visible sociability. Scientists started exploring uncharted areas such as winds and currents. Large atmospheric effects which are the environment of activity rather than activity itself, beyond the usual human habitat, and above all constantly changing rather than based on fixed coordinates, needed the developing technique of infinitesimal calculus because of their fluid nature. Then the investigators needed support

---

[25] See in particular Hooke's preface to *Micrographia* (1665), 'By means of the telescopes, there is nothing so far distant but may be represented to our view; and by the help of microscopes, there is nothing so small as to escape our inquiry' (n.p.).

beyond their own means and that of their immediate circle, on account of both the complexity and the immense number of the phenomena and data, and they had to evolve a new type of scientific sociability.

Halley wrote, in his study of the winds: 'It is not the work of one, nor a few, but a Multitude of observers, to bring together the experience requisite to perfect and compose a perfect History of these Winds.'[26] Because science in these new fields is based on experience, numerous experiments are necessary in order to reach a conclusion, which requires 'a multitude of observers'; the word used by Halley, 'history', had a specific meaning in the scientific writings of the time, referring to the chronological account of a series of experiments, insisting on the number of required attempts. Another area of his work for which he is famous also draws on experiments on a scale beyond the scope of a single man: 'Halley's comet', named after him because he guessed when the comet would reappear (long after his death) by extrapolation, hoping that his successors, when they saw it, would remember that he had predicted its return. This was the moment when science first had to work by extrapolation beyond limits that could be directly experienced, and this called for a new type of sociability in space and time: calling on the observations of different groups of people, both scientists and mariners, known or unknown to the authors, and on the experience of future generations.[27] Although such a phenomenon at large was still a future development, it is important to notice these early isolated examples.

Scientific sociability, past and present modelling
Present-day modelling of scientific networks based on the principle of the 'six degrees' (the assumption that all human beings are connected by sociability networks such that anyone is never more than six links away from any other person)[28] has been retrospectively applied to the scientific networks of the seventeenth century.[29] We see that long-distance relations predominate, across Britain and on the European scale rather than on the

---

[26] 1686, Royal Society vol. 16, shown at exhibition *Beautiful Science* at the British Library in April 2014.

[27] See http://britishlibrary.typepad.co.uk/science/2014/01/beautiful-science-preview.html (accessed June 2018); http://britishlibrary.typepad.co.uk/science/2014/08/beautiful-science-2014-picturing-data-inspiring- insight.html (accessed June 2018); http://britishlibrary.typepad.co.uk/science/2014/05/beautiful-weather.html (accessed June 2018).

[28] After the theory of the 'six degrees of separation' based on Karinthy's hypothesis (1929).

[29] http://flowingdata.com/2013/03/07/six-degrees-of-francis-bacon-a-17th-century-social-network/ (accessed June 2018).

scale of the city area, from the time of Francis Bacon to the late seventeenth century (the former work on Bacon being done by Carnegie Mellon and Georgetown, the latter on the later century being a study by the Geography Department of Loughborough University).

The study of Bacon's network was obtained by 'data-mining existing scholarship that describes relationships between early modern persons'. The new technique of data-mining is applied to text-based scholarship, which makes new patterns apparent, and this creates a new 'representation of the way people in early modern England were connected'. Not only new findings but also new modes of representation are based on data-mining.[30] The visual of the Bacon network was purely diagrammatic; the visual of late seventeenth-century scientific connections is geographically based, the nodes being placed on a map, on the cities inhabited by members of the scientific network; it is thus combined with a cartographical view.

Such phenomena can even serve as a model for our twenty-first-century 'crowd-sourcing', according to Lisa Jardine, who in 2013[31] drew a parallel between seventeenth-century scientific practices and present-day issues. After numerous studies of scientific exchanges in the seventeenth century, she shows that exchange of data enabled scientists to study a comet in 1680 and in 2007 on the same lines. It seems that the problems of scale which appeared with the Scientific Revolution had consequences on sociability which we still encounter through the issues offered by our new tools.

Images of the Restoration urban renewal, implying the structure of society and of sociability networks, thus reveal tensions within visual conventions governing the representation of townscapes and of society, due to emerging modes of social perception caused by changes in sociability and in cognitive modes, with the emergence of scientific perception. We have found a range of artistic practices, from the slight distortions of space meant to accommodate complete views of social groups, to original attempts at reordering views and maps so as to emphasise meeting places, and attempts to visualise scientific networks. With hindsight, we may see how present-day mapping techniques, when applied retrospectively to urban settings of the period, throw light on the evolution of the visual representation of urban society between then and now.

---

[30] P. J. Taylor, M. Hoyler and D. M. Evans, 'A Geohistorical Study of "The Rise of Modern Science": Mapping Scientific Practice Through Urban Networks, 1500–1900', *Minerva* 46(4), 391–410, http://www.lboro.ac.uk/gawc/rb/rb233.html (accessed June 2018).

[31] http://www.bbc.com/news/magazine-21802843 (accessed June 2018).

Chapter 3
Club sociability and the emergence of new 'sociable' practices
Valérie Capdeville

IN 1659 JOHN AUBREY noted, 'we now use the word clubbe for a sodality [a society, association, or fraternity of any kind] in a tavern.'[1] The *Oxford English Dictionary* uses this first occurrence of the term to define the noun 'club' as a rather informal social gathering held in a tavern or in a coffeehouse, during which the expenses were split among the members present. While the first coffeehouses started to develop in London during the Restoration, the first clubs, which consisted of small groups of men, appeared at almost the same time.[2] The English capital experienced important new developments as a consequence of political, social and cultural transformations at work through the Restoration, and especially after the Glorious Revolution. The birth of political parties and the explosion of the press; the emergence of public opinion and of a new public sphere; the expansion of trade as well as the revolution in consumption and leisure; the transformation of London and the development of the West End were all significant drivers of change in urban sociability, as they all encouraged sociable interaction between individuals.

The aim of this chapter is to consider the emergence and development of clubs in London from the Restoration into the reign of Queen Anne, resulting from a combination of various political, social and cultural factors. As supported by a wide range of scholars, the period under scrutiny favoured the emergence of new 'sociable' aspirations, practices and spaces in Britain, and the growth of clubs has to be seen in the context of broader

---

[1]   John Aubrey, *Aubrey's Brief Lives*, ed. Oliver Lawson Dick (Boston, 1999), 46.
[2]   See Valérie Capdeville, *L'Age d'or des clubs londoniens (1730–1784)* (Paris, 2008), 55–7; 'Coffee-houses provided the social and cultural locus for an early modern English public sphere': Steven Pincus, 'Coffee Politicians Does Create: Coffee-houses and Restoration Political Culture', *Journal of Modern History* 67, no. 4 (December 1995), 833.

changes in public sociability.[3] To Peter Clark, the author of *British Clubs and Societies*, 'the decades before 1688 marked the infancy of clubs [...] the first stumbling steps of a new social institution' and their rise 'was boosted by long-term developments after 1688'.[4]

This chapter will provide an analysis of the main reasons why people socialised through these specific new institutions as their various activities and interests determined the function of clubs and their impact on British sociability. What purposes did the club serve at its beginnings and to what extent did it answer new 'sociable' aspirations in post-Restoration Britain? What elements promoted its evolution and success as well as strengthening its social, cultural and political role in the eighteenth century? I will first show how an 'alternative political nation'[5] took shape through public participation and expression as a consequence of both long-term and short-term political and cultural developments. Then I will analyse the impact of the rise of a commercial and urban society on the success of club sociability and on the development of its polite and exclusive character. Finally, the chapter will develop some new insights on the ambiguous function of club sociability in the fashioning of the British gentleman, arguing that the London club can be considered as a key instrument of both self and social construction.

The birth of an 'alternative political nation'

The first significant 'club' was the Rota Club, whose republican members gathered at the Turk's Head Coffee-House as early as 1659. Among them were John Aubrey, Samuel Pepys, who called it the 'Coffee-club', William Petty and James Harrington, its founder. They organised meetings – debates sitting around a large, oval-shaped table. Deriving its name from the project of renewing a third of the members of Parliament each year, in rotation (so that in three years a complete renewal of Parliament would be operated), the club was short lived but became one of the most active political groups of the time. The first aspiration of those early clubmen in creating such an

---

[3] 'As part of a wider development of public sociability after the Restoration of Charles II': Peter Borsay, *The English Urban Renaissance: Culture and Society in the Provincial Town 1660–1770* (Oxford, 1989), 135–7.
[4] Peter Clark, *British Clubs and Societies 1580–1800. The Origins of an Associational World* (Oxford, 2000), 59, 61.
[5] John Brewer, *Party Ideology and Popular Politics at the Accession of George III* (Cambridge, 1976), 160.

institution was to participate in the political life of the nation. As Steven Pincus claimed, they shared 'a thirst for political discussion and a desire to preserve English liberties'.[6]

The political background of the Restoration and the Glorious Revolution generated favourable conditions for the development of 'sociable' practices. In the first chapter of this volume, Brian Cowan, in identifying the political and religious context which helped to forge and modernise the key institutions of sociability, insists on the link between the emergence of political divisions and the ensuing development of partisanship, and the development of new social spaces such as coffeehouses and clubs.

In 1660, with the Restoration of Charles II to the throne of England, government anxiety grew over the threat of political disorder. The 1662 Licensing of the Press Act restored censorship, which had a negative impact on society meetings. Yet, in 1674, a political faction known as the Green Ribbon Club started to meet at the King's Head Tavern in Chancery Lane and counted among its members some wealthy and influential aristocrats such as Shaftesbury, Buckingham and Wharton, all members of the opposition. The Whigs were the first to use the club as a meeting space for debate and opposition and to discover that it could be a useful instrument to influence public opinion. Political tensions in Parliament culminated with the Exclusion crisis (1678–81), which fuelled a violent debate that crossed the boundaries of court and Parliament to take place in public places. This new hub of reflection and agitation played a decisive role in the Whig propaganda campaign, organising petitions and demonstrations in the streets of the capital: twenty-nine other Whig clubs have been identified in London during that period.[7] Several of them were animated by the Earl of Shaftesbury (at the Swan in Fish Street, the Angel Tavern next to the Old Exchange, the Queen's Arms or the Nag's Head) or by the Duke of Buckingham (at the Salutation Tavern in Lombard Street). Their activities were similar to those of the Green Ribbon Club: they organised meetings, processions and petitions in favour of Exclusion. Whereas the Tories did not have any equivalent to the Green Ribbon Club, a few loyalist clubs were formed in the capital during the Exclusion Crisis. For instance, Sir Roger L'Estrange, appointed Surveyor of the Press in 1663, attended a club at Sam's (a coffeehouse in Ludgate). After censorship was temporarily suspended in 1679, the number of pamphlets rose rapidly, inundating the tables of coffeehouses and clubs: 'Pamphlets had become so intermingled

---

[6] Pincus, 'Coffee Politicians Does Create', 811.
[7] David F. Allen, 'Political Clubs in Restoration London', *Historical Journal* 19, no. 3 (1976), 561–80.

with daily life that contemporaries were in danger of eating them at the bottom of their pies or used them to light tobacco.'[8]

The direct consequences of the Glorious Revolution of 1688 were that liberty was then established as a right that resided in the body of the people and that Parliament was assured a crucial place in the governing process of the country. Thus, political activity in the capital increased significantly, in particular during parliamentary sessions: MPs felt the need to meet regularly in convivial spaces, where they could freely discuss and exchange information. Furthermore, pre-electoral activity was quasi-permanent after the Triennial Act of 1694, reinforcing political debate and party rivalry outside Parliament and the court. Daniel Defoe considered this political turmoil as the main drawback of the Triennial Act: 'the certainty of a new election in three years is an unhappy occasion of keeping the divisions and party strife among the people, which otherwise would have died of course.'[9] While that constant election fever reflected great political instability, it nevertheless had an undeniable positive impact on the success of clubs. The political elite was forced to search for political legitimacy outside St James's Palace and Westminster, both parties competing for public support to strengthen their political positions. The tensions between the Whigs and the Tories obviously had a key influence on the intensification of extra-parliamentary political activity and, more precisely, on the multiplication of clubs.

The eighteenth-century club rapidly developed both as an efficient tool to reinforce political partisanship and unity and as a potential counter power, sometimes perceived as a threat to the established order. The October Club, for instance, created in 1710, gathered an important group of Tory dissident MPs who denounced the moderation of Robert Harley's government and wished to act as a 'pressure group'. Jonathan Swift's *Journal to Stella* is interspersed with ironical allusions to that political faction: 'We are plagued here with an October Club, that is, a set of above a hundred parliament-men of the country, who drink October beer at home, and meet every evening at a tavern near the parliament, to consult affairs, and drive things on to extremes against the Whigs, to call the old ministry to account, and get off five or six heads.'[10] The 'October men' became so powerful that Swift clearly considered their club as a sort of counter power: 'the Club

---

[8] Roger L'Estrange, *Tears of the Press* (London, 1681), 4.
[9] Daniel Defoe, *Defoe's Review, Major Single Works*, 22 vols, ed. Arthur W. Secord (New York, 1938), vol. 5, 142.
[10] Jonathan Swift, letter 16 (10 February 1711), *Journal to Stella*, 2 vols (Oxford, 1948), vol. 2, 194–5.

is now growing up to be a party by itself'.[11] Therefore, the fact that politicians could meet freely outside the boundaries of state control fuelled the fears of the government, who in 1675 had already suspected the existence of a secret network when they accused the coffeehouses of fomenting a mysterious plot.[12]

Gradually, the crystallisation of political factions led to the birth of political parties and to better party organisation. It was only from 1714 onwards that the Tories started using the club as a real component of their party, as a means to coordinate their political activity against the Whig supremacy.[13] First coffeehouses, then clubs, had become the headquarters of political parties. As St James's Coffee-House and The Smyrna were reserved to the Whigs, the Tories frequented The Cocoa-Tree Chocolate-House or Ozinda's in St James's Street. In his *Journey through England* published in 1714, the traveller John Macky insisted on the fact that these practices were very strict and that no mixing was possible between politicians of opposite views: 'I must not forget to tell you that the Parties have their different Places, where however a stranger is always well received; but a Whig will no more go to the Cocoa-Tree or Ozinda's, than a Tory will be seen at the Coffee-House of St James's.'[14] This distinction proved enduring, since the Cocoa-Tree Club, whose meetings were held in the coffeehouse of the same name from 1727, was indeed exclusively reserved to the Tories.

An increasingly active opposition against the governing elite through riots or petitions and the multiplication of virulent pamphlets was a sign of the agitation of the time. Yet, political violence could be channelled quite efficiently through debate and convivial gatherings, making of those institutions an alternative political nation. 'In the time of the sitting of the Parliament, there [were] also clubs composed of the different Members of the House of Commons, where most Affairs (were) digested before they are brought into the House,' John Macky reported.[15] As a new space for political discussion and a new way of diffusing political ideas and influencing public opinion, the club not only proved to be a very useful tool for both opposition propaganda and party organisation, but was also considered as an antechamber of power.

---

[11] Jonathan Swift, letter to Peterborough (19 February 1711), *The Correspondence of Jonathan Swift*, ed. Harold Williams (Oxford, 1963), vol. 1, 236.
[12] 'Proclamation Suppressing Coffee-Houses', *London Gazette* (27–30 December 1675).
[13] See Linda Colley, 'The Loyal Brotherhood and the Cocoa Tree: the London Organization of the Tory Party, 1727–1760', *Historical Journal* 20, no. 1 (1977).
[14] John Macky, *Journey Through England* (London, 1714), 188–9.
[15] Macky, *Journey Through England*, 108.

Throughout the second half of the seventeenth century, clubs thus developed into arenas where freedom of expression prevailed and where political discussion and the criticism of power thrived. They became ideal spaces for the emergence of a public opinion. After the Glorious Revolution, the decreasing role of the state and of civic government also contributed to the emergence of 'civil society' and of a 'public sphere'. 'Civil society is that domain in which activities of a collective and individual kind may be freely enacted.'[16] Not subjected to any form of state or monarchical control, civil society was limited only by the private world of the individual, and its authority rested on the consent of those who made up 'the public'. The legitimacy of the institutions of civil society came from the free and voluntary association of private individuals acting as public citizens. The numerous coffeehouses and taverns where diverse political and social clubs gathered allowed for the collective formulation of individual interests and acquired a privileged role as sites for expression of public opinion. Through institutions like the press, the coffeehouse or the club, a new notion of 'the public' arose, one that was composed of private individuals who came together to debate and negotiate matters of public concern, to formulate public opinion.[17] Indeed, the press and sociable spaces such as the coffeehouse and the club had a quasi-organic relationship, since one of their common functions was to raise political awareness among the London population. They both fed the political debate, educated their readers and their members and thus enabled the birth of public opinion.

As a direct effect of the lapse of censorship in 1695, freedom of expression and of political speech was revived through a burgeoning press and owed much to the expansion of this new 'associational world', to use Peter Clark's phrase.[18] The growing interest of Londoners in politics, their thirst for information and the growth of literacy stimulated its development.[19]

---

[16] Richard Price, *British Society 1680–1880, Dynamism, Containment and Change* (Cambridge, 1999), 192. On the evolution of the concept of 'civil society' see Capdeville, *L'Age d'or des clubs londoniens*, 273, note.

[17] Jürgen Habermas, *The Structural Transformation of the Bourgeois Public Sphere: An Inquiry into a Category of Bourgeois Society*, trans. Thomas Burger (Cambridge, 1989), 25–6.

[18] From Peter Clark's title: *British Clubs and Societies 1580–1800. The Origins of an Associational World*.

[19] The literacy rate improved dramatically from the Civil War to 1714: 30% to 45% for men, 10% to 25% for women, knowing that the population of London was far more literate than the rest of the country, with almost 80% of men able to read during the Restoration period. See David Cressy, *Literacy and the Social Order: Reading and Writing in Tudor and Stuart England* (Cambridge, 1980).

News circulated in 'newsletters' written by hand in London and sent down to correspondents in distant towns and villages. London became a communication crossroads *par excellence* with the circulation of the first daily newspapers such as *The Daily Courant* (1702) and *The Evening Post* (1706). The birth of a periodical press, from the creation of the *Tatler* in 1709 and of the *Spectator* in 1711, endowed the club with a more cultural and educational purpose. This new institution not only served as a literary device for Addison and Steele to picture the capital's flourishing sociability practices, but was used as a real instrument of social reformation in a rapidly changing urban environment.[20]

The club as a new urban institution

The second half of the seventeenth century was marked by the modernisation of cities and the introduction of new habits of consumption and leisure, which favoured new sociable practices. Although the 'urban renaissance' and the parallel birth of a 'consumer society' were '*longue durée* processes and both began well before the Restoration', Brian Cowan contends, the rise of new spaces devoted to sociability was a factor of modernisation of post-Restoration urban society.[21] The success of coffeehouses in the Restoration period depended on specific political, economic and social conditions, which made the impact of those 'embryo clubs'[22] on the vitality of the urban community decisive.[23]

In 1700 London had become a huge city with more than one tenth of the population of England. It swelled to 575,000 inhabitants, making it the largest city in Europe, closely followed by Paris with 510,000 inhabitants and three times the size of Naples. After the Great Fire of 1666, the City of London was entirely rebuilt. The first phase of reconstruction started with the adoption by Parliament of a set of laws in 1667.[24] To this first wave corresponded the expansion of the capital westward with the settlement

---

[20] See Alain Bony, *Joseph Addison, Richard Steele: The Spectator et l'essai périodique* (Paris, 1999).
[21] See Chapter 1.
[22] A. S. Turberville, *Johnson's England, an Account of the Life and Manners of his Age*, 1933, 2 vols. (Oxford, 1965), vol. 1, 177.
[23] Peter Clark, *Sociability and Urbanity: Clubs and Societies in the Eighteenth-Century City* (Leicester, 1986).
[24] 'Acts for the Rebuilding of the City of London' (1667). Various accounts of this reconstruction can be found in *The Diary of Samuel Pepys*, 11 vols., ed. R. Latham and W. Matthews (London, 1970–83), vol. 8, 35, 72, 81, 136, 201.

of the aristocrats in the West End.[25] Parallel to this 'westward trek' was the transfer of luxury trades to the same urban districts, close to Westminster. It was at this time that St James's Square was built, taking shape in the 1670s and progressively becoming one of the most prestigious town addresses and a highly fashionable urban space at the heart of London sociability.[26] The second phase of reconstruction of the capital started after the Treaty of Utrecht in 1713 and was associated with the movement of the landed aristocracy, who had their houses built in the West End. In the 1720s Daniel Defoe was surprised by this construction frenzy, reporting 'the prodigious increase of buildings'.[27] These architectural transformations were accompanied by progressive improvement in lighting and sanitation in residential areas. From 1694, oil lamps were lit from 6pm until midnight, and it became safer to walk the streets of London after sunset and to participate in the nocturnal social activities, especially in the West End.[28] Even if it was still reputed dangerous to walk at night in the capital during the reign of Queen Anne, the progress in street lighting had positive effects on the development of 'those little Nocturnal Assemblies, which are commonly known by the name of Clubs'.[29] The 'colonisation of night' had started, and was considered by Peter Clark as 'an essential part of the refashioned world of urban sociability'.[30]

A variety of social events not only increasingly took place at night but, more significantly, multiplied in the capital during the period known as the 'season'. The London 'season' was a concept created before the Restoration but which, as a result of the new constitutional terms following William and Mary's accession to the throne in 1689,[31] henceforth coincided with the annual sessions of Parliament. It developed into an unprecedented social phenomenon which saw a growing tide of landowners come to London each year, most often from November to June, and enjoy a rising number

---

[25] Lawrence Stone, 'The Residential Development of the West End of London in the Seventeenth Century', in *After the Reformation*, ed. B. Malament (Manchester, 1980), 173–82.

[26] In 1720 the square was described as 'a large handsome Place, encompassed with Rails, and graced on all Sides with large Buildings, inhabited chiefly by the Nobility', John Strype, *The Survey of London*, 2 vols. (London, 1720). Book 6, Chapter 6.

[27] Defoe, *A Tour through the Whole Island of Great Britain* [1724–25] (London, 1971), 294.

[28] *London Gazette* (30 December 1706–2 January 1707); *Tatler*, no. 96 (19 November 1709).

[29] Joseph Addison, *The Spectator*, no. 9 (10 March 1711).

[30] Clark, *British Clubs and Societies*, 171.

[31] See Hannah Greig, *The Beau Monde: Fashionable Society in Georgian London* (Oxford, 2013), 4, 6.

of various social activities organised essentially in the West End. From the 1690s onwards the concentration of so many coffeehouses and clubs in the district of St James's testified to the social vitality of the area and its identification with elite sociability.

This metropolitan shift in the life-style of the ruling elite was also a consequence of the development of trade. England's expanding colonial and commercial interests, and the creation of the Bank of England in 1694, favoured the development of finance and trade, which naturally stimulated urban institutions such as coffeehouses, since they provided public spaces for commercial transactions and news circulation. For instance, merchants started to gather in coffeehouses close to the Royal Exchange such as Garraway's, Jonathan's or Lloyd's, in Lombard Street, to meet their clients and reinforce their business networks.

The rise of the commercial and financial classes and the professions also had a direct impact on the success of club sociability. As trade flourished in the 1690s and the rising merchant class grew wealthier, more individuals wanted to take advantage of the economic growth to climb the social ladder and to adopt the manners of their superiors. They began to assume a dominant role in the nation's social and cultural life as well as its economic and political life: '[they formed] that class of leisured and predominantly urban families who, by their manner of life, were commonly regarded as gentry, though they were not supported by a landed estate'.[32] However, if London did not exist, they would be incapable of reaching and maintaining such social status. In the first decades of the eighteenth century, more wealthy Londoners aspired to become club members, belonging to a club being seen as a marker of prestige. Indeed, commerce could buy prestige: families could elevate themselves through trade and finance, which Defoe saw as a potential social 'rejuvenation of the elite'.[33] In *The Complete English Tradesman* he fervently defended the merchant's cause:

> Trade is so far *here* from being inconsistent with a Gentleman, that *in short* trade in England makes Gentlemen, and has peopled the Nation with Gentlemen; for after a generation or two the tradesmen's children, or at least their grand-children, come to be as good Gentlemen, Statesmen, Parliament-men, Privy-Counsellors, Judges, Bishops, and Noblemen, as those of the highest birth and the most ancient families; and nothing too high for them.[34]

[32] Alan Everitt, 'Social Mobility in Early Modern England', *Past & Present* 33 (1966), 71.
[33] Defoe, *Roxana, The Fortunate Mistress* (Oxford, 1981), 164.
[34] Defoe, *The Complete English Tradesman, Major Single Works*, vol. 1, 377.

Rising living standards as well as fashion contributed to the emergence of new behaviours and social practices: leisure and entertainment became part of the wealthy Londoner's everyday life and belonged to a new consumer culture.[35] 'New wealth brought new standards and expectations of comfort',[36] then shared by the members of an expanding gentry as well as some distinguished men of letters, artists and scientists, who came to dwell in the West End and were increasingly associated with the social and cultural development of those new, fashionable sociable practices.

In the second half of the seventeenth century some clubs started to promote knowledge. The diffusion of knowledge was then made easier thanks to the scientific revolution that was symbolised by the creation of the Royal Society in 1660, which obtained a Royal Charter in 1662. The existence of several small clubs and societies in the orbit of the Royal Society favoured scientific specialisation and emulation. The Temple Coffee-House Botanical Club, founded in 1689 by Hans Sloane and his close friends, among whom was James Petiver, drew together some of the most active natural historians of the day.[37] Although the club had quite informal gatherings, it was a significant focal point for scientific virtuosi and for promoting botanical knowledge at a time when the latter was still absent from the curriculum of educational institutions, including the universities.[38] Richard Coulton argues that it was 'a locus of gentlemanly conversation and socialising as much as one of cerebral endeavour and knowledge production'.[39] In the same way, the Club of Royal Philosophers, founded by Edmund Halley in 1731 and later known as the Royal Society Club, was famous for its convivial dinners, which were fertile centres for erudite conversation.[40]

---

[35] See J. Brewer, N. McKendrick and J. H. Plumb, *The Birth of a Consumer Society: the Commercialisation of Eighteenth-Century England* (London, 1983).

[36] E. M. Jones and M. E. Falkus, 'Urban Improvement and the English Economy in the Seventeenth and Eighteenth Centuries', in *The Eighteenth-Century Town 1688–1820*, ed. Peter Borsay (London and New York, 1990), 142.

[37] James Petiver (c. 1665–c. 2 April 1718) was an English botanist and entomologist, a fellow of the Royal Society. An assiduous correspondent and collector, he successfully cultivated sources of natural historical intelligence and material from the Americas to the East Indies. He later became a professional apothecary in London.

[38] See Margaret Riley, 'The Club at the Temple Coffee House Revisited', *Archives of Natural History* 33, no. 1 (April 2006), 90–100.

[39] Richard Coulton, '"The Darling of the Temple-Coffee-House Club": Science, Sociability and Satire in Early Eighteenth-Century London', *Journal for Eighteenth-Century Studies* 35 (2011), 43–65.

[40] See Archibald Geikie, *Annals of the Royal Society Club, the Record of a London Dining-club in the Eighteenth and Nineteenth Centuries* (London, 1917) and the club's manuscript 'Menu Books', kept at the Royal Society Library. On civil conversation

Conversation has often been considered as the best remedy for social tension. For instance, the Earl of Shaftesbury advised avoiding conflicts and harmonising the relationships between individuals by insisting on the equalising function of conversation.[41] Exchange and conversation were some of the clubmen's main motivations. Through these, they not only aimed to improve their knowledge but also to enjoy convivial interactions in their pursuit of happiness. Drinking and dining were obvious means to be happy in good company. Drinking and dining clubs essentially flourished from the 1720s, although the Kit-Cat Club was founded as early as 1700 and remained famous for its toasts celebrating some beautiful ladies of the day.[42] Addison insisted on the central function of food and drink in London club life: 'The *Kit-Cat* itself is said to have taken its original from a Mutton-Pye. The Beef-Steak, and October clubs are neither of them averse to Eating and Drinking, if we may form a Judgement from their respective Titles.'[43] The Kit-Cat was nevertheless a prominent literary as well as political club.[44]

Towards a polite and exclusive sociability

Several historians have agreed that there was an innovative feature in the rise of polite culture after the Restoration. In line with J. G. A. Pocock, Lawrence Klein considers that politeness 'entered its significant career only in the mid-seventeenth century' and that its consolidation was closely associated with a 'reorganisation of culture and social life at the beginning of

---

and scientific knowledge, see Steven Shapin, *A Social History of Truth: Civility and Science in Seventeenth-Century England* (Chicago, 1994).

[41] Lord Shaftesbury (Anthony Ashley Cooper), 'Sensus Communis, an Essay on the Freedom of Wit and Humour in a Letter to a Friend', in *Characteristicks of Men, Manners, Opinions, Times*, ed. Lawrence E. Klein (Cambridge, 1999).

[42] Written by Lord Halifax in 1703, here is an example of the poetic verses engraved on the club's toasting glasses:
The Lady Sunderland.
All Nature's charms in Sunderland appear,
Bright as her eyes, and as her reason clear;
Yet still their force to man not safely known,
Seems undiscover'd to herself alone. (British Library, Mss Add. 40060)

[43] *The Spectator*, no. 9.

[44] 'a social assembly of the leaders and many members of the Whig party [...] a sort of permanent joint committee of the party in the two Houses, meeting regularly to concert political measures in an informal manner', Walter Frewen Lord, 'The Development of Political Parties during the Reign of Queen Anne', *Transactions of the Royal Historical Society* 14 (1900), 117.

the eighteenth century.'[45] Philip Carter sees the emergence of 'an explicitly innovative concept of social refinement – politeness – practised by and within "polite society", by which is meant the people who sought politeness and the locations, broadly defined as the nation and the city, or as specific venues, where refined conduct was expected and encouraged.'[46] As a matter of fact, the emergence of polite culture was central to the development of club sociability, as clubs were the ideal places for the expression of polite behaviour and the recognition of one's social status. Manners, politeness, refinement were key words found in treatises and conduct manuals defining the great principles of the education of the gentleman. Seventeenth-century English courtesy literature provided predominantly elite men with training in the refined accomplishments necessary for the success in court and country life. For example, William Ramsay's *The Gentleman's Companion* (1669) and William Darrell's *A Gentleman Instructed in the Conduct of a Virtuous and Happy Life* (1704) extolled the seventeenth-century civic humanist ideal of virtuous behaviour.

However, the most influential early eighteenth-century theorists of politeness in Britain such as Addison and Steele, as well as Shaftesbury, endeavoured to shape politeness as a means to guarantee political liberty and new moral standards in a commercial society. The *Spectator* and the *Tatler* progressively diffused 'gentlemanly values' to their readers. By upholding the 'gentleman ideal', periodical literature attempted to polish and refine the conduct of the middle classes and to purge the elite of their habits of vice and folly. Reaching out to a larger public, it became a reforming tool, meant to diffuse new standards of politeness for genteel society. According to Carter, 'what mattered about politeness and what distinguished it from earlier modes was its innovative synthesis of relaxed outer polish with inner moral values, to produce a force of superior sociability.'[47] Defining norms of politeness reinforced the structures of the civic community and the quest for social status within the club, in particular. For those aspiring to be accepted in higher social circles, especially affluent merchants, prestige was rooted in new qualifications including fashion,

---

[45] J. G. A. Pocock, *Virtue, Commerce, and History: Essays on Political Thought and History, Chiefly in the Eighteenth Century* (Cambridge, 1976) ; Lawrence E. Klein, 'Liberty, Manners and Politeness in Early Eighteenth-Century England', *Historical Journal* 32, no. 3 (1989), 583; *Shaftesbury and the Culture of Politeness: Moral Discourse and Cultural Politics in Early Eighteenth-Century England* (Cambridge, 1994), 13.

[46] Philip Carter, *Men and the Emergence of Polite Society, Britain 1660–1800* (London, 2001), 1.

[47] Carter, *Men and the Emergence of Polite Society*, 23.

consumption and public display.⁴⁸ The aspiration to social recognition by one's superiors was clearly described by Bernard Mandeville: 'We all look above ourselves, and, as fast as we can, strive to imitate those, that some way or other are superior to us.'⁴⁹ Participation in a club was a decisive step for the young gentleman eager to polish his manners and culture so as to gain recognition from his peers and assert his social status. The various activities provided by clubs were an essential vector of those values and norms of behaviour, to which these exclusive circles were dearly attached. We can already foresee the reaction of the eighteenth-century elite, who would try to exclude the rising merchant classes from their clubs, using politeness as an 'exclusivizing' function.⁵⁰

In his pioneering work, *La Distinction, Critique sociale du jugement* (1979), French sociologist Pierre Bourdieu claimed that the social status of each individual determined a coherent set of practices, values and tastes, on which his social world logically rested.⁵¹ Bourdieu considered that access to some cultural practices was defined by norms which were different for all social classes. Therefore, an individual naturally develops strategies of distinction as he intends to assert his position in society. We can easily apply this concept to clubmen's behaviours, since clubs are powerful vehicles for collective practices and values and are highly representative of their social status. Distinction can also be interpreted as a distancing process, as an intentional quest for exclusiveness or elitism, also a characteristic feature of the gentleman's club.

Socialising among 'equals' was seen as a perfect answer to that need for distinction, community of values and education, so central to the social and governing elites. The club functioned as a sort of laboratory of polite society, providing the young man, eager for new social and intellectual experiences, with the perfect opportunity to polish his education in contact with men who embodied models to imitate.⁵² From the 1730s, a growing demand for distinction and exclusivity started to transform London sociability and

---

⁴⁸ Greig, *The Beau Monde*, 2.
⁴⁹ Bernard de Mandeville, *The Fable of the Bees* [1714], ed. Phillip Harth (London, 1970, 1989), 153.
⁵⁰ Lawrence E. Klein, 'Politeness for Plebes. Consumption and Social Identity in Early Eighteenth-century England', in *The Consumption of Culture*, ed. John Brewer and Ann Bermingham (London, 1997), 262–82.
⁵¹ Pierre Bourdieu, *La Distinction. Critique sociale du jugement* (Paris, 1979).
⁵² 'When a young man, new in the world, first gets into that company, he very rightly determines to conform to and imitate it', Lord Chesterfield (Philip Dormer Stanhope), letter 133, *Letters written by the late Philip Dormer Stanhope, Earl of Chesterfield, to his Son*, 2 vols. (London, 1774), vol. 1, 350–1.

significantly changed the functioning of club life: most clubs adopted more selective election procedures and stricter internal rules. This came from a desire to restrain their access, in a reaction to the openness and publicity of coffeehouse sociability. For example, White's Chocolate-House became a private club in 1736, The Club of Royal Philosophers (future Royal Society Club) appeared in 1731 and the Society of Dilettanti was founded in 1734. The selective membership was not only a means to guarantee social recognition through introduction to the best social circles, and therefore the consolidation of friendships and networks, but also an instrument of social discrimination, with the exclusion of unfortunate candidates from a restrictive group of carefully chosen equals. As one would expect, analysis of the various membership lists confirms that eighteenth-century club sociability was mainly aristocratic, a space for the British social and political elite. Nevertheless, a few eminent merchants were part of the founding members' list of White's Club in 1736: William Fauquier, Robert Bristow, Robert Dingley and Pierre Delmé.[53] Club members also included famous writers, scientists and artists, as they represented the intellectual elite of the nation: for example, Horace Walpole, David Hume, David Garrick, Edward Gibbon, Richard Brinsley Sheridan, Edmund Burke or Joshua Reynolds were all members of Brooks's Club. Being a member of several clubs simultaneously, or multi-membership, was a common practice which increased a clubman's social and political influence.

If eighteenth-century London clubs were reserved for the higher ranks of society, they were above all homosocial spaces. Most of their activities were clearly considered unsuitable for ladies. Dining and drinking, gambling and conversation were the chief motivations for such gatherings, and enabled clubmen to share their political, scientific or artistic interests in a convivial and 'safe' male-only environment. The sense of belonging to a select community was enhanced by the election of a new member, which was frequently followed by an initiation ritual. This shared experience produced as well as strengthened clubmen's ties. The practice of toasting, for example, cemented club membership and was central to gentlemen's club conviviality in the first half of the eighteenth century, although it progressively disappeared.[54] Moreover, the different rituals performed by clubmen, such as initiation ceremonies or the ritual of toasting, had a strong role in promoting masculine collective values.

---

[53] See White's members' lists chronologically arranged in Capdeville, *L'Age d'or des clubs londoniens*, 367–87.

[54] On toasting in clubs, see Capdeville, *L'Age d'or*, 139–45.

The self and social construction of the British clubman

The function of those increasingly exclusive homosocial spaces in shaping men's identities deserves particular attention, since being a member of a gentleman's club was not like any other social practice of the time. The specificity of the club, a social space between the private and public spheres, offered the British gentleman a unique means to reconcile his aspiration to both individuality and society. Alluding to the cohesive dimension of the club in his *Spectator*, Addison pointed to the clubman's double aspiration for self- and social improvement:

> Men are thus knit together, by a Love of Society [...] to enjoy one another, when they are thus combined for their own improvement, or for the Good of others, or at least to relax themselves from the Business of the Day, by an innocent and cheerful Conversation, there may be something very useful in these little Institutions and Establishments.[55]

Born from the free association of private persons in a public place, the London club, like the coffeehouse, was, according to Habermas,[56] a forum for discussion where public opinion was formed, a place where social practices were performed, thus fully following this dynamics of publicity. However, as I have argued in previous work, the British club occupied an ambiguous position within the Habermasian model. Located at the heart of the public sphere, it became, throughout the eighteenth century, an increasingly private institution. Clubs progressively deserted coffeehouses and taverns to dwell in their own private buildings, often re-creating a quasi-domestic universe, which made some often consider their club as their 'second home'.[57] Thus, the club, among other spaces of the eighteenth-century city devoted to social interaction, could be seen as a 'social space', an intermediary space, following Michèle Cohen's argument that 'social spaces were neither fully public nor private but rather a space-between, created in part by the nature of the activities that took place there, and

---

[55] *The Spectator*, no. 9.
[56] Questioning Habermas's model, Nancy Fraser denounced the hegemonic dominance of this male 'bourgeois public sphere', in 'Rethinking the Public Sphere: A Contribution to a Critique of Actually Existing democracy', in *Habermas and the Public Sphere*, ed. Craig Calhoun (Cambridge, 1992), 109–42.
[57] See Capdeville, 'The Ambivalent Identity of Eighteenth-century London Clubs as a Prelude to Victorian Clublife', *Cahiers victoriens et édouardiens* 81 (printemps 2015), https://cve.revues.org/1976.

comprising all the spaces for "society" both inside or outside the home'.[58] This particularity of the club would also be reinforced by its ambivalent function in the shaping of the British clubman's identity. It provided each club member with a space within the limits of which he could not only test but reconcile both his individual and his social selves.

For the British gentleman, the club served as an instrument of self- and social construction, shaping his character both as a private individual and as a public man. However, what challenge was the clubman really confronted with when becoming a member of a club? The constraints of group life with its rules and procedures; the social norms and codes he was expected to conform to; the social prescriptions related to gender expectations. This very challenge raised obvious tensions between self and social, individual and society, exclusive and inclusive. Man's 'unsocial sociability' was, for Immanuel Kant, a powerful way to express the conflicting social nature of man, torn between his sociable drive and his individualistic instinct, yet club life definitely mirrored and somehow reconciled such a paradox.[59] Echoing Kant's theory, developed in 1784 in his *Idea for a Universal History with a Cosmopolitan Aim*, a number of scholars have recently explored the implications of the paradox of collective and personal identity on the construction of social identity.[60] Is the construction of the individual in society a question of self-control or self-discipline, or is it, on the contrary, a matter of enabling the expression of one's true self, whatever the tensions this could generate?

The function of the club was to shape and sustain character or selfhood, as it prepared a clubman to be a productive member of the society he lived in. Jerrold Siegel, in his introduction to *The Idea of the Self*, defines the *self* as 'the particular being any person is, whatever it is about each of us that distinguishes you or me from other, draws the parts of our existence

---

[58] This idea is developed by Michèle Cohen, 'Manliness, Effeminacy and the French: Gender and the Construction of National Character in Eighteenth-Century England', in Michèle Cohen and Tim Hitchcock, *English Masculinities. 1660–1800* (London and New York, 1999), 47. In almost the same way, Amanda Vickery affirmed that those spaces 'resisted the categories of public and private', since 'the very function of sociability [...] is to integrate the two', Amanda Vickery, *The Gentleman's Daughter. Women's Lives in Georgian England* (New Haven, 2003), 196.

[59] The 'unsocial sociability' thesis was developed in Immanuel Kant, *Idea for a Universal History from a Cosmopolitan Point of View* (1784), ed. Lewis White Beck (Indianapolis, 1963).

[60] See Katie Aske and Kimberley Page-Jones, eds., *La Sociabilité en France et en Grande-Bretagne au Siècle des Lumières*. Tome 6 : 'L'insociable sociabilité: résistances et résilience' (Paris, 2017).

together, persists through changes, or opens the way to becoming who we might or should be'. He adds, 'From knowledge of what the self truly is people have hoped to gain greater happiness, deeper fulfilment, liberation from fetters or constraints, better relations with other people, or ways to achieve power over them.' He then concludes: 'Selfhood thus matters to us both as individuals and as social creatures, shaping our personal existence and our relations with those whose lives we somehow share.'[61] To adopt a more psychological stance, we could say that social interaction enables us to develop a sense of who we are.[62] Moreover, if sociability is the projection of self, it is also essential to self-formation. Adam Smith illustrated this process by making the following hypothesis:

> Were it possible that a human creature could grow up to manhood in some solitary place, without any communication with his own species, he could no more think of his own character, of the propriety or demerit of his own sentiments and conduct, of the beauty and deformity of his own mind, than of the beauty or deformity of his own face … Bring him into society, and he is immediately provided with the mirror which he wanted before.[63]

Social interaction and self-construction through club sociability answered the Englishman's aspiration towards individuality, distinction, eccentricity as well as his appetite for social cohesion, community experience and normative behaviour. For example, the coexistence of polite and impolite behaviours reveals that a gentleman's behaviour may adapt, depending on the various situations and on the company. The concept of 'occasional politeness' has been brilliantly analysed by Kate Davison.[64] The extent to which manners are dependent on social context also proves the flexibility of behavioural practices. Company is thus seen as the factor determining the 'habitus' of a social encounter (based on French sociologist Bourdieu's theory),[65] and hence what is considered 'appropriate behaviour'.

---

[61] Jerrold Siegel, *The Idea of the Self. Thought and Experience in Western Europe since the Seventeenth Century* (Cambridge, 2005), 3.
[62] Vivien Burr, *The Person in Social Psychology* (New York, 2002), 71.
[63] Adam Smith, *The Theory of Moral Sentiments* (London, Edinburgh, 1759) Part 3, Chapter 1.
[64] Kate Davison, 'Occasional Politeness and Gentlemen's Laughter in 18th-century England', *Historical Journal* 57, no. 4 (2014), 921–45.
[65] The term 'habitus' refers to the sets of bodily and intellectual 'skills' which allow people to accomplish particular social tasks in specific social settings. Pierre Bourdieu, *Le Sens pratique* (Paris, 1980).

Gentlemen could thus show considerable flexibility in their adherence to polite standards depending on the familiarity they shared with their companions. Their social identities were constantly refashioned by their relationships with others. This argument seems to shed a new light on the famous passage when Mr Spectator goes from one coffeehouse to another, blending into any company of men, by adjusting his behaviour and countenance to fit each place he visits:

> There is no place of general resort wherein I do not often make my appearance: sometimes I am seen thrusting my head into a round of politicians at Will's, and listening with great attention to the narratives that are made in those little circular audiences; sometimes I smoke a pipe at Child's, and while I seem attentive to nothing but the postman, overhear the conversation of every table in the room. I appear on Sunday nights at St. James's coffee-house [...]. My face is likewise well known at the Grecian and the Cocoa-Tree [...]. I have been taken for a merchant upon the exchange far above these ten years, and sometimes pass for a Jew in the assembly of stock-jobbers at Jonathan's.[66]

Gentlemen's clubs were a primary setting for the performance of the self, as they enabled social performances to be confirmed, imitated and even, at times, to surpass the expectations of company. It was in company that people learned 'how and what to speak; to move and to look; to gesture and to listen; to think and to respond; to participate in habitual routines and tasks; to recognise hierarchies and conventions – all according to place and context'.[67] Yet, as John Brewer claimed, 'the requirements that polite people shape their feelings according to their effect on others created a profound anxiety about their identity. Was there some genuine interior self, or was one only an artefact of polite society?'[68] Phil Withington suggests that 'it was through the symbiotic process of learning and acting that skills were embodied and the self was constructed.'[69] Club members gained a sense of their individual identities through participating in a collective identity,

---

[66] *The Spectator*, no. 1 (1 March 1711).
[67] Alexandra Shepard, *Meanings of Manhood in Early Modern England* (Oxford, 2006), 11–12.
[68] John Brewer, *The Pleasures of the Imagination: English Culture in the Eighteenth Century* (London, 1997), 99.
[69] Phil Withington, chapter 6, 'The Sociable Self', in *Society in Early Modern England. The Vernacular Origins of Some Powerful Ideas* (Cambridge, 2010), 200. Also see Dror Wahrman, *The Making of the Modern Self. Identity and Culture in Eighteenth-Century England* (New Haven and London, 2004).

and, perhaps even more socially useful to them, they earned some sort of status, based on the fact that they were part of a group while others were not. The dual function of the club as an instrument of both integration and exclusion takes on its full dimension here as it contributes to shaping clubmen's identities.

Belonging to a group usually takes precedence over the individual. It fulfils any clubman's aspiration for community, so that experiencing the pleasure of association can be considered as an end in itself. The individual is incorporated to the well-being of the social machine, and social interactions thus contribute to the creation of what Simmel calls 'the common consciousness of a group'.[70] But, contrary to what Larry Norman affirms, the self is not supressed in the service of sociability;[71] the self is tamed and integrated without being destroyed. The habit of social exchange strengthened the individual's control over character, encouraging restraint on self-expression and control over self-representation. As I said above, politeness requires a remarkable degree of self-discipline, as prescribed in *An Essay on Polite Behaviour* (1740): 'It requires the Conjunction almost of all Virtues to be polite and complaisant. A Man must be Master of Himself, and his Words, Gestures and his Passions.'[72]

The conviviality of club dinners and gatherings around several glasses of wine or a bowl of punch favoured the expression of the self through sociability and happiness. Many representations of groups of gentlemen sharing sociable moments together in their clubs testify to the importance of gender-exclusive company in the construction of their social identities. Joshua Reynolds's two famous group portraits of the *Dilettanti Society* (1777–78) pictured a constructed image of masculine sociable bliss, illustrating the improvement of the individual through the group as well as the cohesive and socialising functions of drink among gentlemen (Figure 8). Those scenes corresponded to an elite ideal for collective improvement. However, William Hogarth's *A Midnight Modern Conversation* was not meant to be a social performance or a praise of masculine sociability, but to offer a glimpse of the potentially excessive conviviality of club life. Whereas women were thought by some contemporary thinkers as necessary to temper the excess of men in drunkenness and bad language, their exclusion reinforced male bonding and was thought of as a necessary condition

---

[70] Georg Simmel, 'The Sociology of Sociability', in *Simmel on Culture. Selected Writings*, ed. David Frisby and Mike Featherstone (London, 1997), 127.
[71] Larry F. Norman, 'Modern Identity and the Sociable Self in the Late Seventeenth Century', *Nottingham French Studies* 47, no. 3 (Autumn 2008), 35.
[72] Quoted in Brewer, *The Pleasures of the Imagination*, 111.

for the constitution of British masculine sociability. The ambivalence of women's social influence on men was perfectly encapsulated by William Alexander in his *History of Women* (1779), who claimed: 'Of all the various causes which tend to influence our conduct and form our manners, none operate so powerfully as the society of the other sex.' Yet, he continued:

> If perpetually confined to their company, they infallibly stamp upon us the effeminacy, and some other of the signatures of their nature; if constantly excluded from it, we contract a roughness of behaviour, and slovenliness of person, sufficient to point out the loss we have sustained. If we spend a reasonable portion of our time in the company of women, and another in the company of our own sex, it is then only that we imbibe a proper share of the softness of the female, and at the same time retain the firmness and constancy of the male.[73]

Thus, despite the risks implied by the exclusion of the female sex from gentlemen's social gatherings, a major factor of cohesion was in fact the homosocial nature of clubs, based on male bonding, masculine friendship and masculine pastimes. The threat of women's influence on men's character was nevertheless considered as greater.[74] Indeed, if women's conversation could polish the gentleman out of his rude nature, it could also fashion him into an effeminate 'other'.[75] To 'retain manliness', as Alexander put it, men had to remove themselves from women's company and conversation and create or maintain a private space in which to preserve their masculine identity. In such an exclusive social space as the club, a man could perform his masculinity through his activities, his conversations and his behaviour. The visibility of gender and social performance could determine a man's future social and political success. Indeed, by providing its members with the respect and support of their fellow clubmen, clubs played a crucial role in the process of gender identification and social recognition.[76]

---

[73] William Alexander, *The History of Women, from the Earliest Antiquity to the Present Time, Giving Some Account of Almost Every Interesting Particular Concerning that Sex among All Nations*, 2 vols. (London, 1779), vol. 1, 314.

[74] On the threat of feminine or effeminate 'foreign' influences on club sociability, see Capdeville, 'Gender at Stake: The Role of Eighteenth-century London Clubs in Shaping a New Model of English Masculinity', *Culture, Society & Masculinities* 4, no. 1 (Spring 2012), 13–32.

[75] Alexander, *The History of Women*, vol. 1, 314.

[76] As John Tosh observed, homosociality revealed 'the central role of peer approval in confirming masculine status', Michael Roper and John Tosh, 'Hegemonic Masculinity and the History of Gender', in *Masculinities in Politics and War: Gendering Modern History*, ed. S. Dudink, K. Hagemann and John Tosh (Manchester, 2004), 70.

Figure 8. *Members of the Society of Dilettanti*, by William Say (printmaker, 1812–16), after Joshua Reynolds (1777–78).

The period from 1660 to 1715 was a landmark in the history of British sociability as it witnessed the emergence of public opinion, of political parties and of civil society. Such a favourable context encouraged contacts among individuals, stimulated the urban community, raised new common interests and developed sociability. As the first clubs appeared in London during the Restoration period and after the Glorious Revolution, those new institutions answered both an aspiration towards political freedom or defiance and a need for social intercourse. By the death of Queen Anne in 1714, clubs were increasingly considered as necessary components of public sociable activity. Throughout the eighteenth century, this exclusive homosocial space became a powerful socialising institution and an instrument of self- and social identification for the British gentleman. Therefore, the second half of the seventeenth century can be considered as a prequel to the emergence of new 'sociable' practices. Phil Withington's work on the concepts of 'society' and 'company' in early modern England has shed light on the modern concept of sociability.[77] If, in the seventeenth century, the term 'company' was used to describe institutionalised as well as non-institutionalised organisations, formal or less formal associational bodies or communities, it already suggested 'a politics (in the broad sense of the term) of social participation involving inclusions, exclusions and the construction of boundaries'.[78]

As I have demonstrated in this chapter, the advent of club sociability resulted from a combination of various factors, which either implied long-term developments or followed short-term events. It not only stimulated British urban sociability but was especially crucial in the constitution of a choice community of clubmen and in the development of influential social networks.

By favouring the creation of selective circles and networks, 'clubbability' has definitely played a prominent part in the evolution of modern British sociability.[79] Coined from Johnson's adjective 'clubable' in 1783, it is rooted in a historical and cultural national reality, both as a way of interacting with others and as an individual quality in a definite social context, that of the British club. Therefore, clubbability is not equivalent to sociability, since it encapsulates the very essence of the club phenomenon. Referring to the sociable qualities of an individual, his polite manners and friendly skills, clubbability also specifically outlines his ability to be accepted and esteemed in any select and closed circle. Clubs can be considered as key instruments in the fashioning of the identity of those who were members, both as social characters and as individual men, forging their masculine identity as well. The specific features and functions of those institutions

---

[77] Phil Withington, 'Company and Sociability in Early Modern England', *Social History* 32, no. 3 (August 2007), 291–307.
[78] Withington, 'Company and Sociability in Early Modern England', 301.
[79] See Capdeville, 'Clubbability: A Revolution in London Sociability', *Lumen* 35 (2016), 63–80.

would give eighteenth-century British sociability its unique character and favour the exportation of the gentlemen's club model across the British Empire.

Chapter 4
The tea-table, women and gossip in early eighteenth-century Britain
Markman Ellis

THE TEA-TABLE is an object, an event and a concept. In the first iteration, the tea-table is a piece of furniture, a table on which the tea equipage is placed. The term also refers, in a second iteration, to the social gathering at which tea is consumed. It further identifies a third sense, the topic of this chapter: a new and hybrid form of polite sociability in the early eighteenth-century centred around the consumption of tea, that engages both women and men in a liminal zone between public and private spheres. The tea-table as event and concept is imbricated in practices of, and discourse about, talk and conversation. As a location for women's talk and conversation, the tea-table has been consistently identified with, or scapegoated by, gossip and scandal. Each of those aspects is closely embedded in the discourse of sociability as it was practised and understood in Britain in the early eighteenth century. In this sense, the tea-table makes an intriguing and largely under-researched contribution to debate about women's participation in the public sphere in this period. Resituating the tea-table within this debate further requires reconsideration of the discursive formation of gossip and scandal.

The context for tea-table sociability in Britain is the emergence in the late seventeenth century of the consumption of tea, the hot infusion of the oxidised and prepared leaves of *Camellia sinensis*. All tea consumed in Britain in this period was imported from China and Japan: it was in very limited supply and remarkably expensive. Tea drinking was at first especially associated with socialising amongst elite women at the royal court, and retained a symbolic connection with refinement and elite women even after its consumption became common. In this it differed from its main rival in the market for hot beverages, coffee, which, sourced from the Levant, had become almost ubiquitous in London and provincial cities by the 1670s, where it was closely associated with the public socialising of men in the coffeehouse. In the early decades of the eighteenth century, tea consumption rapidly expanded in Britain. Whereas in the seventeenth century tea had been mostly sourced through the Amsterdam sales of the Vereenigde Oost-Indische Compagnie (VOC), in the 1690s and after, increasing quantities were imported into Britain by the English East India Company (EIC), from Canton and other factory ports in China. As tea emerged into wider public consumption in the first half of the eighteenth century, it remained strongly marked by its association with the women's socialising, with polite behavior and with the domestic or private sphere.[1]

The relation of new social practices to political discourse in early eighteenth-century Britain has often been understood within the rubric of the public sphere. The public sphere, as articulated by Jürgen Habermas, points to an area of social life in which ordinary people come together to develop their capacity to have opinions on, and make judgements about, cultural and political topics. In Habermas's account, the emergence of the public sphere points to a historical transformation in which the moral values and cultural ambitions of the middling sort gain ascendancy over those of the court and the monarchy. Hans Speier, a formative influence on this aspect of Habermas's hypothesis, argued that this amounted to a new role for public opinion – the views of ordinary people – in the decision-making processes of the state. The public sphere is closely identified by Speier and Habermas with new forms of sociability that emerged in Britain, France and Germany in the period 1650–1750. Following Speier, Habermas's most particular and winning example is his case study of the coffeehouse in Britain, in which, he argues, men of all stations of life met together for free-ranging discussion on topics that mattered to them, gathered around the common table to consume the exotic hot beverage of coffee.[2] The example of the coffeehouse, as numerous critics have noticed since, is somewhat problematic with regard to gender, as women were almost universally excluded from coffeehouse discussion, although women worked in many coffeehouses.[3] This is a pointed exclusion, as the transformation of manners in early

---

[1] Markman Ellis, Richard Coulton and Matthew Mauger, *Empire of Tea* (London, 2015).

[2] Jürgen Habermas, *The Structural Transformation of the Public Sphere: An Inquiry into a Category of Bourgeois Society*, trans. Thomas Burger (Cambridge, 1989), 32–3; Hans Speier, 'Historical Development of Public Opinion', *American Journal of Sociology* 55, no. 4 (January 1950), 376–88 (381).

[3] Emma Clery, 'Women, Publicity and the Coffee-House Myth', *Women: a Cultural Review* 2, no. 2 (1991), 168–77; Markman Ellis, 'The Coffee-women, *The Spectator* and the Public Sphere in the Early-eighteenth Century', in *Women and the Public Sphere*, ed. Elizabeth Eger and Charlotte Grant (Cambridge, 2001), 27–52; Brian Cowan, 'What was Masculine about the Public Sphere? Gender and the Coffeehouse

eighteenth-century Britain was articulated through a wider understanding of the role of women in defining civility, politeness and modernity. In short, women and ideas of femininity or feminisation were central to the new polite sociability of the public sphere, even though women themselves were excluded from the coffeehouse and the club.

As an article of furniture, the term 'tea-table' specifically identifies a table on which the items associated with tea-making – the tea-equipage – are placed to facilitate tea consumption.[4] In this period, the items of a tea equipage might include a tea-pot, kettle, sugar bowl, slops bowl, sugar tongs, porcelain cups and saucers and tea-spoons, with additional items according to taste. Richard Collins's conversation piece *A Family of Three at Tea*, dated to around 1727, which depicts a family taking tea, provides a useful illustration of the distinct items of the tea equipage and their refined and expensive forms, manufactured variously in silver and porcelain, with a tea-table, almost hidden, below.[5] The tea-table is distinct from the common form of the domestic table, typically by being small, and of a light and elegant make. Surviving evidence suggests that the first tea-tables so designated were imported from China or India, by both the EIC and the VOC. An article in *The London Post* in July 1700, for example, gave notice that among the cargo of the *Sarah Galley*, lately arrived from China, were 2,848 'Tea-Tables', amongst other 'Lacker'd Wares of divers sorts'.[6] Even earlier, Elizabeth Maitland, duchess of Lauderdale (died 1698), had a 'Tea table, carv'd and guilt' in her private closet at Ham House near the Thames at Richmond, as listed in an inventory of 1683, and still preserved in the house.[7] Such tables resembled a tray, set upon legs, made of highly prized exotic hardwoods, and often lacquered or decorated with mother of pearl. Some, such as that of the duchess of Lauderdale, were repurposed or retrofitted from imported oriental serving trays, as found amongst the Chinese

---

Milieu in Post-Restoration England', *History Workshop Journal* 51 (February 2001), 127–57.

[4] 'Tea-equipage' is defined in the *Oxford English Dictionary* as a 'tea-service' or 'tea-things', items discussed below. The first reference is Richard Steele, *The Tatler*, no. 86, 27 October 1709, (ed. Donald Bond, 3 vols. (Oxford, 1987), II, 43). The terms 'tea-things', 'tea-set' and 'tea-service' are first recorded later in the eighteenth century (respectively 1747, 1786, 1809).

[5] Richard Collins (active 1726–32), 'A Family of Three taking Tea' (c. 1727), Victoria and Albert Museum, P.9–1934; and another version: 'The Tea Party' (c. 1727), Goldsmiths' Hall London.

[6] *London Post*, no. 177, 24 July 1700.

[7] Peter Thornton and Maurice Tomlin, *The Furnishing and Decoration of Ham House* (London, 1980), 82, 84, and figs. 88–89.

repertoire of tea utensils, primarily by adding or elongating legs to bring the tray surface to the height required by European chairs. London furniture makers began making their own forms of 'tea-table' for the luxury market in the first decades of the eighteenth century, often using exotic and luxurious materials such as mahogany embellished with brass inlay. Although such highly ornamented tea-tables were obviously very expensive, the form of the tea-table became a central part of the polite equipment of the tea service, alongside porcelain tea-cups and slops bowls, silver tea-pots and tea-spoons and the tea itself. In this sense, the tea-table was not only an item of furniture but also a tea-preparation utensil. The market for tea-tables, and their formal properties, was like that for tea itself, distinctively and importantly shaped by women's taste and patterns of consumption.[8]

Early eighteenth-century conversation paintings that depict groups assembled for tea drinking demonstrate how the tea-table as an item of furniture importantly shaped and defined the arena of tea-drinking sociability. The company are drawn up around the tea-equipage on the tea-table, either seated on chairs or (in the idiom of the conversation piece) standing nearby. The tea-table itself is mostly unrecognised and uncelebrated in these views – although in the second plate of Hogarth's *A Harlot's Progress*, published in 1732, a tea-table commands attention when Moll Hackabout kicks it over, smashing the tea-pot and cups, so as to distract attention from her lover sneaking out of the door on his tip-toes.[9] Although in this case the tea-table has literally upstaged the tea, in general the tea-table occupies a subaltern role. In Richard Collins's *A Family of Three at Tea* the tea-table is an inconspicuous rectangular table with turned legs, made of a dark, polished wood, perhaps mahogany. A similar rectangular table is noted in Joseph Van Aken's *An English Family at Tea* (c. 1720), and an oval pedestal tea-table in black lacquer can be seen in *Two Ladies and an Officer Seated at Tea* (1715), sometimes attributed to Nicolaes Verkoje.[10] As this visual evidence confirms, the social practice of tea taking was centred on the tea-equipage on the tea-table, displayed prominently within the social space

---

[8] Ann Martin, 'Tea Tables Overturned: Rituals of Power and Place in Colonial America', in *Furnishing the Eighteenth Century: What Furniture Can Tell Us about the European and American Past*, ed. Dena Goodman and Kathryn Norberg (London, 2007), 169–81.

[9] William Hogarth (1697–1764), 'Plate II from A Harlot's Progress', 1732, Etching, 31 x 38cm, Victoria and Albert Museum, London, Museum no. F.118:37.

[10] Joseph Van Aken, 'An English Family at Tea', c.1720, oil on canvas, 99.4 x 116.2 cm. Tate Collection, London; Nicolaes Verkoje (attrib.), 'Two Ladies and an Officer Seated at Tea' (1715), oil on canvas, 63.5 x 76.2 cm, Victoria and Albert Museum, London.

of the gathering. It also reminds us that tea was prepared at the tea-table itself by the ranking woman family member, rather than by a servant in an 'off-stage' location. This was unusual, redoubling attention on the tea-table gathering, as women in prosperous families undertook very little labour that was performed in public view.

As the place of a social gathering for tea and conversation, the tea-table also named the company assembled there, and its characteristic sociability. In an essay in *The Spectator* (no. 536, 14 November 1712), for example, Mr Spectator noted a letter from a 'pretty young' woman satirising what she called 'Womens-Men or Beaus', which he said was enough to amuse 'a whole Tea-Table of my Friends'.[11] In such usages, the term 'tea-table' has expanded from its place as an item of furniture, to describe the event of tea drinking, including the company assembled there. It is in this sense, as a synecdoche for the whole performance of tea-taking, that the tea-table is a most relevant example to discussion of sociability in early eighteenth century Britain.

Of the structural social transformations that point to the emergence of the public sphere cited by Habermas, the most appropriate comparison for the tea-table may be with the salon in France.[12] Habermas sees the salon as a social enclave of the town, in which the nobility, the bourgeois and the intellectuals could meet 'on an equal footing' for conversation and discussion. In the dominant account of the salon, these assemblies took place in the private home of an elite woman, to which invited guests, both men and women, would gather in a spirit of equality for polite conversation addressed to political and philosophical topics, as well as the ebb and flow of social gossip and scandal.[13] Recent research has suggested that the participants were drawn more consistently from elite circles close to the court, that the mode of discussion was not always egalitarian or polite, and that as the gatherings were conducted in private they cannot be considered as a constituent of the public sphere.[14] In the same period in Britain, this model of sociability was not unknown, especially among the elite, intellectually oriented women of the bluestocking circle such as Elizabeth Montagu and

---

[11] Joseph Addison and Richard Steele, *The Spectator*, no. 536 (1712), ed. Donald F. Bond, 5 vols. (Oxford, 1965), IV, 412.
[12] Habermas, *The Structural Transformation*, 33–4.
[13] Dena Goodman, *The Republic of Letters: A Cultural History of the French Enlightenment* (Ithaca, NY, 1994).
[14] Antoine Lilti, *The World of the Salons: Sociability and Worldliness in Eighteenth-Century Paris*, trans. Lydia Cochrane (Oxford, 2015).

Elizabeth Vesey in the 1770s and 1780s.[15] But in Britain such assemblies were relatively irregular events, and configured with more formal or theatrical modes of social interaction. Moreover, in both Britain and France gatherings such as salons were not known in the first half of the eighteenth century. The social formation of the tea-table, described here, is furthermore more firmly embedded in the everyday quotidian social world of its participants, and, as such, smaller, more ad hoc and common, and less intellectually ambitious. Like both the coffeehouse and the salon, the tea-table offers a spatial dimension for 'a realm of our social life in which something approaching public opinion can be formed'.[16] The tea-table fulfils some, and exceeds others, of the characteristics of the public sphere which Habermas observed in the coffeehouse and the salon and, as such, makes a distinct contribution to the debate on women in the public sphere.

Whatever the facts about real tables on which actual tea was served, in this period the concept of the tea-table was refined and elaborated in representations across a variety of media, including poetry, essays, satires and, in visual culture, conversation pieces and caricature. In such texts and images a somewhat idealised concept of the tea-table emerged as the location of a free and open discussion of matters of public concern, undertaken by a mixed group of men and women, privileging the voice of the young and of women, interacting with wider moral and religious debate through close proximity to the print culture of occasional essays, newspapers, conduct books, poetry, novels and moral philosophy. At the tea-table, individuals of both sexes gather together to participate in an open discussion uncontaminated by hierarchy or status.

This conception of the tea-table, as a safe place for heterosocial discussion about matters of significance, emerges in early eighteenth-century literature and visual culture. Its emergence is decisively reflected by the noticeable increase in tea-related literature in the first four decades of the eighteenth century. This increase in books about tea was also coincident with the significant increase in tea consumption in that period. While there is some discourse on tea in English in the Restoration, the publication of the Reverend John Ovington's *An Essay upon Tea* in 1699 inaugurated a mini explosion in poems, satires, tracts and essays about tea and its consumption

---

[15] Deborah Heller, 'Bluestocking Salons and the Public Sphere', *Eighteenth-Century Life* 22 (1998), 59–82; Betty Schellenberg, *Literary Coteries and the Making of Modern Print Culture, 1740–1790* (Cambridge, 2016); Susanne Schmid, *British Literary Salons of the Late Eighteenth and Early Nineteenth Centuries* (Basingstoke, 2013).

[16] Jürgen Habermas, 'The Public Sphere: An Encyclopedia Article', *New German Critique* 3 (1974), 49–55 (p. 49).

in the period 1700–40.[17] The abundance of tea texts is a distinctively British phenomenon, as there is nothing similar in European languages at this time, and is also historiographically distinct from publications about coffee and coffeehouses, where the most vigorous period of production was in the late seventeenth century, especially 1660–90.

An important group of texts in this new discourse on tea comprise large-scale poems on tea. These verse satires and didactic poems serve not only to elevate tea drinking, but also to establish and elaborate a new and complex notion of the tea-table. A series of poets published poems on tea in this mode, including Nahum Tate, *Panacea: a Poem upon Tea* (1700); Peter Anthony Motteux, *A Poem in Praise of Tea* (published 1712, first printed c. 1704); *Tea. A Poem. Or, Ladies into China-cups; A Metamorphosis* (1729); Duncan Campbell, *A Poem upon Tea* (1734); and *Tea, a Poem. In Three Cantos* (1743).[18] These poems employ various experimental and hybrid kinds of panegyric, didactic and mock-didactic verse forms to enhance the appeal of tea to consumers, by, for example, noting the high status of its typical consumers, its complex and satisfying flavour landscape and its sanative and medicinal attributes. Furthermore, each poem elevates tea by associating it with the drinking habits of the gods of the classical pantheon, picking up on a punning association between tea and the gods jocularly explored in seventeenth-century scientific writing (the word 'goddess' in Greek ('Thea') is punned with the invented word used to mean 'tea' in early modern scientific Latin ('Thea')).[19] Following Tate's lead, they do this while also providing an account of the origin of tea. In this sense, these poems can be identified as invention poems, a form defined by Ulrich Broich as a kind of mock-heroic developed in the Renaissance, which gave an account of the origin of a natural product or a craft.[20]

In Tate's *Panacea: a Poem upon Tea* (1701), the origins of tea are explored in two lengthy cantos. The first versifies an anecdote from ancient Chinese history that Tate had found in the travel writing of the French Jesuit

---

[17] John Ovington, *An Essay upon the Nature and Qualities of Tea* (London, 1699).
[18] Nahum Tate, *Panacea: a Poem upon Tea: in Two Canto's* (London, 1700); Peter Anthony Motteux, *A Poem in Praise of Tea* (London, 1712); *Tea. A poem. Or, Ladies into China-cups; a Metamorphosis* (London, 1729), Duncan Campbell, *A Poem upon Tea. Wherein its Antiquity, its several Virtues and influences are set forth; and the Wisdom of the sober Sex commended in chusing so mild a Liquor for their Entertainments* (London [1734]); *Tea, a Poem. In Three Cantos* (London, 1743).
[19] Johann Pechlin, *Theophilus Bibaculus, sive de Potu Theae Dialogus* (Frankfurt, 1684), 80.
[20] Ulrich Broich, *The Eighteenth-century Mock-Heroic Poem* trans. by David Henry Wilson (Cambridge, 1990).

Louis Le Compte, published in French in 1696 and translated in 1697.[21] In this narrative, tea is proposed as a palliative beverage with the power to heal internecine conflict, a quality that made it valuable in this period of China, and in post-revolutionary Britain. In the second canto, Tate creatively imagines a new mythic origin for tea, proposing that tea was the subject of debate amongst the gods of classical Roman mythology, who argue between themselves as to which god should be tea's patron. This is in itself ironic: as historians like Le Comte had come to understand, Chinese history could be traced back to before the classical and biblical periods, and yet classical and biblical scholarship evinced no knowledge of China or Chinese culture. Tate's neo-classical myth of tea ironises that moment of historical globalisation. Tate imagines a scene at Jove's palace on Mount Olympus where each of the goddesses proposes herself as the most appropriate patron of tea. Juno, as queen of the gods, claims her right to the 'Queen of Plants'; Minerva, goddess of wisdom and the arts, claims tea as the reward of scholars and the inspiration of the arts; Venus, goddess of love and beauty, claims tea as the associate of youth and beauty; Cinthia, goddess of fertility and virginity, declares that tea is felicitous for women as it encourages chastity; Thetis, a sea nymph, celebrates tea as one of the glories of the arts of commerce and England's 'Ocean-Empire'; Salus, the goddess of health, pleads that tea is hers because it is the panacea, a remedy to cure all diseases. The contest ends when Jove elevates tea itself to the status of a goddess. Tate's neo-classicising imaginary renders tea in a polite and elevated mode appropriate to its high-status social coding.[22] The council of the gods scene became something of a trope in tea poems, repeated in Motteux's *Poem in Praise of Tea*, published in 1712, for example. The trope has an important role to play in the gentle mock-heroic strategy of these poems, but the scene, with the goddesses arranged around the table politely debating their topic, also carries an important echo in this world, suggesting itself as a representation of a conversation around the tea-table. Reversing the metamorphosis, the polite conversation of the council of the gods casts a benevolently aggrandising light on any earthly tea-table party. The debate of the goddesses over tea offers a flattering model of the elite, heterosexual and polite sociability of the tea-table.

Joseph Addison and Richard Steele's *The Spectator* (1711–12), the most influential periodical essay of the early eighteenth century, furthered the

---

[21] Louis Le Comte, *Memoirs and Observations Topographical, Physical, Mathematical, Mechanical, Natural, Civil, and Ecclesiastical. Made in a late Journey through the Empire of China* (London, 1697).

[22] Tate, *Panacea: a Poem upon Tea*, 18, 29.

tea-table's construction as an important location for public sociability. Addison and Steele developed a significant re-evaluation of social manners, gently satirising folly and vice, as well as offering debate on conduct, philosophy and morals. In the tenth essay, published on 12 March 1711, Addison located new forms of sociability as central to the periodical's project:

> It was said of *Socrates*, that he brought Philosophy down from Heaven, to inhabit among Men; and I shall be ambitious to have it said of me, that I have brought Philosophy out of Closets and Libraries, Schools and Colleges, to dwell in Clubs and Assemblies, at Tea-tables, and in Coffee-houses.

In Addison's view, philosophy might be rescued from its scholastic obscurity by a transition both spatial and social, moving from universities and libraries into the new social world of the city: clubs, assemblies, coffeehouses and tea-tables – a list with an amusingly anachronistic Habermasian flavour. As Mr Spectator notes in the previous essay, these distinctive and innovative forms of urban sociability in early eighteenth-century London were all evidence that man is 'a sociable animal'. As Addison develops his thoughts in no. 10, it is the tea-table that he finds most propitious, for there alone his essays will reach an audience of women.

> I would therefore in a very particular Manner recommend these my Speculations to all well-regulated Families, that set apart an Hour in every Morning for Tea and Bread and Butter; and would earnestly advise them for their Good to order this Paper to be punctually served up, and to be looked upon as a Part of the Tea Equipage.[23]

Addison hopes that his periodical will become a routine accompaniment to the quotidian consumption of tea in well-regulated families: simply a part of the tea-equipage along with the cups, saucers, tea-pots, sugar bowls and spoons. Numerous further essays – at least twelve – envisage reading *The Spectator* as a necessary part of a daily habit of domestic sociability and tea-drinking.[24] In these essays, tea-table sociability mingles conversation and discussion on topics relevant to the essay's theme, alongside the consumption of tea and bread and butter. The essays imagine the tea-table routine happening in the morning, between members of the family and their

---

[23] *The Spectator*, no. 10 (ed. Bond), I, 44.
[24] Collective reading of *The Spectator* at the family tea-table is also noted in numbers 92, 140, 158, 212, 216, 246, 276, 300, 323, 395, 488, 536 and 606.

friends, including both men and women, and usually, but not always, both. Although these scenes may be only part of Addison and Steele's imagination, they propose that *The Spectator* was read aloud to other members of the group, allowing the moral question of the essay to be discussed or debated while taking tea. At the tea-table, as in the coffeehouse, consumption of the hot beverage is only a minor aspect of some more significant associated social practices, primarily conversational, but also about engaging in print culture.

In *The Spectator*, the tea-table is a social space and a spoken space. The numerous essays located at the tea-table evidence Mr Spectator's understanding that the tea-table is the location from which he might address women and matters of interest to them. *The Spectator*'s focus on women and their manners, Mr Spectator explains in the fourth essay, is what makes his new essay periodical innovative and significant. The essays, he claims, will examine the codes of behaviour and moral qualities of the 'fair Sex', but his purpose is not to ridicule female manners. His satire will 'not lower but exalt' women: although he will criticise folly and luxury when he finds it, he nonetheless sees women and their manners as the agent for the moral improvement of society. 'In a Word', Mr Spectator says, 'I shall take it for the greatest Glory of my Work, if among reasonable Women this Paper may furnish *Tea-Table Talk*.'[25] That is, he proposes that the moral and philosophical debates rehearsed in the essays should become the actual subjects of conversation around the tea-table, establishing a fluid interpenetration between the public world of *The Spectator*'s moral concerns and the private sphere of women and the family. Mr Spectator sees the tea-table as a kind of feminised analogy to the coffeehouse, as the location for a polite and conversational reformation of manners.

Further essay-periodicals followed *The Spectator* in imagining the tea-table as a social space central to their moral project. One such example is *The Tea Table* (1724), a half-folio essay periodical in the tradition of *The Spectator* that ran for thirty-five bi-weekly issues in 1724, published by James Roberts, and sometimes erroneously attributed to Eliza Haywood.[26]

---

[25] *The Spectator*, no. 4 (ed. Bond), I, 22.

[26] *The Tea-Table* ([London, 1724]). Patrick Spedding, *A Bibliography of Eliza Haywood* (London, 2004), 661–2. Spedding lists *The Tea-Table* periodical amongst Haywood's rejected attributions (as Ca.43). The misattribution probably stems from the title's similarity to another of Haywood's works (Spedding Ab.22), *The Tea-Table: or, A Conversation between some Polite Persons of both Sexes, at a Lady's Visiting Day*, published by the same bookseller, J. Roberts, in 1725. Although the former has been described erroneously as the original issues of the latter, the two works are, as Spedding concludes, clearly 'unrelated'.

The satire of *The Tea-Table* (1724) is primarily directed against populist theatrical spectacles organised by entertainment entrepreneurs – 'mercenary and unhallow'd hands' – whose activities have corrupted true wit and the theatre. In particular, the periodical identifies 'Masquerades, Hocus Pocus Tricks and Dr Faustus: Heidegger, Fawks and Rich' as the target of its satire. Johann Jacob Heidegger (1666–1749) was the masquerade impresario who successfully promoted masquerade balls at the Haymarket Theatre. Isaac Fawkes (d. 1731) was a conjuror who presented magic shows at Fawkes Theatre, adjoining the Tennis Court in St James's Street. John Rich, who ran the theatres at Lincoln's Inn Fields and later Covent Garden, specialised in harlequin roles in popular pantomimes. All these examples of debased forms of popular entertainment, the periodical reiterates, express a vulgar corruption of public taste. With theatre and spectacle as their focus, *The Tea-Table* (1724) essays have little interest in tea consumption or tea-equipage, and the essays do not represent the tea-table as an item of furniture. But the periodical is governed by the idea of the tea-table as an event and a concept. The periodical's consistent scenario describes a coterie of women and men sharing opinions and anecdotes, identified collectively as the 'Tea-Table'. Furthermore, the essays are strongly marked by the residual metaphor of the sociable space around which the members of the coterie meet. So, by reading the essays, the reader establishes that the 'Tea-Table' coterie assembles after prayers in the morning, at an undefined location, where the members take regular seats or places, served by a Gentleman Usher (a waiter or servant) who performs or adjusts 'all the Forms and Ceremonies, and the other Preliminaries that are usually observ'd among us'.[27] As the Tea-Table they engage in discussion and conversation, or read aloud from a newspaper, tract or correspondence, and offer commentary, observations and wit amongst themselves, very much in the model proposed in *The Spectator*. It is a polite and self-regulated space: they listen in silence to the longer 'relations' and narratives, and they are at times attended by two clerks who take down the proceedings in shorthand. Although essays in *The Tea-Table* (1724) describe a wide variety of topics and themes focused on theatrical satire, the periodical never loses sight of its controlling tea-table metaphor of heterosociability.

As Habermas clarifies, one of the attributes of the public sphere encountered in the bourgeois structural innovations of the coffeehouse is that the debate should be rational and critical. This aspect of his argument is presented within his historical digression on coffeehouses: his research did not indicate how this conception was itself an idealisation of the coffeehouse

---

[27] *The Tea-Table*, no. 11 (27 March 1724), 1.

debate, forged in the period in *The Spectator* and its ilk, nor how unusual most contemporaries would have found this as a characterisation of coffee-house debate, which was more often understood to be irrational, exuberant and factional.[28] The case of the tea-table makes an interesting comparison. Widely represented as a location – bourgeois, structural, innovative, transformational – for conversation and debate, to what extent might its talk be described as rational and critical? The answer, it seems, was mostly not much. Even though *The Spectator* finds the tea-table a fruitful location for the reformation of manners, most writers described its characteristic discursive formations as chatter, gossip and scandal. In terms of Habermas's argument that would seem to preclude the tea-table from consideration as a significant part of the public sphere. However, this understanding may significantly and unfairly misrepresent the nature of tea-table talk, especially in a culture that routinely degraded women's opinion and learning by unfairly scapegoating discussion amongst or involving women as gossip.

Tea-table conversation was habitually represented as gossip and scandal. Samuel Johnson, who thought that tea drinkers were 'brought together not by the tea, but the tea-table', claimed that it was nothing but 'a pretence for assembling to prattle, for interrupting business, or diversifying idleness'.[29] The vulgar satirist Tom Brown, in *Essays Serious and Comical* (1707), examined the equivalence between coffeehouses, where men assembled for spirited political conversations consumed by their own intellectual enthusiasms and interests, and tea-tables, a private or domestic space for women's talk, accessible through 'visitings'. In an essay called 'On Tea Tables and Visiting Days', Brown argued that the primary 'Entertainment' of the tea-table was not tea but the talk it occasioned amongst the 'Fair Sex'. There, he said, women are to be observed:

> letting a loose to their Passions and their busie Tongues, which are the Ambassadors of their evil Intentions; the Censures that they without Measure uncharitably fling upon others, and Backbiting the whole World, is the chief Diversion among 'em, and Scandal the principal Dish of the Collation. Ignorance and Pride, Malice and Revenge, set 'em so

---

[28] Habermas, *The Structural Transformation*, 33–4. For a discussion of the historiography of the coffeehouse ideal, see Markman Ellis, 'General Introduction', *Eighteenth-Century Coffee-House Culture*, 4 vols. (London, 2006), I, xi–xxxi.

[29] Samuel Johnson, 'Review of *A Journal of Eight Days' Journey* by Jonas Hanway', *The Literary Magazine; or, Universal Review* 2, no. 13 (April 1757), 161–7 (p. 164).

beside themselves, that they laugh while they are drawing their own Pictures in a back-biting Story on another.[30]

Brown establishes a free-floating equivalence, dependent upon historical tropes of misogyny, between women, gossip and tea, each of which reinforces the conditions for the other, and all of which are seemingly some distance from Habermas's ideal discursive situation of rational and critical debate. The dramatist Colley Cibber reinforced this hypothesis in his comedy *The Lady's Last Stake* (1707): 'Tea! Thou soft, thou sober, sage, and venerable Liquid, thou innocent Pretence for bringing the Wicked of both Sexes together in a Morning; thou Female Tongue-running, Smile-smoothing, Heart-opening, Wink-tippling Cordial.'[31] The character who speaks these lines, though himself no avatar of rational enquiry, enthuses that while tea is a sober and innocent drink, in the social formation of the heterosocial tea-table, it only encourages the exchange of gossip and slander.

Gossip, however, is worth further attention. Historians and literary critics have tended to take complaints against gossip at face value, even when articulated in a satirical mode. In this way, gossip has been routinely derided as both inconsequential and destructive, frivolous and corrupting, though how it can be both at once is unclear. It is also habitually associated with women's oral discourse. In the latter half of the twentieth century, beginning with work by Max Gluckman, sociologists and ethnographers have developed a revised view of gossip as a repository of information about social formations.[32] It is appropriate then to reconsider what it means that tea-table discussion, usually undertaken in feminised but heterosocial situations, is demeaned as nothing but gossip and scandal.

The sociologists and anthropologists begin by observing that gossip is ancient and everywhere in human society, and possesses some positive virtues, even when it is in itself cruel and destructive. Gluckman argued that gossip and scandal 'maintain the unity, morals and values of social groups. Beyond this, they enable these groups to control the competing cliques and aspiring individuals of which all groups are composed.'[33] The

---

[30] Thomas Brown, 'On Tea Tables and Visiting Days', in *Essays Serious and Comical* (London, 1707), 39–40.

[31] Colley Cibber, *The Lady's Last Stake, or, The Wife's Resentment. A Comedy. As it is acted at the Queen's Theatre in the Hay-Market, by Her Majesty's servants* (London, [1707]), 9.

[32] Jörg R. Bergmann, *Discreet Indiscretions: The Social Organisation of Gossip*, trans. John Bednarz, Jr. (New York, 1993).

[33] Max Gluckman, 'Gossip and Scandal', *Current Anthropology* 4, no. 3 (1963), 307–16 (308).

sociologists notice that gossip has an integrative effect, allowing social groups and coteries to define themselves by signalling who is included or excluded from gossip. The limits of a community are defined by (amongst other things) the limits of its gossip circle. Gossip is pre-eminently oral in its formation and circulation, and even in print often adopts the rhetorical structures of oral exchange. Gossip's oral focus reinforces its gendered status. Although sociologists argue that all members of society participate in gossip, women have a particular association with gossip. This association is both etymological and historically enduring.[34] Gossip is also associated with places where people meet to pass the time and engage in conversation, such as the well, the washing-place, the photocopier, the coffeehouse or the tea-table. The sociologists reiterate that gossip is gendered, sociable and spatial.

Gossip typically focuses on people, their actions and the ethical status of those actions: as such, gossip is a discourse on manners and morals. The German sociologist Jörg Bergmann summarises:

> The subject of gossip always consists of observed, conveyed, or suspected stories about personal qualities and idiosyncrasies, behavioural surprises and inconsistencies, character flaws, discrepancies between actual behaviour and moral claims, bad manners, socially unacceptable modes of behaviour, shortcomings, improprieties, omissions, presumptions, blameable mistakes, misfortunes, failures, – preferably from the area of the relations between the sexes.[35]

Bergmann's list of gossip's affinities is interesting, as it points to its closeness to the forms of satire that notice folly, failings and other vices in order, at least ostensibly, to promote reform and improvement. Although the effect of gossip can be cruel and damaging to its victims, sociologists are fond of noticing its complex positive function in the social organisation as a whole. Gossip is useful and productive, disseminating information necessary to society's smooth functioning and reproduction. The moral and philosophical project of gossip is firmly rooted in the quotidian and the practical. Gossip is socially engaged and practical moral reasoning. By participating in gossip, members of a society discover the limits of the shameful and embarrassing. In gossip, social behaviour is examined in public, and

---

[34] Giselle Bastin, 'Pandora's Voice-Box: How Woman Became the "Gossip Girl"', in *Women and Language: Essays on Gendered Communication Across Media*, ed. Melissa Ames and Sarah Himsel Burcon (Jefferson, 2011), 17–29.

[35] Bergmann, *Discreet Indiscretions*, 15–16.

the boundaries of what is acceptable to the group are clarified. As Patricia Spacks has observed:

> Gossip [...] is a catalyst of social process. It provides groups with a means of self-control and emotional stability. It circulates both information and evaluation, supplies a mode of socialization and social control, facilitates self-knowledge by offering bases for comparison, creates catharsis for guilt [...]. It provides opportunity for self-disclosure and for examination of moral decisions.[36]

So, although talk about gossip frequently takes the form of denunciation of gossip and its consequences, gossip itself makes an important contribution to the public sphere and its sociabilities.

Early eighteenth-century satire associated the sociability of the tea-table with women and with gossip, and in doing so scapegoated all three. An

Figure 9. *The Tea-Table* (c. 1710).

[36] Patricia Meyer Spacks, *Gossip* (New York, 1985), 34.

engraved print entitled 'The Tea-Table', derived from verses published in Nathaniel Mist's *Weekly Journal and Saturday Post* in May 1720, exemplifies this triple focus (Figure 9).[37]

The plate depicts six women talking and taking tea in a lavishly decorated room, gathered around a table on which can be seen the tea-equipage comprising a tray with spare cups and a spoon, as well as a series of fashionable objects, including a fur muff, a fan and a book. The open title page of the volume reveals its title, *Chit Chat*, the name of Thomas Killigrew's fashionable play of 1719, signalling that the women's conversation was light and familiar small-talk.[38] While the women converse, they drink tea: one woman pours from the pot, and others hold their handle-less cups between forefinger and thumb in the proper mode of the period. Tea, and the tea-table, this plate argues, was a place for the consumption of precious commodities (tea, porcelain, fashion) alongside a social performance of good manners and polite conversation. The verses published in Nathaniel Mist's *Weekly Journal and Saturday Post*, also engraved below the plate, reinforce these associations. The verses launch a trenchant attack on the moral status of tea-table conversation, describing it as the seat of female empire, as the source of gossip, scandal, slander, falsehoods and lies:

> How see we Scandal (for our Sex too base)
> Seat its dread Empire in the Female Race,
> 'Mong Beaus & Women, Fans & Mechlin Lace.
> Chief Seat of Slander! Ever there we see,
> Thick Scandal circulate with right Bohea.
> There Source of blackning Falshoods, Mint of Lies,
> Each Dame th'improvement of her Talent tries,
> And at each Sip a Lady's Honour Dies.[39]

Gossip codes women's talk as ephemeral, frivolous, false and destructive, but also underscores its focus on the morality of conduct. The engraved image renders this argument iconographically. Beneath the table, a horned devilish man sits drinking tea, over-hearing the women's tea-drinking gossip. The spirit of 'eaves-dropping' (the capacity for others, including men, to participate in the circulation of scandal) is reinforced by two men listening at the window, literally under the eaves. Meanwhile, in the upper

---

[37] *The Tea-Table* (London, [1720]). Image ID: lwlpro2596. Call number 766.0.37
[38] Thomas Killigrew, *Chit-Chat: A Comedy* (London, 1719).
[39] *Weekly Journal and Saturday Post*, 14 May 1720 (Issue 76), reprinted in *A Collection of Miscellany Letters: Selected out of Mist's Weekly Journal*, 5 vols. (London, 1722–27), I (1722), Letter 75, 225–7.

left corner of the plate, the argument is rendered allegorically, in emblem-book fashion. Envy, depicted as a filthy, topless hag carrying a viper and a thorned club, drives out of the room two women, representing Justice, identified by her scales, and Truth, almost but not quite naked. To this satirist, tea-table conversation was not characterised by polite and rational debate, but was subject to the more unruly energies of gossip and scandal.

This argument – that the tea-table encouraged gossip more than conversation – was rehearsed in an anonymous poem called *Tea, a Poem: in Three Cantos*, published in 1743. Although the poem defends tea itself as the 'Best of Herbs', the tea-table assembly is identified as a source of destructive scandal. Emulating Pope's *Rape of the Lock*, the poet adopts a mock-heroic mode to satirise the polite discourse of the tea-table. In the second canto, the poet describes a neoclassical 'Temple of Tea' at which obedient votaries gather to exchange gossip under the watchful eye of the 'saucy Virtues', Folly and Envy. At the altar, the twin goddesses of Scandal and of Pride lead the slaughter of Reputation, who, as she expires, calls fruitlessly for rescue by Truth. The gossipy gathering at the tea-table continues:

> Now all inspir'd, with fell malignant Rage
> (For so the *Goddess* bids) with Warmth engage;
> *Belles* meet with *Belles*, asperse each others Cloaths,
> *Prude* jostles *Prude*, and *Beaux* encounter *Beaux*.
> Determin'd all, to conquer, or to die,
> Gloves, Sword-knots, Fans, in rude Confusion fly.
> The Tumult thickens; now they loudly jar,
> All furiously involv'd in equal War!
> By Turns all conquer; all the Vict'ry claim,
> Triumphant those, who most can mangle Fame.[40]

Tea-table sociability, the anonymous poet suggests, encourages the exchange of gossip, figured as a malignant force, ruinous to virtue, destructive of reputation, driven by base motives and obsessed with the shallow concerns of fashion and appearance.

This essay has proposed that the tea-table was a location for the heterosocial discussion of public opinion, notably in the scapegoated formation of 'gossip'. As numerous scholars have argued, gossip and scandal cover a wide range of topics, but especially include a kind of socially activated debate on moral principles. Although the anonymous poet of *Tea, a Poem: in Three Cantos* lists clothing and other fashionable accoutrements (gloves, sword-knots, fans) as the subject of tea-table conversation, the

---

[40] *Tea, a Poem: in Three Cantos* (London, 1743), 29–30.

mock-heroic diction points to a more significant war over sexuality and gender. More importantly, topics of conversation at the tea-table, as in the coffeehouse, were unregulated, with broadly observed freedoms of expression, consumption of publications and association implying freedom from censorship, economic and political control.

Habermas's public sphere is a speaking space in which private individuals come together as a group to engage in rational debate on matters of importance, such as politics, religion, commerce and culture. Access to that space, Habermas proposed, was open and unregulated, and in this way a coffeehouse may appear more accessible than a domestic tea-table ensconced in the private sphere of the domestic home. The consequence of this conclusion, implied in Habermas's discussion of both the exclusion of women from coffeehouses and the nature of the private sphere, is to exclude women from the public sphere. As Jenny Batchelor and Cora Kaplan argue, 'Habermas's conceptualization of the public sphere served to relegate women to the confines of the domestic household and denied them a role in the formation of public opinion'.[41] But perhaps the assumption that the tea-table is located in the simply private sphere of the domestic world is unfounded. Numerous critics have since suggested that Habermas's assumption of a hard distinction between public and private is hasty and insecure. Amanda Vickery, for example, has pointed to the fluidity between the public and private worlds inhabited by women, both in her histories of domestic manners and in her historiographical examination of the discourse of public and private in eighteenth-century history. Gillian Russell, although examining the late eighteenth century, has described a zone of interaction which she calls 'domiciliary sociability' in which elite women engage in public culture from within the private household.[42] The cultural evidence of the tea-table in the early eighteenth century also proposes it as a domestic location with multiple and overlapping ties to publicness and public opinion.

In conclusion, this chapter has argued that the tea-table is constructed as a gendered sociability, dominated by the discourse of femininity, even when attended by men as well as women. The tea-table establishes connections to the wider world of politics and debate through the consumption

---

[41] Jennie Batchelor and Cora Kaplan, 'Introduction', in *British Women's Writing in the Long Eighteenth Century: Authorship, Politics, and History*, ed. Jennie Batchelor and Cora Kaplan (Basingstoke, 2005), 4.

[42] Amanda Vickery, *Behind Closed Doors: At Home in Georgian England* (New Haven, 2009); Amanda Vickery, 'Golden Age to Separate Spheres? A Review of the Categories and Chronology of English Women's History', *Historical Journal* 36, no. 2 (June 1993), 383–414; Gillian Russell, *Women, Sociability and Theatre in Georgian London* (Cambridge, 2007), 11.

of print culture: newspapers and periodicals especially, but also poetry, verse satire and visual culture. It is also supported by a culture of visiting and gift exchange. Finally, and most importantly, the tea-table is a speaking space, closely embedded in the practices of conversation, talk and debate. That debate has been characterised as unimportant and frivolous, excluded from the rational and critical by being scapegoated as gossip. This chapter suggests that there is good reason to reconsider how that scapegoating embeds its own gendered stereotypes. Gossip codes women's talk as ephemeral, frivolous and destructive, but also underscores its moral focus, especially in the parallel formations of scandal and satire. The tea-table might rather be considered as an embodied metaphor for gossip and, as such, for the participation of women in public debate in early eighteenth-century Britain.

Part 2
Competing models of sociability

IN THE SECOND section, entitled 'Competing models of sociability', the dynamics of transfers and oppositions between continental (especially French) and British social practices, which influences the evolution of forms and networks of sociability, is revealed. British society, through processes of imitation, hybridisation, rejection and redefinition, developed a new model of urban sociability.

The Académie Royale de Peinture, founded in Paris in 1648, acted as a model for the London Academy, created 120 years later, more particularly in the way both institutions dealt with the non-professional world of 'amateurs' in France and connoisseurs in England. The relation of artist members with cognoscenti is first defined by the founding texts of both academies. In chapter 5 **Elisabeth Martichou** examines how such a different approach is also reflected in art theory on both sides of the Channel.

Anglo-French links and rivalry also stepped onto the Masonic stage and informed the structures of British Masonic sociability. While Scotland is said to have been at the origin of some of the forms of French Masonic rituals, they were then transferred back across the Channel to England by English observers of the French practices. However, **Pierre-Yves Beaurepaire** shows in chapter 6 that the English Masons were not ready to give up their national obedience to the French. And some French Masons (in Brest or Strasbourg) decided to keep part of their allegiance with London, thus demonstrating the varieties and limits of strictly national practices of sociability.

His rejection of the continental models of sociability (which he scrutinised in famous cities like Montpellier, Nice, Pisa or Rome) led Tobias Smollett to suggest a different model of British sociability and to adopt a revised opinion on his native country. In chapter 7 **Annick Cossic-Péricarpin** uses Smollett's medical treatise, *An Essay on the External Use of Water* (1752), and his travel book, *Travels through France and Italy* (1766), to challenge the model of sociability that the British had recently forged. To the French model of heterosociability Smollett opposed his own model of British sociability, which extolled the virtues of homosociality, of masculinity, akin to the sociability of the 'rude people' described by the Scottish philosopher Adam Ferguson in his 1767 *Essay on the History of Civil Society*.

Scotland is further analysed by **Jane Rendall** in chapter 9, which explores the distinctive quality of the practices of sociability in Edinburgh between 1790 and 1830 through the life of the autobiographer Eliza Fletcher, 'the Mrs Mongague of Edinburgh', and her circle of friends. Fletcher reformed networks and literary salons, but also inspired elite women's activism in the newly formed voluntary associations of Edinburgh. In a deeply homosocial culture, inherited from the Scottish Enlightenment, Fletcher negotiated her extensive sociability while Edinburgh society defined its practices in reaction to the models of the French salonnière and the English 'bluestocking', sometimes with admiration and sometimes with hostility.

In chapter 8, **Alain Kerhervé** investigates the origins and specificities of epistolary exchange, a British form of sociability in the eighteenth century. Arguing that a British form of epistolary writing developed from the 1740s onwards, the author yet demonstrates that British specificities of that theory are questioned in reference and opposition to continental, more precisely French models. The Britishness of epistolary sociability thus finds its limits in certain manuals, for example in *The Ladies Complete Letter-Writer* and in William Gilpin's letter-writer, which paradoxically manages to combine forms of resistance to sociability with the promotion of epistolary sociability.

Chapter 5
'Amateurs' vs connoisseurs in French and English academies of painting
Elisabeth Martichou

IN THE HISTORY of western art, academies evolved from professional associations, also known as drawing academies, into institutions embodying cultural and artistic sociability. Under the influence of neoclassicism, academies flourished across Europe in the second half of the eighteenth century before institutional teaching of art began to be questioned at the turn of the century.

Moreover, academic institutions were a frequent object of comparison, whose purpose was to introduce a hierarchy between the three capitals Paris, London and Rome,[1] and it has been established that the Paris academy of painting decisively influenced almost all other academies of art. Most academies included honorary members belonging to the aristocracy or coming from the ranks of connoisseurship.[2] However, as the Paris and London academies were founded 120 years apart, the Académie Royale de Peinture in 1648 and the Royal Academy of Arts in 1768, it might be relevant to assess the limits of the Parisian model when it came to opening up to the non-professional world of connoisseurs, a development truly representative of cultural sociability, as it aimed to bring into contact people from different spheres but with a common purpose: defending the fine arts.

The words used to identify those who had an interest in the arts without necessarily having practical experience differ in French and English writings, and this difference is reflected in the dictionaries: there is no entry for 'amateur' in Johnson's *Dictionary* nor in Chambers' *Cyclopaedia*, whereas Pernety's *Dictionnaire portatif de peinture, sculpture et gravure* includes

---

[1] See Christophe Charle (ed.), *Le Temps des capitales culturelles XVIIe–XXe siècles* (Seyssel, 2009), 55.
[2] See Nikolaus Pevsner, *Les Académies d'art*, trans. Jean-Jacques Bretou (Paris, 1990), 103, 141.

a lengthy article defining the 'amateur' as a lover of the arts with enough enlightened taste to encourage artists and, possibly, engrave their works.³

The 'amateur' is portrayed here as a knowledgeable collector, perfectly able to advise the artist, while in the same dictionary the 'connaisseur' is considered as knowing the rules and precepts necessary to pass a sound judgement on a work of art; many try to pass themselves off as connoisseurs who are in fact ignorant.⁴ The ability of the true connoisseur to pass an aesthetic judgement and the existence of frauds are also present in Johnson's quick definition: 'connoisseur: a judge, a critic, it is often used of a pretended critic.'⁵ According to Carol Gibson-Wood, 'connoissance' was the term chosen by Richardson in *The Science of a Connoisseur* and the word 'connoisseurship' began to be used only in the middle of the century.⁶ Meanwhile the meaning of the term 'virtuoso' seems closer to the French 'curieux', a person whose interest expands to all fields of curiosity, while 'vertueux' in French either has the same meaning as 'virtuoso' or is more strictly applied to the true lover of painting.⁷ In spite of this lexical diversity two terms recur: 'amateur' is used almost constantly by the authors of the 'conférences', which were read in the French academy and which constitute the main bulk of theoretical writings on art in France in the seventeenth and the eighteenth centuries, while in English art theory the word 'connoisseur' prevails.

The role given by both academies to 'amateurs' or 'connoisseurs' is first enshrined in the founding texts of these institutions, the statutes of the French academy and the *Instrument of Foundation* of the London academy,

---

3   '[Une] personne qui joint à l'amour pour la peinture, la sculpture ou la gravure assez de goût et de lumières pour favoriser les artistes, encourager leurs travaux et souvent faire un recueil de leurs de leurs ouvrages. On peut être amateur sans être connaisseur et non au contraire [...] Nous avons aujourd'hui en France un grand nombre d'amateurs connaisseurs, qui se font un plaisir d'ouvrir leurs cabinets aux curieux'. Antoine-Joseph Pernety, *Dictionnaire portatif de peinture, sculpture et gravure*, 1757 (Geneva, 1972), 9–10. In Antoine Furetière's dictionary the two terms were in opposition and the 'amateur' lacked knowledge of the arts. See Pamela J. Warner, 'Connoisseur vs Amateur: a Debate over Taste and Authority in Late Eighteenth-Century Paris', in *Penser l'art dans la seconde moitié du XVIIIe siècle: théorie, critique, philosophie, histoire*, ed. Carl Magnusson and Christian Michel (Paris, 2013), 178.
4   Pernety, *Dictionnaire portatif de peinture, sculpture et gravure*, 91.
5   Samuel Johnson, 'Connoisseur', *A Dictionary of the English Language* (London, 1756).
6   Carol Gibson-Wood, *Jonathan Richardson, Art Theorist of the English Enlightenment* (New Haven, 2000), 199.
7   See Jacqueline Lichtenstein and Christian Michel (eds.), *Conférences de l'Académie royale de peinture et de sculpture* (Paris, 2006–15), vol. II, no. 1, 22.

to which must be added the plans that preceded the foundation itself. The differences and similarities in academic attitudes to amateurs or connoisseurs are also founded in the theoretical approaches on both sides of the Channel. Eventually, in late eighteenth-century France and Britain, amateurs were the target of criticism and their privileged connection with artists was questioned in satirical writings.

The role of amateurs or connoisseurs as defined in the statutes

Amateurs were part of the French academic project from the start. In 1648 the request seeking Louis XIV's protection was carried by a distinguished amateur, Martin de Charmois. Lovers of the arts, many of whom were aristocrats, attended the first meetings of the academy. The statutes of 1664 gave them an official position within the institution, as they underlined the importance of preserving harmonious transactions among the members of the academy and created six 'conseillers' with voting rights.[8] They also regulated seating arrangements and stipulated that the members of the aristocracy, the amateurs of the sciences and the arts (who could also be given voting rights) and the counsellors invited by the academy were to be seated on the left of the director.[9] In one of the early 'conférences', dated 20 September 1686, the role of the two monthly meetings of the academy was specified: one was for addressing current affairs and the other for encouraging sociable intercourse and friendship, both being indispensable and praiseworthy in all illustrious societies.[10] Not only did amateurs attend these meetings, whose purpose was not limited to discussing paintings, but they were also present in the drawing sessions after living models.[11]

However, this apparent opening to non-professionals was limited in scope, since between 1648 and 1747 only twenty-nine amateurs of the arts were appointed under varying denominations: 'conseillers honoraires', 'conseillers amateurs', 'amateurs honoraires', 'conseillers amateurs honoraires'. In August 1747 a new category was created, including eight 'associés libres' who would have voting rights only if there were not enough amateurs.[12] Thirty

---

[8] Anatole de Montaiglon, *Procès-verbaux de l'Académie royale de peinture et de sculpture* (Paris, 1875–92), vol. 1, 254.
[9] Montaiglon, *Procès-verbaux*, 256.
[10] 'Pour entretenir [...] cette liaison d'amitié et cet esprit de société qui a toujours été si nécessaire et si louable dans le commerce des compagnies illustres'. Lichtenstein and Michel, *Conférences*, vol. II.1, 152.
[11] Lichtenstein and Michel, *Conférences*, vol. III, 200.
[12] Lichtenstein and Michel, *Conférences*, vol. V, no. 1, 19–20.

years later, in 1777, the declaration from the king, once again confirming the statutes of the academy, conferred on amateurs the extra function of defending the progress of the arts and preserving the academic institution.[13] It was necessary to belong first to the category of 'honoraire associé libre' in order to become 'honoraire amateur'.

In the eighteenth century the 'honoraires' were encouraged to express their views in the 'conférences'. At the turn of the century the most famous art theorist among amateurs was Roger de Piles. Later on Caylus and Watelet occasionally launched into art theory, but most of the time the amateurs' lectures were devoted to biographies of dead academicians or, as in the case of Henri van Hulst, aimed at completing the historiography of the institution.[14] This was a way of serving the interests of the academy as specified in the 1777 Royal Declaration. Amateurs were also expected to commission works from academicians or make gifts to the academy from their own collections: in August 1750 Caylus offered a portrait of Dufresnoy by Le Brun.[15] The acceptance of amateurs within the academy was far from disinterested. They could contribute to the prestige of the institution through their social rank, their erudition or as patrons of the arts. Yet they were not always welcomed by professional artists. On 7 June 1732 so few people attended a lecture by Caylus that it had to be repeated the following month.[16] The engraver Charles-Nicolas Cochin was determined not to leave the monopoly of the 'conférences' to amateurs, and in 1758 he warned them against passing judgements beyond their capacity and considered it necessary for them to be in possession of natural taste as well as knowledge of the arts.[17] Artists tried to limit the role of non-professionals within the institution, thus questioning one of the fundamental tenets of academic sociability as defined in the statutes.

---

[13] 'Les titres d'honoraires, tant amateurs qu'associés libres, sont destinés et seront conférés, par voie d'élection, à des personnes qui, sans exercer les arts comme les académiciens proprement dits, seront distinguées par leurs connoissances dans la théorie des arts et de leurs parties accessoires, par leur goût pour ces mêmes arts et leur amour pour leur progrès, enfin par une intelligence en matière d'affaires qui puisse rendre leur surveillance utile pour le maintien et la conservation des droits et des intérêts de l'académie'. *Déclaration du roi, en faveur de l'Académie royale de peinture et de sculpture* (Versailles, 1777), 10.

[14] Caylus explicitly gave amateurs this mission in a lecture delivered in 1760. See Lichtenstein and Michel, *Conférences*, vol. VI, no. 2, 588.

[15] Lichtenstein and Michel, *Conférences*, vol. V, no. 2, 555.

[16] Lichtenstein and Michel, *Conférences*, vol. V, no. 1, 19.

[17] Lichtenstein and Michel, *Conférences*, vol. VI, no. 2, 544.

At the beginning of the eighteenth century, in the dedication of his *Essay towards an English School*, Bainbrigg Buckeridge regretted the lack of an academy on the French model which would enable the English genius to 'outshine' the rival nation.[18] It seems, however, that if such an academy eventually came into being in 1768, relations between connoisseurs and artists within the academic movement did not follow the French pattern. Indeed, if the Queen Street Academy, founded in 1711, included 'practising artists and interested amateurs', its successors, Thornhill's Academy and Saint Martin's Lane Academy, numbered very few non-professionals among their members.[19] In fact amateurs already had their own societies, such as the Society of the Virtuosi of St Luke created in 1689 or, more famously, the Society of Dilettanti founded in 1732 'for the purposes of friendly and social intercourse'.[20] Sociability played such a part in the latter that, if we are to believe Horace Walpole, to be accepted as a member, 'the nominal qualification is having been in Italy, and the real one being drunk'.[21]

Between 1753 and 1755 the Dilettanti were involved together with a number of artists such as Francis Hayman to elaborate the plan of an academy. The negotiations ended when the committee meeting of the Dilettanti on 20 April 1755 came to the conclusion that the president of the future Royal Academy could not but be chosen 'out of the Society of Dilettanti'.[22] This failure to reach an agreement is confirmed later by Robert Strange, an engraver, in his *Inquiry into the Rise and Establishment of the Royal Academy of Arts*. He maintains that the Dilettanti made the first step towards establishing and financing an academy and then concludes: 'After various conferences, the *dilettante* finding that they were to be allowed no share in the government of the academy, or in appropriating their own fund, the negotiation ended.'[23] The issue of power sharing thus precluded the possibility of mixing the artistic sphere and the world of art lovers, which might have been a strong sign of cultural sociability.

The rivalry for artistic control was to prevail over the imitation of the French model when it came to the opening of the future academy

---

[18] Bainbrigg Buckeridge, 'Dedication', in Roger de Piles, *The Art of Painting*, trans. John Savage (London, 1706), np.
[19] See Sydney C. Hutchison, *The History of the Royal Academy, 1768–1986* (London, 1986), 7.
[20] Lionel Cust, *History of the Society of Dilettanti* (London, 1898), 6.
[21] Horace Walpole, 'Letter to Horace Mann', quoted in Cust, *History of the Society of Dilettanti*, 36.
[22] Walpole, 'Letter to Horace Mann', 55.
[23] Robert Strange, *An Inquiry into the Rise and Establishment of the Royal Academy of Arts* (London, 1775), 61–3.

to amateurs, and this is reflected in the plans that anticipated the act of foundation proper. John Gwynn, an architect, in his *Essay on Design* (1749), included a proposal for a public academy. Like Buckeridge, Gwynn insists on the necessity of an academy to develop English artistic capacities and to promote English art. When he describes the French academic system Gwynn mentions the place given to amateurs:

> Some gentlemen, who are only lovers of arts and discover a taste of what is excellent are admitted to this rank [of Academician]. Artists may then have the honour to be patronized by those of their own body, who, though greatly superior in fortune, cannot rise to the same rank in that body with themselves.[24]

Clearly the situation of amateurs in the French academy is interpreted as one of subordination and social interaction does not give them any right to equality as regards decision making. When it comes to English connoisseurs, Gwynn acknowledges their potential role as advisers to artists: 'A perfect connoisseur, tho' no artist himself, is not only pleased with a fine piece of painting or sculpture but he knows from whence his pleasure arises, and perhaps can see what escaped the artist, how it might have been excited to a higher degree.'[25] Private gentlemen are also expected to finance the academy, a major difference from the French model in which the institution is provided for by the sovereign. Yet, according to the rules that Gwynn imagines as the founding principles of the academy, the 'officers' are all to be chosen from among painters, sculptors and architects and no mention is made of the participation of amateurs.[26]

A few years later, in 1755, a *Plan of an Academy*, emanating from the group of artists close to the painter Francis Hayman already mentioned, included gentlemen for the financing but omitted them for membership of the institution unless they were 'scholars'.[27] In this project, those who contented themselves with collecting were considered as tasteless connoisseurs, preferring old masters to contemporary British art: 'It will necessarily follow, that it must be with a painter as with the Roman Catholic

---

[24] John Gwynn, *An Essay on Design: Including Proposals for Erecting a Public Academy* (London, 1749), 38.
[25] Gwynn, *An Essay on Design*, 19.
[26] Gwynn, *An Essay on Design*, 81 ff.
[27] *The Plan of an Academy for the better Cultivation, Improvement and Encouragement of Painting, Sculpture, Architecture, and the Arts of Design in General* (London, 1755), viii, xii. See also Brandon Taylor, *Art for the Nation: Exhibitions and the London Public 1741–2001* (New Brunswick, 1999), 6.

saints, who are never beatified till a hundred years after they are dead, nor canonised till after a hundred years more.'[28] Indeed a lot, perhaps too much, seemed to be expected of connoisseurs in the years preceding the founding of the academy. Thus the painter Joseph Highmore reminds the reader of his *Essays* published in 1766, two years before the creation of the Royal Academy of Arts, that painters must not be left to be the only judges of their own productions and that they have always had protectors, not just princes and patrons but 'innumerable private persons' who have collected works of art and 'honoured the artists themselves with their esteem and friendship'.[29] The best connoisseurs are 'those who have extraordinary natural and acquired abilities, who have studied nature, and particularly human nature'.[30]

In 1768 the *Instrument of Foundation* of the Royal Academy of Arts specified in its first article that academicians 'shall all of them be artists by profession at the time of their admission'.[31] Unlike the statutes of the French Academy, the *Instrument* does not mention amateurs or connoisseurs. Mere lovers of the arts were thus explicitly excluded and the category of 'associates' created the following year aimed only at integrating practising artists, originally engravers, who had been omitted in the *Instrument*, as well as participants in the annual exhibition.[32] As Ian Pears pointed out: 'Even when the Royal academy was founded, the only place in it for amateurs was to offer specialised lessons, such as in anatomy, for the benefit of the students.'[33] Amateurs could be included only as scholars, well versed in human nature, as Highmore had put it.

Friendship and advice the object of art theory

So, one may wonder if the differences in artistic sociability on both sides of the Channel are related to a different theoretical approach in defining the relations between painters and amateurs. In France these relations were discussed mainly in the 'conférences' in the first half of the eighteenth century, essentially by two amateurs who were also practitioners of the graphic

---

[28] *The Plan of an Academy*, vi.
[29] Joseph Highmore, *Essays* (London, 1766), vol. 2, 84.
[30] Highmore, *Essays*, 89–90.
[31] Quoted in Hutchison, *The History of the Royal Academy*, 245.
[32] Hutchison, *The History of the Royal Academy*, 35–6.
[33] Ian Pears, *The Discovery of Painting: the Growth of Interest in the Arts in England, 1680–1768* (New Haven, 1988), 196.

arts, Roger de Piles and the Comte de Caylus, and by two painters, Antoine Coypel and his son Charles-Antoine Coypel.

As early as 1677, in the first of Roger de Piles's *Conversations sur la connaissance de la peinture et sur le jugement qu'on doit faire des tableaux*, one of the protagonists of the dialogues recommends cultivating the friendship of painters.[34] A few years later, in *L'Idée du peintre parfait*, de Piles grounded the possibility of this friendship in the notion of genius, common both to the amateur and the painter.[35] De Piles was the main orator of the 'conférences' for ten years, from 1699 to his death in 1709, and in one of his lectures, delivered on 4 February 1708, he stresses the importance of an active way of looking at paintings both for the virtuoso and for the painter.[36] Thus, if the amateur has a touch of creative genius, conversely, the painter has a degree of connoisseurship. In his writings de Piles aims to erect a palace for painting.[37] Theory is profitable both to the professional and to the amateur and the image chosen, of a common dwelling, is in itself significant of a wish for social intercourse, certainly within the walls of the academy, where the 'conférences' took place.

Four years later Antoine Coypel seemed more diffident, and eager to set precise boundaries to the influence of the amateur over the painter. The 'curieux' have no superiority of judgement over the other art lovers, regarded as gentlemen, and scholars. For the amateur, an erroneous conception of artistic sociability consists in forging too exclusive a relationship with a particular artist, which can become a source of conflicts and cabals.[38] Those who wish to pass judgement on a painting must always praise it in public and discuss its defects with the artist only in private, and in very civil terms.[39]

---

[34] He advises 'de voir souvent les plus habiles peintres, et de faire en sorte qu'ils soient vos amis. Vous aurez cela de commun avec le Grand Alexandre, qui avait un sensible plaisir de les voir travailler, et de les entendre parler dessus leurs ouvrages.' Roger de Piles, *Conversations sur la connaissance de la peinture et sur le jugement qu'on doit faire des tableaux*, 1677 (Geneva, 1970), 72.

[35] 'Une des choses les plus essentielles dans la connaissance des tableaux, c'est le génie, il en faut dans le bon connaisseur ainsi que dans le bon peintre.' Roger de Piles, *L'Idée du peintre parfait*, 1715 (Paris, 1993), 100.

[36] 'Le curieux y trouve ce qui est proportionné à son goût, et le peintre y observe les diverses parties de son art.' Lichtenstein and Michel, *Conférences*, vol. III, 263.

[37] 'Un palais de la peinture, où les grands, les véritables curieux, les amateurs de la peinture et les gens de bon goût puissent se retirer en sûreté.' Lichtenstein and Michel, *Conférences*, vol. III, 268.

[38] Lichtenstein and Michel, *Conférences*, vol. IV, no. 1, 44–8.

[39] 'Avec la politesse que l'on ne doit jamais abandonner.' Lichtenstein and Michel, *Conférences*, vol. III, 107.

Antoine Coypel's son, Charles-Antoine, gave two lectures, delivered in 1726 and 1730, revealing an interest in defining the relationship between artists and amateurs: one was entitled 'Dialogue sur la connaissance de la peinture' ('Dialogue on Connoisseurship in Painting') and the other 'Sur la nécessité de recevoir des avis' ('On the Necessity of Receiving Advice'). Although Coypel accepted amateurs such as Caylus in 1731, in the ranks of the academy, like his father, he was careful to set limits to their role. He dismisses 'les faux connaisseurs', pretended connoisseurs, who are exclusively focused on details such as the touch or the painter's life, or questions of attribution – unlike professionals who have an interest in the beauties of a work rather than in the identity of its author.[40] If amateurs are requested to express their opinion, the painter should not content himself with only one point of view.[41] In 1747 Coypel added a further restriction, reminding amateurs that they can only offer opinions and not pass judgements, as they are not practitioners of the art of painting.[42]

In the lectures delivered by the two Coypels, the language of sociability does not disguise the fact that the acceptance of amateurs within the ranks of the academicians is only half-hearted. This might be the reason why the Comte de Caylus, after being received in the academy as an 'honoraire', was careful to cast himself in the humble part of the pupil, ready to be taught.[43] He nevertheless underlined that a passion for drawing was a common feature of both the painter and the amateur, and added in his lecture entitled 'De l'amateur', in 1748, that it was indispensable for the amateur to copy, draw and paint after nature.[44] In fact, in the French academy artists and amateurs collaborated in producing engravings for a chosen public.[45] Yet practice for the amateur is only a way of learning about the great masters; there is no ambition to rival contemporary painters, whom he is here to serve without any prejudice in favour of a particular artist, unlike the

[40] Lichtenstein and Michel, *Conférences*, vol. IV, no. 1, 281–3.
[41] 'Rarement est-il possible que les avis d'un seul ami soient suffisants: nous devons donc nécessairement faire société avec des personnes de goûts différents', Lichtenstein and Michel, *Conférences*, vol. IV, no. 2, 406. The phrase 'faire société' suggests that the painting itself, as an object of discussion, creates social intercourse, private here, but also public since the 'conférences' were originally meant to be a critical discussion of a given history painting.
[42] Lichtenstein and Michel, *Conférences*, vol. V, no. 1, 56–7.
[43] 'Je ne suis qu'amateur, et l'amateur et le maître doivent parler bien différemment: l'un peut réfléchir, l'autre doit donner des leçons, et je les attends de vous, messieurs'. Lichtenstein and Michel, *Conférences*, vol. IV, no. 2, 452.
[44] Lichtenstein and Michel, *Conférences*, vol. V, no. 1, 198.
[45] See Charlotte Guichard, *Les Amateurs d'art à Paris au XVIIIe siècle* (Seyssel, 2008), 276.

'curieux' who favours one single artist or school.[46] Sociability through conversation is encouraged and the amateur must complete his studies by frequently meeting painters, whose conversation is always useful.[47] So, even with a few restrictions, French art theory encouraged friendship and advice between artists and amateurs, all the more so since the amateur was considered a potential artist, able to draw and engrave. Sociability was also founded on a shared artistic practice.

In England, the definition of connoisseurship was mainly the work of the painter Jonathan Richardson, who devoted a whole treatise to the question, *The Science of a Connoisseur*, first published in 1719. To a lesser degree, Joshua Reynolds, in his annual *Discourses* as first president of the English Academy, occasionally broached the subject of connoisseurship. Both painters had read Roger de Piles and there are hints in Reynolds's *Discourses* of his being cognisant of the French 'conférences'.[48] So, how far did the French conception of relations between amateurs and painters influence English art theory?

Unlike Roger de Piles and French theorists, when defining connoisseurs Richardson is explicit about the social category they ideally belong to: 'My present business in short is to endeavour to persuade our nobility and gentry to become lovers of painting and connoisseurs.'[49] Encouraging the development of a national taste has a cost which must be met by the richest class. Financial assistance is expected for the creation of academies:

> For if our nobility and gentry were lovers, and connoisseurs, publick encouragement and assistance would be given to the art; academies would be set up, well regulated, and the government of them put into such hands, as would not want authority to maintain those laws, without which no society can prosper or long subsist.[50]

However vague Richardson's academic project was, it can be surmised that gentlemen-connoisseurs would have played an active part in the

---

[46] 'Il ne doit affecter aucun genre, ni aucun goût, il doit être l'ami solide de la peinture et des peintres en général et en particulier.' Lichtenstein and Michel, *Conférences*, vol. V, no. 1, 197.

[47] He will benefit from 'le commerce des peintres, dont la conversation lui sera toujours utile et profitable.' Lichtenstein and Michel, *Conférences*, vol. V, no. 1, 199.

[48] Some of them, in particular those by Antoine Coypel, had been published in 1721 and a few seventeenth- century lectures were translated and published in 1740.

[49] Jonathan Richardson, *A Discourse on the Dignity, Certainty, Pleasure and Advantage, of the Science of a Connoisseur* (London, 1719), 8.

[50] Richardson, *A Discourse*, 56.

administration of such institutions, had they been created. Richardson himself was a member of the Queen Street Academy, which included both amateurs and artists as has already been mentioned. Gentlemen-connoisseurs were also expected to fulfil their role as collectors bringing works of art into England, thus enriching the taste of the nation.[51] The relationship to connoisseurs was envisaged in practical socio-economic terms rather than in terms of intellectual prestige, as was more often the case in the French academic context.

Despite the difference in the definition of amateurs, Richardson was probably inspired by de Piles on some aspects of the relationship between artists and connoisseurs. The high degree of sociability of some members of the nobility suggests that social intercourse with artists is a strong possibility: 'And some such we have of our own nation, who are distinguish'd not only by their births, and fortunes, but by other the most amiable qualities that justly endear them to all that have the honour, and happiness of knowing them, and being known to them.'[52] Richardson goes even further and suggests that gentlemen should encourage their younger sons to become painters.[53] Like de Piles, Richardson denies the strict separation between 'connaissance' and painting, as the former also necessitates a form of genius: 'those who want genius, and a competent measure of understanding in the particular study, however sensible men they may be in general, can never penetrate into the beauties or defects of a picture.'[54] A good connoisseur must have the intellectual qualifications of a painter and is also encouraged to draw.[55] Richardson thus takes up what was already described as a characteristic of the *virtuoso*.[56] Conversely, and for Richardson as well as de Piles, connoisseurship is useful for the artist 'not so much from the knowledge of hands, and how to distinguish copies from originals […] but to know accurately to discover the beauties and defects of a picture.'[57] Because friendly intercourse is based on common knowledge, the connoisseur, as a commissioner of paintings, is entitled to advise the painter: 'A good taste and judgment in those who employ them [the painters] would not only compel painters to study, and be industrious, but put them in a right way if they fell not into it themselves.'[58] While de Piles gave Alexander the Great

[51] Richardson, *A Discourse*, 57–8.
[52] Richardson, *A Discourse*, 93.
[53] Richardson, *A Discourse*, 60.
[54] Richardson, *A Discourse*, 144.
[55] Richardson, *A Discourse*, 47.
[56] See Pears, *The Discovery of Painting*, 182.
[57] Richardson, *A Discourse*, 218.
[58] Richardson, *A Discourse*, 59.

as an example of an illustrious adviser, Richardson chooses Charles I as counsellor of Van Dyck.[59] Unlike the Coypels, father and son, Richardson allows the connoisseur to pass a judgement, not just to express an opinion.

Reynolds later takes up some of the ideas expressed by de Piles and Richardson in his seventh *Discourse*. Friendship for the painter here takes the form of 'the conversation of learned and ingenious men', which category must include enlightened amateurs since the purpose of these conversations is 'a power of distinguishing right from wrong; which power applied to works of art, is denominated *taste*'.[60] Indeed, taste and genius are similar in nature: 'Genius and taste, in their common acceptation, appear to be very nearly related; the difference lies only in this, that genius has super-added to it a habit or power of execution: or we may say that taste, when this power is added, changes its name, and is called genius.'[61] Both the artist and the connoisseur are guided by immutable rules: 'If therefore, in the course of this inquiry, we can show that there are rules for the conduct of the artist which are fixed and invariable, it follows of course, the art of the connoisseur, or, in other words, taste, has likewise invariable principles.'[62] Theory, 'speculative knowledge', is indispensable both to the artist and to the connoisseur. However, this reciprocity does not hold when it comes to the question of advice and Reynolds seems to share the reluctance sometimes voiced in the French 'conférences'. In his eleventh *Discourse* he warns that 'connoisseurs will always find in pictures what they think they ought to find'.[63]

By proclaiming, after de Piles, the similarity in essence of genius and taste, both Richardson and Reynolds give a theoretical foundation to an element of artistic sociability, the possibility for connoisseurs to express friendly advice to artists.

However, in the last *Discourse*, Reynolds states that a professional painter is better able to discuss his art, be it but in a short essay, than an author who will write volumes 'the purpose of which appears to be rather to display the refinement of the author's own conceptions of impossible practice, than to convey useful knowledge'.[64] The attempt to reserve the discourse on art to professional artists was part of the questioning of the role of the amateur

---

[59] Richardson, *A Discourse*, 59.
[60] Joshua Reynolds, *Discourses on Art*, 1769–1790, ed. Robert R. Wark (New Haven, 1997), 118.
[61] Reynolds, *Discourses on Art*, 120.
[62] Reynolds, *Discourses on Art*, 123.
[63] Reynolds, *Discourses on Art*, 200.
[64] Reynolds, *Discourses on Art*, 267.

and of the redefining of artistic sociability from the 1760s in France and from the 1780s in England.

Questioning the link between artists and amateurs

Charlotte Guichard points out that, in France, 1760 was a turning point in the attitude to amateurs.[65] Before that date, what she calls 'sociabilités restreintes' (forms of restricted sociability) had a monopoly on taste. After 1760, amateurs were the target of virulent criticism in many of the writings generated by the 'Salon', the exhibition of academic art that took place every two years and gave rise to art criticism as a specific genre.

The most famous of eighteenth-century critics in France, Diderot, attacked amateurs repeatedly in his *Salons*. Refusing the distinction between 'connoisseurs' and 'amateurs', he considers them as a plague and denies them the right to advise artists elaborating their works.[66] Not only are amateurs described as vermin pestering painters in their studios, but their ability to show good taste in purchasing art is also denigrated.[67] In the following *Salon*, Diderot made direct attacks on such famous 'honoraires' as Caylus or Watelet. The death of the former is announced with scathing brevity[68] and the famous portrait of Watelet by Greuze is allotted only two lines of contemptuous description.[69] These *ad hominem* attacks were also a way of denying amateurs a privileged connection with the artists of the academy. Diderot amplified his attacks in the introduction to the 1767 *Salon*, which includes a violent diatribe against the cursed race of amateurs, who are once more accused of disturbing the artist at work with their stupid advice and also blamed as almighty intermediaries between artists and patrons.[70]

[65] Charlotte Guichard, ' L'Amateur dans la polémique sur la critique d'art au XVIIIe siècle', in Magnusson and Michel, *Penser l'art dans la seconde moitié du XVIIIe siècle*, 123–4.
[66] 'Nos artistes sont fatigués dans leurs ateliers d'une vermine présomptueuse qu'on appelle des amateurs, et cette vermine nuit beaucoup à leurs travaux.' Denis Diderot, *Salon de 1759* (Paris, 1984), 185.
[67] 'Nos amateurs sont des gens à breloques, ils aiment mieux garnir leurs cabinets de vingt morceaux médiocres que d'en avoir un seul et beau.' Diderot, *Salon de 1759*, 249.
[68] 'La mort nous a délivrés du plus cruel des amateurs, le comte de Caylus.' Denis Diderot, *Salon de 1765* (Paris, 1984), 27.
[69] 'Il est terne; il a l'air d'être imbu, il est maussade. C'est l'homme; retournez la toile.' Diderot, *Salon de 1765*, 189.
[70] Denis Diderot, *Salon de 1767* (Paris, 1993), 60–1.

Although Diderot's art criticism was meant for the restricted public of Grimm's *Correspondance Littéraire*, his hostility is nevertheless significant of a change in attitude, which is confirmed in the *Mémoires Secrets*. This work, whose author or authors are unknown, includes an appraisal of the 1787 Salon.[71] In a digressive passage about M. le marquis de Turpin, 'honoraire, associé libre', the critic suggests that there are two categories of 'amateurs honoraires': those who retain their traditional role of protecting, defending and supporting artists and those who want to speculate on art by making some artists fashionable.[72] Amateurs, who used to confine their own artistic attempts inside their cabinets, are now bold enough to exhibit them at the Salon, with limited success.[73]

During the same period, Carmontelle published his famous *Coup de patte sur le salon de 1779*, which gave him the opportunity to attack the academic system as a place of artistic prejudice, frivolous rules and cabals, which could but constrain genius.[74] Four years later, in his *Triumvirat des arts*, he depicted amateurs as extravagant beings who, far from being connoisseurs, were only fickle and strange people, supposed to learn everything and in fact knowing nothing.[75] Artists are more qualified to pass critical judgement on art and, in what might be termed a hierarchy of opinions, the 'hommes de lettres' are at the bottom, with the artists above them and the public at the top.[76] The figure of the amateur is but a grotesque puppet and his special relationship with the painter is a thing of the past.

So, one must not be surprised if, in France, the amateur was a stock character in satirical writings, such as Nicolas-Thomas Barthe's play entitled *L'Amateur: comédie en vers et en un acte* (1764). This was also the case across the Channel in Beaumont Brenan's *The Painter's Breakfast. A Dramatic Satyr* (1756), in which one of the characters is Formal, a connoisseur.[77] In England satire was also present in some of the texts of art criticism

---

[71] The *Mémoires* used to be attributed to Louis Petit de Bachaumont but this is no longer the case. See Bernadette Fort (ed.), *Les Salons des 'Mémoires secrets' 1767–1787* (Paris, 1999), 12–14.

[72] Fort, *Les Salons des 'Mémoires secrets'*, 338.

[73] Fort, *Les Salons des 'Mémoires secrets'*, 338.

[74] Louis de Carmontelle, *Coup de patte sur le salon de 1779* (Paris, 1779), 9.

[75] 'Ces amateurs étourdis qui de tous temps ont jugé les arts avec une indiscrète légèreté, espèce d'hommes bizarres, qui passant jadis pour savoir tout sans rien apprendre, de nos jours apprennent tout pour ne rien savoir.' Louis de Carmontelle, *Le Triumvirat des arts* (Paris, 1783), 43.

[76] 'Les opinions uniformes de la multitude l'emporteront souvent chez moi sur l'opinion de l'artiste.' Carmontelle, *Le Triumvirat des arts*, 6.

[77] Beaumont Brenan, *The Painter's Breakfast* (Dublin, 1756), 6.

inspired by the annual exhibition at the London academy. John Wolcot, alias Peter Pindar, a would-be painter turned art critic, knew immediate editorial success with his *Lyric Odes to the Royal Academicians for 1782*, which were followed by similar 'pindaric' verse in 1783, 1785 and 1786. John Williams, who had studied engraving, took the pseudonym of Anthony Pasquin in 1786 and started publishing satires against Royal Academicians and the annual exhibition. Both writers criticise the Royal Academy as an institution. Pindar blames it for rewarding only insignificant artists, to the detriment of real talent: 'Th' Academy is like a microscope / For, by the magnifying power, are seen / Objects, that for attention ne'er could hope, / No more, alas! than if they ne'er had been.'[78] In *The Royal Academicians. A Farce* Pasquin aims his satire at the professors and the quarrels dividing the members of the academy.

The annual banquet, which from 1771 was to take place on St George's day, 23 April, was exploited by both satirists to shed a critical light on the relationship between artists and illustrious patrons of the arts, aristocrats who were invited for a preview of the exhibition and an 'academic dinner'. Sociability gives way to gluttony in Wolcot's evocation of a banquet in which artists and aristocratic connoisseurs are compared with 'gypsies in a barn, around their king, / That annual meet, to eat, and dance, and sing' and fight for the best morsels: 'Unfortunately for the modest dukes, / The nimble artists, all with greyhound looks, / Fell on the meat, with teeth prodigious able.'[79] In Williams's *Memoirs of the Royal Academicians* (1796) the amateur is reduced to a mouth that has to be fed, as the so-called 'academic oath' includes the following command: 'You shall feed the amateur once a year.'[80] There follows a description of the purchasing of a 'Lincoln-fed ox' whose hide will be used to make a winter gabardine for the porter of the academy and whose tallow 'will feed the lamp in the life academy.'[81]

The grotesque representation of artistic sociability, more pronounced in England than in France, is completed by incidental remarks redefining amateurs' and artists' respective roles. Like Carmontelle, both satirists favour the artist's judgement on art over the amateur's. In *Farewell Odes for the Year 1786*, Pindar simultaneously attacks Horace Walpole and makes

---

[78] Peter Pindar, *Lyric Odes for the Year 1785* (London, 1785), 11.
[79] Peter Pindar, *Farewell Odes for the Year 1786* (London, 1786), 8–9.
[80] Anthony Pasquin, *Memoirs of the Royal Academicians* (London, 1796), 53.
[81] Pasquin, *Memoirs of the Royal Academicians*, 59–60. The banquet had been part of the academic ritual ever since the foundation of the institution, a sociable practice already in use at the Society of Artists or the Foundling Hospital, one of the first places for exhibitions in London.

a general statement: 'The artists should on painting solely write [...] But when the mob of gentlemen / Desert their province, and take up the pen / The Lord have mercy on the art / Their crow-quills can no light impart.'[82] The idea is shared by Pasquin when he deplores that 'all pictorial treatises in this country, are written by persons whose qualifications did not square with their ambition.'[83] Only professionals can write successfully on the arts.[84] Pasquin goes further and denounces the link of economic subservience that binds art and patronage. Like the amateurs in Diderot's 1767 diatribe, patrons are denounced as too powerful: their way of life bars them from passing a valid judgement: 'The people of distinction, here, are too licentious to appreciate ingenuity with truth, and too vain to be great.'[85]

However, if both French and English writers work at weakening the link between artists and connoisseurs by disqualifying amateurs and connoisseurs as knowledgeable advisers, they do not attempt to replace it by a direct connection with the public, even if there are some hints at a possible public sphere for art, at least on the French (pre-revolutionary) side. For Diderot and Carmontelle the general public's opinion was not devoid of a value of its own. Pindar has a fluctuating attitude to the public of the exhibition. Sometimes it is considered as superior in taste to the French public.[86] Elsewhere, it is shown as unable to perceive the meaning of the work of art beyond its physical aspect: 'For people judge not only by the eyes, / But feel your merit by their finger ends; / Nay! closely nosing, o'er the picture dwell, / As if to try the goodness by the smell.'[87] As for Pasquin, he completely disregards the opinion of 'the vile mob, who are eternally in the wrong.'[88] On both sides of the Channel critics and satirists question cultural sociability in its academic form.

To a certain extent, Richardson's and Reynolds's ideas about the relations between artists and amateurs reflect the influence of French academic theory. Yet, while the French institution admitted at least a few amateurs within its walls, the London academy did not grant them official status.

---

[82] Pindar, *Farewell Odes for the Year 1786*, 25.
[83] Anthony Pasquin, *A Liberal Critique on the Present Exhibition of the Royal Academy* (London, 1794), 29.
[84] Pasquin, *Memoirs of the Royal Academicians*, 100.
[85] Anthony Pasquin, *A Critical Guide to the Exhibition of the Royal Academy for 1796* (London, 1796), 28. William Blake shared this critical attitude in his annotations to Reynolds's *Discourses*. See Reynolds, *Discourses on Art*, 291.
[86] Pindar, *Lyric Odes for the Year 1785*, 22.
[87] Peter Pindar, *Lyric Odes for the Year 1783* (London, 1788), 21.
[88] Anthony Pasquin, *A Critical Guide to the Present Exhibition at the Royal Academy, for 1797* (London, 1797), 23.

Holger Hoock offers one possible explanation for this: the refusal to model the English academy on an institution of the French absolutist monarchy.[89] This explanation is in keeping with the wish for the birth of original British art, as voiced by such artists as Hogarth. Yet another explanation may lie in the history of sociability proper to each country. The role devoted to the banquet in each academic institution is significant of this difference in sociability: the prohibition of banquets was stipulated at the beginning of the French academy in the 1648 statutes.[90] Banquets were associated with the 'maîtrise', that category of artisan painters from whom Academicians were eager to distinguish themselves. In the London academy, on the contrary, the annual banquet was anticipated by a similar practice in the Society of the Virtuosi of St Luke.[91] In France, amateurs and artists met outside the academy, in the 'Salons', which were places where art could be commissioned. In England, connoisseurs and painters could also meet on neutral territory, in taverns like the Turk's Head, but in the first half of the eighteenth century they also had their own separate places of social intercourse, societies like the Society of Dilettanti for the connoisseurs and drawing academies for artists, even if some painters, like Reynolds later, belonged both to the Royal Academy and the Society of Dilettanti. Moreover Reynolds, and also Richardson or Highmore, associated with scholars and literary men, be they amateurs or not, for example in Johnson's Literary Club.

However, this privileged connection between artists and amateurs, often viewed as potential patrons, came under radical scrutiny at the end of the century. In pre-revolutionary France mounting criticism of the academy went hand in hand with the tendency to favour the judgement of the public against that of the specialist and finally led to the suppression of the institution, considered as undemocratic, in 1793 and its replacement by the temporary 'Commune des arts', thus putting an end to one form of restricted sociability.[92] In England criticism of Academicians was associ-

[89] Holger Hoock, *The King's Artists: the Royal Academy of Arts and the Politics of British Culture 1760–1840* (Oxford, 2003), 26.
[90] 'Il ne s'y proposera de faire aucun festin ni banquet'. Montaiglon, *Procès-verbaux* 7.
[91] See Peter Clark, *British Clubs and Societies 1580–1800: the Origins of the Associational World* (Oxford, 2000), 63.
[92] See Nikolaus Pevsner, *Les Académies d'art*, 166: in fact French academies were recreated in 1795 under the name 'Institut de France'. In his attempt to defend the academic institution, Antoine Renou had reasserted the simultaneous presence of amateurs and artists as 'conseillers'. See Antoine Renou, *Esprits des statuts et règlements de l'Académie royale de peinture et de sculpture, pour servir de réponse aux détracteurs de son régime* (Paris, 1790), 6.

ated with the lampooning of George III, for Wolcot, and anti-aristocratic opinions, for Williams. Yet, if their political opinions led them to a criticism of artistic sociability they refused to acknowledge the potential role of the public to replace patronage.[93] Besides, in spite of ridicule, the annual banquet was still celebrated on St George's day, even if the number of guests was limited by the beginning of the nineteenth century, thus preserving a form of sociability between artists and distinguished amateurs viewed as potential patrons. Meanwhile the Royal Academy Club, founded in 1813, organised dinners for Academicians exclusively.[94] In revolutionary France, the privileged connection with amateurs was dissolved, to be replaced by a direct connection with the general public, whereas in England a different historical context allowed the link to be maintained although it retained much of the diffidence that had been its characteristic all through the eighteenth century.

---

[93] Significantly, but also in accordance with a common British reaction, both men had a shifting attitude to the French revolution.
[94] Sydney C. Hutchison, *The History of the Royal Academy*, 71, 75.

Chapter 6
Masonic connections and rivalries between France and Britain*

Pierre-Yves Beaurepaire

IN A WORLD of Freemasonry that was used to being fairly discreet and to favouring orality, we find two written documents that are worth opening this chapter with because they reveal the complex relationship that French Freemasons maintained with England, or the British Isles more broadly, during the Enlightenment. The first document was aimed at the profane Masonic population. Just after the signing of the Treaty of Versailles (1783), which put an end to the American War of Independence, the French lawyer, academic and encyclopedist Edme Beguillet, an officer of the newly opened Parisian lodge La Réunion des Etrangers, published his *Discours sur l'origine, les progrès, et les révolutions de la franc-maçonnerie philosophique, contenant un plan d'association et un projet maçonnique de bienfaisance, pour l'erection d'un double monument en l'honneur de Descartes.*[1] It was both a plea in favour of Descartes, who was a national philosophical celebrity,[2] and a violent attack on Newton and all those in France who promoted his theories: 'The Masonic commendation of Descartes will be followed by an exposition of his little-known philosophy, which has almost sunk into oblivion since Anglomania caused us to be infatuated with a foreign system.'[3]

---

* Note: all citations from French sources have been translated.
[1] *Discourse on the origin, progress and revolutions of philosophical Freemasonry, including an association plan and a Masonic charity project to erect a double monument in honour of Descartes.*
[2] Stéphane Van Damme, *Descartes. Essai d'histoire culturelle d'une grandeur philosophique (XVIIe–XXe siècle)* (Paris, 2002).
[3] *Discours sur l'origine, les progrès, et les révolutions de la Franc-maçonnerie philosophique, contenant un Plan d'Association & un Projet Maçonnique de bienfaisance, pour l'Erection d'un double Monument en l'honneur de Descartes*, By Brother Beguillet, Parliament Lawyer and General Secretary of the L(odge) of La Réunion des Etrangers (Philadelphia, 1784), 37: 'L'éloge maçonnique de Descartes sera suivi d'une

The second document was aimed solely at the membership of one of the most prominent lodges in Paris, the Amis Réunis, which was made up of *fermiers-généraux* (tax collectors during the Ancien Régime), high-finance workers, foreign travellers of quality and theatre amateurs plus the artists under their protection. The lodge wrote in its visitors' book that the Brothers 'wanted to form a society of friends much like the English clubs'. The secretary also felt it necessary to specify in the register's margin 'or clubs, or coteries in French' and then on the next folio 'a coterie of respectable people'.[4] To my knowledge, this is a unique case in the documentation currently available. This attempt by the actors themselves to define their own form of sociability is interesting because it resonates with a definition given half a century earlier by René-Louis de Voyer, marquis d'Argenson and future Foreign Affairs Minister from 1744 to 1747, of the famous Club de l'Entresol in his *Mémoires*:

> The ecclesiastic [Alary] formed a small establishment whose history, now already unknown to many, will soon be forgotten by all. It deserves to be recorded nevertheless. It was an English-type club, in other words a wholly liberal political society, made up of people who liked to debate current affairs. They would meet up and express their opinions without fear of being compromised, because they were all acquainted with one another and therefore knew who they were talking with and in front of. This society was called the *Entresol*, because the place where they met was an entresol. It was where the ecclesiastic Alary lived. It had all manner of creature comforts: comfortable seats, a good fire in winter and windows that opened onto a pretty garden in summer. There was no lunch or dinner provided, but there were cups of tea in winter and lemonade and chilled liqueurs in summer. There was also a permanent supply of French, Dutch and even English newspapers. In short, it was a café for respectable folk.[5]

All of this points to the fact that eighteenth-century sociability was not just a social and cultural affair but also an association plan and a reflection

---

exposition de sa philosophie trop peu connue, et qui est tombée presque totalement depuis que l'Anglomanie nous a engoués d'un système étranger'.

[4] National Archives, 177 AP 1, Tailliepied de Bondy papers, Amis Réunis visitors' book, commenced 16 February 1777, fols. 7–8.

[5] René Louis de Voyer de Paulmy, Marquis d'Argenson, *Journal et mémoires du Marquis d'Argenson*, ed. E. J. B. Rathery (Paris, 1859–67), vol. I, 96–100.

on its modalities. It is worth noting that a lodge in Perpignan even deliberately chose to change its name to La Sociabilité.[6]

Conflictual dynamics

Anglo-French Masonic relations – Scotland is a case apart, which I will individuate – thus bore the mark of rivalry and conflict rather than of fraternal emulation, and there were significant interactions in diplomatic circles. This was particularly true in the Baltic and the Levant, where the two countries had been vying with one another since the seventeenth century. The account given by Charles Tullman, provincial English Grand Master for Sweden since 1765 and Secretary to the London Ambassador to the Stockholm Court, is very illuminating in this respect. He had decided 'to force the lodges that are working with French constitutions here [in Sweden] to follow his dictates'.[7] With the support of his superior, Ambassador Sir John Goodricke, who was also a Freemason, he deployed a considerable amount of zeal and proselytised. Similar situations were also to be found in Naples, Warsaw and St Petersburg.

The conflict was political, territorial and symbolic. In fact, from the middle of the eighteenth century until nowadays, the Grand Lodge of England has claimed the 'universal motherhood' of London, the merging of the four London lodges giving birth to the Grand London Lodge in 1717; the writing of Anderson's Constitutions in 1723 and in 1738 are not only considered as reference dates in the history of English Masonry but as the birth marks of 'modern' Masonry around the world.

Paris offered London a treaty of alliance (which was in reality a treaty of mutual non-interference) which stipulated that 'in order to maintain the union and amity between them, the Grand Orient de France and the Grand Lodge of England will maintain a mutual correspondence',[8] and in particular that 'the Grand Orient de France will have complete executive jurisdic-

---

[6] 'Our lodge is almost entirely made up of the cream of Roussillon nobility, who will be happy to set an example of propriety and virtue' (Bibliothèque Nationale de France, Manuscripts Department, Masonic collection, FM^2 349, *Sociabilité* file, 22 March 1783).

[7] '*die hier illegal arbeitenden Logen französischen Systems zu zwingen, sich mir* [Tullman] *unterzuordnen*'. Cited by Roger de Robelin, 'Die Freimaurerei in Schweden im 18 Jahrhundert', *Gold und Himmelblau. Die Freimaurerei, Zeitloses Ideal* (Abo, 1993), 66.

[8] Bibliothèque Nationale de France, Manuscripts, Masonic collection, FM^1 118, fol. 408v, article 3.

tion in its territory'.[9] Paris stated, moreover, that 'the intention of the Grand Orient de France is to negotiate this equality, which has to form the basis of the treaty of alliance, with the Grand Lodge of England on equal terms'.[10] London, of course, rejected their demand for parity and their conception of the Masonic space:

> The equality of the 1st article cannot happen not least because Germany, Sweden and Holland have unanimously recognised the Grand Lodge of England, which can prove that it established the first National Grand Master in France, as their Mother ... It does not understand how the 2nd article wishes to constrict the Grand Lodge, which was established in London within range of the British Government, when its branches extend out into all parts of Europe.[11]

The balance of power and the principle of equality that Paris was trying to impose on London at the beginning of the negotiations had two aims. Internally, it wanted to force the lodges that had been set up in France by London to renounce their English allegiance, and to have them re-established by Paris. The Anglaise in Bordeaux was singled out in particular and ostracised from the national Masonic community during its construction. Externally, Paris was seeking alliances in Europe and was opening up negotiations with Masonic Obediences across the Continent in order to isolate London and promote its own model of independent national Obediences, whose jurisdictions would be merged with state boundaries. The existence of this conflictual dynamic (because it was indeed a dynamic), which brought two conceptions of the Universal Republic of Freemasons into confrontation, is therefore undeniable. One was a 'cosmopolitan' conception, espoused by London, which 'limited' its demands to the recognition of its moral authority over the Order. The other was a 'national' conception, championed by Paris.

---

[9] Bibliothèque Nationale de France, Manuscripts, Masonic collection, FM^1 118, fol. 408v, article 2.
[10] Bibliothèque Nationale de France, Manuscripts, Masonic collection, FM^1 118, fol. 408r, article 1.
[11] Freemasons' Hall, London, Archives of the United Grand Lodge of England.

Intense interactions

This rivalry did not, however, prevent intense interactions and exchanges between the two, which were a notable social connection between the two nations. Although the negotiations between the French and English Grand Lodges were marked by many tensions, they mobilised cultural and scholarly mediators of the first order. This was most notably the case with the astronomer Jérôme Lalande, Professor at the Collège Royal, and the ecclesiastic Rozier, editor of the *Journal de Physique*. Both these men regularly stressed their links with the Royal Society and the English scientific communities, proof once more that Masonic sociability fitted into the social environment with which it had forged close ties. For example, in 1773 Lalande wrote to London:

> The Grande Loge de France – or, rather, the Grand Orient that has now been put in place – has long wished to develop a relationship with the Grand Lodge of England. Mr des Vignoles has sometimes written to us on this subject. As I cannot see him in the directory of grand officers, printed in 1773 at 1 Cole Newgate Street, I thought it best to return to source and contact you.
>
> Mr de Luc, a skilled physician and close friend of mine,[12] who stayed with you last year, has assured me you will be kind enough to honour me with a response and this I earnestly request of you.
>
> My position as Senior Warden of the Grande Loge de France obliges me to ask you some questions. If you do not have the time to respond, I would be grateful if you could send me the name and address of the Grand Lodge's Correspondence Secretary so that I might address myself directly to him. It is no problem for him to write to me in English. In the two years since Freemasonry in France took on a new shape and adopted new activities, we have set up and reformed more than 200 lodges …
>
> I would also like to ask you if the Grand Lodge of England has received the two most recent annual reports that we had printed for you, showing our Statutes, the charts of our lodges and a list of our officers.

---

[12] Jean-André De Luc (1727–1817) was a Genevan geologist of Huguenot origins as well as Queen Charlotte's reader in London from 1773 onwards. The scientific correspondence that De Luc maintained with the queen was published in 1779 under the title Jean-André De Luc, *Lettres physiques et morales sur l'histoire de la Terre et de l'Homme* (La Haye, 1779 and Paris, 1779). I am preparing to publish De Luc's personal papers, preserved at the Sterling Memorial Library of Yale University, New Haven, CT, which contain friendly and scholarly correspondence with Lalande.

I can send you them if you wish and would be grateful if you could send me your reports from London. You could have them taken to the home of the bookseller Elmsley or to Mr Nourse's residence, who both often have occasion to come to France. If you have someone who would like to establish a correspondence between the two Grand Lodges through me, that would be very pleasing for both sides.

I would be interested to know where the Grand Lodge assembles and whether the plan to contribute to the purchase of a house has gone ahead as planned in 1773. Does the Grand Lodge have a building or public establishment in London or Scotland?

Please excuse me for the liberty I have taken in importuning you on account of my zeal for Freemasonry, which must be as dear to you as it is to me judging by the eminent position you hold.

I am with respect

Sir

Your very humble and obedient servant

Delalande

From the Académie des Sciences and the Royal Society of London, at the Collège Royal, Place de Cambrai.[13]

Likewise, in preparation for the 1787 convent (general meeting), the Philalèthes (literally, lovers of truth), who were a mystical Masonic society that brought together the cream of Parisian society and their counterparts from across Europe, decided to question the Grand Lodge of England (which they considered to be the repository of the Order's history) on the origins of Freemasonry and the ancient archives that the English Brothers had preserved. The following extract is from the memorandum addressed to their counterparts in France and abroad:

> It would seem useful to ask England how far back the Archives and Protocols of their first ones [Lodges] go to see if they have proof that Freemasonry existed in the previous century somewhere and also to gather together all the Blue Lodge degrees [Entered Apprentice, Fellowcraft and Master Mason] and more particularly the Catechisms that are not used in their studies.[14]

---

[13] London, Freemasons' Hall, Grand Lodge Library, *Archives of the United Grand Lodge of England*, undated.

[14] Charles Porset, *Les Philalèthes et les Convents de Paris, Une politique de la folie* (Paris, 1996).

While London was seen as the repository or even the model of Freemasonry's origins, France was, in turn, where many English Freemasons generally discovered the Masonry of Adoption (open to women) and where they practised sociable Masonry. The case of Lady Colebrooke, who lived in Boulogne, illustrates this well. In his *Journal*, Abot de Bazinghen, a member of the local nobility, mentions the existence of a Lodge of Adoption in 1781 in Boulogne-sur-Mer, which initiated representatives from the local high society, including his own wife. The Grand Mistress was Milady Colebrooke, and her daughter, Miss Colebrooke the elder, was First Director (the female equivalent of the Senior Warden in the male lodges). The *Journal* states that just after Mrs de Bazinghen's initiation, 'Brother Comte de la Mark – Worshipful Master of the military lodge Parfaite Union – gave a superb banquet, after which, at two o'clock in the morning, the Colebrook ladies left Boulogne for Soissons where they had rented a house.'[15] Mr and Mrs Bazinghen had become acquainted with the Colebrooke ladies a few months earlier when they had helped to distribute a play staged by a selectively recruited amateur theatre troupe. This is a particularly interesting example because, with only a few exceptions (which are scantly documented elsewhere), women were reputed to be absent from the lodges in England. Given their composition in the nineteenth and twentieth centuries, the English lodges can be considered *a priori* to be societies for men, whereas the French Freemasons seem to have followed the example of Brother Choderlos de Laclos (who had penned a plea to open the temples to women)[16] and welcomed Sisters into the temple of the Fraternity more readily. As such, they pioneered the trend for Women's Freemasonry and the Masonry of Adoption and are thought to have been the main contributors to its diffusion on the Continent. It would be worth carrying out a detailed study in this domain to take into account national representations or stereotypes and established memberships.

Leaving France's northern coast behind and travelling down to its capital, we find the famous Lodge of the Neuf Sœurs (a reference to the nine Muses), which was often presented as a symbol of the growing appeal of the Parisian centre in the final third of the eighteenth century. The prestige of this lodge was linked to the memory of *fermier-général* and philosopher Helvétius, who had nurtured a plan before he died to found a 'Sciences' lodge with the support of the astronomer Lalande. His project was taken

---

[15] Alain Lottin (ed.), in collaboration with Louisette Caux-Germe and Michel de Sainte-Maréville, *Boulonnais, Noble et Révolutionnaire. Le journal de Gabriel Abot de Bazinghen* (1779–1798) (Arras, 1995), 68.

[16] Besançon Public Library, manuscript Z 377 (4).

up by the society or 'salon' that his wife had formed in Auteuil. The Neuf Sœurs also owed its reputation to the celebrity of its Worshipful Master, Benjamin Franklin, and to the fact that it had welcomed Voltaire in 1778, a few weeks before his death.[17] Unlike the Neuf Sœurs in Paris, the lodges across the Channel were reputed to be more circumscribed in their public activities in the eighteenth century (this is still the case today). They would limit their interventions in the secular domain (i.e., outside of the Temple, in city life) to charity work for contemporary charitable organisations. However, in reality the picture here too was more nuanced. First of all, three lodges in European capitals (Paris, London and St Petersburg) had adopted the name of the ancient Muses in the 1770s. The Lodge of the Nine Muses in St Petersburg had set the ball rolling in 1774 with its constitutions from the Grand Lodge of England, which gave it the identification number 466. The Parisian lodge followed in 1776, and on 25 March 1777 the London lodge was formed, with the identification number 235. It met at the Thatched House Tavern in St James's Street.[18] All three lodges were linked to their respective science academies. The global environment was undoubtedly favourable to the spread of a sociable Freemasonry, in line with the expectations of the urban elite, across Europe and in the British isles.

Within the context of London Masonry, the Lodge of the Nine Muses was not just another high society lodge. It was majorly connected to the Royal Society, for example, and it claimed to adhere to the Newtonian legacy espoused by Jean-Théophile Désaguliers. It also welcomed many Brothers and visitors from overseas, particularly Italians and Russians. Its founder, Bartolomeo (Bartholomew) Ruspini (1728–1813), a famous surgeon and philanthropist and protégé of the Prince of Wales, was himself of Italian origin.[19] It was Ruspini's intention with the Lodge of the Nine Muses

---

[17] Louis Amiable, *Une loge maçonnique d'avant 1789, la loge des Neuf Sœurs* (Paris, 1897), supplemented with a commentary and critical notes from Charles Porset (Paris, 1989).

[18] Significantly, other societies and clubs would meet in this tavern, which was located in an area that represented the social centre of the London elites. [Lodge of the Nine Muses. no. 235], A centennial sketch of the history of the Lodge of the Nine Muses, 1777–1877. Presented to the Brethren at the centennial festival, held at Long's Hotes, Old Bond Street, London, on Tuesday, May the 8th, 1877, [London: Unwin Brothers, Printers]. Further information is available on the lodge's website: http://www.ninemuses.org.uk/html/library.html and particularly in the e-book published by the lodge in 2012: http://www.ninemuses.org.uk/historybook/.

[19] He is the subject of a biographical note written by Isabelle Krihiff-Aguirre in *Le Monde maçonnique des Lumières (Europe/the Americas & Colonies). Dictionnaire*

to show the influence of the London lodge in Europe and to affiliate the foreign visitors who converged on the English capital. Most notable among them was Pascal Paoli, who was welcomed as a member. The lodge also corresponded with its Parisian sister, the Neuf Sœurs.

English-origin Blue Lodge degrees and French-origin 'Scottish' degrees

In order to understand the importance of Franco-British Masonic interactions, we need also to focus on the success of the French high degrees. These were often perceived as having devalued the three primary degrees of English Masonry (Entered Apprentice, Fellowcraft and Master), which were judged to be too simplistic and not selective enough. The French high degrees emphasised the chivalrous, Christian nature of Freemasonry and allowed orders to organise lavish ceremonies with highly elaborate decors and settings. Once again, though, this situation was not clear cut because it was possible to combine a commitment to the three 'English' primary degrees and the trend for the 'French' high degrees, whose paternity incidentally the French symbolically attributed to the Scottish.[20] This tendency to attribute the Order's origins to medieval Scotland rather than to England descended from Jacobite Andrew Ramsay's 1737 *Discours*. There are numerous (and some unexpected) records of this, not least among which is the account of Jean-Paul Marat, who was doctor at the time to the Comte d'Artois's security entourage. He was welcomed as a Mason in London and admitted into the swanky Temple of the La Bien Aimée Lodge in Amsterdam on account of his French-origin high degrees. On 10 October 1774, with his certificate from the London lodge the Misericorde in hand, he signed the Amsterdam lodge's visitors' book.[21] Fifteen years earlier, in 1759, Casanova had also visited the prestigious Dutch lodge and invented a high degree for himself in his entry in the visitors' book: 'Giacomo Casanova of

---

prosopographique, ed. Charles Porset and Marie-Cécile Révauger (Paris, 2013), III, 2422–4.

[20] This is still the case. Incidentally, the most frequently practised rite in the world is currently the Ancient and Accepted Scottish Rite of Freemasonry. Beyond its symbolic reference, however, its origins lie less in Scotland and more in a broad Atlantic movement that went from Bordeaux to Haïti, on to Charleston and then back again to France.

[21] The Hague, Orde van Vrijmetslaren onder Het Grootoosten der Nederlanden, Archief, carton 4337, 41: Visiteurenboek van de loge La Bien Aimée, minutes dated 10 October 1774.

the Saint André Lodge in Paris, Grand Inspector of all lodges in France.'[22] Moreover, he recounted the episode in *Histoire de ma vie*:

> M. D. O. – a merchant from Amsterdam – invited me to dine with him at the burgomasters' lodge. This was a true honour, because despite all the usual rules of Masonry, it would only admit its twenty-four members. These were the wealthiest millionaires in the Bourse [the Amsterdam Stock Exchange]. He told me he had announced me and that the lodge would be opened in French because of me. They were so happy to have me that they declared me supernumerary for the entire duration of my stay in Amsterdam. M. D. O. told me the next day that the company I had dined with had three hundred million between them.[23]

This was undoubtedly an exaggeration, but it is nevertheless an interesting source because of Casanova's combining of the three English-origin primary degrees, which would have allowed him to be recognised anywhere in the world as a Brother, and the French-origin high degrees, which enabled access to the smartest Masonic cenacles. He wrote, moreover: 'Two months later [after being initiated as a Freemason in Lyons], I became first a Fellowcraft and then a Master in the Duke [sic] of Clermont's lodge in Paris.[24] There is no higher degree in Freemmasonry [sic]. Those who imagine themselves to be higher because of the new titles that have been invented are mistaken, or else they want to deceive.'[25]

This Franco-British combination was not just a characteristic of individuals but was also expressly adopted by those lodges situated at the interface of oceanic and colonial spaces, such as the Heureuse Rencontre in Brest, or at the meeting point of different linguistic areas, such as the Candeur in Strasbourg. Both of these are good illustrations of the dynamics at work

---

[22] The Hague, Orde van Vrijmetselaren onder Het Grootoosten der Nederlanden, Archief, carton 4337, 41: Visiteurenboek van de loge La Bien Aimée, 1759.
[23] Casanova, *Histoire de ma vie*, published under the guidance of Gérard Lahouati and Marie-Françoise Luna, in collaboration with Furio Luccichenti and Helmut Watzlawick (Paris, 2013), II, 225.
[24] Louis de Bourbon-Condé (1709–71), Comte de Clermont, Grand Master of the Grande Loge.
[25] Casanova, *Histoire de ma vie*, I, 590. Casanova's first draft read as follows: 'Two months later, I received the second degree in Paris, and a few months after that the second degree [of Entered Apprentice], and a few months after that the third, which is the Mastery. This is the ultimate. All the other titles that have been given to me over time are pleasant inventions, which although symbolic add nothing to the dignity of the degree of Master' (Casanova, *Histoire de ma vie*, I, 1025–6).

and the plasticity of the different forms of Masonic sociability that existed during the Enlightenment.

English recognition of the Brest and Strasbourg lodges

The 'Livre d'Architecture', which was the register of minutes taken at the assemblies and meetings of Loge Anglaise no. 184, reveals that the Heureuse Rencontre, which numbered many naval officers among its membership (it is important to highlight this point because of the Anglo-French naval rivalry), had a dual identity. Preserved at Finistère's Departmental Archives, the register covers a period from the creation – or 'installation' – of the Brest Lodge on 18 May 1774 to the end of the Revolutionary period.[26] The circumstances of this lodge were original, to say the least, because it was 'known to the Grand Orient de France under the title of Heureuse Rencontre and to the Grand Lodge of England as no. 184'.[27]

The lodge's decision to come under the jurisdiction of two Obediences at the same time, one of which was foreign, represented a considerable amount of additional administrative work. It meant that one community of Freemasons had to actuate two independent lodges, practise different rituals, keep two registers of all minutes, correspondences and accounts, elect two colleges of officers every year and so on. This task was complicated by the fact that London was in the habit of writing in English to its continental foundations while the use of French was common in eighteenth-century European Masonic correspondence (even when documents did not cross the border). The translation of English regulatory texts and of the documents sent by London was therefore a laborious prerequisite. It was also compulsory for all Freemasonry collective reflections and practices to be recorded in French. Trying to match the English and French Masonic uses, or at least to find some similarities between them, also necessitated the

---

[26] Archives Départementales du Finistère, 40 J 47, *Loge Anglaise n°184*, Livre d'Architecture 1774–year VI.

[27] The Masonic collection in the Bibliothèque Nationale de France's manuscripts department holds an identical Livre d'Architecture from the Heureuse Rencontre under the classification FM³ 261: 'the present register containing two hundred and forty-eight pages including the present one has been classified and signed by us on the first and last pages and handed over to the archives of the Heureuse Rencontre Lodge to be used for registering the minutes and deliberations of the symbolic lodges' meetings for the degrees of Entered Apprentice Fellowcraft; and M[aster] Mason. Brest Lodge, Year of Light 5773 – symbolically, the Masonic calendar begins at the world's creation … 4,000 years ago'.

long but interesting task of compiling and comparing all the documents, which was the responsibility of the Commissioners. There is evidence of this in the archives:

1. The lodge adopts in their entirety the Commissioner's comments on lodge no. 184's request for the distinctive title of Heureuse Rencontre should some English lodges have distinctive titles as well as their numbers.
2. On the request to the Very Respectable Grand Lodge of England for the functions attributed to each officer in English lodges and on the delivery to them of those attributed to date to the officers we recognise in our lodge.
3. On the request to the Very Respectable Grand Lodge of England for the degrees that it recognises, their relative ranks, those that are due honours, the type of honours, how they are conferred, how each degree operates (working or banquet lodge) and how each of them is pictured.
4. On the delivery to the Very Respectable Grand Lodge of England of the names of the degrees that we have given to date in the lodge as well as the names of those that we are familiar with.
5. On the request to the Very Respectable Grand Lodge of England for an overview of the lodges that it recognises as being properly constituted.
   ...
10. On the delivery to the Very Respectable Grand Lodge of England of the signs, words and touches that we believe to be the new English recognition with a request to be so kind as to tell us if it is genuine, and if it is not and if there is one, to please pass them onto us.[28]

Some members of the lodge had undoubtedly under-estimated the drawbacks of such a situation, including the Worshipful Master, who was presiding over the work himself, as his declaration to the lodge's Commissioners on 26 June 1776 shows:

[the Worshipful Dudezerseul declares] that the reason for these comments and protestations over the meeting of 25 June was the belief that

[28] Bibliothèque Nationale de France, Manuscripts, Masonic collection, FM³ 261, 'Livre d'Architecture of the Heureuse Rencontre', Brest Lodge, minutes from 16 May 1774, fols. 44–5.

since the French and English lodges form one single lodge under the name of Heureuse Rencontre no. 184, these two lodges must by rights have the same officers. However, having read articles 3 and 17 of the Grand Lodge of England's general regulations and their comments on the articles to the Grande Loge on 16 May, *we accept that the French and English lodges are absolutely distinct and separate and that they are independent of one another.*[29]

Given the risks of confusing the two structures, a meeting was convened to arrive at some clarification. The Commissioners explained to the Brothers that 'since the lodge [no. 184] has considered that it has specific rules that are distinct from those of the Grand Orient de France and, further, that the head of Lodge no. 184 only has authority at the behest of the Grand Lodge of England, this lodge cannot be merged with the Heureuse Rencontre Lodge.'[30]

If the Freemasons in Brest accepted the complexity of such an organisation and, consequently, the uncertainties and awkwardness of the separation, it was clearly because it was in their interests to do so. For them, the English affiliation in 1772 in no way meant a renunciation of almost thirty years of the French Masonic practices which they had been adhering to since 1745, and likewise the lodge's formation through the Grand Orient de France did not imply more of a separation with London. Herein lies the ambiguity, but also the richness, of the Brest Lodge's situation. The matter of the high degrees is a good example of this. One of the keys to the success of French Freemasonry in Europe was without a doubt the existence of these high degrees, which were mainly Christian and chivalrous in essence. So, when they linked up with English Freemasonry, it may have seemed at first glance that they would have had to abandon the high-degree rituals. In reality, the situation was more complex, and the choice of constituent power proved decisive. English Freemasonry was not monolithic. While the Grand Lodge of the Moderns believed, up until the 1813 Act of Union, that 'pure Ancient Masonry comprised three degrees and no more', its rival the Grand Lodge of the Ancients practised the Royal Arch high degree. It was the Ancients who had granted the constitutions to the Brest Lodge, a choice that demonstrates that they had a good knowledge of the Masonic situation in England (arguably through geographic proximity). This

[29] Archives Départementales du Finistère, 40 J 47, *English Lodge no. 184*, Livre d'Architecture, fol. 19, 26 June 1776.
[30] Archives Départementales du Finistère, 40 J 47, *English Lodge no. 184*, Livre d'Architecture, fol. 20, 8 September 1776.

contrasts sharply with the relative lack of knowledge that Lalande showed in his aforementioned 1773 letter, despite the fact that he was Grand Officer of the Grand Orient and a member of the Royal Society.

The Brest Lodge is proof that Freemasons during the Enlightenment knew how to make the most of the opportunities afforded them by a plural Fraternity. They practised supplementary high degrees, whose foreign origins just made them all the more appealing. Once reattached to the Grand Orient, the Heureuse Rencontre's autonomous existence in relation to Lodge no. 184 allowed it, after much skilful manoeuvring during meetings, to simultaneously pursue the practice of the French high degrees. For example, on 7 September 1782 'the Worshipful Master … read out the regulation to be observed in the English lodge no. 184, at the Brest Lodge … and convened an English lodge for the lodge's "chevaliers de l'orient" [one of the principal French high degrees] in order to confer on them the Royal Arch degree on the first Saturday of next month'.[31]

Not only did the Brest Brothers succeed in combining the English and French degrees, they also integrated both of them into a newly created scale of degrees. They clearly found this system to their satisfaction because, when their lodge came out of hibernation in September 1797 after five years of interruption to its work as a result of the Revolution,[32] they were happy to abide with the obligation from the new political regime to change the name Royal Arch to Parfait Arch.[33]

The Breton lodge's decision to have a dual French and English identity also offered the potential to nurture stimulating and enriching relations with lodges in other countries while, at the same time, not isolating itself in regard to its regional Masonic fabric – in contrast to the situation which its mother lodge, the Anglaise in Bordeaux, once found itself in. The Brest Lodge was mainly composed of naval men, but it also regularly welcomed foreign visitors. It offered assistance to shipwrecked sailors, such as Robert Wyneau (a member of the Perfect Amity no. 230 in Bath) and Captain Wreitt from Limerick, and to merchants, all of whom opened up new horizons for the Brest community.[34] Moreover, the lodge was subject to an increasing number of requests from Brothers who wanted to gain access

---

[31] Archives Départementales du Finistère, 40 J 47, *English Lodge no. 184*, 'Livre d'Architecture', fol. 43r, 7 September 1782.

[32] Their work was interrupted in October 1792.

[33] Archives Départementales du Finistère, 40 J 47, *English Lodge no. 184*, 'Livre d'Architecture', fol. 72v. The lodge's minutes made reference at the time to 'la République française une et indivisible' (the French Republic, one and indivisible).

[34] Archives Départementales du Finistère, 40 J 47, *English Lodge no. 184*, 'Livre d'Architecture', fol. 41r, fol. 58v.

to England or another country through an English Masonic certificate. Some of the problematics developed by Renaud Morieux in his thesis on the Channel as the Anglo-French border were therefore visible here in the masonic domain.[35]

The Brest Lodge had proved in its own way that, with adaptability and diplomacy, it was possible to retain a considerable amount of room for manoeuvre in relation to the Obediences and their drive for centralisation. It is worth noting that this approach appeared to comply with the regulations enacted by the Grand Orient: 'all lodges situated within the territory of one Grand Orient will be able to request and obtain aggregation letters from another Grand Orient, but they will only be delivered to those lodges equipped with local constitutions and the consent of the Grand Orient that those lodges depend on'.[36] Moreover, the Heureuse Rencontre never sought to hide the fact that its Brethren also belonged to the Grand Lodge of England. It was a unique case, and the Chambre des Provinces in Paris, which was extremely pernickety in ensuring that respect for Masonic orthodoxy was maintained within the Grand Orient, could not dispute the legality of their decision.[37]

The national logic that was increasingly asserting itself across Masonic Europe at the end of the eighteenth century did not therefore exclude a commitment to the principle of a broad, cosmopolitan space. Neither wholly English Freemasons nor wholly 'French Freemasons' (in the contemporary sense of the expression), the Brest Freemason community had constructed its own identity.

In Strasbourg, the Brothers of the *Candeur*, a lodge that was closely linked to the university and aimed at persons of note, worked under the leadership of Pierre de Guenet. Originally from Languedoc, he had been present at the origins of Freemasonry in France and never missed an opportunity to remind his Parisian interlocutors of the fact: 'About forty years ago,[38] I was received by Milord Darwentwater, who was Grand Master at the time[39] and who received all the court nobles, and I have been witness

---

[35] Renaud Morieux, *Une mer pour deux royaumes. La Manche, frontière franco-anglaise XVIIe–XVIIIe siècles* (Rennes, 2008).
[36] Bibliothèque Nationale de France, Manuscripts, Masonic collection, FM¹ 118, commission for foreign Grand Orients, fol. 408r, 7 March 1775.
[37] A letter from the *Heureuse Rencontre* was in fact read out at the Chambre des Provinces on 4 June 1774. It explicitly mentioned the constitutions granted by the Grand Lodge of the Ancients.
[38] His letter written from Strasbourg is dated 22 April 1773.
[39] Charles Radcliffe, Lord Darwentwater (1693–1746) was Grand Maître from 27 December 1736 until 1738. It is likely he left the post after the pope had fulminated

to all the progressions and variations that the order has undergone. My zeal and steadfastness have led me to the reform [the Templar reform that spread from Dresden in Saxony] that was introduced to me a long time ago.'[40] By 1765, when the Grande Loge de Paris (the Obedience succeeded by the Grand Orient in 1771–77) was in crisis, he could not find words harsh enough to criticise the laxity of French Freemasonry:

> All of Germany, Russia and Italy wholeheartedly reject, through a comprehensive reform, these so-called Brothers, who through either their state of origin or their customs should not be members of this Great Republic. There is no more anarchy than in France. Masonry in this country is just an object of amusement, for the most part seen as an opportunity to swindle or gorge on food and drink. We must only be interested in frivolity, and we will be the last to restore masonry to its first institution. Only by following it can we achieve its aim.[41]

Although the new Obedience intended to impose its law on the provincial lodges, it sought to break with Paris and requested patents from London instead:

> Driven to desperation by the fanciful, self-seeking claims of the so-called Grande Loge, which has resumed its position (under the name of Grand Orient), we deemed it Necessary for the Good of the Order to turn to England where Masonry has been preserved in all its simplicity and purity, and we have obtained constitutions from them.[42]

At the same time, De Guenet made contact with the emissaries of the Templar reform from Saxony, who were bringing with them a plan for the radical reform of the Masonic Order that was chivalrous and Christian in essence. While this was far removed from the English Masonic model, it was known to be thriving in Saxony:

---

the bull *in eminenti* in May 1738. The last mention of his Masonic activity is in December 1739 at a meeting at which he was present in his capacity as former Grand Master. He was executed after the Jacobites' defeat at the Battle of Culloden.

[40] Archives Départementales de l'Hérault, Astruc papers, 1E8, item no. 11.
[41] Bibliothèque Nationale de France, Manuscripts Department, Masonic collection, FM^1 111, Chapelle collection, tome VI, fol. 445r, 22 January 1765.
[42] Bibliothèque Nationale Universitaire de Strasbourg, mss 5437, *Registre des procès-verbaux de la loge de La Candeur constituée mère des loges du Grand Orient de Strasbourg* [sic], 30 June 1772, fol. 271.

Turning Away from the sorry spectacle now on offer to Us as a result of the schism that divides French Masonry and anticipating Only very slow and highly uncertain outcomes from the zealous efforts of the lodges in the Midi to resolve the situation, we have fixed Our attention and pinned our hopes on the operations of Northern Germany.[43]

While Brest chose dual recognition from France and England, Strasbourg chose both the path of Masonic reform with its conversion to Templar Masonry and a return to the Order's English origins as a source of stability. It is clear that French Freemasons were certainly never left indifferent by English Freemasonry in the eighteenth century. Moreover, this is still the case today because Freemasonry worldwide is still split between a self-proclaimed regular Freemasonry, that is, recognised as such by London, and a Liberal or Adogmatic Freemasonry, which is not recognised because it does not respect the landmarks defined by London. Even when they maintain that they have broken with the hegemonic claims of the Grand Lodge of England, the French Freemasons still define themselves in relation to the English. Hence, close attention paid to the different levels of relations in the Order and its management strata at local level would reveal a broad spectrum of attitudes and representations.

---

[43] Bibliothèque Nationale Universitaire de Strasbourg, mss 5437, *Registre des procès-verbaux de la loge de La Candeur constituée mère des loges du Grand Orient de Strasbourg* [sic], 30 June 1772, fol. 272.

Chapter 7
Competing models of sociability: Smollett's repossession of an ailing British body

Annick Cossic-Péricarpin

TOBIAS SMOLLETT is undoubtedly better known as a novelist, but this chapter interrogates two of his lesser-known writings, his medical treatise, *An Essay on the External Use of Water* (1752),[1] and his travel book,[2] *Travels through France and Italy* (1766).[3] These two works testify to the diversity of his skills and the complexity of his career. If Dr Johnson could sarcastically quip 'The noblest prospect which a Scotchman ever sees is the high road that leads him to England!',[4] Smollett went further afield and started as a surgeon in the Navy around 1740. Both the *Essay* and the *Travels* correspond to different stages in his life. He wrote the *Essay* as a result of his stay in Bath, where he had briefly and unsuccessfully tried to start a

---

[1] Tobias Smollett, *An Essay on the External Use of Water* (London, 1752). This edition will be used throughout this chapter.
[2] Smollett plundered from a guidebook, *Roma antica, e moderna* (1750), and also used Joseph Addison's *Remarks on Several Parts of Italy*, according to Louis L. Martz, *The Later Career of Tobias Smollett* (Yale, 1942), 89. The *Travels* was 'the careful composition of one who was not only a vigorous narrator and satirist, but also an accurate historian and an expert man of letters', 89. An opinion partly shared by Richard J. Jones: '*Travels through France and Italy* was an extension of Smollett's historical work [...] a complementary volume to his historical work' (*Tobias Smollett in the Enlightenment, Travels through France, Italy and Scotland* [Lewisburg, 2011], 108–23). Jones concludes his study by comparing Smollett's *Travels through France and Italy* to Voltaire's *Dictionnaire philosophique portatif* (1764) and considers that Smollett has written a similar kind of 'pocket encyclopedia' (p. 136). Smollett is also the author of *A Complete History of England* (1759).
[3] The edition of the *Travels* used in this essay is the Centaur Press edition, *Travels through France and Italy*, 1766, ed. Jan Morris (London, 2006).
[4] James Boswell, *The Life of Dr Johnson* (1791; London, 1962), 1, 264.

practice.⁵ There he must have been caught up the in *sulphur controversy* that opposed the Chemists to the Galenists.⁶ The *Travels*, on the other hand, narrates his tour of the Continent that lasted two years (1763–65), and consists in a series of forty-one letters sent to a limited number of addressees.⁷

In these two books Smollett blew apart a degree of consensus, laying the foundations of the new social practices that were created or recreated in Enlightenment Britain. He wrote the second book in the context of the Seven Years' War (1756–63), during a period of unprecedented English domination which inevitably entailed the possibility of decline. Smollett is generally perceived as an arch-conservative and identified with the benign but cantankerous representative of the landed gentry, Matthew Bramble, who is the main character in his last novel, *The Expedition of Humphry Clinker* (1771). This chapter will challenge this perception, in the wake of Terence Bowers's critical study,⁸ and will redefine Smollett's contribution to a renewal of the recently forged British model of sociability,⁹ through his perception and description of the British body.

---

[5] Little is known about Smollett's medical practice; he may have obtained a medical degree from Aberdeen in June 1750 (Lewis Mansfield Knapp, *Tobias Smollett, Doctor of Man and Manners* (1949; London, 1963), 144–6). The English looked down on Scottish degrees.

[6] Charles Lucas, who published an *Essay on Waters* in 1756, denied the presence of sulphur in the Bath waters; such a contention was challenged by John Rutty in *A Methodical Synopsis of Mineral Waters* (London, 1757) and *The Analyzer Analysed* (London, 1758). See Annick Cossic, *Bath au XVIIIe siècle. Les fastes d'une cité palladienne* (Rennes, 2000), 41.

[7] I have followed a recent trend in criticism that refuses to see the 'I' in the *Travels* as a persona. For Richard Jones, the book 'leaves the domain of the travel book and becomes an encyclopaedic work of a Scottish Enlightenment' (Jones, *Tobias Smollett in the Enlightenment*, 10).

[8] Terence Bowers, 'Reconstituting the National Body in Smollett's *Travels through France and Italy*', *Eighteenth-Century Life* 21 (1997), 1–25.

[9] For the *Oxford English Dictionary*, the word 'sociability' appeared first in the fifteenth century and means 'the character or quality of being sociable, friendly disposition or intercourse'. In the *Transversales Series* (Paris, 2012–16) that examines the interaction of the French and English models of sociability, the definition provided by Georg Simmel in his work, *Soziologie* (Berlin, 1908), has been used as a starting point. For Simmel, the essence of sociability is to be freely consented by individuals and to entail a ludic dimension.

Contesting some new medical and social practices in Britain: the Bath model and the *open society* under attack

The eighteenth century in Britain has been called the 'age of watering places', and the development of new medical practices encouraged sociability. The Pump Room at Bath, designed at the beginning of the century, had become a hotbed of sociability due to its architecture and the ritualisation of both drinking the waters and bathing.[10] The practice of drinking the waters was encouraged by Dr William Oliver in *A Practical Essay on Fevers ... to Which is Annex'd A Dissertation on the Bath Waters*: 'The custom of drinking these waters at the Pump and warm had not prevail'd long, at least had not been made so universal, for tho' some drank them every year, yet above twenty years ago, I remember very few came to Bath for anything but the bathing part.'[11] In the *Travels*, Smollett implicitly recognises the superiority of Bath when he discovers Rocabiliare, a small town not far from Nice, and complains because '[the] waters are at a distance of a mile and a half from the town. There are no baths nor shelter, nor any sort of convenience for those that drink them; and the best part of their efficacy is lost unless they are drank at the fountain-head.'[12] Most remarkably, it is abroad that Smollett admits that the new, mostly Palladian, architecture displayed in Bath in Queen Square, the North and South Parades, Prior Park (designed by John Wood the Elder), the Assembly Rooms (the work of John Wood the Younger), to name but a few examples, was unrivalled elsewhere. In *The Expedition of Humphry Clinker*, published shortly before its author's death in 1771, the main letter writer, Matt Bramble, lambasts the attributes of spa sociability, questions the solidity and sanity of the new buildings and longs for the solitude of his Welsh mountains: he describes the condition of quite a few characters who have been forced to settle and 'lead a weary life in this stewpan of idleness and insignificance.'[13]

On the scientific level, Smollett's heretic contention in the *Essay* is that the cures worked by the Bath waters are not due to the latter's composition but, rather, to their liquidity. Simple water, *aqua simplex*, would do the trick: 'I am inclined to believe, that the Mineral Principles in Hot Springs,

---

[10] As early as the sixteenth century, Dr John Jones in his essay, *The Bathes of Bathes Ayde* (London, 1572), tried to scientifically prove the virtues of the Bath waters and recommended drinking them. See Cossic, *Bath au XVIIIe siècle. Les fastes d'une cité palladienne*, 31.
[11] William Oliver, *A Practical Essay on Fevers ... to Which is Annex'd A Dissertation on the Bath Waters* (London, 1704), 214–15.
[12] Tobias Smollett, *The Expedition of Humphry Clinker* (1771; Oxford, 2009), 168.
[13] Smollett, *Humphry Clinker*, 56.

have often, in the cure of patients by bathing, usurped that praise and reputation which was really due to the simple element.'[14] Smollett then proceeds to praise the virtues of the steam bath, a method that he says was not practised at Bath, which had already become 'the great hospital of the nation.'[15] The charge against the Bath physicians is renewed in the *Travels*, where Smollett presents himself as 'not one of those who implicitly believe in all the dogmata of physic.'[16] Smollett's attempt at working as a physician in Bath is not well documented by his biographers, for lack of reliable sources. What has been established is that he did not stay there for long, and both his fiction and the *Essay on the External Use of Water* draw a somewhat unflattering portrait of the fashionable spa.

His negative assessment of both the medical profession at Bath and the bathing establishment leads him to advocate reform. Reform was urgently needed because the organisation of the cure was lethal, or definitely detrimental to the patient's health. Smollett complains about a number of new social practices such as the 'continual noise of ringing and tolling of bells'[17] to signal the arrival of newcomers. He suggests new 'Regulations', for instance an all-night service of chairs[18] and also inserts Mr Cleland's schemes, i.e. redesigning the King and Queen's Baths, segregating the sexes, using pumping, screening the bathers from the onlookers' gaze.[19] The implementation of reforms raises two issues: that of the resistance of the Bath Corporation, of its conservatism,[20] and that of the international competition between spas. According to Smollett, rival European spas were ready to use Cleland's improvement plans:

> This is far from being a vain apprehension; in as much as some ingenious physicians from *Portugal* have obtained models of Mr Cleland's apparatus, and copies of his plan, with a view to carry it into execution at the *Caldas* near *Lisbon*; and I make no doubt that the people of *Aix la Chapelle*, and the proprietors of the famous Hot Wells in *Bohemia*,

---

[14] Smollett, *An Essay*, 22.
[15] Smollett, *An Essay*, 29.
[16] Smollett, *Travels*, 11.
[17] Smollett, *An Essay*, 46.
[18] Smollett, IX, *An Essay*, 45.
[19] Smollett, *An Essay*, 48. Mr Cleland was a controversial figure, a surgeon: following a quarrel (1743–44), Cleland was dismissed from the Bath General Hospital.
[20] The City Act of 1766 provided for the rehabilitation of the baths and the enlargement of the Pump Room. The Improvement Act of 1789 outlined a plan which envisaged the aggrandisement of some streets and the building of a new Pump Room under the supervision of the architect Thomas Baldwin.

and other parts of *Germany*, will seize the first opportunity of improving those waters, from which they derive such advantage, in the concourse of strangers which they draw together.[21]

Smollett's target in the *Essay* is, above all, the emergence of the new social practices of the *open society*,[22] which involved the redefinition of leisure and of gender relations. As argued by Neil McKendrick, an open society encourages a culture of innovation and novelty and originates in a flexible and open political and social regime.[23] Relations between the sexes were desegregated as a result of the new urban culture at work in places of public assembly like the Assembly Rooms or the Public Gardens, Vauxhall or Ranelagh in London, Spring Gardens in Bath.[24] This desegregation of the sexes could also be observed on the Continent and Smollett sarcastically describes the custom of the *conversazione* between ladies of quality and their *cicisbei* (or official lovers) in Italy, a custom which he associates not with heterosexual friendship but with libertinage, vowing: 'For my part I would rather be condemned for life to the gallies than exercise the office of a *cicisbeo*, exposed to the intolerable caprices and dangerous resentment of an Italian virago.'[25]

The mixing of the sexes[26] causes Smollett's indignation, particularly when the body is half naked and exposed to the voyeurism of onlookers in Bath or by the seaside, as when he describes his bathing experience at Nice and assumes that the fair sex must be excluded from its benefits 'unless they lay aside all regard to decorum.'[27] The sexes were side by side in the therapeutic context of the spa, and also in that of a new leisure culture, which involved the proliferation of *sub dio* entertainments, later satirically depicted by Smollett's persona, Matt Bramble, in *The Expedition of Humphry Clinker*, in a famous description of London's public gardens: 'When I see a number of well-dressed people, of both sexes, exposed to the eyes of the mob; and, which is worse to the cold, raw, night-air, devouring sliced

---

[21] Smollett, *An Essay*, 40.
[22] British society was a commercial society, open to innovation, a trend that started in the late seventeenth century and that was reinforced after the Glorious Revolution of 1688.
[23] See Neil McKendrick, John Brewer and J. H. Plumb (eds), *The Birth of a Consumer Society. The Commercialization of Eighteenth-Century England*, (London, 1992), 9–33.
[24] See Cossic, *Bath au XVIIIe siècle. Les fastes d'une cité palladienne*, 66.
[25] Smollett, *Travels*, 193.
[26] The Baths in Bath were mixed, with the exception of the Queen's Bath.
[27] Smollett, *Travels*, 161.

beef, and swilling port, and punch, and cyder I can't help compassionating their temerity, while I despise their want of taste and decorum.'[28] In the *Travels*, one of the main reasons for the tour – beside the grief induced by the loss of his beloved daughter – is the poor quality of the British air, and the sick Smollett who arrived in Boulogne had been tormented by the *tabes*[29] in England and weakened by frequent colds: 'Another advantage I have reaped from this climate is my being in a great measure delivered from a slow fever which used to hang about me and render life a burden. Neither am I so apt to catch cold as I used to be in England and France.'[30] Smollett's obsession with the air announces the popularity of the miasma theory,[31] which hindered the eradication of epidemics like cholera in the nineteenth century and was successfully challenged by Dr John Snow (1813–58), who is considered to be one of the founders of the germ theory of disease. So, for Smollett, an aching body like his own could find relief or be cured only elsewhere than in Britain. The tour that he undertook for health reasons turned out to have mighty implications for his sociable body.

The cure on the Continent: the questionable impact of continental sociability on Smollett's body

Like most Grand Tourists, Smollett observed his new surroundings and, in particular, the continental sociability which served as a model, since it was imitated by the British, disseminated via conduct books and treatises of civility and reinforced by the Grand Tour itself. The idea of continental superiority in the field of manners and refinement was still alive, and Smollett regrets it from the outset: 'The French preserve a certain ascendancy over us, which is very disgraceful to our nation and this appears in nothing more than in the article of dress. We are contented to be thought their apes in fashion; but in fact we are slaves to their tailors, mantua-makers, barbers and other tradesmen.'[32] He sets out to examine the French and Italians from five angles in a truly holistic approach, using five criteria,

---

[28] Smollett, *Humphry Clinker*, 89.
[29] *Tabes dorsalis* or the general relaxation of the fibres; a cause of consumption. The tabes can be considered as neurosyphilis. Smollett, *Travels*, 163.
[30] Smollett, *Travels*, 164.
[31] At the time, miasma was synonymous with poisonous vapour. In the nineteenth century the miasma theory was contested by John Snow, who drew up a map of London and demonstrated that the outbreaks of cholera were the result of the contamination of the water, not of the inhalation of foul air.
[32] Smollett, *Travels*, 43.

i.e. the natural environment, the built environment (the habitat), economic development, social interaction and the fetishisation of the body.

He is immediately seduced by the southern climate of Nice: while 'the air of Boulogne is cold and moist and, […] of consequence unhealthy',[33] in Nice (which was not part of France at the time) he is 'enchanted'.[34] The whole country was 'cultivated like a garden', 'indeed the plain presents nothing but gardens full of green trees loaded with oranges, lemons, citrons and bergamots, which make a delightful appearance'.[35] Yet the continental (Italian) gardens are deemed inferior to the English ones, because they lack the 'beauties of simple nature and the charms of neatness'.[36] When he leaves Nice for the rest of Italy, and Rome in particular, he is disgusted by the 'filth that disgraces the streets and the palaces' and pollutes the air, and exclaims: 'the Piazza Navona is almost as dirty as West Smithfield, where the cattle are sold in London'.[37] The dirt of the streets and the ensuing stench were partly caused by the 'putrifying carcasses of criminals who had been dragged through them by the heels and precipitated from the *Scalae Gemoniae*, or Tarpeian rock, before they were thrown into the Tyber, which was the general receptacle of the *cloaca maxima* and all the filth of Rome'.[38]

The built environment itself, on the whole, is rather positively perceived by Smollett, who recognises the elegance of a number of buildings in the vicinity of Nice, the 'white *bastides* making a dazzling shew',[39] or in the rest of Italy, the *Porta del Popolo*,[40] the sublime character of the Piazza of St Peter's Church,[41] with a few notable exceptions like the Pantheon, which to him looks like 'a huge cockpit open at top'.[42] But what mostly interests Smollett is the economic and agricultural development of the regions he tours, which has a direct impact on the health of the inhabitants and on their diet: the poverty of the French peasants strikes him, and he states that 'the peasants in the south of France are poorly clad, and look as if they were half starved, diminutive, swarthy and meagre'[43] as a result of the feudal system that prevented the improvement of husbandry and the gen-

---

[33] Smollett, *Travels*, 18.
[34] Smollett, *Travels*, 101.
[35] Smollett, *Travels*, 101.
[36] Smollett, *Travels*, 219.
[37] Smollett, *Travels*, 211.
[38] Smollett, *Travels*, 212.
[39] Smollett, *Travels*, 101.
[40] Smollett, *Travels*, 208.
[41] Smollett, *Travels*, 221.
[42] Smollett, *Travels*, 224.
[43] Smollett, *Travels*, 67.

eralisation of the enclosure system. Smollett notices the absence of black cattle, and when he encounters the latter, as between Luc and Toulon, he is delighted.[44]

He is also charmed by some French banquets like the one he is invited to in Boulogne: 'The *repas* served up in three services, or courses, with *entrées* and *hors d'oeuvres*, exclusive of the fruit, consisted of above twenty dishes, extremely well dressed by the *rôtisseur*, who is the best cook I ever knew in France or elsewhere; but the *plats* were not presented with much order.'[45] Meals offer him the opportunity to observe table manners, and to debunk the myth of French refinement: 'I think it would be better to institute schools where youth may learn to eat their victuals without daubing themselves, or giving offence to the eyes of one another', or later on, 'Our young ladies did not seem to be much used to do the honours of the table.'[46] In the field of social interaction, Smollett scrutinises both endogamous relations and exogamous ones. The adjective 'sociable' is repeatedly used in his portraits of the French or the Italians. Hospitality is one of his measures of sociability, together with cheerfulness. In his view, the Nissard gentry are inhospitable to foreigners: 'You must not expect that I should describe the tables and the hospitality of our Nissard gentry. Our consul, who is a very honest man, told me he had lived four-and-thirty years in the country without having once eat or drank in any of their houses.'[47] On the other hand, the inhabitants of Montpellier 'are sociable, gay and good-tempered,'[48] and the same remark is made in Pisa, for instance, where 'the people in general are counted sociable and polite.'[49] He pays attention to religious sociability too, and to its negative impact on the economy: 'The great poverty of the people here is owing to their religion,'[50] which imposes upon them religious feasts and financial support for the parish or for the monasteries.

The ultimate criterion used by Smollett is the continental treatment of the body. In both France and Italy the body was fetishised, hidden, distorted by an accumulation of clothes and accessories. He narrates the story of a Frenchman who refused to have his hair cut so that his head could be bathed in cold water on the advice of his physician: 'he dismissed his physician, lost his eyesight and almost his senses, and is now led about with his

---

[44] Smollett, *Travels*, 67, 273.
[45] Smollett, *Travels*, 31.
[46] Smollett, *Travels*, 31.
[47] Smollett, *Travels*, 128.
[48] Smollett, *Travels*, 87.
[49] Smollett, *Travels*, 187.
[50] Smollett, *Travels*, 146.

hair in a bag and a piece of green silk hanging like a screen before his face', which leads Smollett to conclude that 'a Frenchman will sooner part with his religion than with his hair'.[51] Smollett thus refuses what Bowers calls 'the entire system of symbolic assemblages that defines the aristocratic body and structures its relations to other classes of bodies'.[52] His relation to fashion is antagonistic and he is more aware of its enslavement of the body and of the mind than of its social function of discrimination. As postulated by Roland Barthes in *The Fashion System*, 'Fashion must project the aristocratic model, the source of its prestige: this is pure Fashion; but at the same time it must represent, in a euphoric manner, the world of its consumers by transforming intra-worldly functions into signs (work, sport, vacations, seasons, ceremonies): this is naturalized fashion [...]'.[53]

Smollett's views on France and Italy have often been dismissed as xenophobic and just another example of Francophobia or French- and Italian-bashing. Yet, in the *Travels* he shows the same obsessions as in the *Essay on the External Use of Water*, namely the desire to cleanse an ailing body. Smollett writes not only as a scientific observer of bodies whose stance is justified by his medical training, but also as a suffering body. His letters are addressed to physicians, and French doctors' letters are also inserted within the travel correspondence sent to Britain. The reader understands that his obsession with breathing a pure air and bathing in a cold sea is directly related to his consumption and his spleen.[54] In the same way as, in Bath, spa sociability endangered the health of the invalids, in Montpellier he shied away from the cheerful sociability of the inhabitants: 'Montpellier will be extremely gay and brilliant. These very circumstances would determine me to leave it. I have no health to enjoy these pleasures. I cannot bear a crowd of company, such as pours in upon us unexpectedly at all hours.'[55]

In that respect, Nice was for him a perfect location because there he could both breathe freely and bathe: 'the air [of the neighbouring Alps] being dry, pure, heavy and elastic, must be agreeable to the constitution of those who labour under disorders arising from weak nerves, obstructed perspiration, relaxed fibres, a viscosity of lymph and a languid circulation.'[56]

---

[51] Smollett, *Travels*, 54.
[52] Bowers, 'Reconstituting the National Body', 9.
[53] Roland Barthes, *The Fashion System* (Oakland, 1983), 290–1.
[54] See Clark Lawlor: 'Smollett's particular solution to his disease of contemporary civilisation, and his attitude to the effeminating effect of that society, is to be found in his keen pursuit of manly cold bathing and hard exercise', *Consumption and Literature. The Making of a Romantic Disease* (London, 2006), 95.
[55] Smollett, *Travels*, 78.
[56] Smollett, *Travels*, 162.

If there was one thing that the French had imported from Britain, it was the cold bath.[57] Smollett is here faithful to the conclusions that he drew in the *Essay*, where he asserted the beneficial effect of the cold bath in cases of hypochondria[58] and predicated the superiority of cold water over hot water, its 'particles being more penetrating than those of hot water'.[59] Nonetheless, contrary to Hoffmann,[60] he recognises the virtues of hot water, which 'will relax the fibres … quicken the circulation and [cause] the discharge of the virus'.[61]

Although the climate of southern France can be seen as a major agent of recovery, the role of the tour as such should not be under-estimated. Even if Smollett tried hard to make his journey comfortable by carefully selecting the inns or lodgings where he was accommodated, he encountered a number of hardships which in fact, against the odds, strengthened his body – 'I may say I was for two months continually agitated either in mind or body, and very often both at the same time'[62] – and 'braced up his relaxed constitution'.[63] The positive outcome of the tour was thus due to the climate of France and Italy and the multiple occasions for bodily exercise that the tour offered, and not to the sociable character of the inhabitants of the host countries. For Smollett, therefore, the tour had reversed consequences, leading to a revised opinion on his own country.

The body repossessed: competing models of sociability and nationhood[64]

By documenting his tour through letter writing (be it fictitious or not), Smollett reasserted his right to judge: as a matter of fact, in classifying

---

[57] Smollett, *Travels*, 42.
[58] Smollett, *An Essay*, 6.
[59] Smollett, *An Essay*, 12.
[60] He mentions Hoffmann in the *Essay* on p. 2 and his analysis of the properties of the waters of Aix-la-Chapelle (Dr Friedrich Hoffmann, 1660–1742); Hoffmann wrote a dissertation on the patient–physician relationship (*Medicus Politicus*, 1738, or *The politic physician*).
[61] Smollett, *An Essay*, 19.
[62] Smollett, *Travels*, 256.
[63] Smollett, *Travels*, 257.
[64] See David Hume's Essay, 'Of National Characters', 1748; David Hume, *Essays Moral, Political, Literary*, ed. Eugene F. Miller (1777), Essay XXI, 204–6: 'We may observe, that, where a very extensive government has been established for many centuries, it spreads a national character over the whole empire, and communicates to every part a similarity of manners', [and Hume adds]: 'The manners of a people change very

the nations that he visited he destroyed the consensus that officially surrounded the tour. Far from admiring the Roman Colosseum, Smollett sees it as tainted by slave work (it was built by Jewish slaves) and by its function, and observes that on the day when it first opened 'fifty thousand wild beasts were all killed in the arena'.[65] Smollett then proceeds to expose the savagery of the Romans, called a 'barbarous people': 'It is not at all clear to me that a people is the more brave, the more they are accustomed to bloodshed in their public entertainments. True bravery is not savage, but humane.'[66] This differs from the classification established by the Scottish philosopher Adam Ferguson, who, in *An Essay on the History of Civil Society* (1767), distinguishes between the 'Rude nations' and the 'Polished' or civilised ones and also defines true bravery (that he attributed to the savage). Ferguson subdivides Rude Nations into Savage ones and Barbarous ones and puts the Romans in the 'Polished'/civilised category.[67] He too, like Smollett, is afraid of the potential effeminacy of polished nations: 'if the individual, not called to unite with his country, be left to pursue his private advantage; we may find him become effeminate, mercenary and sensual'.[68] Smollett heightens the charge by accusing the Romans of being effeminate in their use of warm bathing in the summer – 'a point of luxury borrowed from the effeminate Asiatics'[69] – even if he concedes that their bathing establishments were remarkable and well-regulated spaces of sociability. His vitriolic charge debunks the model of Antiquity and its virtuous citizens.[70] In the *Essay on the External Use of Water* he repeatedly insisted on the superiority of cold water and drove home the same message, indicting the voluptuousness of the Roman bathers, 'the charming indolence or *Languor* [that] steals upon the spirits'.[71]

---

considerably from one age to another; either by great alterations in their government, by the mixtures of new people, or by that inconstancy, to which all human affairs are subject.'

[65] Smollett, *Travels*, 226.
[66] Smollett, *Travels*, 227.
[67] Adam Ferguson, *An Essay on the History of Civil Society* (1767; Cambridge), ed. Fania Oz-Salzberger, 1995, 147–8, 159, 181.
[68] Ferguson, *An Essay on the History of Civil Society*, 237.
[69] Smollett, *Travels*, 229.
[70] The association of classical beauty and virtue has been explored by Philip J. Ayres in his book, *Classical Culture and the Idea of Rome in Eighteenth-Century England* (Cambridge, 2009): 'Very few would have denied the continuing validity of the classical idea of *libertas* or the social virtue obligatory in citizenship or *civitas*. [...] The preference for Roman-republican models then had much to do with political convenience and class affinities', 2–4.
[71] Smollett, *An Essay*, 12, 16. See footnote 56.

The Italians, who could be expected to be the direct heirs to Roman civilisation, have inherited a number of its objectionable characteristics and customs. Smollett takes a number of examples, like spitting, which he depicts thus: 'They had also another filthy custom which still prevails among the modern Italians; I mean that of spitting and hawking incessantly and defiling the floor with slops of every kind.'[72] Contrary to what Bowers asserts,[73] Smollett's condemnation does not target the patricians only but applies to the entire nation, as when he admits that '[he] had imbibed a strong prejudice against the common people of that country.'[74] A general feeling of distrust prevents all lasting forms of social relations and the advice given by the natives proves systematically wrong, such as that volunteered by the banker Barazzi, who insisted on Smollett taking a road that turned out to be the worst one, although 'he [had] assured [him] that the road by Terni was forty miles shorter than the other, much more safe and easy, and accommodated with exceeding good *auberges*.'[75] Most damning of all is their Catholicism, which hampers their economic development and ruins their art, a rejection that is most obvious in some ekphrastic passages where Smollett the art critic lambasts Catholic works of art, telling his reader that the 'the figure of Christ is as much emaciated as if he had died of a consumption. Besides, there is something indelicate, not to say indecent, in the attitude and design of a man's body, stark naked, lying upon the knees of a woman.'[76]

The French do not fare much better, but Smollett makes a fairly perceptive assessment of the situation of France in a pre-revolutionary period. His obsession with dirt goes beyond the pathological, to reach the systemic. According to him, France's ills are economic, societal and political, and are all to be ascribed to its regime, which is a prime example of divine right monarchy. France appears as a country where there is no freedom of speech or of thought – Smollett's books were confiscated when he entered the country – where ideas therefore cannot circulate freely, where heavy taxation oppresses the peasants and where innovation is stifled. In Montpellier, famous for its Faculty of Medicine, a celebrated professor misdiagnoses Smollett's illness, and in the mechanical arts France is shown to be wholly deficient and thus markedly inferior to Britain. Even if the Bath Corporation is accused of conservatism in the *Essay on the External Use of Water*,

---

[72] Smollett, Footnote to Letter 30, *Travels*, 292.
[73] Bowers, 'Reconstituting the National Body', 2.
[74] Smollett, *Travels*, 252.
[75] Smollett, *Travels*, 243.
[76] Smollett, *Travels*, 221.

some British physicians or surgeons are innovative, such as Mr Cleland who 'formed an easy and rational plan for rendering the baths more safe and commodious'.[77] In the *Essay*, Smollett pays tribute to the architect John Wood, 'to whose extraordinary genius they [the Bath Corporation] are indebted for a great part of the trade and beauty of the place: yet they have industriously opposed his best designs'.[78] Smollett is convinced that Bath, if properly managed, could rival 'the Baiae of the ancients', 'for it might easily be brought to excel as much in beauty and convenience, as in the salubrious efficacy of its waters' and 'in point of elegant architecture, [could become] the admiration of the whole world'.[79] A few years later, the British traveller proudly asserts that '[he has not] seen any bridge in France or Italy comparable to that of Westminster, either in beauty, magnificence or solidity; and when the bridge at Blackfriars is finished, it will be such a monument of architecture as all the world cannot parallel'.[80]

The decline of France is also linked to the effeminacy of its male population, most notably its aristocracy: Smollett's description of the ease with which Frenchmen could attend a lady's toilette recalls Ferguson's fear of an effeminate British nation in *An Essay on the History of Civil Society* published a year after Smollett's *Travels*.[81] Paradoxically, this effeminate nation can also indulge in barbarous practices like duelling, which was forbidden by law, yet widespread:

> In England we have not yet adopted all the implacability of the punctilio. A gentleman may be insulted even with a blow, and survive, after having once hazarded his life against the aggressor. The laws of honour in our country do not oblige him either to slay the person from whom he received the injury, or even to fight to the last drop of his own blood.[82]

---

[77] Smollett, *An Essay*, 33–6.
[78] Smollett, *An Essay*, 39.
[79] Smollett, *An Essay*, 39.
[80] Smollett, *Travels*, 206.
[81] Ferguson celebrated the virtues of the warrior and also linked the nature of a political regime with the economy of the country: 'National poverty, however, and the suppression of commerce, are the means by which despotism comes to accomplish its own destruction' (*An Essay on the History of Civil Society*, 263). On the dangers of effeminacy, see Philip Carter, who analyses the emergence of 'new preoccupations such as with the effects of men's foreign travel to French and Italian centres of ostentatious and thus false refinement' in *Men and the Emergence of Polite Society: Britain, 1660–1800* (2001; New York, 2014), 127.
[82] Smollett, *Travels*, 116.

Smollett therefore feels that France is on the brink of a revolution and pays great attention to the country's dysfunctional institutions, noticing that 'all the parliaments or tribunals of justice in the kingdom seem bent upon asserting their rights and independence in the face of the King's prerogative, and even at the expense of his power and authority'.[83]

Smollett complains about the lack of true sociability in France and Italy, but it was this very absence which actually recreated a presence, that of his friends at home to whom he kept writing. He has no friend among the 'Nissards', concluding at the end of his journey that 'the only friendships he had contracted at Nice are with strangers who, like [himself], only sojourn here for a season,'[84] and longs for home, 'the habitation of my friends, for whose conversation, correspondence and esteem I wish alone to live'.[85] The lack of true sociability appears in the absence of hospitality and the imposition on foreigners, particularly in those places of sociability that the inns – very negatively portrayed throughout the book – could have epitomised.

Letter writing in his travel narrative has enabled Smollett to maintain a sort of vicarious sociability with a limited number of countrymen and women. His network is made up of men, many of whom are doctors, with the occasional addition of women:[86]

> Throughout this time Smollett wrote letters home. They were addressed to a circle of friends in London, mostly it appears medical men, and probably including John Moore [...]. This was a worldly enough audience [...] and Smollett could presuppose an educated understanding of his experiences. He was, however, nothing if not a professional, and he designed these essays specifically for later publication. In them he was striking a public pose.[87]

Smollett's readership contributes to the forging of the nation and illustrates the process analysed by Benedict Anderson in his seminal study, *Imagined Communities* (1983). Anderson posits that nations emerged in America in the late eighteenth and early nineteenth centuries against a specific historical context which witnessed the dissemination of print culture: 'these fellow-readers, to whom they [speakers of the huge variety of Frenches, Englishes or Spanishes] were connected through print, formed,

---

[83] Smollett, *Travels*, 260.
[84] Smollett, *Travels*, 263.
[85] Smollett, *Travels*, 283.
[86] Smollett, *Travels*, letter XV, 112.
[87] Smollett, *Travels*, Introduction, viii.

in their secular, visible invisibility, the embryo of the nationally imagined community'.[88]

Smollett abroad did not really relish the company of other Englishmen and complained about their pretentions and gullibility, blaming them for the various types of 'imposition' practised upon him because, 'like simple birds of passage, [they] allow themselves to be plucked by the people of the country'.[89] As part of a new ritual, the English on the Continent paid each other visits of ceremony[90] that Smollett did not seem to be particularly fond of. He was not the only one, since he met a fellow countryman who endeavoured to avoid him 'with great care' and remained on his hired *felucca*.[91] Smollett humorously remarks that 'he never spoke a word to [the English gentlemen he met upon the road] yet in other respects, was a good man, mild, charitable, and humane. This is a character truly British'.[92] On another occasion Smollett observes that 'two Englishmen [who chance to meet abroad] maintain a mutual reserve and diffidence and keep without the sphere of each other's attraction, like two bodies endowed with a repulsive power'.[93] This is the opposite of what Laurence Sterne, Smollett's arch-enemy, advocated in *A Sentimental Journey Through France and Italy* (1768), which, in a way, showed sentimentalism as an avatar of Newton's law of gravitation. It looks even more like a Scottish model of sociability among 'rude people' than an English one, and here partly matches Ferguson's definition of true sociability, which was inspired by clannish, Highland sociability.[94] Smollett's Scottishness regularly surfaces in the *Travels*, and

---

[88] Benedict Anderson, *Imagined Communities* (London, 2006), 44. Anderson explains: 'the convergence of capitalism and print technology on the fatal diversity of human language created the possibility of a new form of imagined community, which in its basic morphology set the stage for the modern nation', 46.
[89] Smollett, *Travels*, 76, 275.
[90] Smollett, *Travels*, 77. Smollett sarcastically describes the mockery of the visit of ceremony in Rome: 'When you arrive at Rome, you receive cards from all your countryfolks in that city. They expect to have the visit returned next day, when they give orders not to be at home; and you never speak to one another in the sequel. This is a refinement in hospitality that the English have invented by the strength of their own genius, without any assistance either from France, Italy or Lapland', 210.
[91] A *felucca* or a wooden sailing boat.
[92] Smollett, *Travels*, 254. Michèle Cohen, in *Fashioning Masculinity: National Identity and Language in the Eighteenth Century* (London, 1996), shows that 'although practices of sociability central to the fashioning of the English gentleman required the mastery of verbal arts evinced by the French, not only was the monosyllabic English tongue lacking in polish but the English as a nation were said to "delight in Silence"', 3.
[93] Smollett, *Travels*, 286.
[94] Ferguson, to the difference of Smollett, clearly highlights the necessity of sociability: 'send him [man] to the desert alone, he is a plant torn from its roots; the form indeed

Richard Jones contends that he targeted various communities as addressees of his theoretically fictitious letters, in particular 'the lodge of Freemasons at Chelsea (with possible Scottish associations)'.[95] True sociability could not exist without a climate of liberty, which at the time when Smollett was writing was greater in Britain than in France. France was then the land of monopolies (of the post in particular),[96] thus a fettered land, from where Smollett renewed his allegiance to Britain, vowing: 'I am attached to my country because it is the land of liberty, cleanliness and convenience. But I love it still more tenderly as the scene of all my interesting connexions; as the habitation of my friends, for whose conversation, correspondence and esteem I wish alone to live.'[97]

The tour generated a feeling of loyalty on the part of Smollett. Far from going home with a nostalgia for France and Italy and with a view to importing their models of sociability, he returned to Britain convinced that a British model was in the making and that the political and technological superiority of the British would soon translate into the recognition of their superiority in manners.[98] This was a tall statement at the time (the middle of the eighteenth century), which was also due to Smollett's dual loyalties to both Scotland and England. The sociability which he ended up celebrating at the end of the tour was a far cry from the cheerfulness and ease of manners associated with continental sociability. By shifting the emphasis from manners, dress and polite behaviour to the body and a purification ritual,

---

may remain, but every faculty droops and withers; the human personage and the human character cease to exist', *An Essay on the History of Civil Society*, 23.

[95] Jones, *Tobias Smollett in the Enlightenment*, 10.

[96] Smollett, *Travels*, 284. Guillaume Daudin in his book, *Commerce et prospérité: la France au XVIIIe siècle* (Paris, 2011), draws a different portrait of the French economy and highlights its growth (see graph on p. 16): 'Plus surprenant peut-être, son dynamisme s'exprimait dans des formes d'organisation industrielle qui semblent archaïques: pas de généralisation du progrès technique, faiblesse de l'accumulation de capital fixe, complicité de l'Etat dans la domination des producteurs par les marchands, importance du travail rural peu qualifié au sein de la proto-industrie', 403.

[97] Smollett, *Travels*, 283.

[98] This recognition of the qualities of the British administration had already appeared in the conclusion of his *Essay on the External Use of Water*: 'In an age like this, when such sums are expended by private persons, upon works of magnificence and decoration; when such considerable aids are granted for the utility and encouragement of commerce; and our administration seems so well disposed to consult, and promote the welfare of the commonwealth; we have reason to believe, that some attention will be paid to those fountains [the Bath waters] flowing with health, which, at a very moderate expence, might be so improved as to become the greatest boast, ornament, and blessing of these kingdoms', 39.

Smollett redefined British sociability along lines that were closer to the sociability of 'rude people' than to that of their foppish counterparts who, more often than not, belonged to what Bowers has called a 'transnational caste'.[99] The Smollett of the *Essay* and of the *Travels* is different from the conservative Matthew Bramble of *Humphry Clinker*, whose misanthropy made him inapt to all types of sociability, except in Scotland and in Wales, the native places of the author and his persona.

Smollett, in his medical and travel writings, shows himself a defender of reform, be it scientific, political, technological or societal. His position and the comparative approach which he uses[100] were often misunderstood: the *Travels* was attacked by Philip Thicknesse[101] – a minor travel writer who spent some time in Bath and was considered as an eccentric by some – who called the book 'Quarrels through France and Italy', but was praised by *The London Magazine*.[102] The unfortunate side to the story is that no sooner had Smollett set foot in Britain again (he went back to London, then Scotland and finally to Bath)[103] than he relapsed and was once more plagued by ill health. If he could try to change the perception that the British had of their sociability, he could do nothing against the inferiority of the British climate, which was why he left Britain again in the autumn of 1768.[104] It is also remarkable that the *Travels* should end with a delayed return home, as if Smollett could not really bring himself to leave the Continent and reunite his divided self: 'I am now in tolerable lodging, where I shall remain a few weeks, merely for the sake of a little repose; then I shall gladly tempt that invidious strait which still divides you from Yours &c. FINIS.'[105]

---

[99] Bowers, *Reconstituting the National Body*, 17.
[100] Like a number of Scottish Enlightenment philosophers who wrote conjectural histories, Smollett also wrote world histories that entailed a comparative dimension, as in *The Present State of all Nations*, published in 1768–69, in which 'he methodizes the subject' (vol. 1, 5). What Paul-Gabriel Boucé writes about Smollett's systemic approach in 'Scotland and France in Smollett's *Present States of All Nations*, 1768–69' applies to the *Travels* too: 'throughout the eight volumes of *PS* Smollett sticks, with more or less copiousness, to a systematic method in his accounts of the known countries of the world', *Scotland and France in the Enlightenment*, ed. Deirdre Dawson and Pierre Morère (Lewisburg, 2004), 37–8.
[101] Philip Thicknesse, *Observations on the Customs and Manners of the French Nation, in a Series of Letters, in which that Nation is vindicated from the Misrepresentations of some Late Writers* (London, 1766), 104–5.
[102] Jones, *Tobias Smollett in the Enlightenment*, 39.
[103] Jones, *Tobias Smollett in the Enlightenment*, 134.
[104] He returned to Italy, and eventually settled in Leghorn, where he wrote *The Expedition of Humphry Clinker* (Jones, *Tobias Smollett in the Enlightenment*, 134).
[105] Smollett, *Travels*, 287.

Chapter 8
A theory of British epistolary sociability?
Alain Kerhervé

IN HER STUDY of Samuel Richardson's correspondence, published in *Transversales* 5,[1] Hélène Dachez explains what she defines as the 'epistolary sociability' of one of the greatest novelists of the century: a relationship in which, if the letter does not replace the immediacy of conversation *in praesentia*, it permits the creation of deeper links between correspondents while establishing, beyond the superficiality of some sociable contacts, true friendly connections. The present chapter will investigate the origins of British epistolary sociability in the eighteenth century by examining the eighty-eight epistolary manuals which were published in Britain between 1700 and 1800, several of which went through many editions, the whole making a total of over 250 manuals published in Britain.[2] In order to determine how epistolary sociability evolved in Britain in the eighteenth century, it will generally interrogate the links between epistolary writing and sociability, pointing to elements of epistolary writing which had become commonly accepted both in France and in Britain in the eighteenth century. It will then highlight how the theory was adapted in Britain, where greater attention was granted to lower social categories, to commercial activities and to women than in France. Finally, limits of the theory of British epistolary sociability will be questioned in two short case studies: *The Ladies Complete Letter-Writer* and William Gilpin's letter-writer.

---

[1] Hélène Dachez, 'Epistolary sociability: Samuel Richardson and his Readers', in *La Sociabilité en France et en Grande-Bretagne au Siècle des Lumières. Tome 5. Sociabilités et esthétique de la marge*, ed. Annick Cossic-Péricarpin and Alain Kerhervé (Paris, 2016), 127–52.
[2] For a general presentation of the manuals, including the links between British and American editions, see Eve Tavor Bannett, *Empire of Letters: Letter Manuals and Transatlantic Correspondence, 1680–1820* (Cambridge, 2006).

Epistolary manuals and sociability

Promoting the art of living in society was one of the numerous functions of epistolary manuals in the eighteenth century. Very few of them were made only of models of letters: some contained grammars, dictionaries, tables of abbreviations; many comprised sections focusing on social manners and habits, as suggested by the frontispieces of the manuals entitled *Academy of complements*. The variety of essays announced from the front pages of the manuals also testifies to the fact that letter-writing manuals were also concerned with the art of socialising. *A New Academy of Complements; or, The Lover's Secretary* (1715) also contained 'The Silent Language; or, A Compleat Rule for discoursing by Motion of the Hand, without being understood by the Company'.[3] *A New Academy of Complements; or, The Compleat English Secretary* (1748) offered 'Dialogues very witty and pleasant, relating to Love, Familiar Discourse, and other Matters, for the improving the Elegancy of the English Speech, and Accomplishment in Discourse' and 'A Treatise on Moles', 'The Interpretation of Dreams', 'The Comical Humours of the Jovial London Gossips'.[4] The third part of *The Entertaining Correspondent* (1759) was entitled 'The Rule of Life, being a Collection of Select Moral Sentences, extracted from the most eminent Authors, both antient and modern, directing not only how to think, but to act justly and prudently in the common Concerns of Human Life'.[5] In 1782, *Every Man his own Letter-Writer* introduced 'a new System of English Oratory, containing the Art of speaking in Public with Propriety and Elegance', followed by 'The Art of pleasing in Conversation, with Rules and Maxims to form the polite and entertaining Companion'.[6] From the beginning to the end of the century, the letter-writers provided the readers with an echo of other manuals or conduct books whose primary concerns were the art of living in society, the cultivation of propriety, the *Wits Cabinet* being one of the most famous.[7] It contained a section on polite behavior, variously called

---

[3] *A New Academy of Complements; or, The Lover's Secretary* (London, 1715).
[4] *A New Academy of Compliments* (London, 1748).
[5] John Tavernier (ed.), *The Entertaining Correspondent; or, Newest and Most Compleat Polite Familiar Letter-Writer* (Berwick, 1759).
[6] James Wallace and Charles Townshend, *Every Man His Own Letter-Writer: Or, The New and Complete Art of Letter-Writing Made Plain and Familiar to Every Capacity* ... (London, [1782]).
[7] See Katherine Gee Hornbeak, 'The Complete Letter Writer in English 1568–1800', *Smith College Studies in Modern Languages* 15, no. 3–4 (1934), 71: 'there is a section on polite behavior, variously called "The School of Good Manners: or, the Newest Rules of Gentile Behaviour" and "General Rules for Behaviour and Genteel

'The School of Good Manners: or, the Newest Rules of Gentile Behaviour' and 'General Rules for Behaviour and Genteel Conversation'.

In that vein, the letter-writing manuals often attempt to establish a link between discourse and writing. For instance, in *The Complete Academy of Complements* (1705) a section reads 'A miscellaneous present of Sentences to be used either in discourse or writing'[8] and the last part of the manual deals with 'the art of courtship and genteel breeding'. Several sociable situations are imagined (pp. 91–114), mostly depending on the social status of the interlocutors, but also occasionally on the places of sociability (p. 114 : 'in the fair', 'at the inn'). In *The Lover's Instructor* (1770) a section entitled 'the politest personal conversation between lovers, &c.' deals more with conversation than with the theory of letter-writing. *The New Letter Writer* (1775) and *The New complete Letter-Writer* (1788) contain 'the principles of politeness' advertised on the front page, focusing on the art of living in society rather than epistolary writing (pp. 225–38). They are adapted from the chameleonic advice provided by the fourth Earl of Chesterfield, Philip Dormer Stanhope, first published in 1775.[9] Taken up in a letter-writing manual, those elements have, in fact, very little to do with the production of letters but clearly focus on various ways of behaving in sociable company.

The learning of codes and rules allows communication in writing in many social situations. This is often suggested on the front pages of the manuals, a tradition dating back to Fulwood's 1578 *Panoplie of Epistles*.[10] While *The New Academy of Complement*[11] distinguishes only three categories of letters – 'letters of business', 'letters of advice', 'letters of counsel' – the title page of *The Young Secretary* offers nineteen, after Milleran's *Nouveau Secrétaire de la cour* (1714):

Conversation"'. Hornbeak shows that the section was translated from Giovanni della Casa's *Galateo*, first printed in 1558, in the seventeenth-century translation of *The Refin'd Courtier, or A Correction of Several Indecencies crept into Civil Conversation*.

[8] *The Compleat Academy of Complements: Containing First, Choice Sentences, with Variety of Similitudes, and Comparisons, also the Best Complemental Letters. Second, The Art of Courtship and Genteel Breeding, with Discourses Proper for this Ingenious Age ... Together with a Collection of the Newest Songs that Are Sung at Court or Play-House* (London, 1705), 16.

[9] Philip Dormer Stanhope, Earl of Chesterfield. *Principles of Politeness, and of Knowing the World; Being a New System of Education, by the Late Lord Chesterfield Containing Every Instruction Necessary to Complete the Gentleman and Man of Fashion, for the Improvement of Youth* (London, 1775).

[10] See Hornbeak, 'The Complete Letter Writer', 14.

[11] *A New Academy of Complements; or, The Lover's Secretary* (London, 1715), 22–3.

Letters of Business, Letters of Advice, Letters of Recommendation, Letters of Command, Letters of Exhortation, Letters of Congratulation, Letters of Remonstrance, Letters of Intreaty, Letters of Counsel, Letters of Complaint, Letters of Reproof, Letters of Excuse, Letters of Congratulation and Consolation, Letters of Thanks and Visit, Letters of Assistance, Letters of Merriment, Mixed Letters and Answers &c.[12]

Although the main trend was to reduce the number of situations advertised on the front pages, as late as 1782 no fewer than seventy situations of writing, most of them being also situations of oral communication, were publicised on the front page of *Every Man His Own Letter-Writer: Or, The New and Complete Art of Letter-Writing* ...[13] More generally, over half the letter-writers of the century comprised a section giving instructions on the way of addressing people either in writing or in discourse: 'Instructions for Addressing Persons of all Ranks either in Writing or Discourse',[14] 'Instructions how to address Persons of all Ranks, either in *Writing* or *Discourse*',[15] 'And necessary Rules for addressing Persons of all Stations both in Discourse and Writing',[16] 'Directions for addressing Persons of Distinction, either in Writing or Discourse',[17] 'Proper Methods of addressing

---

[12] John Hill (ed.), *The Young Secretary's Guide; or, A Speedy Help to Learning* (London, 1719), front page.

[13] James Wallace and Charles Townshend, *Every Man His Own Letter-Writer: Or, The New and Complete Art of Letter-Writing. Made Plain and Familiar to Every Capacity. Containing a collection of upwards of two hundred original letters, On the most interesting, important, and instructive Subjects, and adapted for general Use and Benefit, by directing every Person to indite Letters, without Any other Assistance, on all the various Occasions of Life. But more particularly on the following Heads, viz. Adversity, Advice, Affection, Ambition, Anger, Avarice, Benevolence, Business, Centre, Charity, Confidence, Condolence, Courtship, Dependence, Diligence, Duty, Education, Emulation, Excellence, Fame, Fidelity, Flattery, Folly, Friendship, Frugality, Generosity, Gratitude, Guilt, Happiness, Honour, Hope, Humanity, Indiscretion, Indolence, Integrity, Industry, Justice, Learning, Love, Marriage, Modesty, Moderation, Morality, Negligence, Passion, Patience, Peevishness, Piety, Pleasure, Politeness, Pride, Prodigality, Prudence, Reproof, Religion, Retirement, Secrecy, Shame, Sobriety, Solitude, Temptation, Trade, Truth, Variety, Vice, Virtue, Understanding, Wisdom, Wit, Letter-Writing. To which Is added, A Collection of Complimentary Cards, with Directions for addressing Persons of all Ranks and Conditions* ... (London, [1782]).

[14] *The British Letter-Writer; or, Letter-Writer's Complete Instructor* ... (London, [1765?]).

[15] *The Complete Letter-Writer; or, New and Polite English Secretary* ... (London, 1756).

[16] George Brown (ed.), *The New and Complete English Letter-Writer; or, Whole Art of General Correspondence* (London, [1770?]).

[17] *The Royal Letter Writer; or, Every Lady's Own Secretary: Containing Letters on every Subject that Can Call for Attention Mothers, Daughters, Wives, Relations, Friends or*

Superiours, and Persons of all Ranks, both in Writing and Discourse.'[18] That selection clearly confirms that discourse and writing were considered to be inseparable and that the codes of sociability prevailed as much and in a similar way *in praesentia* as *in absentia*, when one wrote letters. What, then, were the specificities of the forms of epistolary sociability?

What theory of epistolary sociability?

The theory of epistolary sociability includes a number of material aspects; it requires the choice of a style; it relies on a rather immutable rhetorical pattern.

Among the material aspects highlighted in the letter-writing manuals, the paper quality is a first sign of sociability, as first expressed in *The Complete Letter-Writer; or, Polite English Secretary*: 'Letters should be wrote on Quarto fine gilt post paper to superiors; if to your equals or inferiors, you are at your own option to use what sort or size you please.'[19] The sentence is taken up in several works in the following years and until the end of the century.[20] The choice of paper was essential at a time preceding mechanization, when a large variety of papers, of English or foreign origin, was available in Britain.[21] The manuals mainly establish links between the quality of paper and the quality of the addressee. Once the choice of paper had been made, one should also pay attention to the layout of the page, as mentioned from the seventeenth century onwards.[22] At the end of the eighteenth century *The Correspondent* summarises the instructions of its predecessors, highlighting the importance that should be given to the

---

Acquaintance. Not only on the more important religious, moral, and social duties, but on subjects of every other kind that usually interest the fair sex. With various forms of messages by cards (London, [1793?]).

[18] *The London Universal Letter Writer; or, Whole Art of Polite Correspondence ...* (London, 1800).

[19] *The Complete Letter-Writer; or, Polite English Secretary ...* (London, 1757), 53.

[20] James Wallace and Charles Townshend. *Every Man His Own Letter-Writer* (London, [1782]), 12, taken up in *The New Art of Letter-Writing, Divided into Two Parts* (London, 1762), 17. For another example, see John Gignoux (ed.), *Epistolary Correspondence Made Pleasant and Familiar: Calculated Chiefly for the Improvement of Youth* (London, 1759), iv.

[21] Philip Gaskell, 'Notes on Eighteenth-Century British Paper', *Library* 12 (1957), 34–42.

[22] Sue Walker, 'The Manners of the Page: Prescription and Practice in the Visual Organization of Correspondence', *Huntington Library Quarterly* 66, no. 3/4 (2003), 307–29.

margin, the distance from the top of the sheet and the place for the date.[23] It establishes a clear distinction between intemporal rules and fashionable evolutions.[24] Another material aspect is the folding and sealing of letters: 'Neatness in folding up, sealing, and directing letters, is by no Means to be neglected. There is something in the Exterior, even of a Letter, that may please or displease, and consequently deserves some Attention.'[25] The verbs 'please' and 'displease' involve a number of possible persons in the process: the addressee of the letter, but also the entourage of the recipient, including the persons involved in the delivery of the message. The process matters all the more, such that letters addressed to superiors for whom the message ought to be wrapped in a different sheet of paper, according to *The Court Letter-Writer*, while that can be omitted for letters to relatives or inferiors.[26] Another step of importance was the choice of the seal with which the letter was to be closed. There were two possibilities: a wax seal, the nobler of the two, and the wafer, made of a mixture of flour, water, egg white and colouring.[27] Not only did the nature of the seal matter, but its colour was also meaningful. The only example mentioned in the letter-writers was the black seal, which was to be used in the case of mourning and more generally under melancholic circumstances, as explained in *The Art of Letter-Writing*,[28] at a time when several books contained recipes

---

[23] *The Correspondent, a Selection of Letters, from the Best Authors; Together with some Originals, Adapted to All the Periods and Occasions of Life: Calculated to Form the Epistolary Style of Youth of Both Sexes; to Impart a Knowledge of the World and Letters; and to Inspire Sentiments of Virtue and Morality* (London, 1796), vol. 1, 23.

[24] Other manuals, such as *The New and Complete British Letter-Writer*, even provide the distances separating the main constitutive elements of the letter in inches: 'the date line about an inch from the top'; 'then begin your subject about an inch lower than your *Sir*'. See David Fordyce, *The New and Complete British Letter-Writer; or, Young secretary's instructor in polite modern letter-writing* (London, [1790?]), iii.

[25] *The Accomplished Letter-Writer; or, Universal Correspondent, Containing Familiar Letters on the Most Common Occasions in Life...* (London, 1779), iv.

[26] See *The Court Letter-Writer; or, The Complete English Secretary for Town and Country* (London, 1773), 52: 'Letters to a superior should always be folded in the first manner, and enclosed in a cover; as it would be extremely impolite and disrespectful, to send a Letter folded up without one, to a person of high rank. Thus this second method is only proper to be used to inferiors, and between equals who are well acquainted, and reciprocally dispense with ceremony in this respect.'

[27] Most studies on epistolary practices only mention seals, perhaps because they were more resistant. For instance, see Susan Whyman, *The Pen and the People: English Letter Writers 1660–1800* (Oxford, 2009), 22.

[28] *The New Art of Letter-Writing*: 'In the first Place, they must be neatly seal'd with either Wax or Wafer, and the Colour of 'em as best suits the Circumstance of the Writer; but black if the Subject be melancholy', 26.

explaining how to prepare sealing wax and give it the appropriate colour.[29] Several manuals also provide indications on the manner of presenting the 'outward superscription, which is written on the Out-side of Letters when they are folded up',[30] although they tend to provide examples only for letters addressed to equals or superiors[31] and do not provide any advice about the manner in which the address was to be written for inferiors. The exterior and material aspects of a letter carried important messages, which signified the letter's place in society. Moreover, epistolary sociability also depended on the choice of a style.

The tradition of equating epistolary correspondence with conversation dates back to ancient times[32] and was prolonged in France as well as in Britain, in private exchanges as well as in the theory of the genre.[33] The manuals explain it by 'the necessity of conversing one with another so long as we live',[34] 'the indispensable necessity we are under to converse with one another'.[35] As a result, several letter-writers make a rule out of it: 'the most

---

[29] Catharine Kearsley, *Kearsleys' Gentleman and Tradesman's Pocket Ledger, for the Year 1795* (London, 1795), 176. It was printed by Kearsley, who printed several epistolary manuals. In *Valuable Secrets in Arts and Trades; or, Approved Directions from the Best Artists. Containing upwards of One Thousand Approved Receipts* (London, 1797?), there are nine different recipes to make sealing wax and a method to colour it, 61–9.

[30] The phrase 'outward superscription' is used in *A New Academy of Complements* (1715): 'The outward Superscription is that which is on the Out-side of Letters when they are folded up, and containeth the Name and Titles of him to whom we write, and his Place of Abode', 22.

[31] See *Epistolary Correspondence* (1759), vi, *The Complete Letter-Writer Containing Familiar Letters* (1776), 16–17 and in *The Court Letter-Writer; or, The Complete English Secretary for Town and Country* (London, 1773), 44.

[32] See Alain Boureau, 'The Letter-Writing Norm, a Medieval Invention', in *Correspondence: Models of Letter-Writing from the Middle Ages to the Nineteenth Century*, ed. Roger Chartier, Alain Boureau and Cécile Dauphin (Princeton, 1997), 34–5.

[33] Christoph Strosetzki and Bernard Bray, *Art de la lettre, art de la conversation à l'époque classique en France* (Paris, 1995) shows that this tradition, which is often associated with Mme de Sévigné's writing, is also present in the prefaces and introductions of several French manuals, for instance *Le Secrétaire du Cabinet* (1763). On that point, see also Eve Tavor Bannet, 'Printed Epistolary Manuals and the Transatlantic Rescripting of Manuscript Culture', *Studies in Eighteenth Century Culture* 36 (2007), 26 and Clare Brant, *Eighteenth-Century Letters and British Culture* (Basingstoke, 2006), 21–3.

[34] *A New Academy of Complements; or, The Lover's Secretary* (1715).

[35] *An Useful and Entertaining Collection of Letters upon Various Subjects. Several Now First Published from Their Original Manuscripts, by the Most Eminent Hands* (London, 1745).

certain Rule is to write as we speak'.[36] However, one needs to be careful about the nature of the parallel. In *The New Art of Letter Writing*[37] it is suggested to read the letter aloud as we write it: 'In the Placing of Words, we must consult the Ear and judge whether its Satisfaction be complete' (p. 8). But mastering the art of conversation does not necessarily involve *a priori* that one can reach excellence in the art of epistolary writing, as *The Court Letter-Writer* warns: 'Out of an hundred good speakers scarce ten will be found who write in the same degree of perfection, though it should seem nothing more was wanting than to commit our thoughts to paper'.[38] Most manuals still insist on the importance of taking one's addressee into consideration at the moment of writing.

> To be sure the right Way in general is, to entertain a Naturalist out of the natural World and a Courtier out of the Artificial, the Interest of states, Pretensions to Favour and the whole Science of Policy. For we write out of a Complement to our Correspondent, not to please ourselves, as we invite a Friend to dine with Us, not upon Dishes we relish but such as we know suit his Palate.[39]

The metaphor contributes to the irony of the manual entitled *Polite Epistolary Correspondence* aiming to satirise the courtiers. It also shows that when letter-writing is equated with conversation, it involves a refined type of conversation. It leads to the idea that the natural style of courtiers is not the natural style of servants. *The Young Secretary's Guide*, in 1721, introduces the idea that the former evolves with time, 'A select Number of curious Letters suited to the Circumstances and Occasions of all Persons, in a new and elegant Stile, after the modern Way now in Use among the British

---

[36] John Newbery, *Letters on the most common, as well as important, occasions in life, by Cicero, Pliny, Voiture, Balzac, St Evremont, Locke, Ld Lansdowne, Temple, Dryden, Garth, Pope, Gay, Swift, Rowe, and other writers of distinguish'd Merit; with many original letters and cards, by the editor. Who Has also prefix'd, A Dissertation on the Epistolary Stile; With proper Directions for addressing Persons of Rank and Eminence. For the use of young gentlemen and ladies* (London , 1756).

[37] *The New Art of Letter-Writing, Divided into Two Parts: The First containing Rules and Directions for Writing Letters on All Sorts of Subjects: with a Variety of Examples, equally elegant and instructive. The second, a Collection of Letters on the Most Interesting Occasions in Life...* (London, 1762).

[38] *The Court Letter-Writer; or, The Complete English Secretary for Town and Country* (1773), 43.

[39] *The Polite Epistolary Correspondence. A Collection of Letters, on the Most Instructive and Entertaining Subjects ...* (London, 1748), x.

Nobility and Gentry.'[40] In 1773 *The Court Letter-Writer* confirms that the manual addresses an elite whose members are fully aware of the difference between 'superiors' and 'inferiors', while relying on a 'noble' style. However, *The Complete Letter-Writer*, in 1776, defends a familiar style.[41] From the sixteenth century, the adjective 'familiar' had been associated with 'domestic and commercial letters', to pick up Fulwood's definition,[42] letters which did not require any embellishment, written in a style commonly taught in manuals designed for children such as *Letters between Master Tommy and Miss Nancy Goodwill*,[43] the style which *The Universal Letter-Writer*, in 1788, defined as the 'lowest style', in a letter entitled 'A letter from a young woman to her parents, in the lowest stile, concerning her sweetheart'.[44]

Moreover, the rhetorical organisation of a letter follows the ancient model of Cicero and Pliny's letters,[45] with a few evolutions in the terminology: Angel Day's *The English Secretorie* called the three parts of a letter 'invention', 'disposition', 'eloquution [sic]'.[46] The model is used systematically in letter-writing manuals in France and in Britain in the seventeenth and eighteenth centuries, the words 'exordium', 'discourse' and 'conclusion' used in Puget de la Serre's *Secrétaire à la mode*[47] being taken up in *A New Acad-*

---

[40] *The Young Secretary's Guide Compleated: Being the Speediest Help to Learning ...* (London, 1721).
[41] *The Complete Letter-Writer Containing Familiar Letters on the Most Common Occasions in Life. Also, a Variety of Elegant Letters for the Direction and Embellishment of Style, on Business, Duty, Amusement, Love, Courtship, Marriage, Friendship and Other Subjects. With Directions for Writing Letters, and the Proper Form of Address* (Edinburgh, 1776).
[42] William Fulwood, *The Enimie of Idlenesse: Teaching a Perfect Platforme How to Indite Epistles and Letters of All Sorts* (London, 1582), 69.
[43] *Letters between Master Tommy and Miss Nancy Goodwill; Containing the History of Their Holiday Amusements* (London, 1786), 'advertisement': 'The epistolary Style here adopted, is that which little Masters and Misses shou'd use in their Correspondence with each other, as it will help to regulate their Judgements, to give them an early Taste for true Politeness, and to inspire them with the Love of Virtue.'
[44] Thomas Cooke, *The Universal Letter-Writer* (London, 1788), 39.
[45] See William Irving, *The Providence of Wit in the English Letter Writers* (Durham, NC, 1955), 31–137; Alain Boureau, 'The Letter-Writing Norm, a Medieval Invention', in *Correspondence: Models of Letter-Writing from the Middle Ages to the Nineteenth Century*, ed. Roger Chartier, Alain Boureau and Cécile Dauphin (Princeton, 1997), 36–8.
[46] Angel Day, *The English Secretorie Wherin is Contayned, a Perfect Method, for the Inditing of all Manner of Epistles and Familiar Letters, together with Their Diversities* (London, 1586), 10.
[47] See the section entitled 'Instructions for writing letters' in *The Secretary in Fashion* (London, 1654), 34–5.

emy of Complements; or, The Lover's Secretary (1715) and later in *Elegant Epistles* (1791)[48] or in *The Art of Letter-Writing*,[49] even if the manual suggests not to let it show: 'Now, tho' this order may be observed, yet it will be better to disregard, than to endeavour to make it appear' (p. 11). However, the rhetorical structure is evidence in the models of letters produced in the manuals as the necessary condition to establish a form of epistolary sociability.

While those inherited elements may generate a rather elitist vision of epistolary sociability – the theory of letter-writing being extremely codified and aiming most of the time to climb up the social ladder – a few British specificities may help qualify that statement.

The British mode of epistolary sociability

The question of the Britishness of epistolary models was raised from the sixteenth century, when two manuals, *The Enimie of Idlenesse* (1568) and *The English Secretorie* (1586), were published. The latter was a collection of original letters written by Angel Day; the former was a translation by William Fullwood of a manual published two years earlier in France: *Le Stile et maniere de composer, dicter, et escrire toute sorte d'epistre, ou lettres missives* (Lyon, 1566).[50] From then onwards, the two models competed in Britain in the seventeenth century, one series of letter-writers (most famously *The Academy of Complements*) being adapted from French models (mainly Puget de la Serre's and Jean-Louis Guez de Balzac's), another being original English letters (*The Young Secretary's Guide; or, Speedy Help to Learning* (1687) by John Hill),[51] the two being printed many times in the eighteenth century as well. To further complicate matters, one

---

[48] [Vicesimus Knox], *Elegant Epistles; or, A Copious Collection of Familiar and Amusing Letters, Selected for the Improvement of Young Persons, and for General Entertainment ...* (Dublin, 1791).

[49] *The New Art of Letter-Writing, Divided into Two Parts: The First containing Rules and Directions for Writing Letters on All Sorts of Subjects: with a Variety of Examples, equally elegant and instructive. The second, a Collection of Letters on the Most Interesting Occasions in Life ...* (London, 1762).

[50] For additional detail on both works, see Katherine Gee Hornbeak, 'The Complete Letter Writer in English 1568–1800', *Smith College Studies in Modern Languages* 15, no. 3/4, 1934, 3–9 and Jean Robertson, *The Art of Letter Writing: an Essay on the Handbooks Published in England during the Sixteenth and Seventeenth Centuries* (Liverpool, 1943), 13–17.

[51] Lawrence D. Green, 'French Letters and English Anxiety in the Seventeenth Century', *Huntington Library Quarterly* 66, no. 3/4, 2003, 263–74.

might also note that Nicholas Breton's *A Poste with a Packet* (1602), which went through over twenty editions in the seventeenth century, boasted its Englishness, although it was heavily influenced by Guevara's Spanish *Epistolas Familiares*.[52]

The Britishness of the letter-writing manuals of the eighteenth century was first a matter of taking into account writers from all social categories, paying much more attention to the lower social categories than did their French counterparts. The first letters written by servants were printed in *The Young Secretary's Guide*, which contained four examples: 'A Letter of Advice from a Young Gentlewoman, or Maid-Servant, to acquaint her Friends in the Country with her Marriage'; 'A Servant-Maid's Letter to her Friends'; 'A Letter from a Maid-Servant to her Mistress, excusing her Fault'; 'A Letter from one Maid-Servant to another, inviting her to come to London'. In other words, new situations of epistolary sociability were envisaged in the English manual. In 1741 Samuel Richardson was to go further in that direction. Not only was Richardson concerned with the idea that servants needed to be provided with models of letters, but he also estimated that the manuals should be designed for 'the country people', and not just for those living in towns, as was explained in his prefatory words:

> Two booksellers, my particular friends, entreated me to write for them a little volume of Letters, in a common style, on such subjects as might be of use to those country readers, who were unable to indite for themselves. Will it be any harm, said I, in a piece you want to be written so low, if we should instruct them how they should think and act in common cases, as well as indite? They were the more urgent with me to begin the little volume for this hint.[53]

Richardson's letters were the most often plagiarised in the following manuals of the century. They were used in over twenty titles, half of which contained more than ten letters by Richardson – *Newbery's familiar letter*

---

[52] The work, published in 1539 (vol. 1) and in 1545 (vol. 2), was translated several times into English from 1574 to 1697. See William Irving, *The Providence of Wit in the English Letter Writers* (Durham, NC, 1955), 58–61. Irving perceives the possible influence of Antonio de Guevara, who combines formalism and frivolity, on the style of some British writers, but he finds it hard to demonstrate the point (p. 61).

[53] Samuel Richardson, *Letters Written to and for Particular Friends, on the Most Important Occasions. Directing Not Only the Requisite Style and Forms To Be Observed in Writing Familiar Letters; But How to Think and Act Justly and Prudently, in the Common Concerns of Human Life. Containing One Hundred and Seventy-Three Letters* (London, 1746, third edition).

writer (1788) and *The Accomplished Letter-Writer* (1787) more than thirty. Contrary to the images carried in most of the frontispieces of letter-writing manuals, the model of British epistolary sociability was not limited to the world of elites.

Moreover, subject matter is more diversified in British than in French manuals, since they focus more on business affairs and family life than on court matters, more particularly in *The Young Secretary's Guide*, in *The Experienc'd Secretary: or, Citizen and Countryman's Companion* and in *The Secretary's Guide*. Letters of recommendation multiply, as in Richardson's *Letters Written to and for Particular Friends*, where letters XXXI to XXXV are letters recommending 'a superior Man-servant', 'a Wet-nurse', 'a Cook-maid', 'a Chamber-maid', 'a Nursery-maid' (p. 45–4). Those professional considerations tend to go alongside a tendency to give a reduced place to love, gallantry and *billets doux*, which were often essential in manuals inspired by the Continent. Contrary to the French usage, most of Richardson's *Familiar Letters* concerning marriage are between the young people and the girl's parents, rather than between the young people themselves. All this is a part of Richardson's well-defined policy that marriage was a matter of business negotiation to be conducted by the elders of the lovers, contrary to the young persons who, in the French manner, in *The Young Secretary's Guide*, *The Experienc'd Secretary* and *The Secretary's Guide* flout parental authority, never consulting parents or guardians about their romances and coolly notifying them after the event.

A third distinguishing feature of the British manuals is their taking women's writing into account: *The Young Secretary's Guide*,[54] for instance, was the first to introduce the later ubiquitous aunt, who for the next two centuries was to offer gratuitous advice to her nieces. One of its letters is entitled 'A letter of Counsel from an Aunt to her Niece' (p. 93). The earliest model letter from a girl at school is also in *The Young Secretary's Guide*: 'A Letter from a Young Gentlewoman at School to her Mother, or a Letter of Intreaty'. The daughter's request that her Mother would 'give speedy Orders for my Learning to Dance, and play on the Musick' (p. 28) gives a hint of the curriculum of the time. In fact, as early as 1721 *The Young Secretary's Guide* offered twenty-three model letters for women, more than any of its predecessors. In 1741 almost 100 of the 173 *Letters Written to and for Particular Friends* deal with the affairs of women, which marks the climax of that pre-feminist trend in the complete letter-writers.

---

[54] Hill, John (ed.), *The Young Secretary's Guide; or, A Speedy Help to Learning* (London, 1719, twentieth edition). Initially released in 1687, it was reprinted from the end of the seventeenth century onwards.

The main specificities of epistolary sociability as it developed in Britain in the eighteenth century were thus the taking into account of lower social categories, the idea that epistolary sociability was not exclusively a court matter but also concerned business and family matters, and the inclusion of women's writing.

Two examples of British epistolary sociability

The *Ladies Complete Letter-Writer* was initially released in 1763.[55] It is made up of 122 letters, all of which, contrary to one of the initial statements of its preface, were published before their inclusion in the manual.[56] Very few men were involved in the exchanges: only three letters were written by men, and twenty-five are directed to men. They correspond with a desire not to omit the restricted number of situations in which writing to the other sex was absolutely necessary: four are destined to fathers, five to husbands and sixteen to gentlemen to turn advances down or to settle future meetings. The manual's first difference from French models is on that ground. The quality or social status of the women concerned is also worth noticing. At the end of the preface the editor claims the manual to have been written for 'the fair sex, of every age and station' (p. iii). In the introduction some directions are said to be given to 'Persons very ignorant', although 'the generality of Ladies are well acquainted with such things ...' (p. 4). It suggests that persons of various ranks may use the book. The title to part one reads: 'Letters of Advice to Young Ladies and others ...', which also suggests a mixture of quality, which was a second distinguishing feature of British epistolary manuals. As a matter of fact, only a few letters are said to be written by servants: letters 6 and 8, 'From a young woman just gone to service', and letter 25, 'From a maid servant'. Letter 14 ('From a young Woman of Family ...') tells of the hardships a servant had to suffer from her master's offending attitude (pp. 36–7). However, the contents and concerns of the letters reinforce the impression that most were written by idle ladies: the word 'lady' occurs in fifty-three headings to designate the writer of the epistle. In most other cases, the writers worry about going to the opera, Vauxhall, Ranelagh or watering places (letters 74 and 75), they

---

[55] [Edward Kimber], *The Ladies Complete Letter-Writer; Teaching the Art of Inditing Letters on Every Subject That Can Call for Their Attention, as Daughters, Wives, Mothers, Relations, Friends, or Acquaintance ...* (London, 1763).

[56] For more detail about the manual, see the introduction to *The Ladies Complete Letter-Writer* (1763), ed. Alain Kerhervé (Newcastle-upon-Tyne, 2010).

invite a friend to visit their park or garden (letter 106): the letters accompany various sociable activities. And yet, a woman's proper place is in the home. Public appearances are presented as inappropriate concerns for ladies because 'much company assembled together serves rather to confuse our ideas' (letter 3), 'long conversations grow dull, as few of our sex are furnished with a sufficient fund of materials for long discourses' (letter 3). The tone is set up from letter 1, in which a lady writes to her daughter that 'good housewifery is the most commendable quality', the joy of giving birth (letter 60) and the education of children are highlighted as part the domestic concerns of importance. Letter 103, entitled 'Domestic rule the Province of the Wife', tends to demonstrate that the handling of the house is 'a right ... by the Law of Nature' (p. 236). On that point, the manual echoes the ideas of the 'matriarchs' – Frances Burney, Mary Hays, Mary Wollstonecraft – who were not trying to demonstrate any degree of female superiority but aimed to level the family hierarchies, as Eve Tavor Bannett has explained.[57]

If one then wonders about the Britishness of the manual, from the start, the editor, now acknowledged to have been Edward Kimber, asserted:

> I have not borrowed from the French Letter-Writers; the Manners of their Females are such as would fit but ill upon the English Ladies, and there is a flimsy Kind of Gaiety in their Epistolary Correspondence, that would be displeasing to the more grave and sensible Turn of Mind of the British Fair. (p. ii)

Thus French writers were allegedly excluded from the manual because of their 'Manners' and 'Gaiety'. One should remember that 1763, the year when *The Ladies Complete Letter-Writer* was released, was the last year of the Seven Years' War, which opposed France and England. The French model was totally disregarded, for obvious editorial reasons: the selling of a manual boasting the influence of the enemy was bound to be jeopardised in war time. As a consequence, most scenes are set in England, as can be noticed from the names of the towns mentioned. With the exception of a few watering places, Bath in letter 110, Tunbridge Wells in letters 74 and 75, London occupies a central place in the manual, where most epistles refer directly or indirectly to the capital. Activities are situated in the great London parks (Cuper's Gardens, Hyde Park, Saint James's Park, Vauxhall Gardens). A precise geography of London is occasionally resorted to, as in letter 53, whose writer is seen to be moving from St James's Street to

---

[57] It is the main thesis of Eve Tavor Bannett, *The Domestic Revolution. Enlightenment Feminisms and the Novel* (Baltimore, 2000).

Tavistock and Southampton Streets in the Covent Garden area before going to Haymarket and back to Covent Garden. Many London streets are mentioned in the letters. As in the cards at the end of the manual (part 4), those geographical names are systematically italicised, possibly to suggest that those users of the manual who want to copy the models have only to change the emphasised names.

Beyond the creation of a well-known and reassuring geographic context, the manuals expressed a sometimes exaggerated sense of patriotism – for instance when two lines quoted in letter 93 are said to be by the best English poet, whereas they were just translated from Juvenal. Another way to exalt a national feeling is by way of satire of other nations. In letter 73 Miss Paget criticises the attitude of a man at a ball; even though she has difficulty remembering his name, one notes that it starts with 'Sieur', which suggests a French origin, and thus the caricature applies to a French gentleman. Similarly, letter 75 makes a number of derogatory allusions to people dressed in the French fashion and, interestingly enough, the French airs are attributed to a Mrs Macnamara, married to an Irishman, as if the parallel was here established between the two Catholic nations.

In appearance, no reference is made to either France or French letter writers.[58] And yet, the origin of some of the letters has already been traced as being from across the Channel: letters 18 to 20 were written by the Marchioness de Lambert. In that series, letter 19 begins with 'I desire you to be very cautious now you are with your Relations in London'. The reference to London was absent from Lambert's letter. It must have been added to rule out the possibility of any foreign influence and reinforce the Englishness of the letter. So when the introduction to *The Ladies Complete Letter-Writer* reads: 'they will equal, nay exceed the Lamberts ..', it sounds quite ironic, since some of the letters were actually written by Lambert herself.[59] Similarly, when letter 20 was later reproduced in *The Court Letter Writer* in 1773,[60] it was entitled 'From Mr Richardson to a friend, on the Education of Children', which also clearly excluded the possibility of any French origin, although it was by Lambert as well.

---

[58] The interest of being proficient in the French language is mentioned in only two places in the letters. See 16 (letter 1) and 254 (letter 118); one letter opposes the French taste for Gaiety to the English sense of modesty. See 234 (letter 101).

[59] Even though she did not mention the irony, and perhaps did not look into the origin of the letters now clearly translated from Lambert, Clare Brant commented upon the passage in *Eighteenth-Century Letters and British Culture* (Basingstoke, 2006), 9–10.

[60] See *The Court Letter Writer* (London, 1773), 95, letter 26.

Therefore even though some of its components suggest a clearly defined form of British sociability, *The Ladies Complete Letter-Writer* is still partly based on French models, which suggests a continuing proximity between the French and British models of epistolary sociability.

William Gilpin is more famous as one of the theoreticians of the picturesque or as the writer of many tours of Britain than as a letter writer and the author of a letter-writing manual. And yet, the letters comprising William Gilpin's letter-writer are held in the Bodleian Library.[61] The document is made up of 167 numbered folios comprising 139 neatly individualised letters, which were clearly conceived as model letters for young men.

The letters of the manual give guidance to young men beginning independent life, warning them against the vices of society, which may cause their ruin. While the young man is initially good by nature, he occasionally meets people who drive him off the right track. In one example he encounters a colonel who encourages his men to drink to excess:

> Perhaps you do not know that the Colonel is not merely a great drinker himself, but a very violent promoter of drinking in others. I spent an evening lately with him and some other officers. You know I never drink any thing: Upon which the Colonel insisted in so rude a manner that although I was determined to persist in my resolution of not drinking, in spite of him, and did persist in it, yet, he made me spend one of the most disagreeable evenings I ever spent in my life. (WGM 20)

The soldier, writing to his father, resists temptation, to his father's delight. The son assures his father that he can resist the collective pressure of a group of men. Nevertheless, he eventually yields to a temptation which proves fatal, since he is killed when trying to enter a convent to meet the young woman he is trying to seduce. Once again, he is not naturally disposed to evil: he has been enticed by a friend to follow the young woman (WGM 61). Among the other bad habits, many men swear (WGM 17, 127, 131) and spend money on such vices as games or alcohol, but also on nice clothes (WGM 94–97). The social game also leads to duels, a condemnable practice in William Gilpin's words, as he expresses in two letters of the manual (WGM 20, 70) and in

---

[61] Mary Clapinson and Tim D. Rogers, *Summary Catalogue of Post-Medieval Western Manuscripts in the Bodleian Library Oxford. Acquisitions 1916–1975*, 3 vols. (Oxford, 1991) 1: 431 ('42462. A collection of fictional letters'). His manual was edited by Alain Kerhervé, *William Gilpin's Letter-Writer* (Newcastle-upon-Tyne, 2014). In the following pages, 'WGM number' refers to the letter number in the manual.

many other writings.⁶² It should not be surprising that some men, ruined by the world of leisure and appearances, end up in a state of complete destitution. Consequently, the threat of those masculine ills should be learnt from their early youth, at school, as is explained by a father:

> Boys do not consider, that they generally retain for life the characters, which they gain at school. I do not mean, that every little boy fixes his character: I mean only such boys, as are at the upper end of the school. I know at this time many sly, cunning rascals; who were formerly tricking artful boys: and many lawless, insolent, imperious fellows, who were once tyrants at school. (WGM 133)

Scholarly education is thus perceived as the means to learn social life, and must be understood to be so by young children. Moreover, the dangers of contamination derived from unsuitable sociable links should be perceived by children from their schooldays, as fathers' words explain:

> Far am I from accusing any of your young companions of badness: I know nothing of them. But I cannot help, my dear James, taking this opportunity of warning you, that it is not only very possible <151v> but very probable that there may be among your companions, many worthless lads, who may endeavour to corrupt you. The reason why a bad boy corrupts others, and endeavours to make as many as he can, like himself, is, that he has no defence, except in numbers. Vice and idleness, seen naked, and by yourselves, are so disgusting an appearance, that every body would <152> shun them: every body would detest them. Nature teaches the bad boy this lesson; and though perhaps he hardly knows, that he acts upon the principle, yet he certainly does. He makes you vicious, only that you may keep him in countenance. Have the courage therefore, my dear James, to oppose vice, in whatever form it may appear; and endeavour to get the wisdom to detest it, whatever disguise it may assume: the good <152v> will love you for your firmness; and the bad will revere you. Listen, therefore, my dear child, to no suggestions, that you think are bad. And the best way to keep from all bad suggestions, is to form no friendships with bad boys. In some future letter I may mark out to you the characteristics of a bad boy. (WGM 134)

---

[62] See William Gilpin, *Dialogues on Various Subjects* (London, 1807), 217–52 ('On duelling') and Bodleian Library, Ms. Eng. Misc. d. 569, fol. 210, letter to his son William, 22 March 1796: 'I began lately a little dialogue on duelling.' Also see Ms. Eng. Misc. e. 518, fol. 73 and fol. 77.

> Here I am, happy in the company of <160> wits, and ingenious young fellows, and I wish to add you to the number, that I may relish your conversation the more. I should fear, those who are companions for each other can not be friends. At least, this is an opinion of mine: But you see how much more desirous I am to make my friends my companions, than to make my companions my friends: for I declare to you, I have not for any of this society here a tenth part of the affection and tenderness I bear to you. But God knows how long this affection may last. I know, I cannot insure it, if you will make me feel so severely for it – and I may form more agreeable connections with others, whom I may think as worth and more companionable than yourself. At present I can subscribe myself, with the greatest sincerity, your very affectionate etc. (WGM 136 'From a young gentleman at college to his friend at school')

A clergyman in the Anglican Church, William Gilpin was also a schoolmaster renowned for his pedagogical theories and practices. Beyond sheer academic learning, he valued school education as the art of living in society. If the content of his manual is overtly edifying and moralising, its main objective must have been the teaching of letter-writing as a sociable practice.

To finish, this chapter has highlighted both similarities and contradictions between forms of sociability *in praesentia* and the epistolary sociability defined by the theory of the genre in the letter-writing manuals of the eighteenth century. In a nutshell, the letter is perceived as a means to establish links and connections, based on sincerity and trust, with parents and relatives in particular relying on codes and adaptation to a readership with other people. As such, epistolary sociability complements other forms of sociability. The British mode of epistolary sociability clearly shows in the place granted in the epistolary manuals to lower social categories, to commercial activities and to women. Whilst *The Ladies Complete Letter-Writer* confirms the place granted to women in England, it still raises the question of the Britishness of the implied models. William Gilpin's manual includes a British vision of masculine epistolary sociability. On the other hand, epistolary sociability induces a certain degree of isolation on the part of the letter writer, who keeps away from the contamination of the rest of the world. The image of William Gilpin secluding himself in his office even when his grand-children visited him matches perfectly well that of Samuel Richardson, described by Hélène Dachez: some people were little inclined to socialise and resorted to epistolary writing as, perhaps to them, a sufficient form of sociability.

Chapter 9
Gender and the practices of polite sociability in late eighteenth-century Edinburgh
Jane Rendall

IN 1829 WALTER SCOTT contributed his recollections of the eighteenth-century Scottish songwriter and hostess Alison Cockburn to an anthology of Scottish songs. He suggested that 'she maintained the rank in the society of Edinburgh which French women of talents usually do in that of Paris', and that 'the *vieille cour* of Edinburgh rather resembled that of Paris than that of St James's', in laying aside expense and formality to entertain small circles of the Scottish literati at the heart of the Edinburgh Enlightenment.[1] This representation of Cockburn draws upon the tensions experienced in early nineteenth-century Edinburgh around the participation of aspiring literary women in forms of mixed sociability. For those who observed and wrote from this world, both the French *salonnière* and the English bluestocking were constant points of reference. In 1817, Elizabeth Isabella Spence wrote of her visit to the autobiographer and hostess Eliza Fletcher as an encounter with 'the Mrs Montague of Edinburgh, her house being the centre of all that is literary, amiable and distinguished'.[2] But when, in October 1820, John Wilson, editor of *Blackwood's Edinburgh Magazine*, suggested that in the years before his periodical was established in 1817, 'bluestockingism was in its cerulean altitude', he did so in the context of a reactive redefinition of the Edinburgh republic of letters as one to be led by masculine critical authority.[3] That redefinition began with the foundation

---

[1] *The Scottish Songs*, collected and illustrated by Robert Chambers, 2 vols. (Edinburgh, 1829), vol. 1, lvii.
[2] Elizabeth Isabella Spence, *Letters from the North Highlands, during the Summer 1816* (London, 1817), 36–7.
[3] John Wilson, 'An Hour's Tete-a-Tete with the Public', *Blackwood's Edinburgh Magazine* 8 (October 1820), 99.

of the *Edinburgh Review* in 1802, but continued to be asserted throughout this period.[4] These reference points deserve to be understood against the growth of and shifts in polite urban sociability in the eighteenth and early nineteenth centuries. Located in the intermediate spaces between formal public and domestic worlds, and increasingly politicised and diverse, sociable practices need to be understood within their cultural and national contexts, and alongside changing patterns of association in a more clearly public setting.

The history of eighteenth-century salon culture, across France, Britain and Germany, has been the subject of much recent historical discussion, following, in particular, Dena Goodman's discussion of French salons as evolving from aristocratic institutions into sites of sociability, led by women, that embodied the principles of the Enlightenment, allowing women some share in the shaping of transformational ideas, even though they were excluded from other public institutions.[5] Yet, where Goodman saw such salons as ending abruptly with the Revolution, Steven Kale has argued persuasively for their continuity – and increasing politicisation – among the aristocratic elites of early nineteenth-century France.[6] In London also, aristocratic women acted as political hostesses and facilitators throughout the eighteenth and nineteenth centuries.[7] But the 1750s had seen the emergence of salons there led by the small group of women, scholars, writers and translators, later known as the bluestockings, drawn from the gentry and upper classes, with some from the middling and professional classes. They shared a common perspective which was encouraging of female learning,

---

[4] See, for instance, Marilyn Butler, 'Culture's Medium: the Role of the Review', in *Cambridge Companion Guide to British Romanticism*, ed. Stuart Curran (Cambridge, 1993), 120–47; Ina Ferris, *The Achievement of Literary Authority: Gender, History and the Waverley Novels* (Ithaca, NY, 1991), 19–78; Clifford Siskin, *The Work of Writing: Literature and Social Change in Britain, 1700–1830* (Baltimore, 1999), 224–5.

[5] Dena Goodman, *The Republic of Letters: A Cultural History of the French Enlightenment* (Ithaca, NY, 1994).

[6] Steven Kale, *French Salons: High Society and Political Sociability from the Old Regime to the Revolution of 1848* (Baltimore, 2004); Steven Kale, 'Women, the Public Sphere, and the Persistence of Salons', *French Historical Studies* 25, no. 1 (2002), 115–48; see also, for an important argument for continuity in salons as the institutions of an aristocratic elite, Antoine Lilti, *The World of the Salons: Sociability and Worldliness in Eighteenth-Century Paris*, trans. Lydia G. Cochrane (Oxford, 2015)

[7] See Elaine Chalus, *Elite Women in English Political Life, c. 1754–1790* (Oxford, 2005), ch. 3; K. D. Reynolds, *Aristocratic Women and Political Society in Victorian Britain* (Oxford, 1998), ch. 5.

patriotic, philanthropic and interested in politics.[8] As Amy Prendergast has shown, Elizabeth Vesey extended that salon culture to the Anglo-Irish elite.[9]

Other forms of British sociability have also been extensively studied. The masculine, homosocial culture of eighteenth-century coffeehouses and clubs has received much attention, as have the increasingly important voluntary associations, open to all who subscribed, established often for philanthropic or campaigning purposes, and more clearly in the public arena.[10] Women could participate, to some degree, in the latter. There has been considerable interest in the radical sociability of an oppositional culture developing in Britain in the 1790s, from the dinner-table circles of the radical William Godwin to the liberal and familial sociability found among rational dissenters. The editors of an important collection on *Romantic Sociability* have indicated the importance of recognising 'its fluid interplay with other modes of sociability within British sociability as a whole'.[11] This chapter looks at the roles of middle- and upper-class women in different forms of sociability in early nineteenth-century Edinburgh. In these years women began to colonise a variety of intermediate spaces between the familial and the more formal public realms, while always remaining limited by the gendered boundaries placed upon them. Their greater but contested prominence should be considered against its eighteenth-century context.

Edinburgh sociability in the eighteenth century

The city of Edinburgh had been a national capital without a parliament since 1707. Throughout the eighteenth century the Scottish aristocracy became increasingly oriented towards a London-based social timetable,

---

[8] Recent work on this group includes: Sylvia Harcstark Myers, *The Bluestocking Circle: Women, Friendship and the Life of the Mind in Eighteenth-Century England* (Oxford, 1990); Nicole Pohl and Betty A. Schellenberg (eds.), Reconsidering the Bluestockings, *Huntington Library Quarterly* 65 (2002), 1–2; Elizabeth Eger, *Bluestockings: Women of Reason from Enlightenment to Romanticism* (Basingstoke, 2010).

[9] Amy Prendergast, *Literary Salons across Britain and Ireland in the Long Eighteenth Century* (Basingstoke, 2015), ch. 3.

[10] Peter Clark, *British Clubs and Societies 1580-1800: The Origins of an Associational World* (Oxford, 2000); Markman Ellis, *The Coffee House: A Cultural History* (London, 2004); R. J. Morris, 'Voluntary Societies and British Urban Elites, 1780-1850: an Analysis', *Historical Journal* 26 (1983), 95–118.

[11] Gillian Russell and Clara Tuite, 'Introducing Romantic Sociability', in *Romantic Sociability: Social Networks and Literary Culture in Britain, 1770–1840*, ed. Gillian Russell and Clara Tuite (Cambridge, 2002), 19.

following the parliamentary and court seasons. Nevertheless, Edinburgh remained the base for the administration of Scotland, the independent Scottish legal system and the regular annual meetings of the established Presbyterian Church of Scotland, and had its own, outstanding, university. Many aristocrats did maintain a townhouse, or visit regularly, as did the Scottish gentry who played such a major part in the life of the city.[12] When in 1752 Sir Gilbert Elliot of Minto proposed that 'a capital should naturally become the centre of trade and commerce, of learning and the arts, of politeness and refinement of every kind', he expressed the aspirations for social improvement of Edinburgh's urban elite.[13] The creation of the Edinburgh New Town, begun in 1767, exemplified the drive for improvement characteristic of the age of the Scottish Enlightenment, although it also brought the gradual impoverishment of the Old Town of tenement houses and narrow closes. The city was known for the range and vitality of its many clubs and societies, including musical, literary, scientific, medical and improvement-oriented societies, debating clubs and Masonic lodges, and others, sporting or simply convivial. Their membership came especially from the homosocial, professionally oriented, worlds of the university, the law and the church; some were socially or intellectually exclusive, some appealing primarily to university students.[14] Almost all were entirely masculine, as Rosalind Carr has demonstrated; the one exception to this was the Pantheon Society, a debating society to which women were admitted from 1775, and in which they were allowed to vote, although not to speak.[15]

Nevertheless, with the drive to improvement came acceptance of the importance of women's participation in a mixed, polite sociability. The ideas of the Scottish Enlightenment stressed the civilising effects for men of women's companionship.[16] The new urban context offered very different

---

[12] On Edinburgh in these years see: Charles McKean, *Edinburgh: Portrait of a City* (London, 1991), 108–59; A. J. Youngson, *The Making of Classical Edinburgh, 1750–1840* (Edinburgh, 1970).

[13] [Gilbert Elliott], *Proposals for carrying on Certain Public Works in the City of Edinburgh* (Edinburgh, 1752), quoted in Youngson, *The Making of Classical Edinburgh*, 4.

[14] Davis D. McElroy, *Scotland's Age of Improvement: A Survey of Eighteenth Century Literary Clubs and Societies* (Washington, 1969); Clark, *British Clubs and Societies*, 131–2, 213, 459.

[15] Rosalind Carr, *Gender and Enlightenment Culture in Eighteenth-Century Scotland* (Edinburgh, 2014), 76–92.

[16] Mary Catherine Moran, 'From Rudeness to Refinement: Gender, Genre and the Scottish Enlightenment' (Ph.D. thesis, Johns Hopkins University, 1999), and '"The Commerce of the Sexes": Gender and the Social Sphere on Scottish Enlightenment Accounts of Civil Society', in *Paradoxes of Civil Society: New Perspectives on Modern German and British History*, ed. Frank Trentmann (New York and Oxford, 2000).

spaces for such sociability from those of the country houses of the aristocracy and gentry of previous generations. From November to August, the social season, following the sitting of the Court of Session, came to offer ample opportunities for elite women to participate in visiting networks, tea-drinking parties, assemblies, concerts and the theatre. In 1723 Margaret, countess of Panmure, helped, against the opposition of the Church of Scotland, to establish and direct the Assembly, a space for public dancing in the Old Town. When new premises were found in 1746, the management was undertaken by male managers, although Lady Directresses, usually from leading landed families, were responsible for enforcing the rules of politeness. Entrance was limited by entrance fees. In 1787 new Assembly Rooms were opened in the New Town. Women of the social elite were also active in the struggle, against clerical opposition, to establish a theatre in Edinburgh, which was achieved only with the construction of the Theatre Royal in 1767.[17]

Katherine Glover has stressed that this kind of urban sociability was transformative for the lives of elite women, even if she also notes 'the absence in Scotland of the formal, female-headed salons' so characteristic of the French Enlightenment, and of the bluestockings in London and elsewhere.[18] She suggests that through their families and sociable networks Scottish women were able to influence the exercise of patronage in political and literary matters. Betty Fletcher, for instance, who was friendly with several leading members of the literati of the Scottish Enlightenment, was able to provide a route to the favour of her father, Lord Milton, one of the most politically influential judges in Scotland.[19] Other women too provided support and encouragement to aspiring writers. Susannah, countess of Eglinton, in the 1720s maintained a town house in Edinburgh, where she entertained extensively and became a patron to a circle of literary friends, including the poets Allan Ramsay and William Hamilton of Bangour.[20] Alison Cockburn, the songwriter and hostess from a gentry family whose reputation was so praised by Walter Scott, was also from 1753 fully engaged in entertaining and in the balls, assemblies and visiting life of Edinburgh. She

---

[17] Carr, *Gender and Enlightenment Culture in Eighteenth-Century Scotland*, 105–16; Katharine Glover, *Elite Women and Polite Society in Eighteenth-Century Scotland* Woodbridge, 2011), 3–4, 88–101; James H. Jamieson, 'Social Assemblies of the Eighteenth Century', *Book of the Old Edinburgh Club* 19 (1933), 31–91.

[18] Glover, *Elite Women and Polite Society*, 85, 166–72.

[19] Glover, *Elite Women and Polite Society*, 118–21.

[20] Rosalind K. Marshall, 'Montgomerie, Susanna, countess of Eglinton (1689/90–1780)', *Oxford Dictionary of National Biography* (Oxford, 2004) [http://www.oxforddnb.com.ezproxy.york.ac.uk/view/article/66421, accessed March 2017].

was a close friend and correspondent of David Hume, and well acquainted with many of the literati of the Enlightenment, although her reputation as a salon hostess was one constructed by later generations in the light of French and English models. She published very little in her lifetime, choosing rather to share her poems and songs through the common practice of circulating manuscripts among friends.[21]

Scottish elite women read the works of, and corresponded with, the leading figures of the Enlightenment, although they did not tend to enter the world of print themselves; Richard Sher includes no works by women published before 1800 among the 360 works of the Scottish Enlightenment listed in *The Enlightenment and the Book*.[22] Two women who did publish in Edinburgh in the late 1780s were the novelist, playwright and educational writer Jean Marishall and the novelist Elizabeth Keir.[23] One factor that may have been relevant here was the limited interest of Edinburgh publishers in literary genres. Only seven novels were published in Edinburgh between 1770 and 1800; Peter Garside attributes this to the overarching dominance of London as a publishing centre, and to the location of the main market for fiction in southern England, although another reason might lie in distrust of what might have been regarded as an increasingly feminised form.[24] Marishall published her earlier works in London, but in *A Series of Letters*, published in Edinburgh in 1789, she recalled that it had to be explained to her mother 'that there was nothing more common in England than ladies writing novels.'[25] Eighteenth-century Edinburgh hostesses might entertain and encourage male literati, but they did not share the scholarly aspirations and interest in print of the London bluestockings, either for themselves or for younger *protégés*.

By the 1790s there were signs of change and of greater diversity. Earlier political divisions between reform-minded Scottish Whigs, who followed

---

[21] Thomas Craig-Brown (ed.), *Letters and Memoir of Her Own Life by Mrs. Alison Rutherford or Cockburn* (Edinburgh, 1900); John Dwyer, 'Cockburn, Alison (1713–1794)', *Oxford Dictionary of National Biography* (Oxford, 2004) [http://www.oxforddnb.com.ezproxy.york.ac.uk/view/article/5766, accessed March 2017].

[22] Richard Sher, *The Enlightenment and the Book: Scottish Authors and Their Publishers in Eighteenth-Century Britain, Ireland and& America* (Chicago, 2006), 101–3.

[23] Carr, *Gender and Enlightenment Culture in Eighteenth-Century Scotland*, 96–99; Peter Garside, 'The Novel', in *The Edinburgh History of the Book in Scotland. Vol. 2 Enlightenment and Expansion 1707–1800*, ed. Steven W. Brown and Warren Macdougall (Edinburgh, 2012), 475–82; Pam Perkins, *Women Writers and the Edinburgh Enlightenment* (Amsterdam, 2010), 45–53.

[24] Garside, 'The Novel', 476–7.

[25] Jean Marishall, *A Series of Letters*, 2 vols. (Edinburgh, 1789), vol. 2, 173, quoted in Perkins, *Women Writers and the Edinburgh Enlightenment*, 13.

Charles James Fox, and the government majority, organised by the Scottish political manager, Henry Dundas, were very significantly sharpened as a result of the impact of the French Revolution. The Scottish literati did not contribute to the wider British debate around the French Revolution, but they did try to interpret that revolution in terms of their theories of stadial progress towards a modern commercial society.[26] A minority of Whigs continued to identify with a reformist politics at home in the face of government repression, even if they acquiesced in the patriotic consensus of Britain at war after 1802.[27] Among this minority were Eliza Fletcher, who had come to Edinburgh from Yorkshire in 1791 to marry Archibald Fletcher, a lawyer associated with the Foxite Whigs and the defence of radicals tried for treason in 1793. Such political divisions were relevant to, but could to some extent be overcome among, the elite community for whom the expanding Edinburgh New Town was now their chosen residence.[28]

Literature, politics and gender tensions in Edinburgh, 1800–20

After 1800 the role of literary hostesses came to be more clearly identified. In 1810, a liberal contributor to James Hogg's periodical, *The Spy*, lamented the 'splendour, folly, and extravagance' of contemporary entertainments, looking back imaginatively to 'the simplicity and frugality' of the past; but he did suggest three exceptions in the present:

> In these days it was no unusual thing to see a simple and frugal repast given by some woman of taste or genius, the Mrs H—, the Mrs G—, or Mrs F— of her day, graced by the presence of the poet, the historian, the philosopher, the physician, or the divine, who was the ornament of his age.[29]

---

[26] Anna Plassart, *The Scottish Enlightenment and the French Revolution* (Cambridge, 2015).
[27] Emma Macleod 'The Scottish Opposition Whigs and the French Revolution', in *Scotland in the Age of the French Revolution*, ed. Bob Harris (Edinburgh, 2005), 79–98.
[28] For further discussion, see Jane Rendall, '"Women that would plague me with rational conversation": Aspiring Women and Scottish Whigs c. 1790–1830', in *Women, Gender and Enlightenment*, ed. Sarah Knott and Barbara Taylor (Basingstoke, 2005), 326–47.
[29] James Hogg, *The Spy*, ed. Gillian Hughes, *Collected Works of James Hogg*, ed. Douglas S. Mack, 8 (Edinburgh, 2000), 162.

These references are to the novelist and educationalist, Elizabeth Hamilton, the poet and writer on the Highlands, Anne Grant, and Eliza Fletcher, who published very little but did circulate manuscript material. All three were friends, although the liberal Whiggism of Fletcher and Hamilton separated their social circles slightly from those of the Tory Anne Grant.[30]

In the first twenty years of the nineteenth century there were clearly continuities in the sociable life of Edinburgh. The Assembly Rooms continued to flourish, as did the tea drinking, formal dinner parties and visits to the theatre enjoyed by aristocratic, gentry and professional families living in or visiting Edinburgh, and well recorded in correspondence, in diaries and by travellers.[31] But new critical periodicals were to give a sharper edge to literary sociability. In 1802 the *Edinburgh Review* was founded in Edinburgh by the young Whigs Francis Jeffrey, Henry Brougham and others, with whom, Fletcher recalled, she and her husband were 'intimately acquainted'; Fletcher testified to 'the electrical effects of its publication', and the 'large and good' results that followed politically.[32] It was to be followed by the Tory *Quarterly Review*, founded in London in 1809 by the Scot John Murray, and in 1817 by *Blackwood's Edinburgh Magazine*, also Tory but based in Edinburgh. The founders of the *Edinburgh Review*, in particular, have been seen as heirs to the Scottish Enlightenment, with a particular interest in the disciplines of political science, political economy and the shaping of a modern, reforming, commercial society.[33] Literary scholars have stressed, as suggested above, that this periodical, to be conducted by professional, well-paid reviewers, firmly set out to establish masculine critical authority.

In the early years of the *Edinburgh Review* Fletcher entertained the young Whigs and lawyers associated with it, as well as the poets James Grahame and Thomas Campbell.[34] After Elizabeth Hamilton's arrival in Edinburgh in 1803, the two women formed a friendship which helped to persuade others 'that Mrs Fletcher was not the ferocious Democrat she had been represented, and that she neither had the model of a guillotine

---

[30] Jane Rendall, 'Bluestockings and Reviewers: Gender, Power and Culture in Britain, c. 1800–1830', *Nineteenth-Century Contexts* 26 (2004), 355–74, here 360–1.

[31] For a full account of this social scene, see Mary Cosh, *Edinburgh: the Golden Age* (Edinburgh, 2003).

[32] *Autobiography of Mrs Fletcher with Letters and Other Family Memorials*, ed. [Mary Richardson] (Edinburgh, 1875), 82.

[33] Plassart, *Scottish Enlightenment and the French Revolution*, chs. 7–8; Biancamaria Fontana, *Rethinking the Politics of Commercial Society: The Edinburgh Review 1802–32* (Cambridge, 1985), ch. 1.

[34] [Richardson], *Autobiography of Mrs Fletcher*, 82–3.

in her possession nor carried a dagger under her cloak.'³⁵ Fletcher's social circle was growing, and she noted retrospectively that forms of sociability in Edinburgh generally were changing. Large dinners and supper parties were less frequent, replaced by evening parties, meeting at nine and dominated by music and conversation. Tea and coffee were served, and later some light, cold refreshments: 'people did not in these parties meet to eat, but to talk and listen.' She described Edinburgh society as 'delightful', and also distinguished, including among others Walter Scott, Francis Jeffrey, the novelist Henry Mackenzie, academics Thomas Brown and John Playfair and the clergyman and philosopher Archibald Alison.³⁶ Ladies, and the students also admitted to these gatherings, were more likely to listen to the exchanges of these leading figures, although it seems likely that some women conversed more actively, as Anne Grant's praise for Fletcher suggests: 'she has been, for her personal graces, and the charms of her enlightened, animated, and unaffected conversation, the admiration of all Edinburgh for years past.'³⁷ Grant described Fletcher's 'very numerous & fashionable parties', made possible by a substantial legacy left to her in 1806: 'Her house is the resort of scavans, highflying whigs & strangers from the north & west of England who begin to come here in great numbers.'³⁸ The social networks so built crossed national boundaries.

But Fletcher was not the only Edinburgh hostess to attract such numbers. In a posthumous tribute to Hamilton, which she almost certainly wrote, Fletcher recalled that when Hamilton first came to Edinburgh, having published several successful novels and a work on education, 'a female literary character was even at that time a sort of phenomenon in Scotland', and that she soon attracted not only intellectuals but fashionable society. Hamilton limited her entertaining, however, to levees on Monday mornings, while also receiving close friends in the afternoons.³⁹ Grant recalled that at Hamilton's house 'a more selected circle met, where there really was little or no town gossip; the topics were literary or general.'⁴⁰ Grant herself, widowed in 1801, moved to Edinburgh from Stirling in 1810, and although having fewer resources (she wrote, and took in young women as pupils and lodg-

---

³⁵ [Richardson], *Autobiography of Mrs Fletcher*, 86.
³⁶ [Richardson], *Autobiography of Mrs Fletcher*, 102.
³⁷ *Memoir and Correspondence of Mrs Grant of Laggan* ... ed. J. P. Grant, 3 vols., second edition (London, 1845), vol. 1, 232–3.
³⁸ Anne Grant to Catherine Fanshawe, 15 April 1810, Edinburgh University Library La II. 357, fols. 176–8.
³⁹ Elizabeth Benger, *Memoirs of the Late Mrs Elizabeth Hamilton*, 2 vols, London, 1818, vol. 1, 176–8.
⁴⁰ *Memoir and Correspondence of Mrs Grant of Laggan*, vol. 2, 128–30.

ers, to help support her numerous family) nevertheless took an active role in Edinburgh society and its networks. On her arrival she noted: 'Walter Scott and the formidable Jeffrey have both called on me, not by any means as a scribbling female, but on account of links formed by mutual friends'[41] She praised the conversation of the 'enlightened circles' of 'this Northern Athens' as 'easy, animated, and indeed full of spirit and intelligence'.[42]

Another woman whose entertainments were to prove memorable for her many visitors was Helen Stewart, the wife of a dominant figure of the late Enlightenment, Dugald Stewart, Professor of Moral Philosophy at the University of Edinburgh. The couple entertained extensively in their homes in Canongate, their guests including academic colleagues, lawyers and young aristocrats studying at Edinburgh.[43] Their many visitors from outside Edinburgh included Anna Barbauld in 1794, Elizabeth Hamilton in 1802, Maria Edgeworth in 1803 and Maria Graham, later a writer on India, South America and art history, in 1805. Graham recalled, much later, participating as a young girl in a conversation on philosophy with Dugald Stewart and Thomas Brown. Even though she was condescendingly christened 'metaphysics in muslin', she seized every opportunity she had to go there.[44]

Like the earlier bluestockings, these hostesses also participated in literary networks which engaged in mutual support, criticism and mentoring. Pam Perkins has pointed out how extensively earlier modes of circulating manuscripts survived in early nineteenth-century Edinburgh, and has emphasised the difficulties of drawing distinctions between the sociable exchanges of manuscripts and professional authorship.[45] In 1810–11 the young English medical student Henry Holland wrote regularly to his father of his enjoyment of Edinburgh society and of the hospitality and conversation of Grant, Hamilton and Fletcher; the 'visiting and gaieties' were inseparable from literary discussions and the circulation of unpublished work.[46] Anne Grant was accustomed to circulate her poems and ballads

---

[41] *Memoir and Correspondence of Mrs Grant of Laggan*, vol. 1, 225–9.
[42] *Memoir and Correspondence of Mrs Grant of Laggan*, vol. 1, 234–7.
[43] Gordon Macintyre, *Dugald Stewart: The Pride and Ornament of Scotland* (Brighton, 2003), chs. 10–13.
[44] Macintyre, *Dugald Stewart*, 114–17; William McCarthy, *Anna Letitia Barbauld: Voice of the Enlightenment* (Baltimore, 2008), 363–5; Rosamund Brunel Gotch, *Maria Lady Callcott: The Creator of 'Little Arthur'* (London, 1937), 75–6.
[45] Pam Perkins, '"A Constellation of Scottish Genius": Networks of Exchange in Late 18th- and Early 19th-Century Edinburgh', *Lumen* 34 (2015), 39–54.
[46] Henry Holland to Peter Holland, 17 March 1811, NLS MS Acc. 7515; Perkins, *Women Writers and the Edinburgh Enlightenment*, 98–102.

among friends, and was also persuaded to publish her letters to them as *Letters from the Mountains*.⁴⁷ Fletcher was part of this world. Thomas Campbell's poems were circulated in her circle before going to press as *Pleasures of Hope* in 1799.⁴⁸ In 1801 she was invited by her friend Robert Anderson, editor of the *Edinburgh Magazine*, to comment on a manuscript treatise on female education, which she did, unfavourably.⁴⁹ In 1811 the publisher Manners & Miller sent a copy of the first novel by Mary Brunton, *Self-Control*, out to four readers: Walter Scott, Elizabeth Hamilton, Eliza Fletcher and Anne Grant.⁵⁰ Their reaction was generally favourable and Brunton was to become a close friend of Fletcher's. When the same publisher, in 1814, sent a volume of James Hogg's romantic poetry 'among his bluestockings for their verdict', they judged it 'extravagant nonsense'.⁵¹ Fletcher encouraged the aspiring poet Allan Cunningham, introducing him to the antiquarian Robert Hartley.⁵² She supported Thomas Campbell when in 1825 he was daunted by unfavourable reviews, and in 1826 asked him to write or arrange a favourable review in the *Edinburgh Review* for the *Life of Theobald Wolfe Tone*, edited by Wolfe Tone's son under the supervision of his mother, Matilda Tone, her close friend.⁵³ Fletcher's literary opinions were clearly respected, although her own published output was limited to two privately printed verse dramas, *Elidure and Edward: Two Historical Dramatic Sketches* (1824), which she circulated among friends, inviting comments.⁵⁴

Political conflicts between Whig and Tory could appear to shape the character of sociability in Edinburgh; in 1824 the young diarist Helen Graham wrote of an evening party: 'there is a sort of indefinite feeling of gloominess and blackness about the Whigs, certainly not congenial to a

---

⁴⁷ *Memoir and Correspondence of Mrs Grant of Laggan*, vol. 1, 17, 21–3, 54–7.
⁴⁸ *Life and Letters of Thomas Campbell*, ed. W. Beattie, 3 vols. (London, 1849), vol. 1, 240–1.
⁴⁹ Eliza Fletcher to Robert Anderson, 6 November 1801, National Library of Scotland (NLS), Adv. MS 22.4.11, fols. 253–4; Perkins, '"A Constellation of Scottish Genius"', 44–5.
⁵⁰ *Memoir and Correspondence of Mrs Grant of Laggan*, vol. 1, 279.
⁵¹ James Hogg, *Memoir of the Author's Life; and, Familiar Anecdotes of Sir Walter Scott*, ed. Douglas S. Mack (Edinburgh, 1972), 33–7.
⁵² Perkins, '"A Constellation of Scottish Genius"', 45; [Richardson], *Autobiography of Mrs Fletcher*, 145–8.
⁵³ [Richardson], *Autobiography of Mrs Fletcher*, 178–9; Eliza Fletcher to Matilda Tone Wilson, 19 July 1826, NLS MS Acc. 4278.
⁵⁴ Archibald Fletcher to Robert Anderson, 21 November and 9 December 1825, NLS Adv. MS 22.4.11, fols. 246, 248–9; Perkin, '"A Constellation of Scottish Genius"', 46.

Tory'.[55] But Anne Grant, the conservative who saw Fletcher's only personal flaw as her 'political bigotry', or Whig opinions, suggested that 'the social spirit, which still forms so distinguished a part of our Scotch manners', moderated political hostilities in sociable settings.[56] These settings, both Whig and Tory, did, however, reveal gendered tensions, evident in the many references to bluestockings in the literature of the period – tensions which had often to do with the extension of women's interests into public affairs. John Gibson Lockhart, in 1819, contrasted 'Scottish Blue-Stockings' unfavourably with those of France, suggesting, possibly in a reference to Fletcher, that their favourite topics of conversation were less likely to be the latest novel than 'the resumption of cash-payments, the great question of Borough Reform, and the Corn-Bill'.[57] Fletcher recalled Jeffrey's desire to check 'rational conversation' by 'aspiring and ambitious women' on such subjects, and Holland, writing in 1811, noted the tensions between Jeffrey and the Fletchers.[58]

Literary women noted the harshness of treatment shown to women writers in the reviews, which clearly identified the limits of the subject matter thought appropriate to women writers; they were expected to focus on the domestic and the familial and, although they could celebrate national identities and achievements, were not expected to contribute to political debates.[59] Such domestic settings were contrasted with the world of mixed sociability represented by the salons of the French Enlightenment. In reviewing the letters of Mme du Deffand in 1810, Francis Jeffrey noted that 'the superior cultivation of French women' and the absence of employment for aristocratic men accounted for the success of French salons. But he also suggested that those who lived in such worlds had no notion of private and domestic enjoyments, and that they rested on the abandonment of political duty by the elite and the degradation of the population.[60] The hostility

[55] *Parties and Pleasures: the Diaries of Helen Graham*, ed. James Irvine (Perth, 1957), 43.
[56] *Memoir and Correspondence of Mrs Grant of Laggan*, vol. 1, 257.
[57] John Gibson Lockhart, *Peter's Letters to His Kinsfolk*, 3 vols., second edition (Edinburgh 1819), vol. 1, 308; in the same year Archibald Fletcher published his *Memoir concerning the Origin and Progress of the Reform Proposed in the Internal Government of the Royal Burghs of Scotland ...* (Edinburgh, 1819).
[58] [Richardson], *Autobiography of Mrs Fletcher*, 279; Henry Holland to Peter Holland, 24 June 1811, NLS MS Acc. 7515.
[59] For further discussion, see Rendall, 'Bluestockings and Reviewers', 355–74; Moyra Haslett, 'Bluestocking Feminism Revisited: the Satirical Figure of the Bluestocking', *Women's Writing* 17 (2010), 432–51.
[60] Francis Jeffrey, 'Correspondance de Madame du Deffand et de Mademoiselle de Lespinasse', *Edinburgh Review* [ER] 15 (January 1810), 458–85, esp. 460.

of Edinburgh's responses to mixed sociability had some parallels among London literary men in this period; but it may also owe something to Edinburgh's closely knit professional circles and to the legacy of the homosocial clubs of the Enlightenment.[61]

One response to such treatment might be seen as the networks of female friends and correspondents built across Britain by Fletcher and Hamilton, uniting women with political interests, reforming opinions and high aspirations for their own work. Fletcher first met Anna Barbauld in London in 1801, when dining with the poet and dramatist Joanna Baillie, and each was deeply impressed by the other; the three women remained in contact for the rest of their lives.[62] Fletcher later sent her two eldest daughters to stay with Barbauld in Stoke Newington.[63] Barbauld's letters, suggesting an affinity both familial and political, show her deeply interested in Edinburgh events. She assumes that Fletcher shares her interest in French politics. Sadly, Fletcher's letters, referred to as lively and entertaining, have not survived; but she continued to meet and correspond with Baillie until 1850.[64] The correspondence between Fletcher and Matilda Tone, in the United States, similarly demonstrated a mingling of familial, political and literary interests.[65] Hamilton also frequently corresponded with Baillie, writing to her in some detail of the similarity of their analyses of the passions, and with Maria Edgeworth, whom she had first met at Dugald Stewart's, and with whom she had common interests in philosophical and educational subjects. Hamilton visited Edgeworth in Edgeworthstown in 1813.[66] However, women's occupation of the intermediate spaces between public and private worlds in Edinburgh cannot be understood simply through a focus, echoing eighteenth-century models, on sociability in a domestic or social setting, or through epistolary relationships. Other kinds of association were expanding in these years, associations in which both Fletcher and

---

[61] For other examples of bluestocking satires, see Haslett, 'Bluestocking Feminism Revisited', 439–44; Gillian Russell, 'Spouters or Washerwomen: the Sociability of Romantic Lecturing', in *Romantic Sociability*, ed. Russell and Tuite, 134–41.

[62] Joanna Baillie to Anne Millar, 8 August 1801, NLS MS 9236, fols. 1–2; [Richardson], *Autobiography of Mrs Fletcher*, 79–80.

[63] [Richardson], *Autobiography of Mrs Fletcher*, 101, 113–17.

[64] Anna Letitia Barbauld, *Works, with a Memoir by Lucy Aikin*, 2 vols. (London, 1825), vol. 2, 138–45; [Richardson], *Autobiography of Mrs Fletcher*, 284–5.

[65] See Jane Rendall, '"Friends of Liberty and Virtue": Women Radicals and Transatlantic Correspondence 1789-1848', in *Gender and Politics in the Age of Letter-Writing, 1750-2000*, ed. Caroline Bland and Máire Cross (Aldershot, 2004), 77–92.

[66] Benger, *Memoirs of the Late Mrs Elizabeth Hamilton*, vol. 1, 164, vol. 2, 75–110, 131–6, 146–59, 171–92; Marilyn Butler, *Maria Edgeworth: A Literary Biography* (Oxford, 1972), 220, n.

Hamilton played a significant role, from which they were not excluded as they had been from exclusive eighteenth-century clubs.

Women and the associational world of Edinburgh

The late eighteenth century, in Scotland as in England, saw the growth of voluntary associations, open to all who subscribed, established to achieve some common interest, such as the provision of education or poor relief. These associations, like the older ones, had rules and a constitution, but also reported to their members and to the wider public through regular meetings, annual reports and financial statements.[67] They offered a means of engaging with the social problems generated by rapid urban growth, through the discriminating application of charity and the use of the principle of self-help. The growth of these newer associations was encouraged here as elsewhere by the growth of a significant evangelical movement across Protestant denominations, including a minority, known as the Popular party, within the Church of Scotland, smaller or seceding Presbyterian churches and English-influenced nonconformist denominations.[68] And Scottish Episcopalianism, linked to the Church of England, was at the beginning of a revival.[69] Eliza Fletcher attended Episcopalian chapels in Edinburgh. Unlike the English bluestockings, Edinburgh literary hostesses were not necessarily supporters of the established church. The ruling Moderate party in the Church of Scotland was initially unsympathetic to new, often evangelical-inspired, societies. Like older societies, these were at first entirely male governed, but from the late 1790s all-female associations for philanthropic and religious purposes also appeared in Scotland; the earliest were founded in Edinburgh in 1797, with Eliza Fletcher rapidly taking up the call the following year.[70]

In April 1798 Fletcher, with other ladies, founded the Edinburgh New Town Female Friendly Society for domestic servants and other poor women – the first friendly society in Scotland, as Fletcher claimed. She wrote in

---

[67] Morris, 'Voluntary Societies and British Urban Elites, 1780–1850'; Clark, *British Clubs and Societies*, 8–9, 444–6.

[68] Callum G. Brown, *The Social History of Religion in Scotland since 1750* (London, 1987), ch. 2.

[69] Eleanor M. Harris, 'The Episcopal Congregation of Charlotte Chapel, Edinburgh, 1794–1818' (Ph.D. thesis, University of Stirling), 12–31.

[70] For women's associations throughout Scotland in this period, see Jane Rendall, 'Women's Associations in Scotland, 1790-1830', in *Scottish Clubs and Societies 1700-1830: The Need to Belong*, ed. Mark Wallace and Jane Rendall (forthcoming 2020).

her autobiography of the vehement opposition of the deputy sheriff and magistrates of Edinburgh, when these were legally asked to sanction the rules of the Society. She suggested in retrospect that 'for ladies to take any share, especially a leading share, in the management of a public institution, was considered so novel and extraordinary a proceeding as ought not to be countenanced.'[71] She continued the struggle against Edinburgh magistrates until 1825.

Women might become members of male-led societies and might also by invitation form ladies' committees. In August 1797 at the first meeting of the Edinburgh Philanthropic Society its leaders, the seceding minister, James Peddie and the Reverend David Black, an evangelical minister of the Church of Scotland, proposed that they should found a refuge for prostitutes and fallen women, to be reclaimed from the Edinburgh Bridewell and the streets of Edinburgh.[72] In November 1798 a committee of twelve ladies met in the Magdalene Asylum newly established in the Old Town, charged with taking particular care of the women admitted, and especially their work, dress and conduct. Eliza Fletcher was one of the twelve and remained an extremely active committee member until 1810, working with women from different denominations as one of the visitors attending the Asylum weekly, and having a particular responsibility for purchasing clothes for the inmates from their own earnings.[73]

In January 1801 a House of Industry was set up in Edinburgh by the Edinburgh Society for Encouraging the Industry and Increasing the Comforts of the Poor, inspired by a similar London-based society. From its beginning it included an industrial school for girls. In November 1806 the male committee appealed to 'a number of ladies every way qualified for so important a trust' to take charge of what were described as 'the internal arrangements of the house' … 'as this is entirely a female institution.'[74] The

---

[71] [Richardson], *Autobiography of Mrs Fletcher*, 76–7; for further discussion see Jane Rendall, 'Gender, Philanthropy and Civic Identities in Edinburgh, 1795–1830', in *The Routledge History Handbook of Gender and the Urban Experience*, ed. Deborah Simonton (London, 2017), 213–14.

[72] For the London Philanthropic Society, see Donna Andrew, *Philanthropy and Police: London Charity in the Eighteenth Century* (Princeton, 1989), 182–6; David Black, *Christian Benevolence Recommended and Enforced by the Example of Christ: A Sermon Preached before the Edinburgh Philanthropic Society* (Edinburgh, 1798), 26–47.

[73] Edinburgh City Archives [ECA], Magdalene Asylum, Ladies' Committee Minute Book, minute for 23 November 1798, SL 237/2/1; ECA, Ladies' Committee Inspection Report, 1798–1800, minute for 18 June 1799, SL 237/3/1.

[74] *Caledonian Mercury* [*CM*], 27 November 1806.

committee of ladies then set up included Elizabeth Hamilton, who in 1809 published an account of the school.[75] In 1815 the annual report suggested that the committee was solely responsible for its management.[76] Similarly, after the Edinburgh Lancastrian School Society, founded in 1810, set up a new schoolhouse, with space for girls' and boys' schools, it relinquished the superintendence of the girls' school to a group of female visitors, later a Ladies' Committee, which included Fletcher, Hamilton and Brunton.[77]

The Edinburgh Society for the Suppression of Beggars was established in January 1813, at a time when economic distress meant the proliferation of beggars on the streets in Edinburgh. It was modelled on similar societies elsewhere, and its goals included not only suppressing the practice of begging on Edinburgh streets but the relief of 'the Industrious and Destitute Poor', of whom the female poor were 'by far the most numerous class we have'. The committee of the society suggested opening a repository for work to be taken on for the poor to execute and for teaching poor children useful employments, and it looked to 'a Committee of Ladies' to help it execute these schemes.[78] The Repository was opened on March 1813 and the female committee, including Fletcher and Brunton, played a major part in superintending its organisation. In 1813 Eliza Fletcher personally offered premiums to 'the most industrious, cleanly, and sober' of those working in the Repository.[79]

The more conservative Anne Grant wrote in 1818 that she shrank a little from 'Female Societies formed with the very best intention', through wariness of 'officious gossiping characters, who derive a certain imagined consequence by overruling and interfering', but that she was now a very busy member of such a society, set up to support the provision of Gaelic schools.[80] In 1817 she had become a member of the Committee of Management of the Edinburgh Ladies Association in aid of the Society for the Support of Gaelic Schools, whose membership was drawn from many leading

---

[75] 'Account of the Edinburgh House of Industry', *Scots Magazine* 71 (January 1809), 20–2.

[76] *CM*, 9 January 1815.

[77] *Reports of the Ordinary Directors of the Edinburgh Lancastrian School Society to the General Meetings of the Society … on July 2 and November 15, 1813* (Edinburgh, 1813), 7, 24.

[78] *Society for the Suppression of Beggars; for the Relief of Occasional Distress, and the Encouragement of Industry among the Poor, within the City and Environs of Edinburgh* (Edinburgh, 1813), 11–17.

[79] *First Report of the Society, instituted in Edinburgh on 25th January 1813, for the Suppression of Beggars, …* (Edinburgh, 1814), 9–16, 25–8.

[80] *Memoir and Correspondence of Mrs Grant of Laggan*, vol. 2, 173–4.

Edinburgh families; she remained a member of the committee until 1828.[81] This society was typical of the remarkable growth across Scotland of many female Bible and missionary societies in these years; it was less committed to the management of institutions than to fundraising for the purposes of the association. These societies were remarkably successful in collecting money, often making the largest contributions to the funds of parent societies, and developing new modes of fundraising. In 1827 and again in 1828 the Edinburgh Ladies' Association for the Support of Gaelic Schools held sales of work in the Assembly Rooms on George St, raising £220 and £229, respectively.[82]

Those involved in such associations were fully aware that they were participating in a movement that crossed borders. Information was actively shared, and epistolary, visiting and social networks linking Edinburgh with London and English provincial cities were based on common philanthropic as well as literary and political interests. Fletcher grew up near York, and both she and Hamilton were regular visitors there and familiar with the Grey Coat School reinvigorated in 1784 through the energies of Catherine Cappe, the wife of a local Unitarian minister, Faith Gray, an Anglican Evangelical and local female societies. The York Female Friendly Society was founded in 1788 and Cappe's publications on both the school and the friendly society were widely read and influential.[83] In October 1812 Hamilton visited the Grey Coat School in York, spending some time with both Gray and Cappe. Their work was of considerable interest to her both as a writer of educational works addressed to women and girls and as a practical and engaged philanthropist, deeply involved in the management of the school at the Edinburgh House of Industry for poor women and girls.[84] Hamilton wrote to Joanna Baillie of her visits in 1808 to the schools which her hostess, Mrs Dixon, had established for poor children in the Lake District.[85] Of her visit to Ireland in 1813, she wrote, also to Baillie: 'Wherever I went, there were still sights to be seen and people to be introduced to, schools to visit, and schemes of improvement to be examined', as well as of her visit

---

[81] *Seventh Annual Report of the Society for the Support of Gaelic Schools* (Edinburgh, 1818), 39–40; *Seventeenth Annual Report ...* 1828, 72; *Eighteenth Annual Report ...* 1829, 37–40.

[82] *Seventeenth Annual Report ...* 1828, 32–3; *Eighteenth Annual Report ...* 1829, 22.

[83] Entry in Faith Gray's diary for 2 Oct ober 1812, York City Archives, Gray Papers D1b, Book 2, fol. 12; Catherine Cappe, *An Account of Two Charity Schools for the Education of Girls: and of a Female Friendly Society* (York, 1800); *Observations on Charity Schools, Female Friendly Societies, and Other Subjects ...* (York, 1805).

[84] Benger, *Memoirs of the Late Mrs Elizabeth Hamilton*, vol. 1, 178.

[85] Benger, *Memoirs of the Late Mrs Elizabeth Hamilto*, vol. 2, 75–80.

to Maria Edgeworth in Edgeworthstown.[86] In 1819 Eliza Fletcher visited London, where she not only visited Joanna Baillie and Anna Barbauld, but spent some time in Newgate with Elizabeth Fry, escorted by Robert Owen, who also took her to call on William Godwin.[87] This philanthropic tourism also extended the bonds of sociability.

There is as yet no systematic survey of women's philanthropic engagement across Britain in this period, and women's individual participation may be obscured through the loss of the scanty records of female societies. In Scotland as in England, women's involvement in such associations was frequently welcomed and sometimes invited because the energy, time and ability they brought to religious and philanthropic enterprises were invaluable. Their participation was clearly publicly visible, in newspapers, annual reports and meetings in early nineteenth-century Edinburgh. It was acceptable because associations were clearly structured by gender difference. Female societies limited themselves mainly to concern for the poor of their own sex and for children. Ladies' committees in mixed enterprises were also limited, usually to visiting, to appointing female staff and to the day-to-day management of institutions providing for poor women and children. Male authority, oversight and financial control were preserved through management committees and through the conduct of public meetings, although informally women's influence might be brought to bear, especially by leading female patrons. Even so, women's roles in voluntary organisations were sometimes contested; the resistance of Edinburgh magistrates to female friendly societies is an outstanding example which appears to have no parallels elsewhere in Britain. Anxieties expressed were shared by women themselves. In her last educational work, *Hints Addressed to the Patrons and Directors of Schools*, Hamilton, by then a little disillusioned, reflected on the difficulties that could beset ladies' committees, whom she describes as 'restrained by timidity, and by habits of reserve, from openly declaring their individual opinions, when not certain that they will be received with approbation.'[88] Male assistance was sometimes requested, to deal with the auditing of accounts, with investments or to preside over meetings. One significant barrier which women faced was that of speaking in mixed public meetings. It was almost unknown for women to speak in public to mixed audiences in Edinburgh, and the autonomy of their associations within wider movements was limited.

---

[86] Benger, *Memoirs of the Late Mrs Elizabeth Hamilton*, vol. 2, 173.
[87] [Richardson], *Autobiography of Mrs Fletcher*, 135–7.
[88] Hamilton, *Hints Addressed to the Patrons and Directors of Schools* (London, 1815), 44.

In early nineteenth-century London it is possible to trace a wide variety of sociable practices among upper- and middle-class women, from the literary hostesses who invoked their bluestocking predecessors, such as Mary Berry and the countess of Blessington, to overtly political aristocratic hostesses such as Lady Holland and Lady Jersey, extending to the more modest circles that included, for instance, networks of rational dissenting families and a wide variety of associations.[89] The much smaller city of Edinburgh saw a significant expansion in mixed sociability and in its associational worlds in the early nineteenth century; yet, given its small and cohesive elite, and the absence of a court or parliament, there was much less diversity than in London. The much-cited figures of the bluestocking and the *salonnière* might be idealised, as were the English Mrs Montagu and, in 1829, the Scottish Alison Cockburn. These figures might also be deployed in hostile reactions to women's claim to political opinions, or to buttress the male assumption of critical authority in the face of aspiring and able literary women. Yet sociable encounters in the early years of the nineteenth century went beyond the experience of these eighteenth-century exemplars. Fletcher, Hamilton, Grant and Brunton met not only at parties and dinner tables but in committee-rooms, where their claims to participation were also contested and limited. Nevertheless Hamilton, Grant and Fletcher constantly negotiated these tensions – sometimes successfully, sometimes not – at a time of shifting literary and political relationships and the reshaping of gendered identities, applying their talents to staking out a recognised but limited place in the sociable worlds of Edinburgh.

---

[89] Susanne Schmid, *British Literary Salons of the Late Eighteenth and Early Nineteenth Centuries* (New York, 2013); Reynolds, *Aristocratic Women and Political Society*, 161–2; Timothy Whelan, 'Mary Steele, Mary Hays and the Convergence of Women's Literary Circles in the 1790s', *Journal for Eighteenth-Century Studies* 38 (2015), 511–24.

Part 3:
Paradoxes of British sociability

THE LAST SECTION, entitled **'Paradoxes of British sociability'**, highlights the tensions within British sociability, related to social or political behaviour, to gender issues, to public/private dialectics, to the concepts of norm and excess. It examines the mechanisms that challenged the idea of harmonious sociability as a hegemonic form, looking for some signs of the 'unsocial sociability' of men and analysing some forms of resistance to sociability.

The tensions inherent to British sociability can be expressed through the conflicting nature of the private and public selves of major social figures like Samuel Johnson and James Boswell, for instance. Both are shown to have been amongst the most sociable of all the literary men of the eighteenth century, both of them delighting in company and engaging in conversation of all kinds. Out of company, though, as **Allan Ingram** demonstrates in chapter 10, Boswell and Johnson were lifelong depressives, who relished social intercourse and high spirits when in a good frame of mind, just as much as they shunned it and saw it as meaningless during their periods of lowness. Company and conversation, and even the recording of it, helped to keep them publicly sociable.

Kant's idea of 'unsociable sociability' is central to understanding the paradoxes of British sociability. In chapter 11 **Emrys Jones** uses it to trace currents of resistance in pre-Kantian literary works. Specifically, this chapter identifies the 'friendly enemy' as an important recurring figure in literature of the Patriot opposition. The friendly enemy offered a model of sociable connection which in some senses anticipated Kant's carefully balanced external and internal resistances, but the figure could also demonstrate the danger of such resistances failing, of friendships becoming either too unsociable or not unsociable enough. A choice of various literary pieces of the friendly enemy in captivity provides a valuable distillation of the tensions underlying the friendly enemy trope and the potential for resistance to give way. The examples chosen by the author aim to emphasise both the precariousness of oppositional rhetoric and the problematic status of sociability within political discourse.

Norbert Col's chapter 13 prolongs the paradox in political sociability. Even if Edmund Burke was an eminently sociable man, he did not readily accept some of the new political developments that were emerging in his own day and age. Nor did he spend much time depicting clubs or salons. He was more concerned with a combination of personal and public sociability that explains the dramatic nature of his break with Charles James Fox in 1791, based on diverging outlooks on the Glorious Revolution. Burke's views on party government are based on an idealised rendering of the Whig Junto, and the national sociability which he sketches is debunked by his writings on Ireland.

Toasting and the rituals of convivial practice reveal the pressures under which the ideologies of sociability were placed in the aftermath of the French Revolution in Britain, when political opinions frequently punctured illusions of a homogeneous, unified nation. In chapter 12 **Ian Newman** considers the anti-social behaviour of the radical speechmaker John Thelwall at a meeting of the Royal Humane Society at the London Tavern in 1799, when he refused to drink a toast to the standing army and was subsequently expelled from the tavern. The incident thus provides an opportunity to reflect on the differences between public narratives and private experiences of convivial meetings.

While the French Revolution and the impact of Thomas Paine's *Rights of Man* stimulated the development of radical artisan societies from 1792 onwards, such new public ventures revealed the paradoxes of British sociability by opposing respectability and democratic ideals to political agency. The largest and best-known one, the London Corresponding Society (LCS), formulated democratic demands (universal male suffrage and annual parliaments in particular) and, more importantly for the history of sociability, tried to function as a democratic structure, as an example of an authentic people's assembly. In the final chapter **Rémy Duthille** aims to address the question of plebeian respectability and examines the LCS as the prototype of a democratic polity pitted against the existing institutions. The agitated political context of the last decade of the eighteenth century offers a backdrop to a significant evolution of the British model of sociability as defined throughout the previous sections. Tested by growing aspirations for self-improvement and social mobility and animated by democratic and civic ideals, the British not only challenged traditional continental models of sociability but increasingly questioned current national trends towards social segregation in clubs and public venues.

Chapter 10
In company and out: the public/private selves of Johnson and Boswell

Allan Ingram

Sociable conversation

SOCIABLE CONVERSATION, in all periods, but especially in the formal atmosphere and gender-restricted context of the eighteenth century, is the public face of the individual: that which is on display as against that which remains, more or less effectively, hidden from view. It represents the self that we wish to present to the world, even if that world is in the form of friends and family. The private self, certainly, can sometimes be observed through the cracks, and few performances are perfect, but to discover the extent and nature of that private self demands other sources, other more intimate means of inquiry, and other kinds of relationships. With writers like Johnson and Boswell we are unusually privileged, in that the opportunities are there for comparison between the self in performance and the self that can be read in their published and unpublished works. Thanks to Boswell, especially to his journal and his works on Johnson, we are afforded unique insights into both himself and his friend and idol Johnson, their inner selves as against their public and social personalities. In understanding these differences in perspective we can also read something of the nature of eighteenth-century society, of the weight given to social presence and performance and of the generally forbidden territory that was occupied by inner realities. This chapter explores some of those performances and some of that territory.

Samuel Johnson and James Boswell valued sociability as amongst the very highest pleasures of living within a civilised society. The whole business of interchange of ideas, of pleasantries, even of insults – in short, of what had become known in the period as clubbability[1] – are conspicuously present in all accounts of the ways they chose to spend their time, both when together, during Boswell's usually annual visits to London, and in the course of their separate lives. Yet this straightforward truth also conceals personal complexities in each man's case that make their respective attitudes towards company, conversation and sociability a good deal more paradoxical. Much as they genuinely enjoyed sociable companionability, different, and sometimes overlapping, facets of their personalities at times pulled against their clubbable capacities: competitiveness, self-indulgence, depression and world-weariness were all essentially anti-social tendencies that either were in danger of damaging the civilised within society or by their very nature made isolating and self-absorbing demands on each man. In spite of these complexities, both Johnson and Boswell nevertheless retained their appreciation for company, for engaging fully in social activities, and they clearly derived intense personal satisfaction from doing so.

So highly did Johnson regard this facet of human potential that, as is well known, he founded clubs – the Literary Club, instigated with (or strictly by) Sir Joshua Reynolds in 1764, being the best known – for the purpose of enjoying conversation and company – and dining, which they did at the Turk's Head tavern. Boswell was elected to membership in 1773, and thereafter was a frequent attender while in London. His journal for 3 April 1778 gives an extended account of conversation at the club. This is the beginning:

> Then Club. Burke spoke of Scotch mountains not being high. '[I trust] Mr. Boswell [will not] take it amiss.' Said I, 'No objection to your levelling 'em.' Lord Ossery talked of an antique dog in marble, said to be Alcibiades's. Dr. Johnson said his tail must be docked, that was the mark. How he knows small things! BURKE. 'No picture of animal worth much. At this rate, dead dog better than living lion.' JOHNSON. 'Sir, it is not the worth of the thing, but of the skill in forming it. Everything that enlarges human powers, that shows man that he can do what he thought he could not, valuable. First man who balanced straw on nose, Johnson who rode three horses. No use, but skill.' BOSWELL. 'Yet misapplication not to be encouraged. Addison commends king who for reward to man who threw barley corns through needle, gave bushel.' JOHNSON. 'He has been of Scotland, where barley scarce.' (This flat.)[2]

---

[1] On this, see, for example, Valérie Capdeville, '"Clubbability": A Revolution in London Sociability', *Lumen* 35 (2016), 63–80.

[2] James Boswell, *Boswell in Extremes, 1776–1778*, ed. Charles McC. Weis and Frederick A. Pottle (London, 1971), 234–5.

The scene is repeated in polished and worked-up form, thirteen years later, in the *Life of Johnson*:

F. 'I have been looking at this famous antique marble dog of Mr. Jennings, valued at a thousand guineas, said to be Alcibiades's dog.' JOHNSON. 'His tail then must be docked. That was the mark of Alcibiades's dog.' E. 'A thousand guineas! The representation of no animal whatever is worth so much. At this rate a dead dog would indeed be better than a living lion.' JOHNSON. 'Sir, it is not the worth of the thing, but of the skill in forming it which is so highly estimated. Every thing that enlarges the sphere of human powers, that shows man he can do what he thought he could not do, is valuable. The first man who balanced a straw upon his nose; Johnson, who rode three horses at a time; in short all such men deserved the applause of mankind, not on account of the use of what they did, but of the dexterity which they exhibited.' BOSWELL. 'Yet a misapplication of time and assiduity is not to be encouraged. Addison, in one of his *Spectators*, commends the judgement of a King, who, as a suitable reward to a man that by long perseverance had attained to the art of throwing a barley-corn through the eye of a needle, gave him a bushel of barley.' JOHNSON. 'He must have been a King of Scotland, where barley is scarce.' F. 'One of the most remarkable antique figures of an animal is the boar at Florence.' JOHNSON. 'The first boar that is well made in marble should be preserved as a wonder. When men arrive at a facility of making boars well, then the workmanship is no of such value, but they should however be preserved as examples, and as a greater security for the restoration of art, should it be lost.'[3]

Gone is the reference to mountains in Scotland, and gone are the small asides; each participant, apart from Johnson, and Boswell himself, is identified only by a letter, but the truncated form of the journal conversation has become full sentences – in Johnson's case very full, with the familiar Johnsonian cadence of the *Life* in ample evidence. In both accounts the members go on to discuss a still broader mix of subjects – emigration, commodities, Holland, eloquence (and Burke's in particular), the House of Commons, self-interest, place-hunting, the Irish language, Scotland and the Union, taxes on houses, mountains, books of travel, commercial dealings, the honesty of servants and claret.[4] Boswell concludes his journal

---

[3] James Boswell, *The Life of Samuel Johnson, LL.D.*, ed. R. W. Chapman (Oxford, 1980 edition), 900–1.
[4] Boswell, *Life*, 901–6.

entry by declaring that he 'was very happy'. Indeed, so happy and sociable was he that day that he goes on 'to Mrs. Stuart's and had tea tête-à-tête and much intimate conversation'.[5] The volume editors point out that Margaret Stuart, one of Mrs Boswell's closest friends, was 'the object of flirtatious but apparently harmless attention by Boswell',[6] which clearly limits the nature of the 'intimate conversation'. Even then his day of company is not over, for he finally 'Supped Lord Mountstuart, James, Frederick, Elphinstone and Kennedy with him', conceding to his journal as almost the last observation of the day that he 'Was rather too lively.'[7]

The account of the Club, though, pinpoints exactly the qualities of sociability that Johnson and Boswell – and, we assume, their fellow members – prized: the range of topics, the participation of all present, the interspersing of humour and seriousness, the knowledge displayed, the openness to correction, the freedom of flow and direction, and above all the sense of the good nature prevailing between those present. It is hardly a surprise, if this was the general atmosphere of their meetings (and of course we have Boswell's periodic accounts only from 1773), to find Johnson, in writing to his friend and absent member Bennett Langton in March 1766, giving a report of the health of the Club and its attendance:

> However I will tell you, that the Club subsists, but we have less of Burke's company since he has been engaged in publick business ... Dyer is constant at the Club, Hawkins is remiss. I am not over diligent. Dr. Nugent, Dr. Goldsmith and Mr. Reynolds are very constant. Mr. Lye is printing his Saxon and Gothick dictionary‹;› all the club subscribes.[8]

Notwithstanding Johnson's rather dismissive comment about his own dedication to Club attendance, the testimony is to a mutually engaged and supportive community, committed to similar goals and enterprises, in spite of personal differences.

Johnson makes similar points about the conversation proper for general company in writing to Mrs Thrale in July 1775. He had advised her to attend the first London regatta, back in June,[9] and now takes up the event, saying that 'the advantage' of her having attended is that she will

---

[5] Boswell, *Extremes*, 239.
[6] Boswell, *Extremes*, 221, n. 8.
[7] Boswell, *Extremes*, 239.
[8] Samuel Johnson, *The Letters of Samuel Johnson*, ed. Bruce Redford (Oxford, 1992), 5 vols., vol. I: 1731–1772, 264–5.
[9] Johnson, *Letters*, II: 1773–1776, 231, n. 5.

have a subject by which you can gratify general curiosity, and amuse your company without bewildering them. You can keep the vocal machine in motion, without those seeming paradoxes that are sure to disgust; without that temerity of censure which is sure to provoke enemies; and that exuberance of flattery which experience has found to make no friends. It is the good of publick life that it supplies agreeable topicks and general conversation. Therefore wherever you are, and whatever you see, talk not of the Punick war; nor of the depravity of human nature; nor of the slender motives of human actions; nor of the difficulty of finding employment or pleasure ...[10]

While giving a clear idea of what Johnson expected from sociable conversation, and especially, perhaps, from female conversation, the advice is also of interest for what he explicitly rules out – the 'Punick war', yes, but more specifically the 'paradoxes', the 'censure' and the 'flattery', elements that, one would have thought, are more indicative of conversation as a battleground, or at least implicit point-scoring, rather than as something to benefit the general good, as was the case at the Club.

When we look at some of the detail of Johnson's conversational tactics, though, we see particularly clearly the degree of relish which he had for this kind of social intercourse. It is well known that he frequently 'talked for victory'.[11] What is remarkable, though, is the kind of thinking that went into his conversational behaviour. The most obvious example of this is the familiar pattern of Johnson's mode of address – 'Sir, it is not the worth of the thing' – where 'Sir' allows that extra moment of preparation for the mustering of the response and the form of it. We should bear in mind, too, that the 'Sir' mode of address is recorded everywhere in Boswell's journals, written much closer to the event than the *Life*: evidence that this is not later Boswellian polishing, even though some parts of Johnson's reported conversations clearly were made more eloquent in the rewriting, many years on. One particularly revealing moment, though, is recalled in the *Life*, writing of 7 April 1776. The subject of discussion is gaming. Boswell writes:

He would begin thus: 'Why, Sir, as to the good or evil of card-playing—' 'Now (said Garrick,) he is thinking which side he shall take.'[12]

---

[10] Johnson, *Letters*, II, 238–9.
[11] Boswell, *Life*, 421.
[12] Boswell, *Life*, 734.

Johnson, the man of famously fixed principles, solid upholder of duty and Toryism, was in fact quite fluid when it came to conversational strategy. Boswell draws the general lesson:

> The truth ... is, that he loved to display his ingenuity in argument; and therefore would sometimes in conversation maintain opinions which he was sensible were wrong, but in supporting which, his reasoning and wit would be most conspicuous ... He appeared to have a pleasure in contradiction, especially when any opinion whatever was delivered with an air of confidence; so that there was hardly any topick, if not one of the great truths of Religion and Morality, that he might not have been incited to argue, either for or against it.[13]

Johnson, in other words, was capable of coming fully alive in conversation. Talk combined entertainment, display, knowledge and competition. His relish did not even depend entirely upon the composition of the company. This is how he describes to Mrs Thrale, then in Bath, the famous dinner with John Wilkes that Boswell had contrived, and writes up in such triumphant detail in the *Life*:

> For my part, I begin to settle and keep company with grave aldermen. I dined yesterday in the poultry with Mr. Alderman Wilkes, and Mr. Alderman Lee, and Counsellor Lee, his Brother. There sat you the while, so sober, with your Woodwards and your Harringtons and my Aunt and her turnspit. And when they are gone, you think by any chance on Johnson what he is doing? What should he be doing? he is breaking jokes with Jack Wilkes upon the Scots. Such Madam, are the vicissitudes of things.[14]

If Johnson's relish did not depend entirely on the company, a curious stretch of the *Life* makes clear that it did not depend either on the language being spoken, where Johnson could make what appear to be rather odd choices for odd reasons. 'While Johnson was in France', writes Boswell, where he had gone with the Thrales in autumn 1775,

> he was generally very resolute in speaking Latin. It was a maxim with him that a man should not let himself down, by speaking a language which he

---

[13] Boswell, *Life*, 734.
[14] Johnson, *Letters*, II, 331–2.

speaks imperfectly. Indeed, we must have often observed how inferior, how much like a child a man appears, who speaks a broken tongue.[15]

And Boswell adds an illustrative extra or two:

> When Sir Joshua Reynolds, at one of the dinners of the Royal Academy, presented him to a Frenchman of great distinction, he would not deign to speak French, but talked Latin, though his Excellency did not understand it, owing, perhaps, to Johnson's English pronunciation: yet upon another occasion he was observed to speak French to a Frenchman of high rank, who spoke English; and being asked the reason, with some expression of surprise, – he answered, 'because I think my French is as good as his English.'[16]

Clearly, for Johnson, certain forms when in certain companies took priority over actual content: it mattered more to be seen to be speaking with a degree of elegance and propriety than to be properly understood! Yet, in other ways, he was quite unconcerned with, indeed apparently unaware of, his own lack of social appropriateness, as Boswell writes:

> It happened that Foote was at Paris at the same time with Dr. Johnson, and his description of my friend while there, was abundantly ludicrous. He told me, that the French were quite astonished at his figure and manner, and at his dress, which he obstinately continued exactly as in London; – his brown clothes, black stocking, and plain shirt.[17]

Socially variable

Boswell's own pleasure in company was more varied than Johnson's, not least because, in the normal course of his life, he kept more varied company, or at least mixed with a broader social range in a wider variety of places up and down the country. He takes pleasure in a formal but small dinner after church at the Lord Commissioner's (George Ramsay, the eighth Earl of Dalhousie, the Lord High Commissioner to the General Assembly of the Church of Scotland) in Edinburgh on Sunday 4 June 1780:

---

[15] Boswell, *Life*, 659.
[16] Boswell, *Life*, 659–60.
[17] Boswell, *Life*, 659.

> I dined with the Lord Commissioner, who has all along shown me an attention which I felt with pleasing gratitude ... I was for the first time in company with General Mackay, with whom I had a good deal of conversation: upon the merit of his regiment, the Scotch Fusiliers; the advantage of having a good chaplain to attend a regiment; and the pleasure of drinking a little brandy. We agreed very well.[18]

Again, the sociability of the day continues, and it concludes quietly but well:

> I went home after dinner. Miss Susie Dunlop and the Hon. Patrick Boyle drank tea with us, after which he and I paid a visit to my father. In the evening the children said divine lessons.[19]

Everything here scores in the Boswell scale of things that matter: a framework of Sunday religious observance (but not too tight a framework), the attention of the powerful and important, military achievement and propriety, alcohol (but only talked about), and, afterwards, family duties and orderliness.

Less orderly, Boswell also clearly relished an occasion, the showier the better, and not least if he was able to play a prominent part in it. In London in June 1785 he made one of a company dining as guests of the Lord Mayor. The journal entry is understatedly brief: 'THURSDAY 2 JUNE. Dined at Lord Mayor's and rung gong in Egyptian Hall. Quite my early ideas of City of London. Sat by Mrs. ——, pleasing creature. Much singing. Wilkes.'[20] That this is deceptive is made clear by a paragraph that appeared in the *St James's Chronicle* for 11–14 June, 'obviously written', as his editors point out, 'by Boswell himself':

> The Lord Mayor, some days ago, had an agreeable party of musical friends to dine at the Mansion House. Mr. Boswell was of the company; and rung in the magnificent Egyptian Hall an instrument which his Lordship and all his guests but one had never heard before. This was a Chinese gong, or vibrating bell, which, when struck with a kind of baton ... produces a very noble sound, louder than the great bell of St. Paul's but

---

[18] Boswell, *Extremes*, 220.
[19] Boswell, *Extremes*, 220.
[20] James Boswell, *Boswell: The Applause of the Jury, 1782–1785*, ed. Irma S. Lustig and Frederick A. Pottle (London, 1981), 306.

more melodious. Mr. Boswell's gong is one of the largest and best that ever was brought to England.[21]

He even composed an 'Ode on Mr. Boswell's Gong', published in the *Edinburgh Magazine* in July.

> Wonder of Wonders! what is this
> Mankind applaud? You cannot miss.
> Of *Boswell* now shall be my song.
> Nay, Greater still! of *Boswell's Gong.*
> *Boswell*, who's happy if he can contrive
> To see thieves hang'd, and keep the Lords alive.[22]

Boswell, no doubt, had also participated fully in the 'Much singing', as he did on other similar occasions, and the fact that his friend and one-time drinking companion John Wilkes was also there allows a probably accurate filling-in of the bare details from the journal. What is also typical of Boswell, though, is his shameless capitalising on the occasion through published self-promotion afterwards.

Alcohol, frequently, was prominent in Boswell's companionable activities, and often for the worse – as he was himself capable of acknowledging. One sequence of events, from 1777, provides a good example. On Wednesday 19 March he dines in the small town of Newmilns with his friend Bruce Campbell of Mayfield and Milrig:

> We waited dinner till after seven, and I am ashamed to mention that at my instigation we drank too much brandy punch, so that I was intoxicated, and fell from or rolled off my horse on the road back to Milrigs. I had felt a comfortable love of liquor, and just sat on; and I was conscious I uttered nothing improper. But what a gross debauch was this.[23]

On 24 March, in Kilmarnock, he dines at his friend Mitchell's house, and 'after dinner had some of my clients of the Town Council to drink port with me'.[24] But the next day, on his way back to Edinburgh (he has been travelling from the family seat at Auchinleck), with Colonel Richard Montgomery we find:

---

[21] Boswell, *Boswell: The Applause of the Jury*, 306, n. 6.
[22] James Boswell, *Ode on Mr. Boswell's Gong*, in *The Edinburgh Magazine or Literary Miscellany* (Edinburgh, July 1785), Volume II, 181.
[23] Boswell, *Extremes*, 96.
[24] Boswell, *Extremes*, 101.

> Montgomery and I drank outrageously at Whitburn and at Livingstone and at some low ale-house, and arrived at Edinburgh very drunk. It was shocking in me to come home to my dear wife in such a state.[25]

Certainly, we hear nothing of the conversation, or even of the company, on such occasions. It is merely that Boswell drinks, and seems to prefer a social setting in which to do so. More standard, for Boswell in Edinburgh, is the evening of 27 December 1780 which he spends at the house of Robert Cullen, son of the famous doctor and the future Lord Cullen. After 'a very good chat by ourselves for half an hour' they are joined by 'Counsellor Charles Dundas and his friend Counsellor Steele, an Englishman' for whist, and then, when Lord Maitland drops by, for brag. Boswell's fellow advocate, John Maclaurin, the later Lord Dreghorn, then arrives and watches the game. 'We had', reports Boswell, 'a very good comfortable supper ... I drank some glasses of wine.' Maclaurin tells the company of the difference that had taken place that day between Boswell and the Solicitor-General, Alexander Murray (in fact they had come close to fighting a duel), upon which the company to a man sides with Boswell. He concludes his account of the evening by observing: 'Our conversation was neither brilliant nor learned, but did very well at the time.'[26] This is what one is content to settle for: not every company can have the benefit of a Johnson – or a Burke, or a Wilkes. Boswell is happy to make do, and it serves its purpose.

Social fragility

What Boswell adds at the end, though, of the account of the evening at Cullen's is more telling:

> I was in better spirits than I had been for many days. I saw the intercourse of social life with some degree of satisfaction, though life be uncertain and indeed, to an expanding imagination, very short.[27]

Only a few days earlier, at some time between Friday 15th and 27th (the journal pages have been removed) Boswell had written his *Hypochondriack* paper, the thirty-ninth of the series, on the subject of hypochondria:

---

[25] Boswell, *Extremes*, 102.
[26] James Boswell, *Boswell Laird of Auchinleck, 1778–1782*, ed. Joseph W. Reed and Frederick Pottle (Edinburgh, 1993), 280.
[27] Boswell, *Boswell Laird of Auchinleck*, 280.

Could the Hypochondriack see anything great or good or agreeable in the situation of others, he might by sympathy partake of their enjoyment. But his corrosive imagination destroys to his own view all that he contemplates. All that is illustrious in publick life, all that is amiable and endearing in society, all that is elegant in science and in arts, affect him just with the same indifference, and even contempt, as the pursuits of children affect rational men ... Finding that his reason is not able to cope with his gloomy imagination, he doubts that he may have been under a delusion when it was cheerful; so that he does not even wish to be happy as formerly, since he cannot wish for what he apprehends is fallacious.[28]

Usually it is looking foolish that upsets Boswell during or after a spell in company – something that certainly was more likely with him the more that he drank. It is also something that was a hazard of spending time with Johnson. In fact, one of the major hurts of their relationship arose from Johnson's treatment of him on one particular social occasion. When Johnson remarks of an evening's conversation in the summer of 1768 that 'we had good talk', Boswell, famously, rejoins: 'Yes, Sir, you tossed and gored several persons.'[29] The problem was that it was quite often Boswell himself who was 'tossed and gored', leading, in the *Life*, to Boswell's frequent adoption of the 'a gentleman who was present' formula to hide the fact that it was he who had said a foolish thing and was suitably 'tossed' for it. The evening of Saturday 2 May, however, dining at Sir Joshua Reynolds's, was exceptional, not least because 'there were several people there by no means of the Johnsonian school'. As Boswell records in the *Life*:

> upon some imaginary offence from me, he attacked me with such rudeness, that I was vexed and angry, because it gave those persons an opportunity of enlarging upon his supposed ferocity, and ill treatment of his best friends.[30]

The journal record for the event, and even the surrounding days, is missing,[31] so we have no way of knowing exactly how the conversation developed, how Boswell came to feel so badly treated and what the company made of it. But so badly let down did he feel that, as he continues,

---

[28] James Boswell, *Boswell's Column, 1777–1783*, ed. Margery Bailey (London, 1951), 209–10.
[29] Boswell, *Life*, 400.
[30] Boswell, *Life*, 983.
[31] See Boswell, *Extremes*, 328 and n.

'I was so much hurt, and had my pride so much roused, that I kept away from him for a week; and, perhaps, might have ... gone to Scotland without seeing him again, had we not fortunately met and been reconciled.'[32]

Whether Boswell was saying foolish things or not (Johnson, during their reconciliation meeting, suggests that he had 'interrupted him, which I assured him was not the case'[33]), he clearly regards the offence as unwarranted, and his journal silence may well have to do with an onset of the kind of 'indifference, and even contempt' for 'all that is amiable and endearing in society' of which he was to write two years later as the *Hypochondriack* – indeed, any original journal record might well have been destroyed by his own hand with displeasure at the recollection of such a distressing episode. Had he done so, that would have been a major event: Boswell himself almost never destroyed any parts of his journal. As he puts it in his *Hypochondriack* paper on diaries in March 1783, when he found that his Dutch journal had been lost, he 'felt as if a part of my vitals had been separated from me,'[34] and this in spite of the extreme depression which he suffered during much of his time in Holland. To destroy his journal would be like giving up – like acknowledging that nothing mattered after all. It would have meant giving entry to the hypochondriack vision itself.

The social fabric clearly is fragile, and for the self-confessed hypochondriack the dangers of seeing through its pretences, or what can be taken as pretences, are real and far reaching – far reaching enough to drive Boswell, at times, from what he most cherishes, the company of Johnson, or to encourage him in the spiral of deep drinking, of the intensification of social disillusion and of deeper drinking to hide that harsh truth, or assumed truth.

Johnson's case was somewhat different, not least because of his abstinence for much of his life from alcoholic drink – maybe for the very reasons that Boswell indulged in it. We have far less private detail of Johnson's out-of-company self than of Boswell's, but his private attitudes can be gathered from some of his writing, and not least from *Rasselas*. Early in his quest for the 'choice of life', Rasselas, in Cairo, seeks out company and enjoys being part of 'gayety and kindness', 'the song of joy, or the laugh of carelessness.'[35] Before long, however, he begins to doubt, as he explains to Imlac:

---

[32] Boswell, *Life*, 983.
[33] Boswell, *Life*, 983.
[34] Boswell, *Boswell's Column*, 334.
[35] Samuel Johnson, *The History of Rasselas, Prince of Abissinia*, ed. J. P. Hardy (Oxford, 1999), 43.

> I know not, said the prince, what can be the reason that I am more unhappy than any of our friends. I see them perpetually and unalterably cheerful, but feel my own mind restless and uneasy. I am unsatisfied with those pleasures which I seem most to court; I live in the crowds of jollity, not so much to enjoy company as to shun myself, and am only loud and merry to conceal my sadness.[36]

Imlac sagely replies (as he would):

> Every man ... may, by examining his own mind, guess what passes in the minds of others: when you feel that your own gaiety is counterfeit, it may justly lead you to suspect that of your companions not to be sincere. Envy is commonly reciprocal. We are long before we are convinced that happiness is never to be found, and each believes it possessed by others, to keep alive the hope of obtaining it for himself.[37]

The dreadful truth, for Imlac, and, we may justly conclude, for Johnson, is clear:

> In the assembly, where you passed the last night, there appeared such spriteliness of air, and volatility of fancy, as might have suited beings of a higher order, formed to inhabit serener regions inaccessible to care or sorrow: yet, believe me, prince, there was not one who did not dread the moment when solitude should deliver him to the tyranny of reflection.[38]

Johnson was a widower of seven years at this time, 1759, and the recent death of his mother had obliged him to raise money for her funeral, as well as depriving him of his only surviving parent. One might well expect a negative cast to his thoughts. But more generally, it is widely accepted that Johnson did indeed see the advantages – and the shortcomings – of company in this way. As Glenn J. Broadhead put it back in 1980, 'On a personal level ... it is clear that the intensely troubled Johnson sought companionable chat to divert his mind from self-recriminations, doubts, and madness.'[39] Johnson was able to see the chasm of self-reflection beneath the surface of sociable gaiety because he had experienced it himself.

---

[36] Johnson, *The History of Rasselas*, 43.
[37] Johnson, *The History of Rasselas*, 43.
[38] Johnson, *The History of Rasselas*, 43.
[39] Glenn J. Broadhead, 'Samuel Johnson and the Rhetoric of Conversation', in *Studies in English Literature, 1500–1900* 20, no. 3 (Summer, 1980), 461–74, 461.

But Johnson's view of company, of conversation, of social intercourse, is not uncomplicated, any more than Boswell's is. Boswell genuinely loved to be in company, with or without the assistance of alcohol, and in spite of the dangers of self-exposure, of mockery, of being made to look foolish, and in spite, too, of the risks these things brought of becoming for a while disillusioned with the whole business of getting on with mankind. There are major differences where Johnson is concerned: he was certainly not going to be mocked, and no one in company with him ever seems to have succeeded in making him look foolish, in spite of his oddities of body and manners. Johnson might, with Rasselas and Imlac, have had a lively awareness of dread in the face of solitude, and therefore of the need to occupy the attention with company, be it the oddballs he lived with or the intellectuals he clubbed with. He similarly occupied his mind with writing, with reading, with Cocker's arithmetic. But none of these things were simply stand-ins, emergency aids to put off the dread of being alone and obliged to think. He genuinely liked his oddballs, his reading was the lifeblood of his existence and he adored company and what it brought out in human nature. G. F. Parker, in *Johnson's Shakespeare*, writes of the enjoyment Johnson expressed in Falstaff: it is because Falstaff makes us feel part of wider human nature – he connects us with our kind. As Parker puts it:

> What is it like to become aware of nature, to feel oneself to be a species rather than an individual? Part of the answer is that the boundaries of the self seem less absolute: the sense of self is relaxed, the opposition between all that one is and all that one is not becomes less imperious: one finds oneself less a spectator of and more a participant in a life larger than one's own.[40]

This, I contend, is what Johnson found in company: the chance to be supremely himself while experiencing not his own uniqueness, either for intellectual or for conversational superiority, but his connectedness with his own kind.

---

[40] G. F. Parker, *Johnson's Shakespeare* (Oxford, 1989), 46.

Chapter 11
Friendship and unsociable sociability in eighteenth-century literature
Emrys Jones

WHEN COINING the term 'unsociable sociability' in his 'Idea for a Universal History with a Cosmopolitan Aim' (1784), Immanuel Kant was working within a long philosophical tradition that identified human society as a site of conflicting sociable and moral impulses.[1] To recognise resistance to sociability as a necessary quality of sociability itself was in one sense to align oneself with a strand of social thinking that emphasised the positive outcomes of apparently evil inclinations in human nature. Such an outlook had been epitomised in Britain earlier in the eighteenth century by the works of Bernard Mandeville; Kant's insistence on the value of competition for social development likewise had much in common with Adam Smith's analysis in *The Wealth of Nations* (1776).[2] However, in describing the paradox of humanity's sociability – its 'propensity to enter into society ... combined with a thoroughgoing resistance that constantly threatens to break up this society'[3] – Kant also needed to allow for the weight of genuine altruism and virtuous instinct as a counterbalance to self-interest, and in this he was just as much an heir to the optimism of the likes of the third Earl of Shaftesbury and Frances Hutcheson.[4] The intellectual basis for the idea of 'unsociable sociability' was thus variegated and contradictory, in keeping with the tensions inherent in the idea. The aim of this chapter is not to trace the tortuous etiology of Kant's concept through centuries of social philosophy, but instead to demonstrate its applicability to a trope of

---

[1] This chapter uses the phrase as translated by Allen W. Wood in the Cambridge edition of the Works of Immanuel Kant in Translation. See Kant, *Anthropology, History, and Education*, ed. Günter Zöller and Robert B. Louden (Cambridge, 2007), 107–20.
[2] For an account of sociable philosophy prior to Kant and an attempt to set Kant's thinking in this context, see J. B. Schneewind, *Essays on the History of Moral Philosophy* (Oxford, 2009), 320–40.
[3] Kant, *Anthropology*, 111.
[4] Schneewind, *Essays*, 327–8.

political writing that held particular sway in Britain of the 1730s and 1740s: the figure of the friendly enemy. I will argue through an examination of this figure's various guises and its relevance for the Patriot opposition[5] both that it enacts the dramas of social resistance that would so fascinate Kant, and that it operates in itself as a manifestation of those dramas, a recurring point of conflict between the author's will to engage with the world and an unsocial desire for consensus and compliance. By exploring how these opposing impulses are presented and managed within texts of the time, one can gain a new appreciation of the long-standing currency of Kant's assumptions, as well as a more specific understanding of how this political movement navigated issues of sociability, dissension and individual resolve. Viewed in a broader context, the popularity of the friendly enemy also illuminates the distinctive British mode of sociability – its paradoxes, and its relationship to pre-existing French models – with which this collection as a whole is engaged. This is not to say that all eighteenth-century Britons were diligently attempting to act the part of friendly enemies in their everyday lives, but that such characters enacted in the political arena the same quandaries of sociable autonomy, reliability and indebtedness that shaped attitudes and custom more widely.

I define the friendly enemy as a character who overcomes military or ideological difference to testify to the goodness of his opponent and even to seek personal friendship with him.[6] I use male pronouns here, because the figure of the friendly enemy as I am concerned with it is specifically masculine, bound up in centuries of chivalric tradition. It is rooted in a

---

[5] The political movement that arose around Frederick, Prince of Wales in the 1730s and 1740s was fraught with inherent tensions concerning the legitimacy of parliamentary opposition, the value of chivalric codes of honour for eighteenth-century courtly life and the nature of princely friendship itself.

[6] My usage of the term 'friendly enemy' is thus distinguished from the modern concept of the 'frenemy', which the *Oxford English Dictionary* defines as someone 'with whom one is friendly despite a fundamental dislike or rivalry' or more generally as 'a person who combines the characteristics of a friend and an enemy'. See 'frenemy, n.' *OED Online*. June 2017. (accessed July 2017). Although in some cases the friendly enemies discussed in this chapter may fit such descriptions, it is important to note that 'dislike' has no bearing on these relationships, as will become apparent as the chapter continues. As far as I am aware, there has been no scholarly work focusing specifically on this character type before now, although it has some resemblance to the 'intimate enemy' described in Tom MacFaul, *Male Friendship in Shakespeare and his Contemporaries* (Cambridge, 2007), 21. I also discuss the phenomenon in a different eighteenth-century context in 'Sir John Hill and Friendship', in *Fame and Fortune: Sir John Hill and London Life in the 1750s*, ed. Clare Brant and George Rousseau (Basingstoke, 2018).

medieval understanding of knightly qualities that included generosity and courtesy – qualities which had long led exponents of chivalric culture to focus on the honourable reconciliation of apparently stubborn antagonists.[7] Indeed, one of the most notable texts in the formalisation of chivalric norms, the anonymously authored *Ordene de chevalerie*, concerned itself with a probably apocryphal encounter between Hugh, Count of Tiberias and his friendly captor, the Sultan Saladin.[8] The poem has chiefly interested scholars of medieval history for its description of chivalric ordination ceremonies, but the context is just as telling, the sultan granting Hugh his freedom in exchange for knowledge of knightly standards and in recognition of his valour.[9] The ritual that Hugh enacts, with the sultan in the position of knighted subject, is certainly of questionable validity, given Saladin's religious faith, yet it cements as a core, often unarticulated tenet of chivalry the capacity to rise above worldly conflict and to extend courtesy even to one's avowed foes. This is therefore a tradition distinct from related tropes such as the love affair between a knight and his enemy's daughter, although tropes of that sort likewise appear with great regularity in the political literature of eighteenth-century Britain.

In spite of its noble origins, the literary heritage of the friendly enemy is as ambivalent as it is extensive, straddling the heroic and the absurd. Inherent in the figure is a constant tension between two of the most crucial knightly principles, courtesy and loyalty, the need to do justice to one's enemy precariously balanced against the need to remain faithful to one's own king or family or political faction.[10] By the middle of the eighteenth century, an awareness of this tension had led the character type to be at least partially discredited and subject to increased suspicion. Associated

---

[7] In his seminal study of chivalry as both historical and imaginative phenomenon, Maurice Keen lists the key qualities of the knight as '*prouesse, loyauté, largesse* [...], *courtoisie*, and *franchise*', the last of these referring to a 'free and frank bearing.' See Maurice Keen, *Chivalry* (New Haven, CT, 1984), 2. More recently, Nigel Saul has commented on chivalry's 'range of pacific values which limited aggression and rendered it compatible with civil society', for which see Nigel Saul, *For Honour and Fame: Chivalry in England, 1066–1500* (London, 2011), 196.

[8] The text, thought to have been written in the early thirteenth century, is available in translation in *Le Roman de Eles and L'Ordene de Chevalerie*, ed. and trans. Keith Busby (Amsterdam, 1983).

[9] The historical significance of the text is highlighted in Keen, *Chivalry*, 6–8. Detailed discussion of other scholarly approaches is provided in Max Lieberman, 'A New Approach to the Knighting Ritual', *Speculum* 90, no. 2 (2015), 391–423.

[10] Both courtesy and loyalty could also end up in tension with the need to prove prowess. See Eugene M. Waith, *Ideas of Greatness: Heroic Drama in England* (London, 1971), 10.

with French romances of the previous century, the friendly enemy could be seen to pose a threat to the efficient prosecution of military and political activity, and to contaminate masculine prerogatives of warfare with a strain of sentiment and whimsy. Characters like Artaban in La Calprenède's *Cléopâtre* (1647–56), although paraded as exempla of valiant disinterest, had from another perspective undermined their moral integrity through their very inclination to see the goodness in their enemies and to shift allegiance upon doing so.[11] The hero of Madeleine de Scudery's *Artamène* (1649–53), blessed with the convenient ability to charm bloodthirsty foes, had nonetheless earned the derision of contemporary readers such as Boileau for his willingness, in the words of one twentieth-century critic, 'to put his country to the torch'.[12] Arabella, the heroine of Charlotte Lennox's 1752 novel, *The Female Quixote* – and a devoted reader of works by both La Calprenède and de Scudéry – cannot help but expose the ridiculousness of such friendly enemies even as she attempts to praise them:

> [T]here is nothing extraordinary in fighting for one's Father, and one's Country; but when a Man has arrived to such a Pitch of Greatness of Soul, as to neglect those mean and selfish Considerations, and, loving Virtue in the Persons of his Enemies, can prefer their Glory before his own particular Interest, he is then a perfect Hero indeed.[13]

As so often in Lennox's novel, Arabella's formulation of perfect heroism is a recipe for self-destruction. In straining towards a higher 'Pitch of Greatness', it also tends towards the extinction of more fundamental virtues. The hero for whom love of country and love of family are all too commonplace motivations must ultimately prove a traitor in his love and respect for a foe. Moreover, Arabella's paradoxical association of these motivations with meanness and self-interest points us towards the relevance of the friendly enemy as epitome – but also nemesis – of the Kantian social model. Kant would later write that unsociable sociability arises from the individual's

---

[11] See the rebuke which Artaban receives from his sometime ally King Tigranes as it becomes clear that their interests are about to part ways: 'Ah, *Artaban, said he, turning his Head aside*, how little Care you keep to please your Friends!' This translation, by Robert Loveday, is taken from an eight-volume English edition first published 1652–59 and reprinted in the 1730s at the same time that the Patriot movement was gaining momentum. Robert Loveday, *Hymen's Praeludia: Or Love's Master-Piece: Being that So-Much-Admir'd Romance, intitled Cleopatra* (London, 1736), II, 295.

[12] Nicole Aronson, *Mademoiselle de Scudéry* (Boston, 1978), 70–1.

[13] [Charlotte Lennox], *The Female Quixote; or, The Adventures of Arabella* (London, 1752), II, 82.

anticipation of resistance in others. This is an anticipation derived from his own awareness of a similar resistance in himself, 'the unsociable property of willing to direct everything so as to get his own way.'[14] Arabella's nonsensical construction of heroic behaviour is an inversion of this carefully ordered state, with a dangerous lack of inner resistance leading the friendly enemy to an uncivilised rootlessness, a truer unsociability than that tempered by self-interest. Ironically, then, she might be half-correct to describe one's Father and one's country as 'mean and selfish Considerations', but it is selfishness of these respectable varieties that makes it possible for heroism or social allegiance to have any meaning whatsoever.

Pushed to its limit and reduced to absurdity, friendly enmity could thus expose the limits beyond which unsociable sociability ceases to be profitable for society as a whole. Yet the figure was still being deployed sincerely, as a genuine emblem of public spirit and as a spokesman for universal virtues, in British political literature throughout the eighteenth century. Although writers were generally aware of and sensitive to the figure's potential for absurdity, it was hard to ignore the appeal of such characters as propagandistic tools. For the Patriot opposition of the 1730s and 1740s, the friendly enemy offered a particularly attractive channel for political argument. As they constructed ideal representations of their Patriot prince – analogues to oppositional figurehead Frederick, Prince of Wales – they could assert his decency and his ability to transcend partisan disputes through the testament of erstwhile foes who had been dazzled by his integrity.[15] In so doing, they asserted Frederick's independence. It was a vital and contentious quality, given how his father had disappointed the opposition forces of the 1720s by retaining Sir Robert Walpole's services on coming to power. The prince's independence was likewise a point of anxiety when one considered his very obvious financial dependence on the king and Parliament, or, when his allowance was withheld or limited beyond tolerance, his recourse to the generosity of wealthy political allies.[16] It was logical that a prince so vul-

---

[14] Kant, *Anthropology*, 111.
[15] The authoritative account of the rise of the Patriot movement and the typical features of its literary discourse can be found in Christine Gerrard, *The Patriot Opposition to Walpole* (Oxford, 1994).
[16] One twentieth-century biographer of Frederick notes that he 'loved money, not, like his father, for the pleasure of hoarding it, but for the pleasure of scattering it'. See Avery Edwards, *Frederick Louis, Prince of Wales* (London, 1947), 29. In spite of this, or because of it, Frederick's attempts to secure a more generous allowance from the civil list were blocked by his father and by Walpole and became a key issue of political debate in the late 1730s. See Frances Vivian, *A Life of Frederick, Prince of Wales, 1707–1751*, ed. Roger White (Lewiston, 2006), 238–48; also A. N. Newman,

nerable to accusations of neediness on the one hand and partiality on the other should benefit from representations which emphasised disinterested approbation of his talents. However, even here, as the following discussion will show, there was room for anxiety and awkwardness in the approach his supporters adopted. If used too imprecisely, the testimony of a friendly enemy could confirm not the hero's independence but his gullibility or, worse, his traitorous tendencies. While encounters with friendly enemies could provide opportunities for the Patriot prince to demonstrate his own magnanimity, they could also render obvious the imbalances of power that make a mockery of claims to princely friendship.[17] Furthermore, at a time when much of the opposition press was clamouring for war against Spain, the figure of a conciliating and forgiving prince could become just as counter-productive in a political sense as Lennox's friendly enemy was in a social and moral one.[18]

The friendly enemy as prisoner

As in the story of Hugh and Saladin, the friendly enemies of literature are often bred in captivity. After the battle has been won, the combatants meet, converse and finally gain the opportunity to prove themselves as more than mere warriors or military strategists. This scenario recurs with great frequency in Patriot literature from the mid-1730s onwards. At a time when, according to the prevailing critical narrative, the heroic mode was being undermined and abandoned across British literature and theatre, writers aligned to the Patriot cause often seemed to resist this trend.[19] In keeping with Frederick's general appeal to pre-Hanoverian – or even Jacobite – instincts for monarchical romance,[20] many of the literary works that were conceived in his honour were characterised by a fundamentally earnest and

---

'Communication: The Political Patronage of Frederick Lewis, Prince of Wales,' *Historical Journal* 1, no. 1 (1958), 68–75 (70–1).

[17] I have written about the philosophical tradition wherein friendship with princes or kings is held to be impossible, likewise in relation to Frederick, in Emrys D. Jones, *Friendship and Allegiance in Eighteenth-Century Literature: The Politics of Private Virtue in the Age of Walpole* (Basingstoke, 2013), 92.

[18] For discussion of the opposition's growing frustration with Walpole's pacific policy towards Spain, which would eventually necessitate the War of Jenkins' Ear (1739–48), see Gerrard, *Patriot Opposition*, 6–7, 156.

[19] For the rise of the anti-heroic in Hanoverian Britain, see Elaine McGirr, *Heroic Mode and Political Crisis, 1660–1745* (Newark, 2009), 24, 132–3.

[20] Gerrard, *Patriot Opposition*, 194–5.

un-ironic nostalgia for the heroic types of the previous century. While the Patriot prince of the stage and the page tended to share the politeness and public-spiritedness that typified his contemporaries, he also inherited the classic accoutrements of the heroic genre: a tussle, embedded in narrative, between acts of 'usurpation and restoration'; and, most significantly, a view of history dominated by 'expressions of comforting fantasy'.[21] It is in light of this curiously backwards-looking literary temperament that we must come to terms with the Patriot movement's use of friendly enemies, its approach to the problematic subject matter of imprisonment and the modes of confident pageantry or solemn contemplation that could be used to make unsociable sociability politically useful.

Gilbert West's 1742 work, *The Institution of the Order of the Garter*, is a masque-like 'Dramatick Poem', apparently never performed in its original state although adapted for the stage by David Garrick several decades later.[22] Like many Patriot works, it celebrates Frederick in the guise of a historical figure: here the Black Prince, son of Edward III. In an author's note accompanying the text, West explicitly states that he has toyed with the chronology of the historical events he describes, so that the founding of the chivalric order of the Garter can coincide with the presence of King John of France, who was famously captured by the Black Prince and who, as the text's clearest representation of a friendly enemy, also provides its only moments of drama and conflict.[23] The poem demonstrates effectively the dual propagandistic benefits of the friendly enemy trope. King Edward III and the Black Prince can be shown treating their prisoner with 'all the Regard due to the Quality and Virtue of so great a Prince', proving their own disinterested virtue in the process.[24] In his turn, King John is far from a reluctant or grudging witness to the train of candidates who are then considered for first membership of the order. He ends up playing a pivotal role in the decision to grant this honour to the Black Prince himself. When the latter, perhaps taking chivalric courtesy too far, petitions his father to

---

[21] McGirr, *Heroic Mode and Political Crisis*, 15, 18. In her description of the heroic mode, McGirr is herself indebted to Nancy Klein MacGuire, *Regicide and Restoration: English Tragicomedy, 1660–1681* (Cambridge, 1992).

[22] Gilbert West, *The Institution of the Order of the Garter* (London, 1742). Garrick's rewriting was necessary because the work was in his words 'impossible to bring ... on the Stage as it was originally written'. See David Garrick, *The Songs, Choruses, and Serious Dialogue of the Masque called The Institution of the Garter* (London, 1771), [v].

[23] It is perhaps ironic, then, that Garrick's supposedly more dramatically acceptable version of the play removes King John entirely.

[24] West, *Institution*, [4].

appoint King John as the order's first member, the friendly enemy returns the favour, pleading for the King of England to appoint instead his 'conquering Son'.[25] This is a course of action that has already been urged and foretold by the 'Genius' of Britain that presides over events; it is a decision which can be enacted only by Edward III himself, his subsequent praise and embrace for his son offering an obvious contrast with the notoriously strained relations between George II and Frederick. King John's words lack such ceremonial or metaphorical power, and his acknowledgement of the prince's virtue seems all the more significant, more ingenuous, because it is disconnected from the chivalric rituals that shape the rest of the text.

Nevertheless, King John's approbation of his conqueror is not free from awkwardness, and the very powerlessness that lends his words weight is also responsible for exposing problems inherent in friendly enmity as a concept. In refusing the honour of the garter, John focuses the reader upon the limitations of the Patriot prince's power, and by extension the dangers that arise when there is too much or too little resistance on either side of an unsociably sociable friendship:

> Oh generous Youth! in vain thy Goodness strives
> To raise thy Captive thus above his Fortune.
> The King that is not free, is not a King;
> Nor can thy bounteous Favour reconcile
> Honour and Bondage.[26]

The tendency of these lines is to undermine the testimony of the friendly enemy altogether. If the fact of his captivity cannot be ignored for the sake of chivalric honour, and if honour itself has truly been stripped from him in the way he implies, then what value can his praise or his friendship retain? The speech introduces the uncomfortable possibility that the Patriot prince is either a hypocrite or incorrigibly naïve. His plea on behalf of his enemy might be seen as hollow, a superficial tribute scarcely detracting from the reality of the 'chains' that King John will mention a few lines later. But if the Black Prince truly has not seen or has thought trivial the contradiction involved in attempting to honour his prisoner, this is a yet more serious indictment of Patriot idealism. Without the natural resistance, founded on self-interest, that should direct human sociable endeavours, the prince must rely instead on the common sense and generosity of his enemies. His own 'Goodness' is not sufficient to protect his interests or to guard against faults of logic, as John expressly indicates. The Patriot prince is shown to

---

[25] West, *Institution*, 57.
[26] West, *Institution*, 56–7.

be vulnerable, not because of his pursuit of unsociable sociability, but precisely because he is not always unsociable enough.

Such anxieties are also apparent in an earlier portrayal of the captive friendly enemy. The 1736 prose play *The Patriot*, attributed to John Baillie, has at its heart a triptych of enemy soldiers who have been taken prisoner. The play encourages a certain amount of debate as to whether these figures can be relied upon to further the Patriot project. However, the villain of the piece is ultimately their mirror image, a hardened enemy masquerading as an ally. It should be noted when examining this play that its relationship to the Patriot movement was not necessarily straightforward. Its more immediate function was as an intervention in Dutch politics; through retelling the story of his ancestor, the first William of Orange, it celebrates the current Prince of Orange and recommends him to his people. However, at the same time, the play clearly responds to and incorporates the oppositional discourse that was building up around Frederick in Britain. It foregrounds patriotism in its title. Its prologue eagerly twins Frederick with his Dutch brother-in-law, to the extent that they are described together as 'the Darlings of Mankind, / The Props of Truth and Liberty design'd!'[27] The two exempla of Patriot princeliness offered by the play – William of Orange and his son, Prince Frederick-Maurice – therefore have significance in a British context as well as a Dutch one. As in West's garter poem, their harmonious relationship accentuates by contrast the scandal of Hanoverian disunity. And in certain passages of righteous diatribe the message for Sir Robert Walpole's Britain is impossible to ignore. When rejecting the prospect of absolute power, William lingers on the hypothetical scenario of a future court hijacked by 'a cunning Minister' and 'his Creatures'.[28]

The opening of the play finds its first and most significant friendly enemy in soliloquy. The Duke de Medina Sidonia, William's Spanish prisoner, describes his affection for Augusta, the beloved of Frederick-Maurice.[29] He then receives a gracious letter from his captor; it prompts him to praise the Prince of Orange at length, in terms which parallel his infatuation with the Dutch noblewoman:

---

[27] [John Baillie], *The Patriot: Being a Dramatick History of the Life and Death of William the First Prince of Orange ...* (London, 1736), [vi].

[28] *The Patriot*, 39.

[29] Here also the play's relevance to British politics is apparent. The naming of Augusta seems to owe less to any historical precedent in the life of Prince Maurice – who never married – and more to Prince Frederick's marriage in the year of the play's publication to Princess Augusta of Saxe-Gotha.

And when I, who am his Enemy, view him in such a light, how can [...] he miss of being ador'd by all his Countrymen, for whose Happiness each Moment of his Life is spent? Oh! what a pain it is to be laid under such Obligations as I am to his Goodness, when I can scarce have any Prospect to repay them? My Honour and my Duty oblige me to serve my Sovereign, but the Prince, whose Prisoner I am, has stole away my Heart.[30]

Similar to West's King John, the duke is in a position of conflict. Honour again appears incompatible with a true acknowledgement of the Patriot prince's virtues. There is tacit corroboration of this and, by extension, of the frailty of friendly enmity itself, in the duke's eventual fate. His suicide is largely explained as his response to romantic disappointment, an acknowledgement that the better man has won the hand of Augusta and that he has nothing more to live for. Yet his death in the fifth act also coincides with his efforts to save the life of his beneficent captor; before he dies he warns Frederick-Maurice that there will be an attempt upon William's life, arranged by the Catholic church. This is, in the end, a futile warning. The duke provides precious little detailed information and William is assassinated, as was the historical prince, by infiltrator Balthasar Gérard. However, it seems fitting that the moment of the duke's commitment to the prince's friendship should be immediately followed by his demise. The Princess of Orange gives credence to his warning because he is a 'Man of Honour' and has 'professed himself [William's] Friend'.[31] But the friendship of this enemy is shown to be unsustainable as well as ineffectual; it involves a constant degradation of the duke's competing allegiance to Spain, one claim of honour effectively cancelling out another.

Lest one assume the figure of the duke to be an isolated, solitary presence in the play, the Patriot princes themselves draw our attention to the importance of friendly enmity throughout the work. Interestingly anticipating Gilbert West's text, the play presents Frederick-Maurice as an admirer of the Black Prince, and specifically of the latter's treatment of King John of France. His recounting of the historical anecdote at the start of Act Five is given a great deal of attention. According to his version of events, 'the King did own [the Prince] had conquer'd him more by his Goodness and Humanity than by his Arms; he won his Heart in such a way, that he contracted with him a Friendship most sincere'.[32] It is tempting to read such an assertion as redressing those anxieties of friendly enmity already described;

---

[30] *The Patriot*, 3.
[31] *The Patriot*, 55.
[32] *The Patriot*, 51.

the idea of genuine sincerity in friendship might seem to redeem a figure like the Duke de Medina Sidonia from his awkward, conflicted situation. But the allusion to conquest in Frederick-Maurice's language, the sense of one man imposing his goodness on another, even to the extent of teaching him what goodness and humanity look like, serves to mould such relationships as sites of failed resistance. In William of Orange's own encounters with his various friendly enemies throughout the play, hearts are repeatedly being won or stolen rather than shared, and this is often a distressing experience for those involved. The Spaniard Signor Romero speaks like the Duke de Medina Sidonia of 'the Pain Dependence on another's Pleasure brings'.[33] Upon his own capture, General Schinche – a member of the Duke of Parma's army – describes how Frederick-Maurice's bravery 'forces Admiration, and his Goodness Love'.[34] While the friendship is secured by force, we can never be witness to an ideal Aristotelian friendship of moral equals.[35] In fact, the preponderance of honourable, friendly Spaniards in the text starts to make sense when one takes into consideration the process by which their friendship has been acquired. At no point does the text advocate appeasement of the Spanish forces, either in William of Orange's time or in the context of eighteenth-century Britain. On the contrary, friendship prosecuted with aggression and self-certainty becomes a weapon in itself, exposing Spain's lack of sociable or moral authority.

I noted earlier in this chapter that the figure of the friendly enemy acts not just as a proving ground for ideas of unsociable sociability but also as a manifestation of the phenomenon itself. By this I mean that the deployment of the trope, particularly in the case of these captive characters, can stem from the political author's need to acknowledge difference of opinion while effectively minimising and dismissing it, insisting on an inherently unsociable consensus. Aaron Hill's translation of Voltaire's play *Alzire* provides an intriguing example of this in that the original text's interrogation of the friendly enemy as prisoner did not necessarily lend itself to Patriot co-option. First performed in Paris in January 1736, Voltaire's work was accompanied in at least one printed edition by a dedicatory epistle naming, among other praiseworthy women of Europe, 'la Reine d'Angleterre':

---

[33] *The Patriot*, 35–6.
[34] *The Patriot*, 41.
[35] For discussion of Aristotle's idealistic model of friendship, as detailed principally in his *Ethica Nicomachea*, and of other classical concepts of perfect friendship, see Dirk Baltzly and Nick Eliopoulos, 'The Classical Ideals of Friendship', in *Friendship: A History*, ed. Barbara Caine (London, 2009), 1–64.

The Queen of England, who has acted as mediator between the two greatest metaphysicians of Europe, Clarke and Leibnitz, and who is able to appreciate them, has not because of this neglected for one moment the cares of a queen, of a woman and of a mother.[36]

The possibility of Queen Caroline's neglect of her first-born son and of her culpability in the family feud which was becoming all the more apparent to personal acquaintances and the public at large, was an issue which would dominate Patriot discourse in the years before her death (in late 1737) and after.[37] While Voltaire's praise for her in his epistle should not necessarily be viewed as partisan in nature, it was in keeping with his long-standing admiration for the queen and the mixed political company he had kept during his time in Britain in the previous decade.[38] Hill's decision to dedicate his translation of *Alzire* instead to Prince Frederick therefore appears in an awkward light. Although he presents himself as still honouring 'the ROYAL MOTHER' through her illustrious son, his determination to 'congratulate [Frederick] on the human Glories of [his] *future* Reign' cannot help but look like an indictment of the current political regime.[39]

Hill's *Alzira* is a hostage text. Like the friendly enemies already cited and like several of the characters that inhabit the play itself, it is forced to bear witness to political lessons and to corroborate ideological stances that are foreign to its original purpose. The play revolves around two manifestations of friendly enmity, as does Voltaire's original. At the start, the character of Alvarez lectures his son, Carlos, on the virtue of forgiveness, impressed as he has been by the mercy of a particular Peruvian chief who treated him with dignity and freed him from captivity. According to Alvarez, conciliatory behaviour towards one's enemies is both a moral good in itself and a practical one. Since 'the *forc'd* Heart, submitting, still *resists*'

---

[36] The epistle was included in the Amsterdam edition of the French text. See *Alzire, ou les Américains* (Amsterdam, 1736), ix. The translation provided here is my own.

[37] I have discussed the political currency of these issues in Emrys D. Jones, 'Royal Ruptures: Caroline of Ansbach and the Politics of Illness in the 1730s', *Medical Humanities* 37 (2011), 13–17.

[38] Voltaire was apparently on good terms with both the Tory Lord Bolingbroke and Walpole himself. See Roger Pearson, *Voltaire Almighty: A Life in Pursuit of Freedom* (London, 2005), 79; also Eva Jacobs, *Theatre in Focus: Voltaire and Tragedy* (Cambridge, 1987), 22–4.

[39] Aaron Hill, *Alzira. A Tragedy* (London, 1736), iv, x. For Hill's ambitions of patronage from Frederick and the tensions that his political allegiances caused for his several translations of Voltaire, see Christine Gerrard, *Aaron Hill: The Muses' Projector 1685–1750* (Oxford, 2003), 182–3, 190–2.

– a lesson just as applicable to Carlos's attempts at imposing peace on his South American territory as it is to his amorous inclinations towards the eponymous heroine – it is strategically advisable and in one's own interests to court genuine friendship instead.[40] As in this chapter's other examples, then, the doctrine of friendly enmity encapsulates an appropriately Kantian paradox. One does away with external resistance, and answers the needs of one's own internal resistance, by adopting the stance of the non-resistant and opening oneself up to sociable possibility. In the closing stages of the play, these lessons are called into question, however. Mortally wounded by his father's erstwhile saviour, Zamor, Carlos has no practical motive for offering forgiveness, nothing to gain besides the moral high ground and the brief opportunity to demonstrate his decency to a shocked Alzira. Carlos tells Zamor that he will not leave him until he has 'soften'd *Envy*, into *Friendship*', an ambition which one might expect to require rather more time and reciprocal engagement than the Spaniard's deathbed speeches permit.[41] In these final moments of the play, the idea of friendly enmity as mutually rewarding is undermined by the extent of Carlos's selflessness, the redundancy of the term 'friendship' itself and the obvious moral failure of the play's other friendly enemy, Zamor, in assassinating the son of the noble Alvarez. The scene is yet more problematic in light of Hill's political agenda. If Carlos stands for Frederick in the English translation, then his practice of friendly enmity is shown to be faulty on several fronts, self-sacrificial rather than sensibly negotiated, and establishing order only through the relinquishment of worldly power. Hill, following Voltaire, envisages a friendly enmity that can paper over differences and impose a peaceful consensus on the divided political world.[42] But the flaws in this peace and the potential for tragedy in disregarding one's own interest are all the more evident, thanks to the work's strained re-contextualisation.

The friendly enemy as ally

The Patriot texts considered so far have all revolved around happily aligned father–son pairings. In such instances, the friendly enemy seems to pose little threat to royal hierarchy or order of succession; the Patriot prince

---

[40] Hill, *Alzira*, 5.
[41] Hill, *Alzira*, 55.
[42] Jacobs sums up the 'underlying humanitarian message of universal brotherhood and mutual tolerance' in both this play and Voltaire's earlier *Zaïre* (1733). See Jacobs, *Theatre in Focus*, 28.

is often shown to have learned virtue from the example of a Patriot king (or, in the case of Carlos and Alvarez in *Alzira*, a Patriot governor). The main potential for political controversy in these works rests in ironic readings, which would emphasise the disparity between such happy families and the true discord of the house of Hanover. However, the friendly enemy could manifest in more inflammatory, politically provocative ways in other Patriot texts, works which seek to pit the values of a prince against those of a reigning monarch and which court legal objections and enduring notoriety when doing so. In these works, we find the friendly enemy imagined not as a powerless prisoner in confinement but as a potential ally of son against father.

James Thomson's play *Edward and Eleonora* (1739), famously forbidden from performance under Sir Robert Walpole's Stage Licensing Act of 1737, includes two such friendly enemies, influencing the prince in similar ways throughout the text, although they possess very different religious and political backgrounds.[43] The Earl of Gloster, accompanying the future Edward I on the ninth crusade, makes clear his historically conflicted allegiance at an early point in the play. He had been involved in Simon de Montfort's attempted rebellion against Edward's father, Henry III, and he is all the more appreciative of the prince's virtue, due to the way he has managed to overlook this former transgression:

> One Instance it becomes me to recount,
> That shows the genuine Greatness of his Soul.
> Tho' I have met him in the bloody Field,
> He fighting for his Father, I for Freedom;
> Yet bears his Bosom no remaining Grudge
> Of those distracted Times: to me his Heart
> Is greatly reconcil'd – Virtue! beyond
> The little unforgiving Soul of Tyrants![44]

If this encomium in one sense gives the impression of a man who has seen the error of his ways, from another viewpoint it suggests a curious entrenchment on Gloster's part. While he recognises goodness in Edward, he is not ready to acknowledge that his own cause was unjust; his characterisation of Edward's father as in effect the antithesis of freedom's cause remains relevant in less 'distracted' times. In an earlier scene, he

---

[43] For background on the Stage Licensing Act, see John Loftis, *The Politics of Drama in Augustan England* (Oxford, 1963), 128–53.

[44] James Thomson, *Edward and Eleonora. A Tragedy* (London, 1739), 5–6.

has highlighted the need for Edward to 'save [his father] from his Ministers.'[45] Slightly later he will directly oppose the rationale for the crusade itself, describing it as 'a kind of persecution.'[46] It is clearly Gloster's view that Edward's virtue would be more sensibly and humanely exercised by toppling the corrupt political regime back in Britain.

Thus, the friendly enemy urges a more active and potentially more rebellious role upon his Patriot prince. The treasonous aspect of his counsel has become something of a moot point by the end of the play, when news arrives of Henry's death and Edward is able to return to Britain and resolve its political troubles from a position of constitutional legitimacy. However, this should not obscure the controversy implicit in the adviser's interventions. It is only when taking such controversy into account that one can see the true propagandistic intricacy of a play whose political agenda has sometimes been dismissed as more simplistic and unquestioning than Thomson's other dramas.[47] We have here the prospect of Frederick siding with his father's avowed enemies, a prospect not only explored but welcomed and central to the satisfactory resolution of the plot. More drastic even than Edward's reconciliation with Gloster are the eventual bonds of friendship which he develops with his Muslim foe, Sultan Selim; in this friendship, Edward follows in the footsteps of Sir Hugh from the *Ordene de chevalerie*, but the play goes further than the medieval poem in consolidating the relationship between British knight and Muslim sovereign, allowing the one to influence and perhaps inspire the other. For all that Selim proves himself worthy of Edward's appreciation by saving the princess's life and by speaking eloquently on the subject of religious tolerance, his final truce with the prince nevertheless constitutes a defiance of the recently deceased father's commands. There is also a worrying sense in which this exotic friendship exceeds the bounds of decency established in other encounters between Patriot princes and their friendly enemies. Selim fixates on Edward's 'noble Heart', his 'beautiful Disorder', and his susceptibility to 'human Passions'.[48] These are qualities described elsewhere in the play as weaknesses that Edward should resist or tame in order to become a more

---

[45] Thomson, *Edward and Eleonora*, 3.
[46] Thomson, *Edward and Eleonora*, 7.
[47] Such is the interpretation presented in Åke Eriksson, *The Tragedy of Liberty: Civic Concern and Disillusionment in James Thomson's Tragic Dramas* (Uppsala, 2002), 23. In refuting this approach, I build on my previous discussion of Thomson's work in Jones, *Friendship and Allegiance*, 101–4.
[48] Thomson, *Edward and Eleonora*, 93.

devoted servant to his nation.[49] The fact that the Sultan homes in on these very characteristics implies that friendly enmity may have a more complex function here than as a simple corroboration of princely goodness. The capacity for friendship with Selim might also be read as a warning sign. It would not be acceptable for the Patriot prince to be too easily befriended by his despotic, Oriental counterpart.

In William Paterson's *Arminius* (1740), another play denied a licence under the terms of the Stage Licensing Act, a proliferation of friendly enemies likewise leads to confused loyalties and unease concerning the basis for Patriot resistance. As with Hill's *Alzira*, the play's plot was imported and distorted; Paterson's work builds on a narrative that had been popularised in operatic culture of the preceding forty years – most recently in Handel's *Arminio* of 1737.[50] Nonetheless, the play's marshalling of its friendly enemies and its frequent expatiations on the topic differentiate it from its source material. The drama's central conflict between first-century Rome and the Germanic tribes is not simply a matter of brave defiance, nor the trivial backdrop to courtship that it had sometimes resembled in operatic iterations. For Paterson, it is explicitly a proving ground for notions of friendship and alliance whose political meanings are decidedly unstable. At the play's outset, the title character's former ally and would-be father-in-law, Segestes, has struck up a new allegiance with Rome, one portrayed as unjust not only because it involves the betrayal of Arminius but because, in so doing, it demeans even those who are party to the alliance. It is, as Segestes's own daughter describes it, the wrong kind of friendly enmity, driven by convenience rather than mutual respect, and conditional above all on obedience:

Accursed *Rome*! unjust imperious Power!
Is this the sad Condition of thy Friendship?
If it be thus thou dost extend thy sway;
Thus to control our best domestic Joys;

---

[49] Gloster himself comments that he aims 'to moderate his Heat, / to guide his fiery Virtues.' See Thomson, *Edward and Eleonora*, 6.

[50] Handel's opera, first performed at Covent Garden Theatre on 12 January 1737, used a 1703 libretto by Antonio Salvi. For details of the libretto's various settings prior to Handel, see Reinhard Strohm, *Essays on Handel and Italian Opera* (Cambridge, 1985), 73. Strohm notes that the hero and heroine of Handel's opera were intended to parallel Prince Frederick and Princess Augusta, but he seems to understand this more in the context of general flattery than as indicative of ulterior political motives on Handel's part.

> Then thy Allies are Slaves, whatever Name,
> Or gaudy Title may adorn their Chains.[51]

Artesia's speech encourages us to anticipate more positive formulations of friendly enmity that will define and validate the cause of the play's Patriot hero. This appears to be the function of one character who had not been part of the story's operatic tradition. Egbert, a henchman to Segestes, is instrumental in Arminius's escape from imprisonment in Act Three. When the two men have a chance to catch their breath, Arminius asks, 'to what Cause / Owe I your generous Friendship and Assistance?' And Egbert replies, as a dutiful model of friendly enmity ought: 'To your own Virtues; to th'Injustice done you; / And to that Love I bear my sinking Country.'[52]

However, this is to prove the high point of Egbert's dramatic and thematic significance in Paterson's play. When Arminius is recaptured towards the end of Act Four, he informs us that his new-found ally has been killed off-stage.[53] If this were the full extent of the play's engagement with the trope of the friendly enemy, it would be a fairly unremarkable piece of propaganda, a comforting reminder that the Patriot prince's virtue is inspirational and that his friendships operate in a different way to those of tyrannical Rome. But in practice, Egbert's role is overshadowed by two friendly enemies with rather more problematic connotations. The first of these is the son of Segestes, Sigismund, who likewise joins with Arminius, an act which he justifies to his father as being in the best interests of their own family's honour and future reputation.[54] For the broad strokes of this characterisation, Paterson is indebted to the operas that had gone before him, but, as in Hill's *Alzira*, the weight of the characters' decisions shifts with the story's new political context. Although Arminius is the recognisable Patriot prince at the heart of the narrative, we might pause occasionally to consider whether Sigismund is also a substitute for Frederick, and a more candid representation of the filial disobedience and treason sometimes necessitated by patriotic virtue:

> If this, my Lord, deserves the Name of Traitor,
> Your Son is one; and Glory's in the Name.[55]

It is easier to voice such sentiments in a play than to make them the foundation of a respectable political campaign; easier also for an apparently

---

[51] William Paterson, *Arminius. A Tragedy* (London, 1740), 6.
[52] *Arminius*, 35.
[53] *Arminius*, 53.
[54] *Arminius*, 47.
[55] *Arminius*, 47.

subsidiary character to celebrate treason in these terms than to have the Patriot prince sully his own lips with the idea. Still, the Patriot cause is infected by the admission that treachery may in some contexts be not only necessary but desirable. By understanding Sigismund's awkward situation – his status as both a friendly enemy and something like a Patriot prince himself – we can also perhaps explain the play's dedication to Frederick's younger brother, William, Duke of Cumberland. What at first seems an odd dedicatory strategy, targeting an individual with no obvious association to the Patriot cause, instead starts to look like an invitation to wider disloyalty, a way of probing the applicability of Patriot discourse to figures besides Frederick himself.

The other character who reveals himself as a friendly enemy as the play proceeds is yet more surprising, and complicates Paterson's agenda even further. In spite of Artesia's earlier attack on Roman friendship, the leader of Rome's forces in Germany, Quintilius Varus, recognises Arminius's worth and ultimately decides to free him so as to face him on the battlefield. This again had precedent in operatic versions of the tale, but there Varus had quickly changed his mind and ordered Arminius returned to prison again. Here the Roman general is as good as his word, much to the exasperation of his ally Segestes and to the astonishment of Arminius himself:

> Now, on my Soul, did not superiour Ties
> Forbid all Friendship with our Countries Foes,
> I could embrace thee, *Roman*, for thy Virtues.[56]

They will never reach a truce as Edward and Selim did in Thomson's play. Arminius's words make clear that friendship as such is out of the question. However, the conventions of friendly enmity are very clearly implicated in this attempt to preserve virtue on both sides, and Paterson, in doing justice to Roman decency, seems to go beyond the mutual recognition of virtue found in Baillie and West's works. Here it is not a single representative of an enemy power overcoming hostility to testify to the Patriot prince's goodness; rather, Varus sees himself as embodying all that is good about Roman culture as he releases Arminius – he does it more for himself and his nation than out of admiration for his rival. His decision leads one to question whether the war and, by extension, Arminius's supposedly singular patriotism are necessary at all; it threatens to undermine the binary oppositions on which much Patriot rhetoric was founded. Thus, even as the play worries us with the possibility that patriotic action may involve

---

[56] *Arminius*, 54.

what others call treason, it simultaneously implies that this action may be pointless, a distraction from more fundamental commonalities.

We observe again in the friendly enemies of *Arminius* and *Edward and Eleonora* both the appeal and the pitfalls of the trope, its obvious propagandistic value set alongside its treasonous implications and, in Varus's case, its potential to undercut political certainties. The trope anticipates a carefully balanced Kantian sociability at the same time that it makes us aware of sociability's less rational or governable aspects, the qualities that make it such an unreliable tool in political discourse. In all of these works, the use of the friendly enemy cuts against the reputation of the Patriot movement for earnest, aesthetically bland panegyric and a lack of wit or ironic sensibility. For the literary use of the friendly enemy is always an occupation rife with ironic possibility, one which depends on a balance of internal and external resistance as already described throughout this chapter, but which may also encourage covert resistance on the part of readers and audiences. Even as the friendly enemy urges us to admire the Patriot prince, or as the Patriot prince praises his own opponent, each can steer us to greater scepticism concerning the boundaries of duty, the price of consensus, and the value of emotional or sociable passions in the midst of political struggles.

In *The Memoirs and History of Prince Titi* (1736), an uncharacteristically satirical Patriot work originally published in French and sometimes attributed to Frederick himself, the hero strikes up 'the sincerest Friendship' with his father's enemy, the neighbouring King Forteserre.[57] Titi successfully petitions for this enemy's freedom when he has been taken prisoner. At a later point in the narrative, it seems like Forteserre will repay this generosity with counter-productive military zeal; he becomes a rallying point for the rebellious soldiers of Titi's homeland and considers bestowing sovereignty on Titi himself. His name at moments like this might be seen as evoking Shakespeare's Fortinbras and that character's welcome, albeit belated, conquest of Denmark in the closing scenes of *Hamlet*.[58] However, typical of the friendly enemy's awkward political resonance, Forteserre cannot be allowed to do the Patriot prince's work for him. In fact, his friendship

---

[57] *The Memoirs and History of Prince Titi* (London, 1736), 105. The text has sometimes been attributed to Themiseul de Saint-Hyacinthe, but Christine Gerrard asserts Frederick's involvement in *Patriot Opposition*, 61. For details of a rival English edition, also of 1736, see, Jones, *Friendship and Allegiance*, 194.

[58] Ros Ballaster comments on the significance of *Hamlet* as a touchstone for prose romances of the 1730s, in an article which also discusses Prince Titi's place in this genre. See Ros Ballaster, 'Satire and Embodiment: Allegorical Romance on Stage and Page in Mid-Eighteenth-Century Britain', *Eighteenth-Century Fiction* 27, no. 3/4 (2015), 635–6, 645.

causes additional trouble for Titi, since the Prince cannot honourably allow his father to be dethroned, and widespread knowledge of his growing friendship with Forteserre makes him ever more vulnerable to charges of treachery.[59] Rather than simply holding out the friendly enemy as a guarantee of the prince's virtue, *Prince Titi* thus uses the figure to expose the conceptual fragility of the nascent Patriot movement, the fundamental conflict between its need for widespread, ideologically diverse support and its onus on princely self-sufficiency. As has been shown throughout this chapter, the friendly enemy is a figure particularly well positioned to represent and invite reflection on these tensions. When Titi politely declines Forteserre's offer of the throne, he epitomises not just the peculiar, clumsy tone of this little-known text, but the anxieties inherent in the Patriot movement and in the tradition of the friendly enemy itself:

> Surely your Royal Magnanimity and Prudence will not suffer you to support Rebels against their lawful Prince; and you are too wise to take a Son's part against his Father; I dare flatter myself that you will not oblige me to quit those Sentiments of an inviolable Respect with which I always desire to be [...] Your Majesty's most humble and most obedient Servant, Titi.[60]

Here Titi insists on the fundamental bonds of honour, common sense and self-interest that serve to put chivalric largesse in its place. He restrains and resists the excesses of friendly enmity with a caution that Kant would surely have admired. But he also lays bare, as so many of his Patriot successors were to do in one way or another, the challenges of a friendship that must neither ask for too much nor heed worldly concerns too little.

---

[59] Titi's parents seek to have him arrested on the grounds that 'he never spoke of [Forteserre] but with Praises such as became him not to give to the Enemy of his Country'. *Prince Titi*, 124.

[60] *Prince Titi*, 142–3.

Chapter 12
The anti-social convivialist: toasting and resistance to sociability[1]
Ian Newman

THE LATE EIGHTEENTH century saw the flourishing of new ideas about sociability that went by the name 'conviviality'. While drawing on much older ideas about eating and drinking together, convivial practice developed distinctive characteristics in the later part of the century, challenging earlier models of sociability described most famously by Joseph Addison and associated with the coffeehouse. Thanks in part to the work of Jürgen Habermas, coffeehouse sociability has come to be associated (however accurately) with political discussion, newspaper reading and the rise of public opinion, a process by which ideas were shaped through rational critical debate.[2] The idea of conviviality, whose spiritual home was the tavern,

---

[1] I would like to express my gratitude to Rémy Duthille, who generously shared with me his (at the time) unpublished work on toasting as I prepared this chapter for publication. See Rémy Duthille, 'Toasting and the Diffusion of Radical Ideas, 1789–1832', in *Radical Voices, Radical Ways: Articulating and Disseminating Radicalism in Seventeenth- and Eighteenth-Century Britain*, ed. Laurent Curelly and Nigel Smith (Manchester, 2016), 179–89, and Rémy Duthille, 'Political Toasting in the Age of Revolutions: Britain, America and France, 1765–1800', in *Liberty, Property and Popular Politics: England and Scotland, 1688–1815. Essays in Honour of H. T. Dickinson*, ed. Gordon Pentland and Michael Davis (Edinburgh, 2015), 73–86. While it would have been cumbersome to acknowledge every moment that our work intersects, my arguments in this essay build on his insights and could not have been possible without his work.

[2] Jürgen Habermas, *The Structural Transformation of the Public Sphere: An Inquiry Into a Category of Bourgeois Society*, trans. Thomas Burger and Frederick Lawrence (Cambridge, MA, 1991), 41–59. Although still influential, Habermas's account of the coffeehouse's importance to the rise of the bourgeois public sphere has since been refined and challenged by numerous critics, notably Anthony Clayton, *London's Coffee Houses: A Stimulating Story* (London, 2003); Brian Cowan *The Social Life of Coffee: The Emergence of the British Coffeehouse* (New Haven, 2005); and Markman Ellis, *The Coffee-house: A Cultural History* (London, 2004).

is fundamentally different because of its emphasis on warm-hearted good humour. At convivial meetings argument was by-passed. The goal was not the shaping of opinion, but a celebration of ideas already affirmed. Tavern gatherings consolidated already existing beliefs and promoted harmony through their avoidance of contention, and by their ritualised celebrations of collective belief such as convivial singing and – the focus of this chapter – toasting.

Toasting formally enacted the central principles of convivial agreement. First a toast was proposed, often a pithy, witty idea or opinion intended to reflect the feelings of all those gathered; then everyone responded, signalling their assent by drinking. Differences were set aside, unanimity was asserted, and indeed unanimity, or 'social harmony', was the precondition for the form. This observation, obvious though it may seem, challenges much of what has been written about toasting, which usually emphasises the oppositional nature of the eighteenth-century toast. In the Jacobite toasting mentioned by Peter Clark in his book on the English Alehouse, the Spencean toasts discussed by Iain McCalman in *Radial Underworld*, John Barrell's discussion of toasts used in evidence during the 1794 treason trials, or Georgina Green's discussion of the Duke of Norfolk's scandalous toast to the 'Majesty of the People', the emphasis has most frequently been on the way toasts take up a political position, either loyalist or radical, in order to counter a perceived problem with an established system of belief.[3] My interest in this chapter is to consider why this might be so. Given that the form of the toast is precisely *not* oppositional, that it is a fundamentally consensus-building form, what might the difference between its formal function and its historical instantiation reveal?

This chapter focuses primarily on a particular instance in which the consensual promise of toasting goes wrong: at a meeting of the Royal Humane Society in 1799 in the London Tavern on Bishopsgate Street. Here, in the midst of a peaceful gathering that celebrated the benevolent activities of a charitable organisation, the presence of the radical orator John Thelwall caused a disturbance that official accounts of the meeting attempted to cover up. I want to suggest that at issue was a collision between individual belief and the collective principles of the gathering. Thelwall's stubborn

---

[3] Peter Clark, *The English Alehouse: A Social History, 1200–1830* (London, 1983), 156; Iain McCalman, *Radical Underworld: Prophets, Revolutionaries and Pornographers in London, 1795–1840* (Cambridge, 1988), 122; John Barrell, *Imagining The King's Death: Figurative Treason, Fantasies of Regicide, 1793–1796* (Oxford, 2000), 212–13; Georgina Green, *The Majesty of The People: Popular Sovereignty and the Role of the Writer in the 1790s* (Oxford, 2014), 17–23.

refusal to sacrifice his own principles to the collective and publicly broadcast beliefs of those gathered was tantamount to a rebellion against the principles of conviviality that his presence at the meeting tacitly endorsed. The disturbance at the London Tavern was the result of technically anti-social behaviour, by which I mean that Thelwall enacted a form of resistance to a mode of sociability that had become hegemonic, and to which he refused to capitulate. Furthermore, the absence of any mention of the disruption in newspaper accounts of the meeting draws our attention to the limitations of relying on official reports of public meetings and the discrepancy between the apparently consensual unanimity of public reporting on convivial meetings and the individual experiences and beliefs of those who attended.

Thelwall's behaviour can help us to see an important distinction between the covert, subversive and potentially seditious potential of the toast, which has been the focus of much scholarly attention, and properly anti-social behaviour, which offers resistance to forms of sociability as such. The former is most often acceptable to the company in which it is originally proposed, but meets with controversy once it has moved beyond its original audience and into the public sphere; the latter is a disruption of the principles upon which conviviality itself was founded.

The Royal Humane Society meeting

On 16 April 1799 the Royal Humane Society held their annual dinner in the London Tavern on Bishopsgate Street. The society had been established by the physicians William Hawes and Thomas Cogan, who had been concerned that drowning people who could be easily resuscitated were frequently taken for dead, and were sometimes buried alive, and had established what was originally called the 'Society for the Recovery of Persons Apparently Drowned' at the Chapter Coffee House in St Paul's Churchyard in 1774.[4] By the end of the eighteenth century the society had established chapters throughout Britain, and indeed the world, that provided life-saving equipment near bodies of water and established a series of 'receiving houses' where apparently drowned bodies could receive medical attention from volunteers. At the 1799 annual dinner John Beaumont, the society's secretary, calculated that the society had saved the lives of 2,319 persons, many of whom 'were Children when rescued from the watery grave' and

[4] See Royale Humane Society website: http://www.royalhumanesociety.org.uk/, (accessed February 2014).

now, having arrived to mature years 'are either settled in useful occupations, or defending their Country in the Fleets and Armies of the Nation'.[5] As this description indicates, the society was an explicitly loyalist institution, whose patron was the king and whose utility was measured not only in terms of personal value but in terms of the benefit to the nation. The treasurer's annual report proudly proclaimed that the rescued victims had been 'restored to Life, to their Parents, to their Families, and *to the State*' (my italics).

The annual dinner at the London Tavern was a sombre affair, held at 4pm on a Tuesday, with over 400 attendees. This, however, did not prevent participation in the rites associated with tavern conviviality, including speech-making, singing and toasting. *The Times* reported that the first toast that was drunk was 'the King's Health', which was followed by 'almost unparalleled applause' concluding with 'God Save the King', sung by Charles Dignum, the celebrated actor and singer, who had made a name for himself at Drury Lane and had been a popular fixture at Ranelagh and Vauxhall, as well as at convivial societies such as the Prince of Wales' Je Ne Scai Quoi Club [*sic*] and the Anacreontic Society.[6] Next, there was a procession, accompanied by solemn music, of 'City Marshalls, Stewards &c.' who led out survivors who had been saved by the society as odes were recited. The survivors carried banners with messages of thanks for the society, the first carried by Mrs Leigh of Newington, which read 'Behold my infant Child and my Niece restored'. Mr Lardner then addressed the President, saying 'I thank you for my own life and the lives of my three children'. Another toast, 'prosperity to the Humane Society', was then proposed and one of the society's founders, William Hawes, gave an address which emphasised the utility of the society and its progress since it was originally founded, and commented on the preservation of the lives of shipwrecked mariners. The report in *The Times* concluded by declaring the anniversary dinner truly the Feast of Reason realised, and observing that at about eleven o'clock

---

[5] *True Briton*, 26 April 1799.

[6] The Je Ne Scai Quoi club was a relatively short-lived club that met at the Star and Garter Tavern in the mid-1790s. The Prince of Wales was the Chairman, and the well-known song-writer Captain Morris was the secretary. Leading actors and singers were regularly invited to entertain the members, who were largely members of the nobility. The spelling of the club's name varies between 'Je Ne Scai Quoi' and 'Je Ne Sais Quoi'; critics tend to prefer the latter, but the former is more common in sources from the 1790s, and I suspect that bad French was something of a running joke in these circles, as the spelling of Captain Morris's name as 'Morrice' in letters to the Duke of Norfolk and the song 'Dans Votre Lit' and its sequel 'Dans Son Lit' suggest.

– seven hours after it had begun – the company retired to enjoy in private 'the feelings which must ever arise in the breasts of those who by their philanthropy are a blessing to the indigent, a consolation to the afflicted, and guardians to the lives of the people'.[7]

The lives saved are those of the 'indigent' and 'afflicted', the poor and sick apparently being the only ones foolish enough to end up in bodies of water. The suspicion that some of these saved souls might have preferred to be left where they were (as Mary Wollstonecraft had been) rather than return to a life of such indigence and affliction is raised, although quickly suppressed.[8] Any such ethical ambiguity is elided in *The Times*' account of the dinner, where the public proclamations of loyalty and national duty are seamlessly contiguous with the patriotic, benevolent and humble feelings which inevitably arise in the breasts of all present when they retire. The public declarations of the dinner, the toasts proposed and the write-up in the newspaper all carefully manage the public representation of the society and cast it as the loyal guardian watching out for the unfortunate.

In many respects there is nothing at all exceptional about the report in *The Times*. The loyalism expressed is conventional enough for the late 1790s as the radicalisms of the early part of the decade had been effectively suppressed, at least for the time being, in public discourse. The juxtaposition of the serious work of the society with convivial rituals that we would normally associate with something more light-hearted might strike us as odd but in fact was a perfectly ordinary occurrence, and the report in *The Times* is indistinguishable from thousands of newspaper reports of such dinners held in London's major taverns in the second half of the eighteenth century. In fact, the occasion would hardly be worth our attention were it not for a note in the Home Office records in The National Archives, indicating that among the attendees of the meeting was the notorious orator, and figurehead for radicalism, John Thelwall.

Thelwall's anti-social behaviour

Having made a name for himself as a speech-maker for various radical causes in the early 1790s, Thelwall had been one of the defendants accused

---

[7] *The Times*, 22 April 1799.
[8] Wollstonecraft's attempt to commit suicide by drowning herself in the Thames was prevented by a stranger who rescued her. She pointedly wrote that she had been 'inhumanely brought back to life and misery'. Janet Todd, *Mary Wollstonecraft: A Revolutionary Life* (London, 2000), 357.

of treason, and gloriously acquitted, during the 1794 treason trials. Despite this victory, the subsequent crackdown by Pitt's ministry on seditious meetings had forced Thelwall to leave London, and he spent the final years of the decade touring Britain, during which period he visited Coleridge and Wordsworth as they worked on *The Lyrical Ballads*, before eventually settling in Llyswen in Wales. He would not return to London until after Pitt's death in 1806. To find him at the London Tavern in April 1799, then, is a surprise, partly explainable by the fact that Thelwall was interested in medicine, had regularly attended lectures at St Guy's and St Thomas's hospitals during his London years and knew William Hawes, one of the founders of the Royal Humane Society well, considering him his 'medical mentor', to use Judith Thompson's phrase.[9] But, biographical details aside, what is most intriguing about the Home Office note is what it reveals about the failures of conviviality. The note, written by Mr Lawless to his sister, claims that Thelwall was 'hooted' out of the tavern for refusing to drink a toast:

> Thelwall was sitting the last but one to the door, seemingly dubious of his reception. By degrees a parcel of them got together, and got him to talk. One of them toasted 'The Army of England.' Thelwall put his hand over his glass, said, he could not drink that toast for it had a dubious meaning, unless it came direct from the Chairman. The alarm was given, and all the endeavors of Dr Chamberlain and his other friends to stem the foment against him were futile, even a good song was hissed in the struggle for his expulsion. He was obliged to retire most uncommonly chagrined.[10]

By refusing to drink a toast to the Army, Thelwall violates the tacit codes of convivial ritual, and by doing so is expelled from what is in theory a charitable sociable gathering.

The contrast between the well-regulated politeness emphasised by *The Times* and the fractious expulsion of Thelwall recorded in the private note Lawless sent to his sister is striking, and indicates the differences between public narratives and private experiences of convivial assembly. The disparity between these two accounts can alert us to the limitations of our ability to recreate the complex dynamics of meetings from newspaper reports. Frank O'Gorman has argued that 'piecing together the innumerable toasts

[9] John Thelwall, *Selected Poetry and Poetics*, ed. Judith Thompson (Basingstoke, 2015), 275.
[10] National Archives, HO 42/47/84 fol. 201.

at election dinners, it is sometimes almost possible to reconstruct the entire belief system of those present.'[11] This is true not only of explicitly political dinners, but of other kinds of convivial gathering. But we should also be alert to the partial and hesitant nature of O'Gorman's claim. It is *sometimes, almost* possible to reconstruct the belief systems of those present, but not quite.

Toasts and public relations

As the report in *The Times* makes clear, the meeting of the Royal Humane Society was a 'public' dinner, in one of the city's most prestigious taverns, designed, as the *Picture of London* reminds us, as a venue for 'public meetings'.[12] In the report this 'public' is contrasted with the privacy of 'feelings' that arise in the breast, produced by the satisfaction of knowing that benevolent philanthropy has contributed to saving lives. The recipients of this charity are then prevailed upon to publicly perform their gratitude, paraded around in the opulent surroundings of the tavern in order that the society can receive the public acknowledgement of a report on the dinner in the newspapers, with the hope that this publicity will raise awareness of the society and bring in further resources to finance more rescues.

As Craig Barclay has shown, the society cultivated relationships with several high-profile newspapers and magazines, including the *Gentleman's Magazine*, to which Hawes sent numerous reports of society activities, with sycophantic covering notes, in order to publicise their work more widely.[13] Public dinners were one of a series of strategies for raising awareness that included both physical assembly and print. Indeed physical meeting and newspaper publicity are inseparable aspects of the overall publicity effort, as, typically for the period, the annual dinner was promoted by placing classified advertisements in newspapers to generate ticket sales for the dinner which would then benefit from the reports which would later appear in

---

[11] Frank O'Gorman, 'Campaign Rituals and Ceremonies: The Social Meaning of Elections in England', *Past and Present* 135 (1992), 113.
[12] Feltham's *Picture* lists five taverns 'chiefly used for public dinners', of which the London Tavern is one. John Feltham, *The Picture of London, for 1806; Being a Correct Guide to all the Curiosities, Amusements, Exhibitions, Public Establishments, and remarkable Objects in and near London; with a Collection of Appropriate Tables* (London, 1805), 355.
[13] Craig Barclay 'Heroes of Peace: The Royal Humane Society and the Award of Medals in Britain, 1774–1914' (unpublished Ph.D. Thesis, Department of History, University of York, September 2009), 54–5.

those same newspapers. Much might be inferred, too, from the newspapers within which reports about the Humane Society occurred. Classified advertisements for the society, both for the anniversary dinner and for sermons preached on the subject of the society, were placed in *The True Briton*, *The Sun* and *The Times* – all loyalist papers. Reports of the activities of the society, their annual dinners and their rescues, appeared in these same papers, contributing to its reputation as a loyalist society.

The standard journalistic practice of reporting the toasts that were proposed at a given meeting made controlling the public image of a society relatively straightforward. Toasts were one of the ways in which clubs and societies of the late eighteenth century aimed to control and manage their public image. They provided the aphoristic structure around which narratives about a given meeting developed. As such, toasting should be seen as a practice that, along with the kinds of rational-critical debate typified by the coffeehouse conversation and discussed by Jürgen Habermas, played a pivotal role in the development of public opinion. But for this reason also, toasts should be viewed with suspicion as authentic beliefs of a particular gathering, because they were often made with a consciousness of the impact they might have on a public audience. Moreover, what was publicly acceptable at one historical conjuncture might very quickly become objectionable at a proximate moment. As Rémy Duthille has argued, '"the liberty of the press, the bulwark of English liberty" had as much urgency, but a different resonance in the time of Wilkes and general warrants, and that of the taxes on knowledge and the unstamped press'.[14] This was a lesson that the recent history of toasting had taught with remarkable clarity, as conventional toasts that bordered at times on platitudes were suddenly challenged, their formerly static meanings abruptly opened up to dramatic redefinition.

Redefining principles

Seven years before the Humane Society meeting at the London Tavern, the same venue was the scene of a more widely publicised controversy over toasting. On 4 December 1792, a few days before Thomas Paine's libel trial for the second part of *The Rights of Man*, Fox made an explicit declaration of his political principles to the members of the Whig Club, an association of Fox's supporters formed in 1784. In his speech Fox declared

---

[14] For a similar argument see Duthille, 'Toasting and the Diffusion of Radical Ideas', 173.

his attachment to 'the House of Brunswick', and to the principles of the constitution asserted at the Revolution of 1688. He also declared himself to be an advocate of 'the *Rights of the People*, upon whose *Rights* alone can ... be founded any real, sound and legitimate Government', and that he would 'act most cordially and steadfastly with *the Friends of Freedom*'.[15] As was common practice, the speech was printed in full in the daily newspapers, appearing in the *Star* the next day. The importance of the speech as an admirable articulation of Foxite values was recognised by James Ridgway, the radical bookseller, who quickly published it in pamphlet form.[16] Four days later, the ministerial paper the *Sun* printed a verse satire of Fox's speech called 'Mr. Fox's Speech to the Whig Club; or, his own exposition of his Political Principles'. The parody of Fox's speech was typical of the kind of reactionary political poetry for which newspapers of the latter part of the decade, such as the *Anti-Jacobin*, came to be known.[17] The thirty quatrains that comprise the poem claim that the intoxicating effects of wine inspired Fox's speech, and attribute the scandalous sentiments of Fox's words to the spirit of sedition fostered in the tavern:

> Here you have touched at the *Times and Measures*,
>   Drawn, like their *Tavern Bill*, from *Tavern Book*:
> For, when he feels an ebb of mental Treasures,
>   Fox drinks a glass, then takes another look.

Drawing on the familiar trope of the inspiration found in altered states, when Fox's 'mental Treasures' fail him he can find a muse in his wine. Convivial practice is simultaneously too predictable and too unregulated. Fox's political philosophy, inspired by the convivial licence, is merely a rote recitation of standard tavern principles, but the principles are at the same time extemporised under the influence of 'the glass' and are an imprudent expression of Fox's true values.

In addition to its depiction of the tavern as a site of political discourse debauched by the consumption of wine, the poem also engages in a more substantive critique of the speech, by allegedly quoting Fox but rewriting each of his principles to reveal what the *Sun* considered as the true

---

[15] *Star*, 5 December 1792.
[16] For accounts of Ridgway's activities see Lucyle Werkmeister, *The London Daily Press, 1772–1792* (Lincoln, 1963), 129, 175–6, 202; Ralph A. Manogue, 'The Plight of James Ridgway, London Bookseller and Publisher, and the Newgate Radicals, 1792–1797', *Wordsworth Circle* 27 (1996), 158–66.
[17] Kevin Gilmartin, *Writing Against the Revolution: Literary Conservatism in Britain, 1790–1832* (Cambridge, 2009), 96–7.

motivations that Fox had sought to conceal. Where Fox had declared himself loyal to the House of Brunswick, the *Sun*'s version emphasises that Fox's loyalties remain with the Prince of Wales, rather than the king:

> So, Here's the House of Brunswick! Not so fast, Sir ---
> My meaning's deep, and worthy your attention:
> I give the House, d'ye see, but not the *Master*;
> There's reason for it, which I need not mention.

The political alliances of Fox, one of the Prince's convivial companions, were the cause of much comment in the press, which during the early 1790s consistently associated the Foxite Whigs with the Prince of Wales and a culture of heavy drinking, while the king and Pitt were prudish and reserved, the antithesis of Whiggish convivial liberality.

Where Fox had declared his allegiance to the 'friends of freedom', the *Sun* identified these 'friends' as the regicidal French:

> Our friends the *French* have perfectly defin'd
> The *sort* of Freedom which we all admire---
> To kick down Thrones, to plunder unconfin'd.
> To pillage, rob, and set the World on fire.

The poem continues, undermining each of Fox's declared philosophies until it culminates with Fox declaring that his beliefs depend on '*Tom Paine's* Doctrine' to 'Knock down the Fences which the State preserve, / And level all which Monarchy defends'. The poem then ends with a depiction of the assembled Whig Club members, gullibly accepting Fox's doctrines and drinking heartily until they stumble to the ground:

> The zealous *Whigs*, obedient to command,
>   Drink till they stare, and call again for more:
> Nor does the Bottle quit their ready hand,
>   Till *Whigs* with *Whigs* lie tumbling on the floor.[18]

According to the *Sun*, tavern rituals, aided by the effects of wine, provide a convenient screen behind which Fox can obscure his seditious political intentions.

After the publication of the *Sun*'s poem, Fox's speech came to be regarded as an imprudent celebration of the cause of popular reform and the rights of man, articulated at a time when Britain was on the brink of war with the

---

[18] *Sun*, 8 December 1792. Reprinted as *Speech at the Whig Club; Or, A Great Statesman's Own Exposition of his Political Principles with Notes Critical and Explanatory* (London, [1793?]).

French Republic, and two weeks before the opening of the trial of Thomas Paine for libel, an assessment that has held currency among political historians ever since.[19] While the strategic wisdom of the speech may be open to debate, however, it is important to acknowledge that Fox's speech was based on the nine standing toasts that traditionally opened each meeting of the Whig Club:

1. The Glorious and immortal Memory of King William the Third.
2. The Constitution, according to the Principles asserted at the Revolution.
3. The Rights of the People.
4. The Friends of Freedom.
5. The Cause for which Hampden bled in the Field and Sydney on the Scaffold.
6. May the Names of Russel and Cavendish be ever united in Defence of the Liberties of their Country.
7. May it be the character of the Whig Club, never to slacken in their Efforts in Adversity, nor to forget their Principles in Prosperity.
8. The House of Brunswick, and may they never forget the Principles which placed their Family upon the Throne of Great Britain.
9. May the Example of one Revolution prevent the Necessity of another.[20]

Although reframed as a speech, Fox's declared principles were direct quotations of the toasts that had been drunk at every monthly meeting of the club since its formation in 1784, claiming that these were the principles that governed his behaviour. Suddenly in 1792, after eight years, what had previously been regarded as acceptable patriotic principles had become a contentious expression of seditious intent. In what we might think of as historical homophony, the words themselves were identical but their meanings had been altered by the change in political circumstances.

In a letter to *The General Evening Post*, Robert Adair, a founding member of the Whig Club and close associate of Fox, called the satire in the *Sun* a 'most false, wicked and seditious Libel', clearly with Paine's forthcoming

---

[19] See E. A. Smith, *Whig Principles and Party Politics: Earl Fitzwilliam and the Whig Party, 1748–1833* (Manchester, 1975), 152. For the connection between the satire in the *Sun* and the Thomas Paine trial see Jon Mee, *Print, Publicity, and Popular Radicalism in the 1790s: The Laurel of Liberty* (Cambridge, 2016), 50.

[20] John Bellamy, *Whig Club Instituted in May 1784, by John Bellamy.* (London, 1792), ix–x.

trial in mind.[21] Another of Fox's supporters, St Andrew St John, wrote a public letter to the Attorney General (also printed in the *General Evening Post*) saying that the satire had overstepped boundaries that separated the domains of public and private: 'The characters of public men are public property and as such are entitled to all the protection of the law.'[22] According to Fox's supporters, satires such as those published in the *Sun* that misrepresent the attitudes of 'public men' are punishable offences because they take as their target not just an individual but an entire system of beliefs and are thus detrimental to the harmony of the nation.

The *Sun*'s mockery of Fox's speech was not simply a personal attack on Fox's private character, but an attack on the doctrines and rituals of the Whig Club, consisting of around 700 of Fox's supporters. The attack, however motivated by a suspicion of Fox's personal stance towards French affairs, was an attack on the (public) values of all those who drank the Whig Club toasts. It was in this sense that Fox was public property; the value systems that he publicly articulated were those also professed by a broader public body. The Foxite Whigs' principles, that is to say, were based on the conviviality that the *Sun* lampooned and dismissed as drunken carousing. But from the perspective of his political opponents, the conviviality that had formerly been considered a continuation of the Whigs' political principles was now understood as dangerously out of touch with the political realities of the post-revolutionary moment. Whatever else this disagreement between Whigs and the loyalist press may have clarified, the back-and-forth structure of the debate made it abundantly clear that a long-standing consensus reached at gatherings of like-minded individuals and celebrated through the ritualised speech of the toast was no guarantee of the final legitimation of that idea. And while this might sound like an obvious point – ideas are always open to challenge – it was a point that was nevertheless obscured by the form of the convivial toast, which emphasised consensus, and a stability imparted by general assent.

The anti-social convivialist

There is, then, an important distinction between the kinds of historical homophony that I have been describing, where the words remain the same but their meanings have changed by an evolving situation, and the quarrel at the Humane Society in 1799. For the majority of controversies surrounding

---

[21] *General Evening Post*, 8–11 December 1792.
[22] *General Evening Post*, 8–11 December 1792.

toasts discussed by scholars, the process involves a toast that is taken out of its original context and made more public. Typically, the toasts were perfectly acceptable at the moment when they were first given, as accurate articulations of the unanimously held sentiments of the gathered convivialists. It was only when these toasts were later reported in newspapers or published in proceedings that they became controversial. Such is clearly the case in Fox's speech of 1792. The Duke of Norfolk's scandalous toast to 'The Majesty of the People' at a celebration of Fox's birthday in 1798 was similarly banal to those gathered, and it was several days before the controversy erupted in the newspapers.[23] Even in the case of Charles Piggott and William Hodgson's arrest for sedition after making a series of republican toasts in the London Coffee House (including calling the king a German hog butcher), the trouble begins when toasts are *overheard* by someone not involved.[24] In each case the toasts were made to cement already existing bonds, declaring principles that would reflect the attitudes of all those gathered and, indeed, that pithily articulated the already acknowledged reason for the gathering.

John Thelwall's refusal to toast at the meeting of the Humane Society, then, is a particularly intriguing example of toasts going wrong, as the implied contract of convivial good humour has been broken. While people must have frequently disagreed with the sentiments proposed in toasts, the convivial contract was such that it was unusual to make a show of refusing a toast, and at convivial meetings presided over by a spirit of unanimity and intolerance to contention it was more rare still that such a refusal should provoke the ire of those gathered.

The two toasts which *The Times* reports – 'the King's health' and 'prosperity to the Humane Society' – are in themselves entirely conventional and, from a certain perspective, unexceptional. Nevertheless, what is

---

[23] See *Morning Chronicle*, 25 January 1798, for a write-up of the meeting that detects nothing amiss. *True Briton*, 26 January 1798, has a satirical account of the meeting that lampoons much of the activities but fails to mention the toast to 'The Majesty of the People'. For the controversy itself, which begins a week later, see *Lloyd's Evening Post*, 31 January–2 February 1798; *True Briton*, 2 February 1798; and a more sympathetic account in the *Morning Post and Gazetteer*, 7 February 1798. See also Green, *The Majesty of the People*, 17–23.

[24] For discussions of this episode see John Barrell, *The Spirit of Despotism: Invasions of Privacy in the 1790s* (Oxford, 2006), 86–95; James Epstein, '"Equality and No King": Sociability and Sedition: the Case of John Frost', in *Romantic Sociability: Social Networks and Literary Culture in Britain 1770–1840*, ed. Gillian Russell and Clara Tuite (Cambridge, 2002), 46; Mee, *Print, Publicity, and Popular Radicalism*, 140–1; and Duthille, 'Toasting and the Diffusion of Radical Ideas', 181–2.

meaningful about them, as with many political toasts of the 1790s, is not the toasts themselves but the context in which they were articulated. Ever since the regency crisis the king's indifferent health had been a matter of considerable concern, in part because of the alliances between the king and Pitt, on the one hand, and the Prince of Wales and Fox, on the other. The king's health was indeed a matter of national political concern, made all the more pointed by the symbolic functions of the king in the decade following the French Revolution and in the midst of the war with France – a country which had six years earlier sent its king to the guillotine, and which under the direction of Napoleon was emerging as an increasingly powerful threat with global ambitions. In 1799 to toast the health of the king was not a straightforward proposition, but a toast that carried with it a great deal of political freight.

The second toast, 'prosperity to the Humane Society', meanwhile should be understood alongside the first toast, as an expression of loyalism. The toast to the society's prosperity is not a vague wish, but an idea that is pointedly associated with the king's health, itself dependent on success in the war with France. At issue here are the metaphorical resonances of the term 'health', an alternative name for 'toast', derived from the ancient practice of honouring a monarch or patron by drinking wine and wishing for their ongoing vigour and well-being. But, given the medical interests of the Humane Society, this is both an abstract wish and a hint that the kind of medical assistance and scientific knowledge that the Humane Society was interested in might be the vehicle by which the king's health, and the health of the nation, might be accomplished.

With much of this Thelwall, who took a keen interest in medicine, might have agreed. No fan of the king as a figurehead, he might nevertheless have been supportive of the medical interest in 'health' more generally. On the other hand, a toast to the Army, especially one proposed not by the chair but by a smaller group who had gathered to goad him into radical expressions, was a step too far for Thelwall. This was the point at which convivial mandate had already begun to be compromised, thus justifying his anti-social refusal of the toast. Furthermore, this smaller community within the larger gathering was ambiguously positioned as an unofficial subgroup within the more public and hence better-regulated domain of the official dinner. It was to the unofficial form of the toast, which assumed the acknowledgement of all the participants in the toast, but not the meeting as a whole, that Thelwall objected.

This was not the first time that Thelwall's toasting practices had got him into trouble. Most famously, it was alleged that Thelwall had made two seditious toasts after an open-air meeting of the London Corresponding

Society (LCS) at Chalk Farm in April 1794. Following the meeting, a group of fifty or sixty men had repaired to 3 New Compton Street, a coffeehouse owned by LCS member John Barnes, where Thelwall apparently made a toast to 'the lampposts of parliament street' and blew the head of his pint of porter, announcing 'this is the way I would serve all tyrants' (or, depending on the version you believe, 'this is the way I would serve Kings'). In the context of a radical meeting, where all the attendees were assumed to share the same political beliefs, it was a witty, amusing gesture, but it was only by being taken out of context that it could be seen as potentially treasonous.

This was a point that Thelwall himself made. He claimed that his charge of treason was supported by little more than some scraps of private conversation, 'A violent word in the moment of irritation, and debate; a ridiculous toast, perhaps suggested by the spies themselves, and repeated in the hour of conviviality, without thought or meaning.' Thelwall claims that the whimsical, amusing toast made off the cuff is not adequate evidence of the long-standing beliefs of that individual. But the claim is, I think, a little disingenuous, because few understood the power of a well-made toast better than Thelwall himself. He had participated in many meetings – both those of the LCS and of other radical groups in which he was involved – in which toasts were made and then subsequently published, demonstrating the utility of the toasts as a powerful communicative device. In the hands of radicals, toasts became manifestoes for political ideals, and indeed in many cases they enabled powerful utopian thinking. The toasts given at meetings of the LCS nearly always contain the verb 'may'. 'THE RIGHTS OF MAN; and may Britons never want spirit to assert them'; '*Citizen Thomas Paine* – May his virtue rise superior to calumny and suspicion, and his name still be dear to Britons.'[25] Toasts were not only opportunities for the display of wit and humour, nor were they bland expressions of political platitudes; they could also be deadly earnest, providing an opportunity for people to project possible futures, to indulge in wishful fantasising about how the assembled group wanted the world to operate. So, while it may be true that the convivial mandate decreed that the only already agreed-upon principles should be proposed in a toast, this did not necessarily mean that a meeting could not also assist in the development of the convivialist's political subjectivity.

---

[25] These were two of the toasts made at a general meeting of the LCS at the Globe Tavern on 23 January 1794. See London Corresponding Society, *A General Meeting of the London Corresponding Society, Held at the Globe Tavern Strand on Monday the 20th January 1794* ([London], [1794]).

Thelwall's rejection of the toast at the London Tavern is a pointed rejection of the yoking of medicine to the loyalist doctrines expressed in public accounts of the Humane Society. While he may have agreed in principle with the promotion of good health, he objected to the logic that the best reason to save people from drowning was to populate the Army of England as the rejected toast implied, and as John Beaumont, the Society's Secretary, had suggested more explicitly in his speech. And even then Thelwall suggests that he would have been willing to obey the convivial mandate for good humour if the toast had been given by the chairman, but was absolved from the necessity by the size of the gathering, a smaller coterie within the larger group of 400 present at the London Tavern. These are the kind of complex dynamics which the publicly sanctioned reports of toasts that appear in newspapers are unable to register.

The episode at the London Tavern, then, can alert us to the difficulties of trying to reconstruct systems of beliefs from the toasts that appear in newspapers, as O'Gorman suggests they might.[26] It is perhaps better to regard lists of toasts not as authentic indices of belief but as expressions of the idealised fantasy of collective agreement. The public articulations of political consensus found in toasts are always provisional expressions of possible beliefs that must encounter the contingent beliefs of the individual.

In this way it is helpful to see toasts *as an idealised form* as aligning with Habermas's notion of legitimation through consensus – the 'competition of private argument [that] came into being as consensus about what was practically necessary in the interests of all'.[27] Toasts in their *historical instantiations*, on the other hand, operate along the principles of Jean-François Lyotard's notion of legitimation by paralogy, that is, by recognising that 'consensus is only a particular state of discussion, not its end'.[28] In the pragmatics of knowledge, consensus offers a provisional proposition with which we can then take issue and begin further discussion. Consensus is important, but it is not the ultimate horizon of discussion; it provides the illusion of finality, but it closes down the search for new ideas. Paralogy, on the other hand, is the ongoing creation of meaning, which is, according to Lyotard, ultimately more enriching than static agreement. We might then see Thelwall's refusal to participate in the toast at the London Tavern not just as a refusal to accept the publicly constructed image of the Royal Humane Society but as a recognition that the idea of consensus implied

---

[26] O'Gorman, 'Campaign Rituals and Ceremonies', 113.
[27] Habermas, *Structural Transformation*, 82–3.
[28] Jean-François Lyotard, *The Postmodern Condition: A Report on Knowledge*, trans. Geoff Bennington and Brian Massumi (Minneapolis, 1997), 65.

by the form of the toast is only partial; the image of the society remains available to be renegotiated. Thelwall's rejection of the toast represents a moment when the political beliefs of the individual take precedence over the imagined consensus of the room; it is a rejection of the synecdochical logics of conviviality. The part, Thelwall says, cannot speak on behalf of the whole. His anti-social behaviour signals the inadequacies of the assumption that everyone's sentiments can be neatly aligned, and that individual belief can be forced into submission by the pressures of public opinion.

This marks a turning point in debates about sociability, one that is bound up in a larger shift in understandings of the relationship between public and private beliefs. It is not merely a coincidence that this moment, April 1799, is closely proximate to the development of Romanticism, an ideology of creative expression that, among other things, placed new emphasis on the individual at the expense of more collective and collaborative practices. That Thelwall had visited Wordsworth and Coleridge at Nether Stowey just eighteen months earlier, as they were at work on *The Lyrical Ballads*, one of the foundational texts of Romanticism, is perhaps just a coincidence of biography, but it nevertheless might alert us to connections between the development of British literary Romanticism and changes in sociability, both of which were responding in different ways to the tilting of the scale away from collectivities and towards individualism in the aftermath of the Revolutionary decade. If, as I have suggested here, toasting was the form that best encapsulated the convivial mandate towards mutual, good-humoured assent, it makes much sense that toasting would come under pressure during the political upheavals of the 1790s, when consensus building could be seen as a seditious, if not treasonable, practice. What this necessitated was a fundamental reassessment of which ideas one could silently submit to, or could let go unchallenged.

At issue is the ambiguous nature of the form of the toast, which is simultaneously an expression of personal belief and a form which lent itself to public relations efforts in newspaper reports on convivial gatherings. Ultimately, the discrepancy between the consensual nature of toasts as a form and their historical instantiation as a controversial political tool reveals the difficulties inherent in coordinating systems of belief so that all concerned might reach consensus. Not only is the coordination of belief a complex problem in itself, but even when it is successful there will always be a new context, or another public to which the group must adjust. To put that another way, it reveals the problems of Habermas's idealisation of the public sphere. The public, as Habermas himself asserts, is 'made up of private people coming together to form a public'.²⁹ To assume that consensus is a possible, or even desirable, aim of public gathering is to assume that individuals will be able and willing to stifle their personal beliefs in order to uphold the unity of the public. And for much of the eighteenth century, despite much evidence to the contrary, it was assumed that this was a desirable and feasible goal. The privileging of collective over individual belief was certainly the ideology that promoted and maintained convivial life, albeit in a form that omitted the burden of debate. But it is at the point when individuals want to assert their own principles over those of the group that this ideology breaks down. It is when the balance of the scale tips from the collective towards the individual that consensus is revealed to be merely 'a particular state of discussion, not its end', just one possibility in the ongoing language games of sociability.³⁰

---

[29] Habermas, *Structural Transformation*, 176.
[30] Lyotard, *Postmodern Condition*, 65.

Chapter 13
Sociability and the Glorious Revolution: a dubious connection in Burke's philosophy
Norbert Col

EDMUND BURKE was never without friends[1] and was highly valued by some of the most eminent among them. That was practical sociability, but, apart from his membership of Samuel Johnson's Literary Club, does it tell much about the significance in his life of those new modes of sociability that were developing at the time? Such new modes went quite a long and potentially dangerous way. Analysing the 'rejuvenation of the ancient doctrine of the social contract', setting up new and ultimately confusing notions of what 'the people' meant, while depriving the same people of older landmarks about their relationship to political power, Yves-Marie Bercé admits that 'the new sociability created in the 1760s nursed all the potentialities of regimes calling on the spirit of democracy', adding that 'one is not the dupe of the jolts of political chronicles when one acknowledges that the late eighteenth century was an entrance into another historical era'.[2] Although Bercé's concern is with the political level, not with those clubs and *salons* that contributed so much to the 'new sociability', the two phenomena – social contract theories and the emerging fashionable sociability – easily connect. In this respect one can profitably turn to Augustin Cochin and his positive reassessment by François Furet.[3] Indeed Bercé does not suggest – which would have been grotesque – that there existed waterproof partitions

---

[1] His 'commitment to sociable intellectual exchange in his early years' is mentioned by Richard Bourke, *Empire and Revolution: The Political Life of Edmund Burke* (Princeton, 2015), 54.
[2] Yves-Marie Bercé, *Révoltes et révolutions dans l'Europe moderne*, 1980 (Paris, 2013), 250–1. My translation.
[3] Augustin Cochin, *La Révolution et la libre-pensée*, posth. 1924 (Paris, 1955); François Furet, *Penser la Révolution française* (Paris, 1978), 257–316.

between the more political and the more social aspects. Beyond Bercé, Furet and Cochin, one can also remember Tocqueville's analyses of a common tendency towards abstraction, the blank slate and rationalism characterising the whole of the new mood in the eighteenth century.[4] This sheds light on what, in those related political and social aspects, created something new with which Burke was even more uneasy than Tocqueville ever was.

It was not simply the best-known aspects of abstraction that worried Burke. They did exist and engaged him much more than he might plausibly have wished. But they may also, indirectly at least, have helped him, albeit sketchily so, to realise that sociability was best left unsystematised. As a result, his diffidence with all expressions of a 'new sociability' went together with a little-noted, though identifiable enough, approach to the Glorious Revolution that was both extolled and demythologised. The end of the line was Burke's instinctive though, again, unsystematic awareness that politics and sociability should be dissociated, since the joint emergence of a specific form of social practice and of a specific form of political practice might well spell havoc. Their combination was, in Burke's eyes, one of the most loathsome manifestations of the new trend towards abstraction, with social practice being made subservient to the demands of political practice. That emerged with the French Revolution. The latter clearly altered the meaning of Burke's recognition of France as Britain's 'gentis incunabula nostrae', or 'the cradle of our people'.[5] If Britain could no longer learn safely from France, what she could learn from herself was no foregone conclusion. Indeed, Burke indicated that 'political' and 'social' sociability hardly went together in 1688–89 in the way they did in the run-up to revolutionary France.

Unsystematic sociabilities

To Burke, 'political Men of Letters' in France ranked among the prime movers of the political revolution. Their calling made them 'rarely averse to

---

[4] Furet also addresses Tocqueville, who insisted on the monarchical trend towards centralisation and mentioned that such abstract views coloured those of the *literati*. See Alexis de Tocqueville, *L'Ancien Régime et la Révolution*, 1856, ed. J.-P. Mayer, 1964 (Paris, 1986), III, i, 229–41; iii, 261–2. While Tocqueville's classic analysis bridges the gap between Ancien Régime and Revolution, since the former had already pulled down whatever remained of earlier, more or less medieval institutions, Jacob Laib Talmon's just as nearly classic approach dismisses any continuity from Ancien Régime to Revolution and is closer to the drift of Burke's thinking than Tocqueville's.

[5] Edmund Burke, *Reflections on the Revolution in France*, 1790, ed. Conor Cruise O'Brien, 1969 (Harmondsworth, 1982), 174.

innovation', they were less pampered after the death of Louis XIV and, in their thirst for an alternative, had 'a regular plan for the destruction of the Christian religion' and courted both 'the late king of Prussia' – Frederick the Great (d. 1786) – and 'the monied interest'.[6] But one should not confuse the wood for the occasionally telling tree. Burke singled out those phenomena that caught his censorious eye, and was far less attentive to those earlier forms of sociability that continued to manifest themselves. Instances of such earlier forms are provided by John Dryden's 'An Essay of Dramatic Poesy' (1668), narrating a learned conversation on a barge on the Thames in June 1665, at the time of the second Anglo-Dutch War, or by significant features from Tobias Smollett's *Roderick Random* or Captain Cook's journal together with accounts by Georg Forster.[7] A new sociability may have been emerging, but earlier forms did not collapse for that. The novel, for instance, provided examples of an instinctive sociability, especially among those who could not have been deemed likely to perform charitable actions.[8] In short, more or less codified, developing forms of intellectual and quasi-political sociability coexisted with instinctive practice, and the latter undercut those pompously benevolent claims that culminated with the tabula rasa of extreme social contract forms such as Rousseau's.

But it would be sketchy to divide things even along such lines, since they engaged Burke's mind only circuitously. The paradox of actual, or potential, criminals rescuing their fellows in need is replaced by a comparison between the ordinary exhilaration derived from attending a play and the much greater exhilaration of witnessing the execution of a criminal.[9] This was a far cry from celebrating natural charity and, although Burke was evidently critical of the mob, he did not work out a dialectic of a gruesome, sacrificial sociability under the Terreur and the new fashionable

---

[6] Burke, *Reflections*, 211–13. Denunciation of the 'monied interest' shows Burke at his least Whiggish.

[7] Bärbel Czennia, 'Floating Communities', in *La Sociabilité en France et en Grande-Bretagne au Siècle des Lumières : L'émergence d'un nouveau modèle de société*. Tome 4. *Utopie, individu et société*, ed. Norbert Col and Allan Ingram (Paris, 2015), 223–63.

[8] Gerald J. Butler, 'Defoe's Moll Flanders vs. Social Illusion', in *Utopie, individu et société*, ed. Col and Ingram, 67–8, connecting *Moll Flanders* with similar traits in Tobias Smollett's *Roderick Random* (1748) and in Henry Fielding's *Joseph Andrews* (1749).

[9] Burke, *A Philosophical Enquiry into the Origins of our Ideas of the Sublime and Beautiful*, 1757, 1759, *A Philosophical Enquiry into the Sublime and Beautiful and Other Pre-Revolutionary Writings*, ed. David Womersley (London, 1998), I, xv, 93–4. Luke Gibbons suggests that the young Burke was impressed by reports of the 1747 execution of Lord Lovat (*Edmund Burke and Ireland: Aesthetics, Politics, and the Colonial Sublime* [Cambridge, 2003], 25).

rites that had gained sway. He performed in the new modes of sociability simply because they were there at his disposal. He seems to have had little time to scrutinise clubs or *salons*, and the only place where he remotely did so was against the background of his second journey to France.[10] The author of *Sublime and Beautiful* was lionised by Madame du Deffand and her *salon* in early 1773, but he returned to Britain in dismay. He implicitly bracketed the Parisian *salons* with the rise of that atheism which was the line he wished to draw to his toleration of Protestant Dissenters.[11] Given his apparent embarrassment with Parisian activities, he could have been in a mood to accept Rousseau's preference for all-male meeting places, but he was no Rousseau and would have laughed at the latter's programmatic cultivation of manly virtue and citizenship.[12] He said nothing about *salonnardes*,[13] and it was Rousseau, Voltaire and Helvetius or, more generally, 'Atheistical fathers' with 'a bigotry of their own', that he shortlisted in his later disapproval.[14]

Be that as it may, the cynosure of 1773 was embarrassed, and at this juncture one can turn to other views of him. It would be difficult to build up, on their basis, a convincing psychological portrait of Burke or of those who moved about him. What can be gleaned does not reach much beyond what is expectable from the ups and downs of friendly intercourse. James Boswell reports that in 1783 Samuel Johnson praised 'Burke's talk' as 'the ebullition of his mind', not springing 'from a desire of distinction, but because his mind is full'.[15] The year after, Johnson joked about 'an

---

[10] The first one was c. 1757.

[11] Burke, *Speech on a Bill for the Relief of Protestant Dissenters*, 1773, *The Works of the Right Honourable Edmund Burke*, 6 vols. (London, 1907–10), VI, 112–3. O'Brien (ed. of *Reflections*, 389) notes that Burke's 'immediate impressions' of Parisian 'intellectual society' are not recorded in what remains of his letters of the time. Frederick P. Lock avers that Burke, by 1792, had grown far more hostile to 'Socinians, Unitarians, and other such sects', now viewing them 'as atheists lightly disguised' (*Edmund Burke*, 2 vols., I, 1998 [Oxford, 2008]; II, 2006 [Oxford, 2009], I, 343).

[12] On Rousseau and the futility of female-dominated *salons*, see Géraldine Lepan, 'Politesse et sociabilité selon Rousseau', in *Utopie, individu et société: la sociabilité en question*, ed. Col and Ingram, 193. Montesquieu was quite snappy about women (Marjolaine Badufle, 'La sociabilité dans les *Pensées* de Montesquieu: Regard sur les femmes', in *Utopie, individu et société*, ed. Col and Ingram, 73–92), but never went so far as Rousseau was to do.

[13] Burke, *Reflections*, 181.

[14] Burke, *Reflections*, 212. In their editions of *Reflections*, O'Brien, Pocock and Clark all point to a footnote where Burke attributes the passage to his son Richard.

[15] James Boswell, *Boswell's Life of Johnson, in two volumes*, 1791, third edition 1799 (London, 1904), II, 458.

extraordinary man' to whatever ostler might listen to him,[16] while in 1778 being 'strangely unwilling to allow to that extraordinary man the talent of wit'.[17] He had distanced himself from Burke's political alignments as early as 1772: 'I would not talk to him of the Rockingham party'.[18] But Boswell also mentions the moving circumstances in which Burke and Johnson last met before the latter's death in 1784,[19] which suggests that politics was no major embarrassment to the two men. Nor could it be seriously argued that Burke was impatient with that other member of the Literary Club, Oliver Goldsmith, according to whom Burke had given to 'party' what 'was meant for mankind',[20] in other words literature. Conversely, Bromwich suggests that, although Goldsmith's criticism was 'written partly to entertain Burke' and 'spares any imputation of dishonourable compromise', 'yet the sting remains'.[21] Goldsmith's Toryism and Burke's Whiggism may have interfered in Goldsmith's judgement, and one can also accept Cone's suggestion that Burke's *Thoughts on the Cause of the Present Discontents* (1770) fired Goldsmith's pistol,[22] but it is safer to wonder whether party affiliations really go a long way towards explaining genuine beliefs. No matter the stridency of political divisions, tags have relevance for those alone who value them and, on top of it, Burke's affiliation with the Whigs sheds rather little light on the intricacies of his thinking. This is where doubts arise respecting the connection of his sociable qualities and his politics, more specifically when the latter come to bear on the heritage of the Glorious Revolution. *Prima facie*, little need be said about the issue, since Burke glories in his membership of several clubs that kept alive the spirit of the Glorious Revolution:

> I certainly have the honour to belong to more clubs than one, in which the constitution of this kingdom and the principles of the glorious Revolution, are held in high reverence: and I reckon myself among the most forward in my zeal for maintaining that constitution and those principles in their utmost purity and vigour.[23]

---

[16] Boswell, *Life of Johnson*, II, 537–8.
[17] Boswell, *Life of Johnson*, II, 243.
[18] Boswell, *Life of Johnson*, I, 460.
[19] Boswell, *Life of Johnson*, II, 639.
[20] Oliver Goldsmith, *Retaliation; a poem* (London, 1774), line 31.
[21] David Bromwich, *The Intellectual Life of Edmund Burke: From the Sublime and Beautiful to American Independence* (Cambridge, MA, 2014), 112.
[22] Carl B. Cone, *Burke and the Nature of Politics*, 2 vols. (Lexington, 1957 and 1964), I, 208. Goldsmith may have viewed Burke's construction of party as factional.
[23] Burke, *Reflections*, 85–6.

He also made sure that Charles-Jean-François de Pont, the French recipient of what was originally intended as a private letter, should not mistake him for a supporter of the views forwarded by the Constitutional Society and the Revolution Society, specifically by Dr Richard Price in his *Discourse on the Love of Our Country* (1789). However, Burke may have slightly exaggerated the number of those clubs that he prided himself on belonging to. Symptomatically enough, O'Brien, Pocock and Mitchell do not list them in their editions of *Reflections*. Clark does mention Brooks's and the Whig Club, but adds that both were soon to incur Burke's displeasure, respectively in 1791 and 1793; Burke left the Whig Club with 'forty-two of his supporters' because he regarded it as supportive of the French Revolution.[24] Cone specifies that Burke was never an active member of Brooks's and that his subscription had not been paid from 1785; but he had been on the committee of the Whig Club.[25] In other words, these two clubs may have been closer than others to his feelings in 1789–90, but the rift was not long in opening, and there is a sense that the politically sociable Burke was less successful than the literary sociable Burke. In a word, the latter must have realised that embarking on a political career to make ends meet[26] tallied with Goldsmith's appreciation; much more must he have felt the sting of his departed friend's cutting remark when he found himself in political isolation.

Much of Burke's most rewarding sociability seems to have remained at the private level of an extended household. This is apparent from one of the worst moments in his late life, when young men volunteered to be his secretaries for free after his son Richard's death, which was evidence of Burke's charisma.[27] Even so, one cannot leave matters at that, since there is quite a different point of view in Mrs Thrale's earlier account of a visit to Beaconsfield in 1774 in the company of her husband and Samuel Johnson. She provides a shocking description of Burke as 'the first man [she] had ever seen drunk or heard talk obscenely', living among statues and paintings in a filthy house with a servant attending to his task 'with a cut wrapped in rags'.[28] It is refreshing to learn about a later episode when that other visitor

---

[24] Edmund Burke, *Reflections on the Revolution in France*, ed. Jonathan C. D. Clark (Stanford, CA, 2001), 145n.

[25] Cone, *Burke and the Nature of Politics*, II, 72–3, 290.

[26] Michel Fuchs, *Edmund Burke, Ireland and the fashioning of self* (Oxford, 1996), 298–9.

[27] Lock, *Edmund Burke*, II, 479.

[28] See Isaac Kramnick, *The Rage of Edmund Burke: Portrait of an Ambivalent Conservative* (New York, 1977), 191, referring to Charles Hughes, *Mrs Piozzi's 'Thraliana'* (London, 1913), 33–4. Kramnick also uses Hester Lynch Piozzi, *Autobiography*,

to Beaconsfield, Mary Shackleton, wrote about 'this famous Senator, this admired author, this inimitable man ... mixing with his own hands pills for the sick Poor.'[29] Burke's own hands were, hopefully, cleaner than his servant's, but what the two anecdotes suggest is that, if anything, Burke's sociability was excessive rather than defective.

Whatever one wishes to think of Kramnick's glosses that the Thrale episode was indicative of Burke's avarice and bourgeois leanings, one cannot but acknowledge the existence of two strikingly opposite approaches to Burke's private sociability, and the same holds true of his political sociability. The two sociabilities, in fact, were not kept in tight compartments, as indicated by Copeland, for whom Burke 'always marched at the head of a clan.'[30] This sheds some light on his friendship with, and mentorship to, the younger man, Charles J. Fox; then on the dramatic break with the same Fox in the House of Commons on 6 May 1791; and finally on both men's obdurate refusal to patch up their resentment.[31] Similarly, Burke never forgave Sir Philip Francis for his disparaging reaction to *Reflections*.[32] Such a complex combination of personal and public sociability in Burke's political activities explains why the conflict with Fox was so heart-rending to him as to discourage any resumption of contact across the new political divide. But this did not lead Burke to put that much to paper, barring the subdued account of the break in *An Appeal from the New to the Old Whigs*.[33] One does not find, in the 1790s, any sustained, conceptualised account of a fully fledged political sociability, let alone in the light of the legacy of the Glorious Revolution. This is intriguing, since it is a step back from what the younger Burke wrote in *Present Discontents*. In the 1790s, the Glorious Revolution was a most conspicuous prop to his political philosophy at a time when he was deprived of political friendship on account of those conflicting exegeses respecting what the same Glorious Revolution actually

---

Letters, and Literary Remains of Mrs. Piozzi (Thrale), ed. Abraham Hayward, 2 vols. (London, 1861), II, 17–18. Lock's biography has nothing about the episode. Thomas W. Copeland, *Edmund Burke: Six Essays* (London, 1950), 50–6, shows more sympathy than either Thrale or Kramnick.

[29] Mary Shackleton, 7 September 1784, to an unknown correspondent, in Lock, *Edmund Burke*, II, 547. Mary was daughter to Richard, who was Burke's close friend in boyhood and later.

[30] Copeland, *Edmund Burke: Six Essays*, 58.

[31] Leslie G. Mitchell, *Charles James Fox* (Oxford, 1992), 115.

[32] Yet, Francis was the only Foxite who attended Burke's funeral, although uninvited: see O'Brien, *The Great Melody: A Thematic Biography and Commented Anthology of Edmund Burke* (London, 1992), 592.

[33] Edmund Burke, *An Appeal from the New to the Old Whigs*, 1791, ed. Norbert Col (Rennes, 1996), 34–6, 50.

signified. Burke's reverence for the hallowed episode is so well known as to discourage further comment. Yet there is much more than meets the eye, which is where one enters slippery ground.

Demythologising the Glorious Revolution?

It may not go amiss to take stock of these two major moments when he rather precisely addressed the Glorious Revolution, since they illuminate his views on political sociability. With *Present Discontents* and its innovative conception of party government, Burke voiced principles that coloured his attitude to Fox; at the time of the French Revolution, he laments the end of the 'age of chivalry'[34] and suggests how widely different things are in Britain, with the felicitous consequences of the Revolution Settlement.[35] However, his views on party government, in 1770, are based on an idealised rendering of the Whig Junto that hardly resists investigation. The Junto, which he terms 'the great connexion of Whigs under Queen Anne', comprised 'Lord Sunderland, Lord Godolphin, Lord Somers, and Lord Marlborough'.[36] It is impossible, for the sake of brevity, to follow the composition of the Junto from the days of William of Orange: suffice it to say that Burke leaves out Wharton and Orford and, which is far more telling, silently subsumes the two Tories, Godolphin and Marlborough, under a Whig tag to which they were clearly not entitled. This suggests some embarrassment with his proposals of a homogeneous government, and his stress on the Junto's cultivation of Roman virtue in the form of political and private friendship may have done some turn in distracting attention from the shaky bases of his proposal. However, his insistence that the state should not be 'a bloody idol' demanding the sacrifice of family affections and friendship'[37] was mapping out what he voiced again at the time of the French Revolution when letting fly at the absorption of all private affections by the emerging monstrous state: 'They think everything unworthy of the name of public virtue, unless it indicates violence on the private'.[38]

In this, the French Revolution connected what *Sublime and Beautiful* still kept in neatly separated apartments: what was, presumably, apolitical relish of human suffering was replaced by what threatened political and

---

[34] Burke, *Reflections*, 170.
[35] Burke, *Reflections*, 180–90.
[36] Burke, *Thoughts on the Cause of the Present Discontents*, 1770, Works, I, 374–5.
[37] Burke, *Present Discontents*, 375.
[38] Burke, *Letters on a Regicide Peace*, 1796–97, Works, V, 209.

religious orders. It also was a sudden awareness that the construction of *Present Discontents*, with its close connection of political technique and foundational friendship, and the later calls for the 'little platoon' extolled in *Reflections*, were changing into wishful thinking. Ideal party politics, as in *Present Discontents*, would make an elective society an equivalent of the instinctive moves of that later 'platoon', which was a society that one had been born into and that developed into love of the whole of mankind;[39] in 1791, Burke's description of the 'true natural aristocracy' relied heavily on a sociability that comprised family background, upbringing and education and whence one moved on to the broader sociability of devotion to the public. He added that without such a natural aristocracy 'there is no nation'.[40] Between the lines, one detects a possible debate between 'new' and 'older' forms of sociability. Burke's considerations certainly lack the raw vigour of Defoe, Fielding or Smollett's descriptions of instinctive and compassionate sociability; they do not rule out the latter but, rather, politicise it in accordance with some presumed order of the universe, and help him to stigmatise the new developments unleashed by the French Revolution.

The passage about a 'natural aristocracy' is the best instance of Burke's elitism, one that was of wide currency and brought together Fielding's Squire Allworthy, arguably a Whig, and Smollett's Sir Launcelot Greaves, arguably a Tory.[41] But it can also be pronounced just as disingenuous as *Present Discontents*, since the two stages are both lofty ideals and party manifestos. Although Burke's views of party were ultimately successful in the nineteenth century, after much revamping of political identities in the wake of the Revolutionary and Napoleonic Wars, his 1770 efforts were a legerdemain whereby he roundly equated the Rockingham faction that he served with the real sense of the nation. Just as strikingly, this was achieved in a manner strangely reminiscent of Bolingbroke's own theories about the Country Party and the Patriot King[42] that Burke was targeting, albeit silently so. With Bolingbroke, what could never have been more than a faction among others – and a divided one at that, though outwardly united

---

[39] Burke, *Reflections*, 135.
[40] Burke, *Appeal*, 154–6.
[41] Paul Langford, *Public Life and the Propertied Englishman: 1689–1798* (Oxford, 1991), 368, referring to *Tom Jones* (1749) and *The Adventures of Sir Launcelot Greaves* (1762).
[42] See Bolingbroke, *A Dissertation upon Parties* (1734), *The Works of Lord Bolingbroke in four Volumes* (London, 1967), II, 5–6, and *The Idea of a Patriot King* (1749), II, 372–429.

against Sir Robert Walpole[43] – posed as the whole. Burke's construction was hardly different, with the proviso that it was even more overtly exclusive than Bolingbroke's. The latter, after all, had tried to bridge the gap between the habitual divide of Whigs and Tories. The Burke who, on the basis of personal friendship, easily rubbed shoulders with Tories like Johnson or Goldsmith would have found it intensely difficult to do the same in political activity, and it took the French Revolution for him to insist that he would 'break with his best friends, and ... join with his worst enemies' to combat any attempt to import French revolutionary principles into British politics.[44] Yet he had to wait for quite some time before those former 'worst enemies' took his views on France seriously. As for his counter-revolutionary accounts of sociability, they offer an equation of 'natural aristocracy' and his own views, in oblivion that a sizeable portion of his natural aristocrats held rather different opinions from his on France.

The kind of sociability that Burke enlarges on in *Reflections* aims at justifying a political order both that he attributes to the Glorious Revolution and that predates it. But the essence of this sociability is religious: 'We know, and it is our pride to know, that man is by his constitution a religious animal.'[45] Burke is less concerned with an Aristotelian political animal, and hardly at all by the developments of sociability in his day and age. One of his best-known passages is about an eternal order, 'a partnership not only between those who are living, but between those who are living, those who are dead, and those who are to be born', in other words 'the great primaeval contract of eternal society, linking the lower with the higher natures, connecting the visible and invisible world',[46] complemented by an allusion to 'the source and original archetype of all perfection'[47] that combines Platonism and Christianity. But such pronouncements shed no real light on post-1688 sociability. Thomas Paine derided his views on religious precedence in the state, considering them as heavily indebted to Roman Catholicism.[48] To what extent Paine erred is quite another matter, but it is impossible to argue

---

[43] Eveline Cruickshanks, 'Le XVIIIe siècle: de la Glorieuse Révolution à la Révolution française', in *Histoire des îles Britanniques du XVIe au XVIIIe siècle*, trans. Mariette Martin, ed. Bernard Cottret, Eveline Cruickshanks and Charles Giry-Deloison (Paris, 1994), 199.

[44] Burke, *Appeal*, 50, referring to his warning to Fox in *Speech on the Army Estimates* (9 February 1790).

[45] Burke, *Reflections*, 187.

[46] Burke, *Reflections*, 194–5.

[47] Burke, *Reflections*, 196.

[48] Thomas Paine, *Rights of Man*, 1791 and 1792, ed. Eric Foner, 1984, notes Henry Collins, 1969 (Harmondsworth, 1985), I, 43, 67. See Burke, *Reflections*, 202–3.

that, in Burke's eyes, the Glorious Revolution brought about any form of novelty whatever. Another passage simply suggests that Freethinking had lost its momentary sway.[49] Even then, Burke never indicates that such aborted novelties had anything to do with a spirit that was nursed by the Glorious Revolution. He contents himself with dismissing Richard Price's notion that the Glorious Revolution called for a completion inspired by France's move towards a religious freedom that Britain would be fortunate to emulate.[50] Burke's Glorious Revolution simply pacified things political and religious. But his political sociability is, at bottom, unconcerned with the Glorious Revolution itself. Interestingly enough, the hallowed phrase hardly appears in *Reflections*. It does indeed, as in the opening pages, but it generally comes as 'the Revolution of 1688' or, simply, 'the Revolution', as it also does in *Appeal*. By shunning an idiom that had been in use at least from Gilbert Burnet right after the events,[51] Burke tried to abstain from mythologising the event. This was already observable in *Present Discontents*, where the 'Revolution' is never given the tag 'Glorious'.

The most compelling explanation, although it is one that Burke rarely puts into so many words, has to do with his Irishness. Tellingly enough, *Appeal* makes no reference to his struggles in favour of Ireland, including her Catholics.[52] It would have been suicidal to do so at a time when he was posing as 'an Englishman',[53] but the national, British sociability that he sketches in the 1790s is debunked by his writings on Ireland with their residual Jacobitism. The Irish had been just as right in resisting William of Orange as the English and Scots had been right in supporting him[54] – by English and Scots, Burke obviously limited himself to those who put their Protestantism first, and he explicitly associated Irish Jacobitism and Catholicism. Doing so, he did not enter into the intricacies of the religious

---

[49] Burke, *Reflections*, 185–6.
[50] Richard Price, *A Discourse on the Love of Our Country*, 1789 (Oxford and New York, 1992), 16–18 and Appendix, 9–10; Burke, *Reflections*, 95–6.
[51] See Bernard Cottret, *La Glorieuse Révolution d'Angleterre: 1688*, 1988 (Paris, 2013), 297, drawing from James R. Hertzler, 'Who Dubbed It "The Glorious Revolution"?' *Albion* 19 (1987), 579–85.
[52] Burke, *Appeal*, ed. Col, 303–4, 308–9.
[53] Burke, *Appeal*, 20.
[54] Burke, *Letter to Richard Burke*, 1792, *Works*, VI, 79. A dismissive voice against 'Irish' readings of Burke is that of Clark in his edition of *Reflections* (25–6). For 'Irish' readings, both before and after Clark's edition, see O'Brien's edition of *Reflections* (22–49) and *The Great Melody*; Fuchs, *Edmund Burke, Ireland and the Fashioning of Self*; Gibbons, *Edmund Burke and Ireland*, and Seamus Deane, *Foreign Affections: Essays on Edmund Burke* (Cork, 2005). Bourke has his doubts about 'psychobiographical accounts' of Burke and Ireland (*Empire and Revolution*, 34).

components of Jacobitism in the three, then two kingdoms, but it is significant that his Irish heritage should have been such a fault-line in his outlook on the events starting in 1688.

Disconnecting politics and sociability

Ultimately, Burke never paused to argue that the Glorious Revolution paved the way for the changes in sociability that the eighteenth century in Britain has come to be associated with. The Glorious Revolution was so much of a restoration, not an innovation, to him that it would have been contradictory to regard it as a landmark even in the history of 'social' sociability. This is Burke at his most conservative. But he also sensed a handful of fishy developments. His lines on the disappearance of the 'age of chivalry' derive from his revisiting the views of the Scottish Enlightenment on commerce, and they suggest embarrassment with some contemporary mores.[55] As for his *juvenilia*, *Vindication of Natural Society* and *Sublime and Beautiful*, they address sociability from vantage points that cast some doubt on the virtues and/or centrality of the Glorious Revolution. *Vindication* indicts Lockean and Rousseauistic views, thus obliquely, but obliquely only, connecting the Glorious Revolution with dramatic developments in political philosophy; *Sublime and Beautiful* pre-eminently relates sociability with bodily, not political passions.[56] In a word, the Glorious Revolution was, at best, of little relevance to Burke's conception of sociability and, at worst, a disquieting feature in history, and *Reflections* tried to smooth things down at a time when such considerations would have been counter-productive.

Trying, as Burke did, to offer a vision of a pacified and unified Britain against revolutionary France led him to recapture something of a maverick tradition, one that he must have considered distinctly wild and adventurous, since it was that of Lord Bolingbroke, with whose writings he had such a conflictive relationship in *Vindication*. But things are more intricate. If *Vindication* claimed to complement Bolingbroke's religious heterodoxy by his alleged heterodox politics, the real targets were Locke and Rousseau – and indeed Bolingbroke's politics had little to do with Burke's satire.[57]

---

[55] John G. A. Pocock, 'The Political Economy of Burke's Analysis of the French Revolution', 1982, *Virtue, Commerce, and History*, 1985 (Cambridge, 1991), 210.

[56] On the centrality of these bodily passions in *Sublime and Beautiful*, see Gerald J. Butler, *Love and Reading: An Essay in Applied Psychoanalysis* (New York, 1989), 57–62.

[57] Norbert Col, 'Burke's Target in *A Vindication of Natural Society*: From Bolingbroke to "this sort of Writers", or an Early Burkean Defense of Church and State', *1650–1850: Ideas, Æsthetics, and Inquiries in the Early Modern Era* 20 (2013), 89–112.

Reflections offered a reluctant reconsideration. Although Bolingbroke still ranked among those Freethinkers who had fortunately sunk into oblivion, Burke's treatment of his political views was more favourable: Bolingbroke preferred monarchy 'because you can better ingraft any description of republic on a monarchy than any thing of monarchy upon the republican forms'.[58] In other words, Bolingbroke was a predecessor in what one would fain call the sociability of constitutional wheels and cogs, but in no way can this be viewed as an acknowledgement that political sociability was transformed by the Glorious Revolution. Burke's language can be, in fact, easily fitted to Stuart rhetoric, and indeed at times it reads strikingly close to Charles I's *Answer to the Nineteen Propositions from Parliament*.[59]

There is more, again, although Burke never really discussed central aspects of Bolingbroke's politics. Even *Present Discontents* is vague enough, contenting itself with referring to the circle around Frederick, Prince of Wales,[60] who had been briefly courted by Bolingbroke as a possible embodiment of his Patriot King. But Bolingbroke himself, although he is clearly identifiable, goes unmentioned, since Burke insisted that personalities – in this case, about Lord Bute – would detract attention from the real evil, namely building up an evil system that survived its inspirers.[61] Yet he tallies with Bolingbroke's stress, against Walpolean Whigs, that one could not view the Glorious Revolution as inaugurating a new era of liberties just because the latter were handed out by some benevolent political power. Burke's liberties were, one ought to remember, immemorial and thus did not depend on a political *fiat* that might suppress them just because it had granted them. True, Bolingbroke's statements were indebted to his trying to distance himself from a Jacobitism that he never fully divorced, and to his turning the tables against Walpole and his hack writers who, paradoxically, revived the old, more or less paternalistic views developed by pro-Stuart historians and propagandists like Sir Henry Spelman and Robert

---

[58] Burke, *Reflections*, 230.
[59] Extracts from the latter are in J. P. Kenyon, *The Stuart Constitution: Documents and Commentary* (Cambridge, 1966), 21–3. Fuchs regards 'Bolingbroke''s jibes at the tripartite constitution, in *Vindication*, as indeed aimed at Charles I, but it is unclear where Burke himself stands (*Edmund Burke, Ireland and the fashioning of self*, 137). Strangely, Fuchs considers that Charles's *Answer* was to the 'British [sic] Parliament'.
[60] Burke, *Present Discontents*, 315.
[61] Burke, *Present Discontents*, 330. On Bolingbroke and *Present Discontents*, see Harvey C. Mansfield, Jr, *Statesmanship and Party Government: A Study of Burke and Bolingbroke* (Chicago, 1965). On Bolingbroke, see Cottret, *Bolingbroke: Exil et écriture au siècle des Lumières. Angleterre-France (vers 1715–vers 1750)*, 2 vols. (Paris, 1992).

Brady.[62] Burke was revisiting Bolingbroke when insisting on the unbroken chain of liberties restored, not instituted, by the Glorious Revolution. In this, the two were Old, not New Whigs – obviously barring all that, in the Old Whigs, smacked of a Cromwellian heritage.

Paradoxically, this vision of the Glorious Revolution, while stressing its centrality, also played down what it offered the country. It was just an encouragement to discover what could remedy constitutional ailments. Bolingbroke held up his Country Party, then his Patriot King, as such solutions. In Burke's case, the solution would have been provided by party government. Rather dangerously so for the coherence of his tenets, he suggested that some completion was desirable. Thus, the Glorious Revolution became part of a continuum that was just as beneficial as it was embattled. Nor can one leave out Burke's pro-Catholic pronouncements, and those were clearly at odds with the Revolution Settlement. In so doing, he was unintentionally finding himself in the loathsome company of that Dr Price, a critic of the Revolution Settlement from the angle of Protestant Dissenters, who was gaining the unenviable status of Burke's new pet hate, in replacement of Bolingbroke, for arguing that Britain should complete the Glorious Revolution by imitating the early stages of the French Revolution. Price's stress on an extension of toleration, which Burke might have accepted but for the compromises of such reformers with revolutionary politics and political atheism, would have laid the foundations of a broader political sociability. This was exactly what Burke came to refuse, although he was just as equally fitted for such perspectives. In any case, his silences illustrate that political changes – if they are changes at all – do not necessarily connect with changes in society. This is no surprise when one remembers the findings of the 'Ecole des Annales' and later historians,[63] but Burke's stone to the edifice cannot be undervalued.

---

[62] On Spelman and Brady, see J. G. A. Pocock, *The Ancient Constitution and the Feudal Law: A Study of English Historical Thought in the Seventeenth Century. A Reissue with a Retrospect*, 1987 (Cambridge, 1990), 91–123, 182–228.

[63] See Jacques Le Goff on Fernand Braudel's *La Méditerranée et le monde méditerranéen à l'époque de Philippe II* (1949): there are three times: 'geographical time', 'social time' and 'individual time', the latter comprising events, implicitly of a political nature (*Histoire et mémoire* [Paris, 1988], 330); and Jacques Rancière on the same Braudel's *Civilisation matérielle et capitalisme* (1967), where time falls into the timeless 'world of repetition', in other words that of the 'defeated', then the 'loquacious' time of 'exchanges' and, finally, that of the capitalistic winners (*Les Mots de l'histoire: Essai de politique du savoir* [Paris, 1992], 131). My translations.

Chapter 14
Respectability vs political agency: a dilemma for British radical societies
Rémy Duthille

PLEBEIAN SOCIETIES, and especially the most famous of them, the London Corresponding Society (LCS),[1] were a novelty and a defining feature of the political landscape of Britain in the 1790s. Those societies sprouted across London, the Midlands and the North of England and many Scottish towns and cities when the publication of Thomas Paine's *Rights of Man* (in two parts, 1791 and 1792) gave an impetus to reform movements and articulated a republican, anti-aristocratic, popular ideology. Drawing their membership largely but not exclusively from among the disenfranchised artisan classes, popular societies agitated for a thoroughgoing reform of parliamentary representation, including universal manhood suffrage, annual (or very frequent) elections, a fair representation of cities, the abolition of rotten boroughs, pensions, sinecures and other forms of royal, aristocratic and government patronage. Although extra-parliamentary politics existed, and popular participation in political rituals such as elections was usual, and indeed expected, in England before the 1790s, the LCS and similar societies challenged the established order, as the initiative came from disenfranchised subjects. They were no longer expressions of a deferential political culture monitored by local élites, but posed a challenge to it. The government and conservative sectors of public opinion could not believe that mere artisans could set up political associations by themselves and they suspected that they were manipulated by aristocrats or wealthy individuals. In the history of political sociability, large popular societies are of interest because they tried, with a considerable degree of success, to devise democratic rules of procedure, to attract new members among the disenfranchised and to educate them into citizenship. But those attempts at a democratic sociability were fraught with difficulties, because the norms of respectability – which were to be followed in order to be considered

---

[1] Referred to as LCS in the rest of the chapter.

respectable and, by implication, worthy of the suffrage and a legitimate political opinion – constrained the radicals' room for manoeuvre, their agency. They were faced with the choice of adhering to middle-class norms in order to be taken seriously and earn their badges of citizenship, or to act up and flout conventions. The LCS, or at least its official instances and its authorised spokesmen, adopted the respectable strategy – a precarious one, given that the context of war with France made the expression of deviant political expression more and more difficult and, after December 1795, virtually untenable.

This chapter will start with a brief reminder of the history of the LCS and a review of current historiographical trends which emphasise the rifts and contradictions in plebeian culture. The contention here is that there is a need to stress some aspects that were better captured in earlier accounts: the resilience of the society and its ability to follow viable rules. The LCS was able to build a bureaucracy even if its forms of sociability were enmeshed in contradictions of several kinds, which are explored in successive sections on respectability and social inclusiveness; the accommodation of plebeian and genteel codes of behaviour; the LCS's role as a school for citizenship and, finally, the relationship, both symbolic and actual, between the LCS and official institutions.

Historians and the paradoxical sociability of the London Corresponding Society

The starting point of Edward Thompson's *The Making of the English Working Class* was the foundation of the LCS in January 1792. The story has become a familiar one: a shoemaker, Thomas Hardy, met with eight other like-minded artisans in a tavern off the Strand to discuss political writings, especially Thomas Paine's *Rights of Man*. All of them, save one, agreed to meet again the next week and subscribe one penny each to cover expenses for fuel, lighting, books and correspondence materials. Hardy soon devised rules, the first of them stating 'that the number of our Members be unlimited'.[2] Thompson famously considered this rule as a fundamental break with exclusive elite politics, heralding a democratic project: it was no less than 'one of the hinges upon which history turns'.[3] This rule and others, such as the rotation of members as chairman of the meetings, were

---

[2] E. P. Thompson, *The Making of the English Working Class* (Harmondsworth, 1980), 19.
[3] Thompson, *The Making of the English Working Class*, 24.

meant to avoid any oligarchic tendency and ensure democratic debating and decision-making procedures. The society was open, in Thomas Hardy's words, to 'all classes and descriptions of men (criminals, insane and infants excepted)'.[4] The same phrase was used in formulations of the society's main goals: the achievement of male universal suffrage and annual elections. The rules of the LCS, which regulated its pattern of sociability, were tightly linked to the society's democratic ideology. For instance, the equality of all members (corresponding to the equality of citizens in LCS ideology and to universal suffrage in its demands) manifested itself by rules such as the obligation for all members to speak during a given debate, or the rotation of the chairmanship, which as noted above, were democratic practices meant to put into practice the ideal of equality and to prevent any oligarchic or aristocratic tendency. It is therefore apt that Thompson should have started with a discussion of the procedural rules rather than with ideology.

The destiny of the LCS[5] exemplifies the hopes and predicament of the English radicals who mustered the people to press for reform but failed to pass reform through Parliament and finally fell victims of government repression and various forms of harassment on the part of self-styled 'loyal' associations.[6] In 1792 and 1793 the LCS expanded rapidly and its infrastructure developed and ramified. It was divided into 'sections' that contained up to thirty members. Once this figure was reached a new section was created, and in this way a network grew across the boroughs surrounding the City of London and expanded eastwards.[7] Besides organising political readings,

---

[4] Albert Goodwin, *The Friends of Liberty: The English Democratic Movement in the Age of the French Revolution* (London: Hutchinson, 1979), 192.

[5] Accounts include: Michael T. Davis, 'London Corresponding Society (*act.* 1792–1799)', *Oxford Dictionary of National Biography*, Oxford University Press, 2004; online edition, January 2008; Albert Goodwin; *Selections from the Papers of the London Corresponding Society, 1792–1799*, ed. Mary Thale (Cambridge; New York, 1983); Michael T. Davis, 'Introduction', in *London Corresponding Society, 1792–1799*, ed. Michael T. Davis, 6 vols. (London and Brookfield, VT, 2002), vol. I.

[6] Loyalism spread across Britain in 1792–93, then resurfaced under various guises (e.g. in the support for recruitment for the war). There is evidence of widespread popular participation far down the social spectrum, but historians are unsure whether the mass of loyalist propaganda distributed to the lower orders changed their opinions in the long run. See Robert R. Dozier, *For King, Constitution and Country: the English Loyalists and the French Revolution* (Lexington, KY, 1983); Mark Philp, 'Vulgar Conservatism, 1792–3', *English Historical Review* 110 (1995), 42–69.

[7] On the geographical distribution of LCS sections, see John Barrell, 'London and the London Corresponding Society', in *Romantic Metropolis: The Urban Scene of British Culture, 1780–1840*, ed. James Chandler and Kevin Gilmartin (Cambridge and New York, 2005), 85–112.

publishing pamphlets and corresponding with societies in Britain and the Jacobin club of Paris, much of the activity in the LCS in 1793 was concerned with the management of such an overgrown network; heated debate on the appropriate degree of autonomy or centralisation led to the rejection of a 'constitution' that was deemed tyrannical.

Although many historians have studied the LCS[8] and the chronology of its activities is well charted, some aspects of the society remain 'elusive', as Michael T. Davis wrote in his entry on the LCS in the *Oxford Dictionary of National Biography*. Contradictory claims were made about membership figures; it is safe to follow Davis's of a low point of 241 paying members in mid-1794 and a peak of 5,000 men in 1795. What is known of the professional activity of a small fraction of the society suggests that artisans were most numerous but rubbed shoulders with members of the professions, medical doctors, lawyers, printers and publishers, who often played a key role in managing the society's activities. Beyond its fluctuating membership, the LCS was able to voice its message to a much larger audience through pamphlets, a magazine, handbills and meetings. This was an uphill struggle. 'Loyalist' associations fought hard to eradicate the LCS, bringing economic pressure to bear on members and publicans who housed LCS meetings in their precincts. In May 1794, several members of the LCS were rounded up. Three leaders were indicted: Thomas Hardy, the founder of the society; the genteel reformer John Horne Tooke; and the orator John Thelwall. Although the much-publicised treason trial resulted in acquittals, the society was reeling from the blow. It could still put on shows of strength, gathering monster meetings to protest against two Bills meant to crack down on the liberty of assembly.[9] On one such occasion, on 12 November 1794, LCS leaders addressed a crowd of 300,000 to 350,000 gathered in a

---

[8] The pioneering study was Thompson. Subsequent studies and publications of primary sources include Thale; Benjamin Weinstein, 'Popular Constitutionalism and the London Corresponding Society', *Albion: A Quarterly Journal Concerned with British Studies*, 34, no. 1 (2002), 37–57; Barrell, 'London and the London Corresponding Society'; Davis, I; Michael T. Davis, 'The Mob Club? The London Corresponding Society and the Politics of Civility in the 1790s', in *Unrespectable Radicals? Popular Politics in the Age of Reform*, ed. Paul A. Pickering and Michael T. Davis (Aldershot, 2008), 21–40.

[9] The Treasonable Practices Act (36 Geo III c.7) and the Seditious Meetings Act (36 Geo III c.8), variously known as the 'Pitt and Grenville Acts' or the 'Gagging Acts', became law on 18 December 1795. The first redefined and extended the existing law on treason and sedition. The second required magistrates to authorise meetings of more than fifty people, in effect criminalising popular political meetings and outlawing LCS meetings. Inciting hatred against the king, the government or the constitution could be punished by transportation of up to seven years. On the legal

field near Copenhagen House – an audience that went considerably beyond LCS membership.[10] Popular agitation (such as several 'monster meetings' held in Sheffield and, in London, by the LCS on 26 October and 12 November 1795 near Copenhagen House and on 7 December 1795 in Marylebone Fields) and parliamentary interventions failed to halt the passing of the two Bills. From then on, the LCS started to decline because the liberty of association, petition and speech was severely curtailed; splinter groups of the LCS dabbled in underground revolutionary activity and the society was formally banned, together with other societies, in 1799.

The most remarkable fact about the LCS, however, is not so much its demise as its survival in the face of such odds. Following E. P. Thompson's insights, research carried out in the 1970s and 1980s by Günther Lottes and Mary Thale demonstrated that this resilience depended on the painstaking building of a viable society through procedures and everyday administrative chores such as the collection of weekly dues, account-keeping and the management of correspondence and printing. Mary Thale insisted, quite rightly, that '[t]he orderly functioning of the Society – indeed their remarkable continuance for over six years – owed much to the members' adherence to rules of procedure'.[11] Voting on a variety of issues (including on rules of procedure), rotation of offices, the choice of extracts to read out and discuss, debating rules such as the obligation of speaking in turn without breaking in on speeches, may have been more fundamental and more formative in the members' experience than any ideological content conveyed by the society.

Today, historians of British radicalism[12] in the 1790s pay close attention to sociability, but have largely moved away from Thompson's focus on class

---

and ideological background of the acts, see John Barrell, *Imagining the King's Death: Figurative Treason, Fantasies of Regicide, 1793–1796* (Oxford and New York, 2000).

[10] Goodwin, *The Friends of Liberty*, 391.

[11] Thale, *Selections*, xxvi. By far the most complete account of the LCS's rules of procedures is to be found in Lottes's untranslated monograph in German (Günther Lottes, *Politische Aufklärung und Plebejisches Publikum: Zur Theorie und Praxis des Englischen Radikalismus im späten 18. Jahrhundert* [Munich and Vienna, 1979]). The gist of the argument is accessible in English in an article by Lottes and in work by Geoff Eley: Günther Lottes, 'Radicalism, Revolution and Political Culture: an Anglo-French Comparison', in *The French Revolution and British Popular Politics*, ed. Mark Philp (Cambridge, 1991), 78–98; Geoff Eley, 'Nations, Publics, and Political Culture: Placing Habermas in the Nineteenth Century', in *Habermas and the Public Sphere*, ed. Craig J. Calhoun (Cambridge, MA and London, 1993), 289–339.

[12] See in particular Jon Mee, *Conversable Worlds: Literature, Contention, and Community 1762 to 1830* (Oxford, 2011); Ana M. Acosta, 'Spaces of Dissent and the Public Sphere in Hackney, Stoke Newington, and Newington Green', *Eighteenth-Century*

formation and his heroic narrative of the endeavours of stern, respectable, artisan and later working-class societies.[13] Since the mid-1980s, writing on the LCS has been informed by the linguistic turn, and postmodern scepticism about the stability of signifiers and the possibility of an ultimate assignation of meaning. Mark Philp stressed the fragmented nature of radical ideology, and the unstable, fissiparous character of a radical sociability that was fraying at the edges and caved in under government repression, loyalist harassment and internal contradictions as the 1790s wore on.[14]

Three largely overlapping tendencies can be discerned in recent literature. In the wake of the English translation of Jürgen Habermas's *Structural Transformation of the Public Sphere* (1962, transl. 1989), a vast literature has been concerned with the emergence of 'plebeian' or 'counter public spheres'.[15] The concept of the public sphere was diffracted and pluralised into competing, internally contentious and overlapping spheres.[16]

More recently, some researchers have focused on the way that space informed sociability, articulating different scales ranging from microspaces (the layout of a particular room or a tavern such as the Crown and Anchor) to the urban environment of London and on to transnational networks.[17] As David Featherstone argued, '[t]he LCS's political identities and practices developed in relation to various transnational networks' because they were shaped in international circulations, for example by adapting French republican practices and symbols (the most notorious was their

---

Life 27, no. 1 (2003), 1–27; John Barrell, *The Spirit of Despotism: Invasions of Privacy in the 1790s* (Oxford and New York, 2006); Micah Alpaugh, 'The British Origins of the French Jacobins: Radical Sociability and the Development of Political Club Networks, 1787–1793', *European History Quarterly* 44, no. 4 (2014), 593–619.

[13] Thompson was careful to define the LCS as a 'popular Radical society' rather than a working-class society (Thompson, *The Making of the English Working Class*, 22).

[14] Mark Philp, 'The Fragmented Ideology of Reform', in *The French Revolution and British Popular Politics*, ed. Mark Philp (Cambridge, 1991), 50–77.

[15] Jon Klancher, *The Making of English Reading Audiences, 1790–1832* (Madison, WI and London, 1987); Kevin Gilmartin, *Print Politics: The Press and Radical Opposition in Early Nineteenth-Century England* (New York, 1996).

[16] For an overview of this historiography, see the introduction of Alex Benchimol, *Intellectual Politics and Cultural Conflict in the Romantic Period: Scottish Whigs, English Radicals and the Making of the British Public Sphere* (Aldershot, England and Burlington, VT, 2010).

[17] Acosta; Ian David Newman, 'Tavern Talk Literature, Politics and Conviviality' (Ph.D. thesis, University of California, Los Angeles, 2013); D. Featherstone, 'Contested Relationalities of Political Activism: The Democratic Spatial Practices of the London Corresponding Society', *Cultural Dynamics* 22, no. 2 (2010), 87–104.

self-styling as 'citizens') and in turn spreading practices to popular societies in America and elsewhere.[18]

Interdisciplinary studies have taken their cue from Iain McCalman's foundational work on the 'radical underworld' of Spencean societies. Thomas Spence, a proponent of a utopian land plan involving democratic institutions and parish ownership of land, had many disciples who gathered in 'a loosely-linked, semi-clandestine network of political organisations, groups, coteries and alliances'. The Spencean underworld overlapped with the LCS and hovered in a 'fluid, ambivalent position', forming 'a long and intricate overlap between the allegedly separate spheres of "respectability" and "roughness"'.[19] McCalman drew attention to the specific venues (Spencean taverns, 'free and easies', debating clubs), forms of sociability and ritual practices. Although debating clubs were vehicles for serious political and anti-religious argument, entertainment was an integral dimension of plebeian sociability. 'The ritual "hullaballoo" of singing, toasting, chanting, and cheering' involved a high degree of theatricality: ritual behaviour in plebeian taverns was bound up with notions of male honour and competitiveness. 'Some Spenceans probably attended them for purely expressive purposes – to enjoy the social ritual and to experience a release of tensions.'[20] McCalman's book opened up a new field, dubbed 'plebeian studies' by Anne Janowitz, with major books by Jon Mee, David Worrall and Kevin Gilmartin, among others.[21]

In 2000, John Barrell's extensive study of treason law, *Imagining the King's Death*, made an exemplary and highly influential use of literary analysis to probe the complex political and cultural landscape of the 1790s.[22] Several cross-disciplinary case studies informed by literary analysis, sociology and anthropology have stressed fault-lines, fluid affiliations and the transvaluation of signifiers. The radicals acted as wordsmiths and playwrights, staging disruptive performances in various arenas of power. Coffeehouses, courtrooms such as the Old Bailey and prisons such as Newgate became

---

[18] David Featherstone, 'The Spatial Politics of the Past Unbound: Transnational Networks and the Making of Political Identities', *Global Networks* 7 (2007), 441.
[19] Iain McCalman, *Radical Underworld: Prophets, Revolutionaries and Pornographers in London, 1795–1840* (Oxford, 1998), 2–3.
[20] McCalman, *Radical Underworld*, 121.
[21] Anne Janowitz coined the term in a review of David Worrall's *Radical Culture: Discourse, Resistance and Surveillance, 1790–1820* and Jon Mee's *Dangerous Enthusiasm: William Blake and the Culture of Radicalism* in *Studies in Romanticism* 32, no. 2 (1993), 297–303. Kevin Gilmartin accepted this label for his own work. Gilmartin, *Print Politics*, 4.
[22] Barrell, *Imagining the King's Death*.

contested sites in which outrageous 'performances' were played out.[23] The histrionic character of many radical leaders, which Thompson deplored,[24] was now seen as a weapon of cultural and political destabilisation.[25] Much attention has been paid to clashes and incidents that occurred in the course of plebeian sociability, or when plebeian and polite codes collided. A case in point is John Thelwall's *King Chaunticlere; or, The Fate of Tyranny*. Published as it was in 1793, in the aftermath of Louis XVI's decapitation, this comic fable about the beheading of a tyrannical cock led to a trial in the course of which Thelwall and his publisher, Charles Pigott, used the legal conventions of the courtroom – the prosecutor was obliged to name King George III whenever he uttered the word 'Chaunticlere' – in order to elicit laughter and destabilise loyalist discourse.[26] Another well-documented incident started with John Frost's scandalous toast calling the King 'a German hog butcher' in a coffeehouse, which again led to prosecution after Frost was overheard by a loyalist customer (or spy?). The case raised issues of respectability, the limits of acceptable speech and the blurred boundaries between public and private spheres. The coffeehouse was an intermediate space between the public sphere and the private realm, a contested space where sociability could either develop or, more likely in the 1790s, be monitored and thwarted by the government.[27]

---

[23] Michael T. Davis, Iain McCalman, and Christina Parolin, *Newgate in Revolution: An Anthology of Radical Prison Literature in the Age of Revolution* (London; New York, 2005).

[24] 'Citizen' Groves's 'speech was moving, if a trifle histrionic, in its sincerity'. Thompson, *The Making of the English Working Class*, 147; Thelwall 'had a dash of the histrionic in his character' (149); there was an 'excess of the histrionic in Margarot's character' (139).

[25] James Epstein and David Karr, 'Playing at Revolution: British "Jacobin" Performance', *The Journal of Modern History* 79, no. 3 (2007), 495–530; John Barrell, '"An Entire Change of Performances?" The Politicisation of Theatre and the Theatricalisation of Politics in the Mid 1790s', *Lumen: Selected Proceedings from the Canadian Society for Eighteenth-Century Studies* 17 (1998), 11–50.

[26] Barrell, *Imagining the King's Death*, 104–5; Michael Henry Scrivener, *Seditious Allegories: John Thelwall and Jacobin Writing* (University Park, PA, 2001), 111–18; James Epstein, *In Practice: Studies in the Language and Culture of Popular Politics in Modern Britain* (Stanford, CA, 2003), 99–103.

[27] James Epstein, '"Equality and No King". Sociability and Sedition: The Case of John Frost', in *Romantic Sociability: Social Networks and Literary Culture in Britain, 1770–1840*, ed. Clara Tuite and Gillian Russell (Cambridge, 2002), 43–61; Barrell, *The Spirit of Despotism*, ch. 2; Newman, 'Tavern Talk Literature, Politics and Conviviality', 3–13.

This historiographical tendency culminated in a festschrift for Iain McCalman, aptly entitled *Unrespectable Radicals?*[28] In this collection, Michael T. Davis discussed the issues of the LCS's respectability on the basis of *The Times*'s reviling of the LCS as a 'mob club'. Davis argued that the government and the conservatives did not merely try to uphold the established order, but sought to root out plebeian clubs by redefining respectability and thus labelling them as deviant. They instigated a moral panic to polarise society into the respectable loyalists and the unrespectable 'Jacobins', who must be marginalised and ultimately eliminated.[29] While conservatives defined the LCS as unrespectable, i.e. inclined towards 'hysteria, excitable, disorderly and passionate, and given to fantasy', the LCS retorted with their own 'politics of civility', a symbolic code in which they defined themselves as respectable, or 'autonomous, rational, reasonable, self-controlled and sane'. In other words, the LCS 'needed to present itself as inclusive, autonomous, as a rule-regulated organisation based upon the principle of equality and rational deliberation in order to invert the political messages of loyalists'.[30] Reviewing the above-mentioned coffeehouse scandals, Davis spelled out a central paradox of LCS sociability: the tension between the necessary rules of self-restraint and the excesses provoked by an unruly, tavern-based sociability. Taverns were key sites because they formed the organisational basis of the LCS, and they were central to artisan sociability: the society could build on this already-existing network to maintain and expand its membership. But rules for keeping the LCS respectable, and especially the ban on drinking and smoking, were in stark contradiction with traditional tavern sociability, thus causing tensions, and occasionally incidents, when a member's personal agenda clashed with the society's rules.

A democratic, inclusive sociability in search of respectability

Michael Davis's account of the LCS's stigma-management strategies is very illuminating and enriches Günther Lottes's earlier account of the

---

[28] Paul A. Pickering and Michael T. Davis (eds.), *Unrespectable Radicals? Popular Politics in the Age of Reform* (Aldershot, England and Burlington, 2008).

[29] By 1792 'Jacobin' came to designate in England supporters of the French Revolution. The loyalists used it as a term of abuse against all English reformers, exploiting the French origin of the word, serving to show the foreignness of radicals. The word also carried a connotation of atheism or religious heresy. Few reformers accepted it; John Thelwall was a notable exception. On the word 'Jacobin' and Thelwall: Scrivener, *Seditious Allegories*, 21–42.

[30] Michael T. Davis, 'The Mob Club?', 25.

contradiction between the rational-discursive ideal of the LCS and its grounding in unruly traditional culture.[31] However, it tells one side of the story, that of the society's difficult relations with the outside world (especially the social-political elites) and the need for managing the society's public image. Seen from the point of view of the rank and file, however, the social benefits of membership probably offset the social stigma. The scandals dissected in recent historiography typically involved gentlemen reformers or *déclassé* intellectuals acting out in exclusive or socially mixed venues. Importantly for the study of LCS sociability, those incidents usually happened outside the meetings of the society rather than in the humdrum meetings of local sections. This intellectual intelligentsia did exist and it left many traces of its activities in print, manuscript and court records – far more than did rank-and-file LCS members. In linguistically informed analyses focusing on print culture this very vocal minority is bound to attract a disproportionate share of attention, and possibly eclipse the more mundane everyday working of the LCS. How representative were they of the several thousand artisan members of the LCS? While reformers who ventured into the world of print or engaged in 'seditious' talk in mixed company could be harshly punished, the artisans who attended LCS meetings might go unscathed and enjoy the benefits of radical sociability.

This contrast raises the question of democratic inclusiveness at a time when sociability became increasingly stratified and compartmentalised. LCS meetings held up a promise of free, rational and egalitarian discussion. Günther Lottes interpreted the society's ethos as a plebeian-democratic derivation of Habermas's Kantian ideal of the enlightened public sphere.[32] For the history of sociability, the LCS's insistence on social inclusiveness mattered because it went against a major trend that had started in the decades preceding the French Revolution – what Jon Mee called 'a broader historical process emptying out or segregating many of the mixed public places through which the vivifying conversation of culture had been perceived to be circulating'.[33] Gentlemen's clubs became exclusive preserves, and free speech in taverns and coffeehouses was threatened by constant monitoring by loyalist informers. The LCS, by contrast, offered social mixing in its meetings and this impacted on the members' lives and prospects. As Mark Philp noted, involvement in reform politics had very different implications for the members of different social classes. Gentlemen-reformers like Horne Tooke were most vulnerable to social stigma. Aristocrats could

---

[31] Davis, 'The Mob Club?'; Lottes, *Politische Aufklärung Und Plebejisches Publikum*.
[32] Lottes, *Politische Aufklärung und Plebejisches Publikum*.
[33] Mee, *Conversable Worlds*, 132.

dabble in Jacobinism with relative impunity. Conversely, 'for people like [Francis] Place and [Thomas] Hardy, reform offered a more practical kind of emancipation or empowerment, together with a degree of social mobility.'[34] This sense of opportunity pervades the classic autobiographies of the LCS leaders. 'After his acquittal, in 1794, John Binns noted, Hardy opened a boot store in Fleet Street, London. The friends of Parliamentary Reform, and the Radicals, liberally patronised him, and he acquired considerable property.'[35] Francis Place, a breeches maker, retrospectively wished that he had exploited his position and connections in the LCS to expand his business. He had been held back by the fear of being accused of making a profit out of his position, but the LCS secretary, John Ashley, was 'less scrupulous,'[36] according to Place, and gained many customers.

Yet Place recognised that he derived some benefits, financial but mainly intellectual, from his involvement in the LCS. Ashley passed on to Place books from some rich customers' 'considerable collections', and the frequentation of men of superior abilities was an exhilarating experience that helped him to engage in business more confidently.[37] In retrospect, Place was satisfied with, not to say complacent about, the influence of the LCS: 'the moral effects of the society were very great indeed; it induced men to read books, instead of spending their time at public houses, it induced them to love their own homes, it taught them to think, to respect themselves, and to desire to educate their children.'[38] In this statement, self-respect is intertwined with moral righteousness, abstinence, family life and a desire for social mobility for one's children.

Place's autobiography, a major source for the history of radicalism, is a good site to explore Jacobin 'respectability.'[39] This retrospective account is notorious for its concern with respectability. As Mary Thale noted, Place never failed to remind his readers that his wife and he tried to dress and act in respectable ways, and castigated those who did not.

---

[34] Philp, 'The Fragmented Ideology of Reform', 73.
[35] John Binns, *Recollections of the Life of John Binns: Twenty-Nine Years in Europe and Fifty-Three in the United States: With Anecdotes, Political, Historical, and Miscellaneous* (Philadelphia, 1854), 42.
[36] Francis Place, *The Autobiography of Francis Place, 1771–1854*, ed. Mary Thale (Cambridge, 1972), 143.
[37] Place, *The Autobiography*, 42–3.
[38] British Library, Add MS 27, 808, fo.60, quoted in Lottes, *Politische Aufklärung Und Plebejisches Publikum*, 209.
[39] Place, *The Autobiography*, 43.

> If a preoccupation with respectability seems repellent to us, Thale proceeded, Place's autobiography may help us to understand how the significance of the word has changed. For us it is an external matter, the good repute which, rightly or wrongly, other people accord us. But for Place it was primarily an internal disposition, even though such externals as clothes may have helped create it. Respectability meant having a good self-image, a sense of one's self as an important being.[40]

Thale went on to comment that for Place and like-minded artisans respectability was not a given but 'a hard-won and perilous acquisition'.[41] Thale's comments capture what might have been the core of the experience of participating in the LCS for artisans and disenfranchised subjects: a process of building self-respect and agency, which in twenty-first-century terms could be called empowerment.

Lack of respectability was a stumbling block, as Thomas Hardy was later to explain in his autobiography (published in 1832; ironically, the year of his death and of the passing of the Great Reform Act). Hardy explained that opponents of the radicals often asked

> who was the founder of the Society [...]. The question was always evaded, because of the obscurity and unimportance in Society of the founder, and that it might be better esteemed by the public, and more respectable, *agreeably to the received idea of respectability*, and that they might attend more particularly to the object which the thing formed had in view.[42]

Hardy's low social origin – he was a shoemaker – diverted the public's attention from the professed goal of the society, parliamentary reform. Hardy distances himself from 'the received idea of respectability',[43] which meant that the lower orders had no say in politics. Significantly, the first occurrence of the word in the *Oxford English Dictionary* appeared in 1775, in the comments by Virginian Arthur Lee on the 'respectability' of petitions

---

[40] Place, *The Autobiography*, xxi.
[41] Place, *The Autobiography*, xxi–xxii.
[42] Thomas Hardy, *Memoir of Thomas Hardy, Founder of, and Secretary to, the London Corresponding Society* (London, 1832), 100 (emphasis added).
[43] Hardy, *Memoir of Thomas Hardy*, 100.

sent from northern English cities to the Westminster Parliament concerning the coercion of the colonies.[44]

LCS sociability: a school for citizenship and respectability

All this suggests that respectability was bound up with citizenship, and achieving a degree of it entitled a social group to voting rights and political representation. The radicals of the LCS thought that attendance at meetings and the respect of procedural rules would educate the artisans into citizenship while building up their self-respect. For Lottes, the process was fraught with difficulty because of contradictions between three factors: the LCS leaders' ideal of an educated, enlightened, autonomous citizenry (involving democratic decision making and, inevitably, lengthy debates) was at odds with the need for operational efficiency (which meant that there should be a strong central executive in the LCS to make quick, authoritative decisions) and with the immaturity of plebeian masses partaking in a traditional culture that valued rowdy pastimes and encouraged a degree of violence. Eley commented that the LCS also presumed the political maturity of the masses that it was intended to create: it was a chicken-and-egg situation.[45]

Admittedly, the reality of LCS meetings was much messier than Place's idealised retrospective vision, as Thompson, Lottes, Thale, and probably Place himself, knew full well. But the contradictions were not as intractable as Lottes suggested. He acknowledged that the LCS had to mould its political expression into plebeian forms of sociability so as not to alienate the masses, but he tended to present this accommodation as a constraint rather than an opportunity.[46] The tavern-based culture of the London artisans possessed features that were conducive, rather than hostile to, the educational work of the LCS. As Jon Mee noted, some members of the LCS, like Place, clearly perceived the contradictions between rational ideals and traditional entertainment but others, including John Thelwall, Daniel Isaac Eaton and

---

[44] 'respectability, n.' *Oxford English Dictionary Online*. Oxford University Press, September 2016 (accessed March 2019). The reference is to Arthur Lee, *A Second Appeal to the Justice and Interests of the People, on the Measures Respecting America. By the Author of the First* (London, 1775), 12.

[45] Lottes, *Politische Aufklärung Und Plebejisches Publikum*, 336; Eley, 'Nations, Publics, and Political Culture'.

[46] Lottes, *Politische Aufklärung Und Plebejisches Publikum*, 337.

Thomas Spence, did not.[47] Levity need not be incompatible with serious political argument; toasts and songs performed the function of community building – a crucial one in the case of a marginalised, repressed group.[48] In a semi-literate world singing could also be a more efficient method of political sensitisation than reading and discussing abstract texts; nor are the two activities mutually exclusive.

Rather than rejecting existing practices of artisan sociability, the LCS tried to build on them. True, some prominent members of the LCS, like Place, professed to hate tavern culture. But Place himself was heavily indebted to a pre-existing artisan sociability. Before he joined the LCS in June 1794 he had been involved in several artisan clubs. He became a leader in the Breeches Makers Society, a benefit club whose activities were akin to those of a trade union. He also formed a society of carpenters, a benefit club of journeymen plumbers; he 'drew up articles for several other clubs, and assisted in their formation, for all which [he] was paid'.[49] There is a clear continuity between Place's earlier activities and his rapid rise in the LCS. The skills he had acquired were precious in the management of the LCS. He was repeatedly elected to the position of chairman, which he described as a difficult one that involved keeping order and pushing business forward without offending members' sensibilities. Place immediately adds that it was later decided that the chairman should be elected for three months rather than every evening.[50] At this point the constraints of bureaucratic efficiency were at odds with the democratic imperative, but a sensible compromise was found.

LCS sociability, a blueprint for a democratic citizenship borrowing from established parliamentary forms

A final tangle of homologies and contradictions must be explored: the relationship between the LCS (as a bureaucratic and political structure) and official (national and local) representative institutions. The LCS had given itself rules meant to ensure fair debating, liberty and equality of speech,

---

[47] Jon Mee, 'Thomas Spence and the London Corresponding Society, 1792–1795', in *Thomas Spence: The Poor Man's Revolutionary*, ed. Alastair Bonnett and Keith Armstrong (London, 2014), 53–63 (59).

[48] Davis, 'Meet and Sing', 123. See also Iain Newman's chapter on toasting in this volume.

[49] Place, *The Autobiography*, 126.

[50] Place, *The Autobiography*, 151.

and a structure topped by a representative leadership. It claimed that those structures, and the mode of sociability they made possible – fair, orderly, democratic, 'manly' in the sense of bold and responsible – demonstrated the civic maturity of the people and could be applied to the official representative institution, Parliament. In a sense, then, the LCS was functioning as a counter-parliament. Much of its activity was engrossed with the business of running the society democratically, which suggests that debating rules, observing them and changing them if needed may have been as important as debating national political issues. A mode of sociability that made it possible for mechanics to debate political topics in an orderly way was by itself a rebuttal of loyalist depictions of democracy as mob rule or anarchy. John Barrell pointed out a tantalising correlation between the geography of LCS divisions in London and the structure of local government. There were few divisions in the City, which was akin to 'a ratepayers' democracy' offering wide opportunities for political participation. Therefore, tradesmen may have felt less urgent need to vent grievances in the LCS than other men of similar social standing living in boroughs ruled by local oligarchies. Inhabitants of the City felt that they were active citizens already, and significantly, despite low LCS activity there, the City protested against the Seditious Meetings Act.[51] If Barrell's surmise is true, which is very plausible, then the LCS offered a much-needed opportunity for political debate to men of the lower and middling orders who felt entitled to citizenship.

There was a homology between the LCS as an unofficial arena and official institutions. For the loyalists and the government, the LCS was trying to usurp sovereignty, especially when it sent delegates to the Edinburgh British Convention in the autumn of 1793 (in the government's view the word 'convention' was indicative of a Jacobin plot).[52] Perhaps they were not

---

[51] Barrell, 'London and the London Corresponding Society', 96–7.
[52] Loyalists claimed that the LCS and similar societies were part of a French Jacobin plot to prepare for an overthrow of the British state and/or a French invasion. The loyalists took the use of French forms such as the word 'convention' as evidence of such a plot. See for example this comment on the British Convention held at Edinburgh in November–December 1793 with delegates from across Scotland, Sheffield and the LCS: 'We have seen an assembly in the metropolis of Scotland, borrowing its name, its inflated jargon, its sanguinary measures, from the records of Gallic anarchy, and ready to erect the standard of revolt in the fields of happy Britain' (*Dundee Repository, of Political and Miscellaneous Information*, 13 December 1793, quoted in John D. Brims, 'The Scottish Democratic Movement in the Age of the French Revolution' [Ph.D. thesis, University of Edinburgh, 1983], 510.). However, it 'was probably not so intentionally provocative or not insidiously revealing of an intention to assume the status or powers of a French republican convention' (Goodwin, *The Friends of Liberty*, 302).

so far off the mark: at least some English reformers considered the LCS as a microcosm, or a blueprint, of an ideal British democratic polity. This can be inferred from an 'anecdote of Thomas Paine' recounted by John Thelwall in *The Tribune*, a periodical based on his political lectures. The anecdote is worth quoting in full:

> It was observed in company to Thomas Paine, that the British and Irish were naturally inclined to Monarchy; so much so, that in their convivial meetings they always had a toast master; and that if six of them went to a tavern to drink a bottle of wine, one would be put into the chair who would collect the bill and pay the waiter, and the rest would benefit by his attention.
>
> Very true, Sir, says Paine, suppose your six men met every day to drink their bottle, and that they had no more and the chairman always took a pint to himself: They would soon contrive to drink without one; that is, if they were fond of wine, and had common sense.[53]

A country could be run as a club. The people club together their resources in the form of taxes and spend them after a democratic decision-making process. The implication is clear: the LCS's orderly proceedings prove the viability of a democratic plebeian polity. Revealingly, 'Paine' counters a conservative argument that also posits a homology between tavern sociability and the English political proclivities. Indeed, the analogy was generally assumed and fought over: whether in the loyalist press, pamphlets, parodies or graphic caricature, conservative discourse in the 1790s always emphasised the 'disorder' and 'anarchy' which supposedly pervaded 'Jacobin' societies.[54]

The government had a stake in the failure of the LCS, while the LCS had to prove that they could adopt procedures that were not those of Pitt's despotism. But, ironically, quite the reverse also held true to some extent: it was in the government's interest to keep the LCS going at least for some time, and the LCS took up some forms and procedures of the British Parliament even while criticising it. A report on a division meeting

---

[53] *The Tribune, a Periodical Publication, Consisting Chiefly of the Political Lectures of J. Thelwall*, ed. John Thelwall, I (London, 1795), 71.

[54] See for example loyalist stories about a Jacobin's intrusion wreaking havoc in an orderly English tavern, ending with the ejection of the outsider and the return to order: Kevin Gilmartin, 'Counter-Revolutionary Culture', in *The Cambridge Companion to British Literature of the French Revolution in the 1790s*, ed. Pamela Clemit (Cambridge, 2011), 129–44 (137).

will serve to illustrate these points.⁵⁵ On 9 June 1794, under the chairmanship of 'Citizen' Groves, Division 2 of the LCS debated the publication of resolutions in the press. After 'a confused conversation' it was decided to publish ten thousand copies. 'A squabbling Conversation for an Hour & an half ensued respecting the Order of putting the Motions.' It was finally decided to discuss the motions in the order that they were made, following the practice of the House of Commons. This decision (and many similar ones in other debates) gives credibility to Place's claim that '[t]he forms of the house of Commons were as nearly as possible observed' in the LCS.⁵⁶ The LCS experimented with procedures and, while adopting some French words, it also imitated the Commons in form and phraseology (the LCS meeting is 'called to order' by the chairman, much as the Commons is by the Speaker). This shows that English 'Jacobinism' was no mere French import but, rather, experimented new forms of organisation and debated fresh ideas, be they of English or French revolutionary origin. The meeting went on:

> A Citizen (who was a Visitor) was very warm – he said that the Movers did not understand their own Motions, and that they were all Stupid
> He was called loudly to order, & the Good Sense of the Division No. 2 was defended by Citizen Groves [...].

Groves 'charged the Author of the Calumnies on that Division with coming there for the express purpose of creating a Confusion.' Another member added that 'it would be a glorious triumph for Pitt and Dundas if they should learn of such a clamour and quarrelling amongst the Members.'⁵⁷ LCS members knew that they were monitored and this self-consciousness shaped their discourse and practices. The fear of infiltration by spies and *agents provocateurs* made it particularly difficult to manage visitors, because the necessity of opening the society to visitors and new members (if only to prove that they were no conspirators) facilitated governmental and loyalist infiltration.

The supreme irony is that Groves was an informer.⁵⁸ The narrative quoted above is taken from his report, which was included in the Treasury Solicitor's papers.⁵⁹ During the division meeting, Groves found himself in

---

⁵⁵ Thale, *Selections*, 181–82.
⁵⁶ Place, *The Autobiography*, 141.
⁵⁷ Thale, *Selections*, 141–2.
⁵⁸ Thompson, *The Making of the English Working Class*, 147.
⁵⁹ The National Archives, Kew, England, TS 11/954/3498.

the position of chairing a division meeting, keeping order, defending the honour of the society and expelling a troublemaker. If Pitt and Dundas read this report, they must have gloated indeed. It was in the government's interest to keep the LCS working as a bureaucratic institution, at least for some time. Of course, the government employed *agents provocateurs* in order to undermine the movement from within and provoke indictable behaviour for the courts to punish. But the government probably gained even more by keeping the bureaucratic structure working. It was easier to monitor a clearly defined society than a shadowy underground like the world of Spencean taverns. The society's official hierarchy made it easier to identify leaders, and the considerable archive it produced served as evidence for the sedition trials of 1794. The employment of *agents provocateurs* and the use of material produced by the LCS bureaucracy could thus substantiate the two apparently contradictory charges levelled by the government and loyalists: that radicals were a bunch of 'incendiaries' bent on causing 'confusion', 'tumult', 'anarchy' and that the LCS plotted to subvert the monarchy.

This chapter has tried to bring out some complexities of the specific kind of 'plebeian' sociability that managed to survive repression and harassment for a remarkable seven years in the LCS. In the polarised atmosphere of the 1790s, clashes and scandals inevitably erupted, sometimes inside meetings, often in external venues. As recently dissected in remarkable studies, those incidents have shed invaluable light on the shrinking limits of acceptable behaviour and norms of political expression in the 1790s. They testify to the degree of hostility which the LCS and other similar societies had to face. This level of aggression, in turn, stemmed from the seriousness of the challenge posed to the *Ancien Régime*. It was no mean objective, and no easy task, to maintain a democratically run society when Britain was at war with France and 'French principles'. Such resilience could be achieved only thanks to LCS leaders' and rank-and-file members' stints of hard work of community building; but alongside painstaking administrative chores, ritual practices like drinking, toasting and communal singing were also crucial. Those activities were no mere impositions from above of the prescriptions of a rational public sphere; many activities in the LCS were continuous with, rather than disruptive of, artisan sociability. If Place's trajectory is in any way representative of that of other, anonymous members, then the LCS, opening its doors to wide sections of the London population and not just artisans, managed to instil some self-respect and self-confidence by rejecting social stigma and redefining 'respectability'. This chapter has suggested that debating, letter-writing, collective pamphlet-reading, the collection of dues and the many other practices was as significant as the ideology that was conveyed by the LCS. On the face of it, the society was a failure: it lasted a mere eight years and never achieved any of its political goals. Many of the debates that agitated it concerned procedures and self-discipline. Debating the order in which motions should be tabled, or discussing whether to follow the customs of the House of Commons, might seem futile. On the contrary, this was no loss of time, no distraction from the LCS's goal, but an essential part of the process of political education and self-fashioning of the members. The disciplining features of LCS sociability – attending weekly debates, waiting in turn to speak out, electing chairmen, performing various duties in rotation – must have had a transforming effect on the LCS members – at least those who attended on a regular basis. In the absence of a study of the life of a cohort of LCS members – an impossible task to perform, given the state of sources – one can only speculate about the importance of this transforming effect. The autobiographies of Francis Place and Thomas Hardy suggest, however, that radical sociability opened up business opportunities and occasions for intellectual advancement and the honing of social, organisational, oratorical and writing skills; for many members the entertainment provided in taverns must have also cemented bonds and friendships. All those skills and social relations that were enhanced by LCS sociability built up a man's agency in the sense that he could get more professional opportunities and had more skills to grasp them. Although this kind of self-advancement was not the goal of the LCS, it was a welcome result, building a sense of respectability and community that could be passed on to a new generation of reformers.

Conclusion
Valérie Capdeville

THIS VOLUME has explored British sociability in the long eighteenth century through a wide range of perspectives and case studies. The authors of the collection have used a combination of macro and micro analyses of sociability to define British sociability as distinctive from other national models and have raised the question of its hybrid nature. The singularity of British sociable practices justifies a close investigation of their emergence, of their evolution and of some of their inherent resisting forces and paradoxes. Therefore, an argumentative and chronological thread has guided our examination of British sociability, shedding new light on a phenomenon that transformed eighteenth-century British society and mentalities.

While male gatherings mainly conducted in public drinking houses were a central forum for the art of conversation in this period, as exemplified by social institutions such as coffeehouses, taverns, clubs, Masonic lodges and art academies, female sociable practices were also instrumental in the definition of distinctive British trends in sociability, as shown through the tea-table phenomenon, their predominant role in epistolary sociability or their involvement in networks and literary circles in late eighteenth-century Scotland. Moreover, the link between sociability, gender and education definitely played a central part in the fashioning of a national model of sociability. Various examples of hetero-social practices existed in eighteenth-century Britain; yet, as this volume has proved, the prominence of gendered practices and spaces of sociability as a characteristic feature of British social life should not be under-estimated. Education remained a fundamental tool for the formation of sociable practices. If public sociability has largely been associated with masculine sociability in Britain, recent scholarship has questioned the theory of separate spheres and underlined a more complex mapping of sociable practices across both spatial and gender lines.[1] For instance, Michèle Cohen has reassessed the role of domestic

---

[1] The concept of the separation of spheres was theorised and developed for the first time by Martha Vicinus, *Separate Spheres* (Bloomington, 1974). Michèle Cohen,

sociability in the education of women, and especially the key function of accomplishments, including conversation, in the sociable education of British women as well as children.[2]

In the eighteenth century, France was still considered as the 'sociable nation' *par excellence*. In a famous passage from his *Lettres Persanes*, Montesquieu suggested the superiority of the Frenchman's sociable nature over other nationalities.[3] At the same period, the Swiss traveller Béat-Louis de Muralt shared the philosopher's view, insisting of such dominant attributes of the French character, such as manners and politeness: 'The things they would have us admire in them above the rest, are their Wit, their Sprightliness, Politeness and Behaviour.'[4] Indeed, politeness, refinement and conversation were strongly associated with France and became characteristic features of French society, thus helping to assert the superiority of a French model of sociability. After imitating French standards and fashions in the first half of the eighteenth century, Britain started to criticise, question and finally reject the French model. The relationship between France and England, especially, has always been characterised by fruitful exchanges as well as fierce and complex tensions. This volume has demonstrated that the emergence of a British model of sociability in the long eighteenth century followed the same pattern, thus challenging the Anglo-French connection by redefining the form which that connection took.

The complementary outcomes provided by the historical and literary approaches chosen by the various contributors to this volume have shown the need to follow new research paths by interrogating widely accepted thinking on the historiography of sociability or by broadening previous ideological debates on the British sociable character. How could England, often described as an uncouth nation by foreign travellers, become a sociable nation and challenge the French hegemonic model? Again, this volume

---

Fashioning Masculinity: National Identity and Language in the Eighteenth Century (Routledge, 1996).

[2] Michèle Cohen, 'The pedagogy of conversation in the home: "familiar conversation" as a pedagogical tool in eighteenth and nineteenth-century England', *Oxford Review of Education* 41, no. 4 (2015), 447–63.

[3] 'On dit que l'homme est un animal sociable. Sur ce pied-là, il me paraît qu'un Français est plus homme qu'un autre,' Charles-Louis Secondat de Montesquieu, lettre LXXXVII, *Lettres persanes*, in *Œuvres completes*, ed. Roger Callois, 2 vols. (Paris, 1949–51) vol. 1, 261.

[4] 'A tous les égards les Français semblent être faits pour la Société [...] Ce qu'ils veulent surtout que nous admirions d'eux, c'est l'Esprit, la Vivacité, la Politesse, les Manières,' Béat-Louis de Muralt, *Lettres sur les Anglois et les François et les Voiages* [1728], ed. Charles Gould (Paris, 1933), 176–7.

has shown that the specificity of British sociability lay in its ability to benefit from tensions and to reconcile contradictions, thus forging a unique national model of sociability which would then be exported to the British Empire and to Europe.

As early as the beginning of the eighteenth century, British sociability was disseminated to the North American colonies, to the Caribbean and later to the Indian and African continents. Colonial sociability was extremely rich and varied as it took multiple forms throughout the British Empire. The expansion of British sociability in the colonial world was driven by a dual force and underwent a complex process of both transfer and adaptation. On the one hand, this process reflected a strong attachment to the values of Britishness and a desire to reproduce the same original social practices around the globe. On the other hand, it revealed an aspiration towards the creation of a new cultural identity depending on the variations of the political, social and economic local contexts in which sociability would flourish.[5] In that respect, British travellers and colonists, as well as the Americans who had an experience of British social life, were particularly important agents in the diffusion of the British model of sociability in colonial America, for instance, and in the constitution of wider social transatlantic networks.[6] In the British American colonies and in the rest of the Empire, despite the weight of imperialist motives, the encounter with colonial realities naturally favoured the hybridisation of this pre-existing model.

A fascinating extension to this study would consider the further evolution of British sociability due to the various social and cultural transformations at work during the Victorian and Edwardian periods. To what extent have social and political movements (Chartism, the struggles for democracy and equality)[7] and new literary and cultural trends (Romanticism

---

[5] On the shaping of national identities in the colonial context, see Linda Colley, *Britons: Forging the Nation, 1707–1837* (New Haven, CT, 2005); Jack P. Greene, 'Search for Identity: An Interpretation of the Meaning of Selected Patterns of Social Response in Eighteenth-Century America', *Journal of Social History* 3, no. 3 (Spring 1969/Spring 1970), 189–220; Élise Marienstras, *Nous, le Peuple. Les origines du nationalisme américain* (Paris, 1988).

[6] Valérie Capdeville, 'Transferring the British Club Model to the American Colonies: Mapping Spaces and Networks of Power (1720–70)', *RSEAA XVII–XVIII* 74 (2017), https://journals.openedition.org/1718/867.

[7] On Chartism and new forms of sociability in the nineteenth century, see D. Craig and J. Thompson, *Languages of Politics in Nineteenth-Century Britain* (Basingstoke, 2013); Margot C. Finn, *After Chartism: Class and Nation in English Radical Politics 1848–1874* (Cambridge, 2003).

and sensibility) transformed social interactions within the British world?[8] Opening new historical and sociological perspectives, such research would also interrogate the possible persistence of a British model of sociability up to our times and assess what remains of Enlightenment sociable practices today.

[8] On the influence of romanticism on sociable practices, see Gillian Russell and Clara Tuite (eds.), *Romantic Sociability: Social Networks and Literary Culture in Britain, 1770–1840* (Cambridge, 2002); Kevin Gilmartin, *Sociable Places: Locating Culture in Romantic-Period Britain* (Cambridge, 2017).

Bibliography

Primary sources

Addison, Joseph and Richard Steele, *The Spectator*, ed. Donald F. Bond, 5 vols. (Oxford, 1965).
A New Academy of Complements; or, The Lover's Secretary (London, 1715).
A New Academy of Compliments (London, 1748).
Anon., *Le Roman de Eles and L'Ordene de Chevalerie*, trans. and ed. Keith Busby (Amsterdam, 1983).
An Useful and Entertaining Collection of Letters upon Various Subjects. Several Now First Published from Their Original Manuscripts, by the Most Eminent Hands (London, 1745).
[Baillie, John], *The Patriot: Being a Dramatick History of the Life and Death of William the First Prince of Orange ...* (London, 1736).
Beguillet, Edme, *Discours sur l'origine, les progrès, et les révolutions de la Franc-maçonnerie philosophique, contenant un Plan d'Association & un Projet Maçonnique de bienfaisance, pour l'Erection d'un double Monument en l'honneur de Descartes Par le F[rère] Béguillet, Avocat au Parlement, Secrétaire Général de la L[oge] de la Réunion des Etrangers* (Philadelphie, 1784).
Bellamy, John, *Whig Club Instituted in May 1784* (London, 1792).
Bolingbroke, Henry St John, Lord, *A Dissertation upon Parties*, 1734, *The Works of Lord Bolingbroke in four Volumes* (London, 1967), II, 5–172.
——, *The Idea of a Patriot King*, 1749, *The Works of Lord Bolingbroke in four Volumes*, II, 372–429.
Boswell, James, *Boswell: The Applause of the Jury, 1782–1785*, ed. Irma S. Lustig and Frederick A. Pottle (London, 1981).
——, *Boswell in Extremes, 1776–1778*, ed. Charles McC. Weis and Frederick A. Pottle (London, 1971).
——, *Boswell Laird of Auchinleck, 1778–1782*, ed. Joseph W. Reed and Frederick Pottle (Edinburgh, 1993).
——, *Boswell's Column, 1777–1783*, ed. Margery Bailey (London, 1951).
——, *Boswell's Life of Johnson, in two volumes*, 1791, third edition 1799 (London, 1904).
——, *The Life of Dr Johnson* (1791; London, 1962).

——, *The Life of Samuel Johnson, LL.D.*, ed. R. W. Chapman (Oxford, 1980 edition).
——, *Ode on Mr. Boswell's Gong*, in *The Edinburgh Magazine or Literary Miscellany* (Edinburgh, July 1785), Volume II, 181.
Brenan, Beaumont, *The Painter's Breakfast* (Dublin, 1756).
Brown, George, ed., *The New and Complete English Letter-Writer; or, Whole Art of General Correspondence* (London, [1770?]).
Brown, Thomas, *Essays Serious and Comical* (London, 1707).
Buckeridge, Bainbrigg, 'Dedication', in Roger De Piles, *The Art of Painting*, trans. John Savage (London, 1706).
Burke, Edmund, *An Appeal from the New to the Old Whigs*, 1791, ed. Norbert Col (Rennes, 1996).
——, *A Philosophical Enquiry into the Origins of our Ideas of the Sublime and Beautiful*, 1757, 1759, *A Philosophical Enquiry into the Sublime and Beautiful and Other Pre-Revolutionary Writings*, ed. David Womersley (London, 1998), 49–199.
——, *Letter to Richard Burke*, 1792, *The Works of the Right Honourable Edmund Burke*, 6 vols. (London, 1907–10), VI, 61–80.
——, *Letters on a Regicide Peace*, 1796–97, *The Works of the Right Honourable Edmund Burke*, V, 152–354 and 358–433.
——, *Reflections on the Revolution in France*, 1790, ed. Conor Cruise O'Brien, 1969 (Harmondsworth, 1982).
——, *Reflections on the Revolution in France*, ed. John C. D. Clark (Stanford, CA, 2001).
——, *Reflections on the Revolution in France*, ed. John G. A. Pocock, 1987 (Indianapolis and Cambridge, 2005).
——, *Speech on a Bill for the Relief of Protestant Dissenters*, 1773, *The Works of the Right Honourable Edmund Burke*, VI, 102–13.
——, *Thoughts on the Cause of the Present Discontents*, 1770, *The Works of the Right Honourable Edmund Burke*, I, 306–81.
——, *Vindication of Natural Society*, 1756, 1757, *A Philosophical Enquiry into the Sublime and Beautiful and Other Pre-Revolutionary Writings*, ed. David Womersley (London, 1998), 1–48.
Campbell, Duncan, *A Poem upon Tea. Wherein its Antiquity, its several Virtues and influences are set forth; and the Wisdom of the sober Sex commended in chusing so mild a Liquor for their Entertainments* (London, [1734]).
Carmontelle, Louis de, *Coup de patte sur le salon de 1779* (Paris, 1779).
——, *Le Triumvirat des arts* (Paris, 1783).
Casanova, Giacomo, *Histoire de ma vie*, ed. Gérard Lahouati and Marie-Françoise Luna, with Furio Luccichenti and Helmut Watzlawick (Paris, 2013).
Cibber, Colley, *The Lady's Last Stake, or, The Wife's Resentment. A Comedy. As it is acted at the Queen's Theatre in the Hay-Market, by Her Majesty's servants* (London, 1707).
Comte, Louis Le, *Memoirs and Observations Topographical, Physical, Mathematical, Mechanical, Natural, Civil, and Ecclesiastical. Made in a late Journey through the Empire of China* (London, 1697).

Day, Angel, *The English Secretorie Wherin is Contayned, a Perfect Method, for the Inditing of all Manner of Epistles and Familiar Letters, together with Their Diversities* (London, 1586).
Defoe, Daniel, *Defoe's Review, Major Single Works*, ed. Arthur W. Secord, 22 vols. (New York, 1938).
——, *A Tour through the Whole Island of Great Britain* [1724–25] (London, 1971).
——, *Roxana, The Fortunate Mistress* (Oxford, 1981).
——, *The Complete English Tradesman* (London, 1726).
De Luc, JeanAndré, *Lettres physiques et morales sur l'histoire de la Terre et de l'Homme* (La Haye, 1779 and Paris, 1779).
De Piles, Roger, *Conversations sur la connaissance de la peinture et sur le jugement qu'on doit faire des tableaux*, 1677 (Geneva, 1970).
Dictionnaire de l'Académie françoise (1798), fifth edition (Paris, 1798).
Diderot, Denis, *Salons 1759–1781*, 4 vols. (Paris, 1984–95).
Feltham, John, *The Picture of London, for 1806; Being a Correct Guide to all the Curiosities, Amusements, Exhibitions, Public Establishments, and remarkable Objects in and near London; with a Collection of Appropriate Tables* (London, 1805).
Ferguson, Adam, *An Essay on the History of Civil Society*, 1767, ed. Fania Oz-Salzberger (Cambridge, 1995).
Fordyce, David, *The New and Complete British Letter-Writer; or, Young secretary's instructor in polite modern letter-writing* (London, [1790?]).
Garrick, David, *The Songs, Choruses, and Serious Dialogue of the Masque called The Institution of the Garter* (London, 1771).
Gignoux, John, ed., *Epistolary Correspondence Made Pleasant and Familiar: Calculated Chiefly for the Improvement of Youth* (London, 1759).
Goldsmith, Oliver, *Retaliation; a poem* (London, 1774).
Granville, Mary, *The Autobiography and Correspondence of Mary Granville, Mrs Delany* (London, 1862).
Gwynn, John, *An Essay on Design: Including Proposals for Erecting a Public Academy* (London, 1749).
Hardy, Thomas, *Memoir of Thomas Hardy, Founder of, and Secretary to, the London Corresponding Society* (London, 1832).
Highmore, Joseph, *Essays* (London, 1766).
Hill, Aaron, *Alzira. A Tragedy* (London, 1736).
Hill, John, ed., *The Young Secretary's Guide; or, A Speedy Help to Learning* (London, 1719).
Hoffmann, Friedrich, *Medicus Politicus* (Lugduni Batavorum, 1738).
Hume, David, *Essays Moral, Political, Literary*, 1777, ed. Eugene F. Miller (Indianapolis, 1985).
Johnson, Samuel, 'Connoisseur', *A Dictionary of the English Language* (London, 1756).
——, 'Review of *A Journal of Eight Days' Journey* by Jonas Hanway', *The Literary Magazine; or, Universal Review* 2, no. 13 (April 1757), 161–7.
——, *The History of Rasselas, Prince of Abissinia*, ed. J. P. Hardy (Oxford, 1999).

——, *The Letters of Samuel Johnson*, ed. Bruce Redford, 5 vols. (Oxford, 1992), vol. I: 1731–1772; vol. II: 1773–1776.
Jones, John, *The Bathes of Bathes Ayde* (London, 1572).
Kant, Immanuel, *Anthropology, History, and Education*, ed. G. Zöller and Robert B. Louden. (Cambridge, 2007).
——, *Idea for a Universal History from a Cosmopolitan Point of View* (1784), ed. Lewis White Beck (Indianapolis, 1963).
Killigrew, Thomas, *Chit-Chat: A Comedy* (London, 1719).
[Kimber, Edward], *The Ladies Complete Letter-Writer; Teaching the Art of Inditing Letters on Every Subject That Can Call for Their Attention, as Daughters, Wives, Mothers, Relations, Friends, or Acquaintance* ...(London, 1763).
L'Estrange, Roger, *Tears of the Press* (London, 1681).
Lee, Arthur, *A Second Appeal to the Justice and Interests of the People, on the Measures Respecting America. By the Author of the First* (London, 1775).
[Lennox, Charlotte], *The Female Quixote; or, The Adventures of Arabella* (London, 1752).
Locke, John, *An Essay Concerning the True Original Extent and End of Civil Government* (London, 1690).
London Corresponding Society, *A General Meeting of the London Corresponding Society, Held at the Globe Tavern Strand on Monday the 20th January 1794* (London, 1794).
Lottin, Alain, Louisette Caux-Germe and Michel de Sainte-Maréville, eds., *Boulonnais, Noble et Révolutionnaire. Le journal de Gabriel Abot de Bazinghen (1779–1798)* (Arras, 1995).
Loveday, Robert, *Hymen's Praeludia: Or Love's Master-Piece: Being that So-Much-Admir'd Romance, intitled Cleopatra* (London, 1736).
Lucas, Charles, *Essay on Waters* (London, 1756).
Macky, John, *Journey Through England* (London, 1714).
Malton, Thomas, *A Compleat Treatise on Perspective, in Theory and Practice* (London, 1775).
Mandeville, Bernard de, *The Fable of the Bees*, 1714, ed. Phillip Harth (London, 1970, 1989).
Montaiglon, Anatole de, *Procès-verbaux de l'Académie royale de peinture et de sculpture*, 10 vols. (Paris, 1875–92).
Montesquieu, Charles-Louis Secondat (de), *Lettres persanes*, in *Œuvres complètes*, ed. Roger₁Callois, 2 vols. (Paris, 1949–51).
Motteux, Peter Anthony, *A Poem in Praise of Tea* (London, 1712).
Muralt, Béat-Louis (de), *Lettres sur les Anglois et les François et les Voiages* [1728], ed. Charles Gould (Paris, 1933).
Ogilby, John, *Britannia* (London, 1675).
Oliver, William, *A Practical Essay on Fevers ... to which is Annex'd A Dissertation on the Bath Waters* (London, 1704).
Ovington, John, *An Essay upon the Nature and Qualities of Tea* (London, 1699).
Paine, Thomas, *Rights of Man*, 1791 and 1792, ed. Eric Foner, 1984, notes Henry Collins, 1969 (Harmondsworth, 1985).

Pasquin, Anthony, *A Critical Guide to the Exhibition of the Royal Academy, for 1796* (London, 1796).
——, *A Critical Guide to the Present Exhibition at the Royal Academy, for 1797* (London, 1797).
——, *A Liberal Critique on the Present Exhibition of the Royal Academy: Being an Attempt to Correct the National Taste; to Ascertain the State of the Polite Arts at this Period; and to Rescue Merit from Oppression* (London, 1794).
——, *Memoirs of the Royal Academicians, Being an Attempt to Improve the National Taste* (London, 1796).
——, *The Royal Academicians: a Farce* (London, 1786).
Paterson, William, *Arminius. A Tragedy* (London, 1740).
Pechlin, Johann, *Theophilus Bibaculus, sive de Potu Theae Dialogus* (Frankfurt, 1684).
Pepys, Samuel, *The Diary of Samuel Pepys*, ed. R. Latham and W. Matthews, 11 vols. (London, 1970–83).
Pernety, Antoine-Joseph, *Dictionnaire portatif de peinture, sculpture et gravure, 1757* (Geneva, 1972).
Pindar, Peter, *Farewell Odes for the Year 1786* (London, 1786).
——, *Lyric Odes for the Year 1783* (London, 1783).
——, *Lyric Odes for the Year 1785* (London, 1785).
Place, Francis, *The Autobiography of Francis Place, 1771–1854*, ed. Mary Thale (Cambridge, 1972).
Price, Richard, *A Discourse on the Love of Our Country*, 1789 (Oxford and New York, 1992).
Reynolds, Joshua, *Discourses on Art, 1769–1790*, ed. Robert R. Wark (New Haven, CT, 1997).
Richardson, Jonathan, *A Discourse on the Dignity, Certainty, Pleasure and Advantage, of the Science of a Connoisseur* (London, 1719).
Richardson, Samuel, *Letters Written to and for Particular Friends, on the Most Important Occasions. Directing Not Only the Requisite Style and Forms To Be Observed in Writing Familiar Letters; But How to Think and Act Justly and Prudently, in the Common Concerns of Human Life. Containing One Hundred and Seventy-Three Letters*, third edition (London, 1746).
Robertson, William, *The History of the Discovery and Settlement of America* [1777] (New York, 1857).
Royal Academy of Arts, *Abstract of the Instrument of Institution and Laws of the Royal Academy of Arts in London, Established December 10, 1768* (London, 1797).
Rutty, John, *A Methodical Synopsis of Mineral Waters* (London, 1757).
——, *The Analyzer Analysed* (London, 1758).
Shaftesbury, Lord (Anthony Ashley Cooper), 'Sensus Communis, an Essay on the Freedom of Wit and Humour in a Letter to a Friend', in *Characteristicks of Men, Manners, Opinions, Times*, ed. Lawrence E. Klein (Cambridge, 1999).
Smith, Adam, *The Theory of Moral Sentiments* (London, Edinburgh, 1759).
Smollett, Tobias, *An Essay on the External Use of Water* (London, 1752).
——, *A Complete History of England* (London, 1758–59).
——, *Travels through France and Italy*, 1766, ed. Jan Morris (London, 2006).

——, *The Expedition of Humphry Clinker*, 1771, ed. Lewis M. Knapp and Paul-Gabriel Boucé (Oxford, 2009).
——, *The Present State of all Nations* (London, 1768–69).
Stanhope, Philip Dormer, Earl of Chesterfield, *Letters Written by the Late Philip Dormer Stanhope, Earl of Chesterfield, to His Son*, 2 vols. (London, 1774).
——, *Principles of Politeness, and of Knowing the World; Being a New System of Education, by the Late Lord Chesterfield Containing Every Instruction Necessary to Complete the Gentleman and Man of Fashion, for the Improvement of Youth.* (London, 1775).
Steele, Richard, *The Tatler* (1709–1711), ed. D. F. Bond, 3 vols. (Oxford, 1987).
Sterne, Laurence, *A Sentimental Journey and Other Writings*, 1768 (Oxford, 2003).
Strange, Robert, *An Inquiry into the Rise and Establishment of the Royal Academy of Arts* (London, 1775).
Strype, John, *The Survey of London*, 2 vols. (London, 1720).
Swift, Jonathan, *Journal to Stella*, 2 vols. (Oxford, 1948).
——, *The Correspondence of Jonathan Swift*, ed. Harold Williams (Oxford, 1963).
Tate, Nahum, *Panacea: A Poem upon Tea: in Two Canto's* (London, 1700).
Tavernier, John, ed., *The Entertaining Correspondent; or, Newest and Most Compleat Polite Familiar Letter-Writer* (Berwick, 1759).
Tea-Table: or, A Conversation between some Polite Persons of both Sexes, at a Lady's Visiting Day, The (London, 1725).
Tea, a Poem. In Three Cantos (London, 1743).
Tea. A Poem. Or, Ladies into China-cups; a Metamorphosis (London, 1729).
Thale, Mary, ed., *Selections from the Papers of the London Corresponding Society, 1792–1799* (Cambridge and New York, 1983).
Thelwall, John, *Selected Poetry and Poetics*, ed. Judith Thompson (Basingstoke, 2015).
——, *The Politics of English Jacobinism: Writings of John Thelwall*, ed. Gregory Claeys (University Park, PA, 1995).
——, ed., *The Tribune, a Periodical Publication, Consisting Chiefly of the Political Lectures of J. Thelwall*, 3 vols. (London, 1795), vol. 1.
Thicknesse, Philip, *Observations on the Customs and Manners of the French Nation, in a Series of Letters, in which that Nation is vindicated from the Misrepresentations of some Late Writers* (London, 1766).
Thomson, James, *Edward and Eleonora. A Tragedy* (London, 1739).
Tocqueville, Alexis de, *L'Ancien Régime et la Révolution*, 1856, ed. J.-P. Mayer, 1964 (Paris, 1986).
Voltaire, *Alzire, ou les Américains* (Amsterdam, 1736).
Voyer de Paulmy, René Louis de, *Journal et mémoires du Marquis d'Argenson*, ed. E. J. B. Rathery (Paris, 1859–67).
Wallace, James and Charles Townshend, *Every Man His Own Letter-Writer: Or, The New and Complete Art of Letter-Writing Made Plain and Familiar to Every Capacity...* (London, 1782).
Walpole, Horace, *The Yale Edition of Horace Walpole's Correspondence*, ed. W.S. Lewis, 48 vols. (New Haven, 1960).
West, Gilbert, *The Institution of the Order of the Garter* (London, 1742).

Secondary sources

Acosta, Ana M., 'Spaces of Dissent and the Public Sphere in Hackney, Stoke Newington, and Newington Green', *Eighteenth-Century Life* 27 (2003), 1–27.
Allen, David F., 'Political Clubs in Restoration London', *Historical Journal* 19, no. 3 (1976), 561–80.
Alpaugh, Micah, 'The British Origins of the French Jacobins: Radical Sociability and the Development of Political Club Networks, 1787–1793', *European History Quarterly* 44 (2014), 593–619.
Amiable, Louis, *Une loge maçonnique d'avant 1789, la loge des Neuf Sœurs*, second edition (Paris, 1989).
Anderson, Benedict, *Imagined Communities. Reflections on the Origin and Spread of Nationalism* (1983; London, 2006).
Aronson, Nicole, *Mademoiselle de Scudéry* (Boston, 1978).
Aske, Katie and Kimberley Page-Jones, eds., *La Sociabilité en France et en Grande-Bretagne au Siècle des Lumières*. Tome 6: 'L'insociable sociabilité: résistances et résilience' (Paris, 2017).
Ayres, Philip J., *Classical Culture and the Idea of Rome in Eighteenth-Century England* (Cambridge, 2009).
Badufle, Marjolaine, 'La sociabilité dans les *Pensées* de Montesquieu: Regard sur les femmes', in *La Sociabilité en France et en Grande-Bretagne au Siècle des Lumières: L'émergence d'un nouveau modèle de société*. Tome 4. *Utopie, individu et société : la sociabilité en question*, ed. Norbert Col and Allan Ingram (Paris, 2015), 73–92.
Baird, Ileana, *Social Networks in the Long Eighteenth Century: Clubs, Literary Salons* (Newcastle-upon-Tyne, 2014).
Ballaster, Ros, 'Satire and Embodiment: Allegorical Romance on Stage and Page in Mid-Eighteenth-Century Britain', *Eighteenth-Century Fiction* 27, no. 3/4 (2015), 631–60.
Bannett, Eve Tavor, *Empire of Letters: Letter Manuals and Transatlantic Correspondence, 1680–1820* (Cambridge, 2006).
——, 'Printed Epistolary Manuals and the Transatlantic Rescripting of Manuscript Culture', *Studies in Eighteenth Century Culture* 36 (2007), 13–32.
Barclay, Craig, 'Heroes of Peace: The Royal Humane Society and the Award of Medals in Britain, 1774–1914' (unpublished Ph.D. thesis, Department of History, University of York, September 2009).
Barrell, John, '"An Entire Change of Performances?" The Politicisation of Theatre and the Theatricalisation of Politics in the Mid 1790s', *Lumen: Selected Proceedings from the Canadian Society for Eighteenth-Century Studies* 17 (1998), 11–50.
——, *Imagining The King's Death: Figurative Treason, Fantasies of Regicide, 1793–1796* (Oxford and New York, 2000).
——, 'London and the London Corresponding Society', in *Romantic Metropolis: The Urban Scene of British Culture, 1780–1840*, ed. James Chandler and Kevin Gilmartin (Cambridge and New York, 2005), 85–112.
——, *The Spirit of Despotism: Invasions of Privacy in the 1790s* (Oxford and New York, 2006).

Barthes, Roland, *The Fashion System* (Oakland, 1983).
Bastin, Giselle, 'Pandora's Voice-Box: How Woman became the "Gossip Girl"', in *Women and Language: Essays on Gendered Communication Across Media*, ed. Melissa Ames and Sarah Himsel Burcon (Jefferson, 2011), 17–29.
Batchelor, Jennie and Cora Kaplan, eds., *British Women's Writing in the Long Eighteenth century: Authorship, Politics, and History* (Basingstoke, 2005).
Beaurepaire, Pierre-Yves, ed., *La Communication en Europe de l'âge classique aux Lumières* (Paris, 2014).
Beljame, Alexandre, *Le Public et les Hommes de Lettres en Angleterre au Dix-huitième Siècle, 1660–1744* (Paris, 1881).
Benchimol, Alex, *Intellectual Politics and Cultural Conflict in the Romantic period: Scottish Whigs, English Radicals and the Making of the British Public Sphere* (Aldershot, England and Burlington, VT, 2010).
Bercé, Yves-Marie, *Révoltes et révolutions dans l'Europe moderne*, 1980 (Paris, 2013).
Bergmann, Jörg R., *Discreet Indiscretions: The Social Organisation of Gossip*, trans. John Bednarz, Jr. (New York, 1993).
Binns, John, *Recollections of the Life of John Binns: Twenty-Nine Years in Europe and Fifty-Three in the United States : With Anecdotes, Political, Historical, and Miscellaneous* (Philadelphia, 1854).
Blanning, Tim, *The Culture of Power and the Power of Culture: Old Regime Europe 1660–1789* (Oxford, 2000).
Borsay, Peter, *The English Urban Renaissance: Culture and Society in the Provincial Town 1660–1770* (Oxford, 1989).
Boucé, Paul-Gabriel, 'Scotland and France in Smollett's *Present States of All Nations*, 1768–69', in *Scotland and France in the Enlightenment*, ed. Deirdre Dawson and Pierre Morère (Lewisburg, 2004).
Bourdieu, Pierre, *La Distinction. Critique sociale du jugement* (Paris, 1979).
——, *Le Sens pratique* (Paris, 1980).
Boureau, Alain, 'The Letter-Writing Norm, a Medieval Invention', in *Correspondence: Models of Letter-Writing from the Middle Ages to the Nineteenth Century*, ed. Roger Chartier, Alain Boureau and Cécile Dauphin (Princeton, 1997), 24–59.
Bourke, Richard, *Empire and Revolution: The Political Life of Edmund Burke* (Princeton, 2015).
Bowers, Terence, 'Reconstituting the National Body in Smollett's *Travels through France and Italy*', *Eighteenth-Century Life* 21 (1997), 1–25.
Braddick, Michael, *State Formation in Early Modern England, c. 1550–1700* (Cambridge, 2000).
Brant, Clare, *Eighteenth-Century Letters and British Culture* (Basingstoke, 2006).
Brant, Clare and George Rousseau, eds., *Fame and Fortune: Sir John Hill and London Life in the 1750s* (Basingstoke, 2018).
Breuninger, Scott & David Burrow, *Sociability and Cosmopolitanism: Social Bonds on the Fringes of the Enlightenment* (London, 2012, 2015).
Brewer, John, *The Pleasures of the Imagination: English Culture in the Eighteenth Century* (London, 1997).

——, *Party Ideology and Popular Politics at the Accession of George III* (Cambridge, 1976).
Brewer, John, Neil McKendrick and J. H. Plumb, eds., *The Birth of a Consumer Society: The Commercialization of Eighteenth Century England* (London, 1982).
Brims, John D., 'The Scottish Democratic Movement in the Age of the French Revolution' (Ph.D. thesis, University of Edinburgh, 1983).
Brioist, Pascal, 'Hooke et Pepys. Deux espaces-vécus du Londres du XVIIe siècle', in *Images et imaginaires de la ville à l'époque moderne*, ed. Claude Petitfrère (Tours, 1998), 15–34.
Broadhead, Glenn J., 'Samuel Johnson and the Rhetoric of Conversation', *Studies in English Literature, 1500–1900* 20, no. 3 (Summer, 1980), 461–74.
Broich, Ulrich, *The Eighteenth-century Mock-Heroic Poem*, trans. David Henry Wilson (Cambridge, 1990).
Bromwich, David, *The Intellectual Life of Edmund Burke: From the Sublime and Beautiful to American Independence* (Cambridge, MA, 2014).
Bryson, Anna, *From Courtesy to Civility: Changing Codes of Conduct in Early Modern England* (Oxford, 1998).
Burr, Vivien, *The Person in Social Psychology* (New York, 2002).
Butler, Gerald J., 'Defoe's *Moll Flanders* vs. Social Illusion', in *La Sociabilité en France et en Grande-Bretagne au Siècle des Lumières: L'émergence d'un nouveau modèle de société. Tome 4. Utopie, individu et société : la sociabilité en question*, ed. Norbert Col and Allan Ingram (Paris, 2015), 55–71.
——, *Love and Reading: An Essay in Applied Psychoanalysis* (New York, 1989).
Caine, Barbara, ed., *Friendship: A History* (London, 2009).
Capdeville, Valérie, *L'Âge d'or des clubs londoniens (1730–1784)* (Paris, 2008).
——, 'Clubbability: A Revolution in London Sociability', *Lumen* 35 (2016), 63–80.
——, 'The Ambivalent Identity of Eighteenth-century London Clubs as a Prelude to Victorian Clublife', *Cahiers victoriens et édouardiens* 81 (printemps 2015), https://cve.revues.org/1976.
——, 'Gender at Stake: The Role of Eighteenth-century London Clubs in Shaping a New Model of English Masculinity', *Culture, Society & Masculinities* 4, no. 1 (Spring 2012), 13–32.
——, 'Transferring the British Club Model to the American Colonies: Mapping Spaces and Networks of Power (1720–70)', *RSEAA XVII–XVIII* 74 (2017), https://journals.openedition.org/1718/867.
Capdeville, Valérie and Eric Francalanza, eds., *La Sociabilité en France et en Grande-Bretagne au siècle des Lumières*, vol. 3. Les Espaces de sociabilité (Paris, 2014).
Carr, Rosalind, *Gender and Enlightenment Culture in Eighteenth-Century Scotland* (Edinburgh, 2014).
Carter, Philip, *Men and the Emergence of Polite Society, Britain 1660–1800* (London, 2001; New York, 2014).
Charle, Christophe, ed., *Le Temps des capitales culturelles XVIIe-XXe siècles* (Seyssel, 2009).
Chartier, Roger, 'Loisir et sociabilité: lire à haute voix dans l'Europe moderne', *Littératures classiques* 12 (1990), 127–147.

Clark, J. C. D., *English Society, 1660–1832: Religion, Ideology and Politics during the Ancien Régime* (Cambridge, 2000).
Clark, Peter, *British Clubs and Societies 1580–1800. The Origins of an Associational World* (Oxford, 2000).
——, *Sociability and Urbanity: Clubs and Societies in the Eighteenth-Century City* (Leicester, 1986).
——, *The English Alehouse: A Social History, 1200–1830* (London, 1983).
Clayton, Antony, *London's Coffee Houses: A Stimulating Story* (London, 2003).
Clery, Emma, 'Women, Publicity and the Coffee-House Myth', *Women: a Cultural Review* 2, no. 2 (1991), 168–77.
Cochin, Augustin, *La Révolution et la libre-pensée*, posth. 1924 (Paris, 1955).
Cohen, Michèle, *Fashioning Masculinity: National Identity and Language in the Eighteenth Century* (London, 1996).
——, 'Manliness, Effeminacy and the French: Gender and the Construction of National Character in Eighteenth-Century England', in *English Masculinities. 1660–1800*, ed. Michèle Cohen and Tim Hitchcock (London and NY, 1999), 44–61.
Col, Norbert, 'Burke's Target in *A Vindication of Natural Society:* From Bolingbroke to "this sort of Writers", or an Early Burkean Defense of Church and State', *1650–1850: Ideas, Æsthetics, and Inquiries in the Early Modern Era* 20 (2013), 89–112.
Colley, Linda, *Britons: Forging the Nation, 1707–1837* (New Haven, 2005).
——, 'The Loyal Brotherhood and the Cocoa Tree: the London Organization of the Tory Party, 1727–1760', *Historical Journal* 20, no. 1 (1977), 77–85.
Cone, Carl B., *Burke and the Nature of Politics*, 2 vols. (Lexington, 1957 and 1964).
Copeland, Thomas W., *Edmund Burke: Six Essays* (London, 1950).
Cosh, Mary, *Edinburgh: the Golden Age* (Edinburgh, 2003).
Cossic-Péricarpin, Annick, *Bath au XVIIIe siècle. Les fastes d'une cité palladienne* (Rennes, 2000).
Cottret, Bernard, *Bolingbroke: Exil et écriture au siècle des Lumières. Angleterre-France (vers 1715–vers 1750)*, 2 vols. (Paris, 1992).
——, *La Glorieuse Révolution d'Angleterre: 1688*, 1988 (Paris, 2013).
Coulton, Richard, '"The Darling of the Temple-Coffee-House Club": Science, Sociability and Satire in Early Eighteenth-Century London', *Journal for Eighteenth-Century Studies* 35 (2011), 43–65.
Cowan, Brian, 'Geoffrey Holmes and the Public Sphere: Augustan Historiography from Post-Namierite to the Post-Habermasian', *Parliamentary History* 28, no. 1 (2009) 166–78.
——, 'News, Biography, and Eighteenth-Century Celebrity', in *Oxford Handbooks Online*, ed. Thomas Keymer, general ed., Colin Burrow (Oxford, 7 September 2016), doi: 10.1093/oxfordhb/9780199935338.013.132.
——, 'Public Spaces, Knowledge and Sociability', in *The Oxford Handbook of the History of Consumption*, ed. Frank Trentmann (Oxford, 2012), 251–66.
——, *The Social Life of Coffee: The Emergence of the British Coffeehouse* (New Haven, CT, 2005).

——, 'What Was Masculine about the Public Sphere? Gender and the Coffeehouse Milieu in Post-Restoration England', *History Workshop Journal*, 51 (February 2001), 127–57.

Cressy, David, *Literacy and the Social Order: Reading and Writing in Tudor and Stuart England* (Cambridge, 1980).

Cruickshanks, Eveline, 'Le XVIIIe siècle: de la Glorieuse Révolution à la Révolution française', in *Histoire des îles Britanniques du XVIe au XVIIIe siècle*, ed. Bernard Cottret, Eveline Cruickshanks and Charles Giry-Deloison, trans. Mariette Martin (Paris, 1994), 157–233.

Cust, Lionel, *History of the Society of Dilettanti* (London, 1898).

——, *L'Idée du peintre parfait*, 1715 (Paris, 1993).

Czennia, Bärbel, 'Floating Communities', in *La Sociabilité en France et en Grande-Bretagne au Siècle des Lumières : L'émergence d'un nouveau modèle de société. Tome 4. Utopie, individu et société : la sociabilité en question*, ed. Norbert Col and Allan Ingram (Paris, 2015), 223–63.

Dachez, Hélène, 'Epistolary sociability: Samuel Richardson and his Readers', in *La Sociabilité en France et en Grande-Bretagne au Siècle des Lumières. Tome 5. Sociabilités et esthétique de la marge*, ed. Annick Cossic-Péricarpin and Alain Kerhervé (Paris, 2016), 127–52.

Daudin, Guillaume, *Commerce et prospérité : la France au XVIIIe siècle* (Paris, 2011).

Davis, Michael T., 'Introduction', in *London Corresponding Society, 1792–1799*, ed. Michael T. Davis, 6 vols. (London and Brookfield, VT, 2002).

——, '"Meet and Sing, and Your Chains Will Drop Off Like Burnt Thread": The Political Songs of Thomas Spence', in *Thomas Spence: The Poor Man's Revolutionary*, ed. Alastair Bonnett and Keith Armstrong (London, 2014), 109–25.

——, 'The Mob Club? The London Corresponding Society and the Politics of Civility in the 1790s', in *Unrespectable Radicals? Popular Politics in the Age of Reform*, ed. Paul A. Pickering and Michael T. Davis (Aldershot, 2008), 21–40.

Davis, Michael T., Iain McCalman and Christina Parolin, *Newgate in Revolution: An Anthology of Radical Prison Literature in the Age of Revolution* (London; New York, 2005).

Davison, Kate, 'Occasional Politeness and Gentlemen's Laughter in 18th-century England', *Historical Journal* 57, no. 4 (2014), 921–45.

Deane, Seamus, *Foreign Affections: Essays on Edmund Burke* (Cork, 2005).

Dozier, Robert R., *For King, Constitution and Country: the English Loyalists and the French Revolution* (Lexington, 1983).

Dunan-Page, Anne and Beth Lynch, eds., *Roger L'Estrange and the Making of Restoration Culture* (Aldershot, 2008).

Duthille, Rémy, 'Toasting and the Diffusion of Radical Ideas, 1780–1832', in *Radical Voices, Radical Ways: Articulating and Disseminating Radicalism in Seventeenth and Eighteenth-century Britain*, ed. Laurent Curelly and Nigel Smith (Manchester, 2016).

——, 'Political Toasting in the Age of Revolutions: Britain, America and France, 1765–1800', in *Liberty, Property and Popular Politics: England and Scotland, 1688–1815. Essays in Honour of H. T. Dickinson*, ed. Gordon Pentland and Michael Davis (Edinburgh, 2015).

Edwards, Avery, *Frederick Louis, Prince of Wales* (London, 1947).
Eley, Geoff, 'Nations, Publics, and Political Culture: Placing Habermas in the Nineteenth Century', in *Habermas and the Public Sphere*, ed. Craig J. Calhoun (Cambridge, MA and London, 1993), 289–339.
Ellis, Markman, 'General Introduction', *Eighteenth-Century Coffee-House Culture*, 4 vols. (London, 2006), I, xi–xxxi.
——, *The Coffee-house: A Cultural History* (London, 2004).
——, 'The Coffee-women, *The Spectator* and the Public Sphere in the Early-eighteenth Century', in *Women and the Public Sphere*, ed. Elizabeth Eger and Charlotte Grant (Cambridge, 2001), 27–52.
Ellis, Markman, Richard Coulton and Matthew Mauger, *Empire of Tea* (London, 2015).
Epstein, James, '"Equality and No King": Sociability and Sedition: the Case of John Frost', in *Romantic Sociability: Social Networks and Literary Culture in Britain 1770–1840*, ed. Gillian Russell and Clara Tuite (Cambridge, 2002), 43–61.
——, *In Practice: Studies in the Language and Culture of Popular Politics in Modern Britain* (Stanford, Ca, 2003).
Epstein, James and David Karr, 'Playing at Revolution: British "Jacobin" Performance', *The Journal of Modern History*, 79 (2007), 495–530.
Eriksson, Åke, *The Tragedy of Liberty: Civic Concern and Disillusionment in James Thomson's Tragic Dramas* (Uppsala, 2002).
Everitt, Alan, 'Social Mobility in Early Modern England', *Past & Present* 33 (1966), 56–73.
Featherstone, D., 'Contested Relationalities of Political Activism: The Democratic Spatial Practices of the London Corresponding Society', *Cultural Dynamics* 22 (2010), 87–104.
——, 'The Spatial Politics of the Past Unbound: Transnational Networks and the Making of Political Identities', *Global Networks* 7 (2007), 430–52.
Fort, Bernadette, ed., *Les Salons des 'Mémoires secrets' 1767–1787* (Paris, 1999).
Fraser, Nancy, 'Rethinking the Public Sphere: A Contribution to a Critique of Actually Existing democracy', in *Habermas and the Public Sphere*, ed. Craig Calhoun (Cambridge, MA, 1992), 109–42.
Fuchs, Michel, *Edmund Burke, Ireland and the Fashioning of Self* (Oxford, 1996).
Furet, François, *Penser la Révolution française* (Paris, 1978).
Geikie, Archibald, *Annals of the Royal Society Club, the Record of a London Dining-club in the Eighteenth and Nineteenth Centuries* (London, 1917).
Gerrard, Christine, *Aaron Hill: The Muses' Projector 1685–1750* (Oxford, 2003).
——, *The Patriot Opposition to Walpole* (Oxford, 1994).
Gibbons, Luke, *Edmund Burke and Ireland: Aesthetics, Politics, and the Colonial Sublime* (Cambridge, 2003).
Gibson-Wood, Carol, *Jonathan Richardson, Art Theorist of the Enlightenment* (New Haven, CT, 2000).
Gilmartin, Kevin, 'Counter-Revolutionary Culture', in *The Cambridge Companion to British Literature of the French Revolution in the 1790s*, ed. Pamela Clemit (Cambridge, 2011), 129–44.

——, *Sociable Places: Locating Culture in Romantic-Period Britain* (Cambridge, 2017).
——, *Print Politics: The Press and Radical Opposition in Early Nineteenth-Century England*, Cambridge Studies in Romanticism 21 (New York, 1996).
——, *Writing Against the Revolution: Literary Conservatism in Britain, 1790–1832* (Cambridge, 2009).
Glover, Katharine, *Elite Women and Polite Society in Eighteenth-Century Scotland* (Woodbridge, 2011).
Gluckman, Max, 'Gossip and Scandal', *Current Anthropology* 4, no. 3 (1963), 307–16.
Goldie, Mark, Tim Harris and Paul Seaward, eds., *The Politics of Religion in Restoration England* (Oxford, 1990).
Goodman, Dena, *The Republic of Letters: A Cultural History of the French Enlightenment* (Ithaca, NY, 1994).
Goodwin, Albert, *The Friends of Liberty: The English Democratic Movement in the Age of the French Revolution* (London, 1979).
Gordon, Daniel, *Citizens without Sovereignty: Equality and Sociability in French Thought, 1670–1789* (Princeton, 1994).
Green, Georgina, *The Majesty of The People: Popular Sovereignty and the Role of the Writer in the 1790s* (Oxford, 2014).
Green, Lawrence D., 'French Letters and English Anxiety in the Seventeenth Century', *Huntington Library Quarterly* 66, no. 3/4 (2003) 263–274.
Greig, Hannah, *The Beau Monde: Fashionable Society in Georgian London* (Oxford, 2013).
Guichard, Charlotte, 'L'Amateur dans la polémique sur la critique d'art au XVIIIe siècle', in *Penser l'art dans la seconde moitié du XVIIIe siècle: théorie, critique, philosophie, histoire*, ed. Carl Magnusson and Christian Michel (Paris, 2013), 113–26.
——, *Les Amateurs d'art à Paris au XVIIIe siècle* (Seyssel, 2008).
Habermas, Jürgen, 'The Public Sphere: An Encyclopedia Article', *New German Critique* 3 (1974), 49–55.
——, *The Structural Transformation of the Bourgeois Public Sphere: An Inquiry into a Category of Bourgeois Society*, trans. Thomas Burger and Frederick Lawrence (Cambridge, 1989; Cambridge, MA, 1991).
Harris, Tim, *Politics under the Later Stuarts: Party Conflict in a Divided Society, 1660–1715* (London, 1993).
Haslett, Moyra, 'Bluestocking Feminism Revisited: the Satirical Figure of the Bluestocking', *Women's Writing* 17 (2010), 432–51.
Heller, Deborah, 'Bluestocking Salons and the Public Sphere', *Eighteenth-Century Life* 22 (1998), 59–82.
Herbert, Amanda E., *Female Alliances: Gender, Identity, and Friendship in Early Modern Britain* (New Haven, 2014).
Hirst, Derek, 'Locating the 1650s in England's Seventeenth Century', *History* 81 (1996), 359–83.
Holmes, Geoffrey, *Politics, Religion, and Society in England, 1679–1742* (London, 1986).
——, *British Politics in the Age of Anne*, revised edition (London, 1987).

Hoock, Holger, *The King's Artists: The Royal Academy of Arts and the Politics of British Culture 1760–1840* (Oxford, 2003).
Hoppit, Julian, *Britain's Political Economies: Parliament and Economic Life, 1660–1800* (Cambridge, 2017).
Hornbeak, Katherine Gee, *The Complete Letter Writer in English 1568–1800. Smith College Studies in Modern Languages* 15, no. 3/4 (1934).
Hutchison, Sydney C., *The History of the Royal Academy 1768–1786* (London, 1986).
Innes, Joanna, 'Jonathan Clark, Social History and England's « Ancien Régime »', *Past & Present* 115 (1987), 165–200.
Irving, William, *The Providence of Wit in the English Letter Writers* (Durham, NC, 1955).
Jacobs, Eva, *Theatre in Focus: Voltaire and Tragedy* (Cambridge, 1987).
Jones, E. M. and M. E. Falkus, 'Urban Improvement and the English Economy in the Seventeenth and Eighteenth Centuries', in *The Eighteenth-Century Town 1688–1820*, ed. Peter Borsay (London and New York, 1990), 116–58.
Jones, Emrys D., *Friendship and Allegiance in Eighteenth-Century Literature: The Politics of Private Virtue in the Age of Walpole* (Basingstoke, 2013).
——, 'Royal Ruptures: Caroline of Ansbach and the Politics of Illness in the 1730s', *Medical Humanities* 37 (2011), 13–17.
Jones, Richard, *Tobias Smollett in the Enlightenment* (Bucknell, 2011).
Keen, Maurice, *Chivalry* (New Haven, CT, 1984).
Kenyon, John P., *The Stuart Constitution: Documents and Commentary* (Cambridge, 1966).
Klancher, Jon, *The Making of English Reading Audiences, 1790–1832* (Madison, WI and London, 1987).
Klein, Lawrence E., 'Coffeehouse Civility, 1660–1714: An Aspect of Post-Courtly Culture in England', *Huntington Library Quarterly* 59, no. 1 (1996), 30–52.
——, 'Liberty, Manners and Politeness in Early Eighteenth-Century England', *Historical Journal* 32, no. 3 (1989), 583–605.
——, 'Politeness and the Interpretation of the British Eighteenth Century', *Historical Journal* 45, no. 4 (December 2002), 869–98.
——, 'Politeness for Plebes. Consumption and Social Identity in Early Eighteenth-century England', in *The Consumption of Culture*, ed. John Brewer and Ann Bermingham (London, 1997), 262–82.
——, *Shaftesbury and the Culture of Politeness: Moral Discourse and Cultural Politics in Early Eighteenth-Century England* (Cambridge, 1994).
——, 'The Figure of France: The Politics of Sociability in England, 1660–1715', *Yale French Studies* 92 (1997), 30–45.
Knapp, Lewis Mansfield, *Tobias Smollett, Doctor of Man and Manners* (1949; London, 1963).
Knights, Mark, *Representation and Misrepresentation in Later Stuart Britain: Partisanship and Political Culture* (Oxford, 2005).
Kramnick, Isaac, *The Rage of Edmund Burke: Portrait of an Ambivalent Conservative* (New York, 1977).
Langford, Paul, *Public Life and the Propertied Englishman: 1689–1798* (Oxford, 1991).

Lawlor, Clark, *Consumption and Literature: The Making of a Romantic Disease* (London, 2006).
Le Goff, Jacques, *Histoire et mémoire* (Paris, 1988).
Lepan, Géraldine, 'Politesse et sociabilité selon Rousseau', in *La Sociabilité en France et en Grande-Bretagne au Siècle des Lumières : L'émergence d'un nouveau modèle de société.* Tome 4. *Utopie, individu et société : la sociabilité en question*, ed. Norbert Col and Allan Ingram (Paris, 2015), 167–96.
Lichtenstein, Jacqueline and Christian Michel, eds., *Conférences de l'Académie royale de peinture et de sculpture* (Paris, 2006–15).
Lieberman, Max, 'A New Approach to the Knighting Ritual', *Speculum* 90, no. 2 (2015), 391–423.
Lilti, Antoine, *Le Monde des salons, sociabilité et mondanité à Paris au XVIIIe siècle* (Paris, 2005).
——, *The World of the Salons: Sociability and Worldliness in Eighteenth-Century Paris*, trans. Lydia Cochrane (Oxford, 2015).
Lock, Frederick Peter, *Edmund Burke*, 2 vols., I, 1998 (Oxford, 2008); II, 2006 (Oxford, 2009).
Loftis, John, *The Politics of Drama in Augustan England* (Oxford, 1963).
Lord, Walter Frewen, 'The Development of Political Parties during the Reign of Queen Anne', *Transactions of the Royal Historical Society* 14 (1900), 69–121.
Lottes, Günther, *Politische Aufklärung und Plebejisches Publikum: Zur Theorie und Praxis des Englischen Radikalismus im Späten 18. Jahrhundert* (Munich and Vienna, 1979).
Lottes, Günther, 'Radicalism, Revolution and Political Culture: An Anglo-French Comparison', in *The French Revolution and British Popular Politics*, ed. Mark Philp (Cambridge, 1991), 78–98.
Lyotard, Jean-François, *The Postmodern Condition: A Report on Knowledge*, trans. Geoff Bennington and Brian Massumi (Minneapolis, 1997).
Manogue, Ralph A. 'The Plight of James Ridgway, London Bookseller and Publisher, and the Newgate Radicals, 1792–1797', *Wordsworth Circle* 27 (1996), 158–66.
McCalman, Iain, *Radical Underworld: Prophets, Revolutionaries and Pornographers in London, 1795–1840* (Cambridge, 1988; Oxford, 1998).
Macaulay, Thomas Babington, *History of England from the Accession of James II*, 5 vols. (London, 1848).
McElroy, Davis D., *Scotland's Age of Improvement: A Survey of Eighteenth Century Literary Clubs and Societies* (Washington, 1969).
MacFaul, Tom, *Male Friendship in Shakespeare and his Contemporaries* (Cambridge, 2007).
McGirr, Elaine, *Heroic Mode and Political Crisis, 1660–1745* (Newark, 2009).
MacGuire, Nancy Klein, *Regicide and Restoration: English Tragicomedy, 1660–1681* (Cambridge, 1992).
McKellar, Elizabeth, *The Birth of Modern London* (Manchester, 1999).
McKendrick, Neil, John Brewer and J. H. Plumb, eds., *The Birth of a Consumer Society. The Commercialization of Eighteenth-Century England* (London, 1992).
Mansfield, Harvey C. Jr., *Statesmanship and Party Government: A Study of Burke and Bolingbroke* (Chicago, 1965).

Martin, Ann, 'Tea Tables Overturned: Rituals of Power and Place in Colonial America', in *Furnishing the Eighteenth Century: What Furniture can tell us about the European and American Past*, ed. Dena Goodman and Kathryn Norberg (London, 2007), 169–81.

Martz, Louis L., *The Later Career of Tobias Smollett* (New Haven, CT, 1942).

Mee, Jon, *Conversable Worlds: Literature, Contention, and Community 1762 to 1830* (Oxford, 2011).

——, *Print, Publicity, and Popular Radicalism in the 1790s: The Laurel of Liberty* (Cambridge, 2016).

——, 'Thomas Spence and the London Corresponding Society, 1792–1795', in *Thomas Spence: The Poor Man's Revolutionary*, ed. Alastair Bonnett and Keith Armstrong (London, 2014), 53–63.

Mitchell, L. G., *Charles James Fox* (Oxford, 1992).

——, ed., *The French Revolution: 1790–94*, vol. VIII of *The Writings and Speeches of Edmund Burke*, general editor Paul Langford (Oxford, 1989).

Montandon, Alain, *Dictionnaire raisonné de la politesse et du savoir-vivre* (Paris, 1995).

Moran, Mary Catherine, '"The Commerce of the Sexes": Gender and the Social Sphere on Scottish Enlightenment Accounts of Civil Society', in *Paradoxes of Civil Society: New Perspectives on Modern German and British History*, ed. Frank Trentmann, revised second edition (New York and Oxford, 2003), 61–84.

Morieux, Renaud, *Une mer pour deux royaumes. La Manche, frontière franco-anglaise XVIIe–XVIIIe siècles* (Rennes, 2008).

Morineau, Michel, 'La Douceur d'être inclus', in Françoise Thélamon (ed.), *Sociabilité, pouvoirs et société. Actes du colloque de Rouen, 24–26 nov. 1983* (Rouen, 1987), 19–32.

Neufield, Matthew, *The Civil Wars After 1660: Public Remembering in Late Stuart England* (Woodbridge, 2013).

Newman, Ian David, 'Tavern Talk Literature, Politics and Conviviality' (Unpublished Ph.D. Diss., University of California, Los Angeles, 2013).

Newman, A. N., 'Communication: The Political Patronage of Frederick Lewis, Prince of Wales', *Historical Journal* 1, no. 1 (1958), 68–75.

Norman, Larry F., 'Modern Identity and the Sociable Self in the Late Seventeenth Century', *Nottingham French Studies* 47, no. 3 (Autumn 2008), 34–44.

O'Brien, Conor Cruise, *The Great Melody: A Thematic Biography and Commented Anthology of Edmund Burke* (London, 1992).

O'Gorman, Frank, 'Campaign Rituals and Ceremonies: The Social Meaning of Elections in England', *Past and Present* 135 (1992), 79–115.

Parker, G. F., *Johnson's Shakespeare* (Oxford, 1989).

Pears, Ian, *The Discovery of Painting: The Growth of Interest in the Arts in England, 1680–1768* (New Haven, CT, 1988).

Pearson, Roger, *Voltaire Almighty: A Life in Pursuit of Freedom* (London, 2005).

Peck, Linda Levy, *Consuming Splendour: Society and Culture in Seventeenth-Century England* (Cambridge, 2005).

Peltonen, Markku, 'Politeness and Whiggism, 1688–1732', *Historical Journal* 48, no. 2 (June 2005), 391–414.

—, *The Duel in Early Modern England: Civility, Politeness and Honour* (Cambridge, 2003).
Perkins, Pam, *Women Writers and the Edinburgh Enlightenment* (Amsterdam, 2010).
—, '"A Constellation of Scottish Genius": Networks of Exchange in Late 18th- and Early 19th-Century Edinburgh', *Lumen* 34 (2015), 39–54.
Pevsner, Nikolaus, *Les Académies d'art*, trans. Jean-Jacques Bretou (Paris, 1990).
Philp, Mark, 'The Fragmented Ideology of Reform', in *The French Revolution and British Popular Politics*, ed. Mark Philp (Cambridge, 1991), 50–77.
—, 'Vulgar Conservatism, 1792–3', *English Historical Review* 110 (1995), 42–69.
Pickering, Paul A. and Michael T. Davis, *Unrespectable Radicals? Popular Politics in the Age of Reform* (Aldershot, England and Burlington, VT, 2008).
Pincus, Steven, '"Coffee Politicians Does Create": Coffeehouses and Restoration Political Culture', *Journal of Modern History* 67, no. 4 (December 1995), 807–34.
Plassart, Anna, *The Scottish Enlightenment and the French Revolution* (Cambridge, 2015).
Plumb, John H., *The Origins of Political Stability, England 1675–1725* (Boston, 1967).
Pocock, John G. A., *The Ancient Constitution and the Feudal Law: A Study of English historical Thought in the Seventeenth Century. A Reissue with a Retrospect*, 1987 (Cambridge, 1990).
—, 'The Political Economy of Burke's Analysis of the French Revolution', 1982, *Virtue, Commerce, and History*, 1985 (Cambridge, 1991), 193–212.
—, *Virtue, Commerce, and History: Essays on Political Thought and History, Chiefly in the Eighteenth Century* (Cambridge, 1976).
Porset, Charles, *Les Philalèthes et les Convents de Paris, Une politique de la folie* (Paris, 1996).
Porset, Charles and Marie-Cécile Révauger, eds., *Le Monde maçonnique des Lumières (Europe/the Americas & Colonies). Dictionnaire prosopographique* (Paris, 2013).
Porter, Roy, *English Society in the Eighteenth Century*, second edition (Harmondsworth, 1990).
—, *Enlightenment Britain and the Creation of the Modern World* (London, 2000).
Prendergast, Amy, *Literary Salons Across Britain and Ireland in the Long Eighteenth Century* (Basingstoke, 2015).
Price, Richard, *British Society 1680–1880, Dynamism, Containment and Change* (Cambridge, 1999).
Rancière, Jacques, *Les Mots de l'histoire: Essai de politique du savoir* (Paris, 1992).
Rasmussen, Steen Eiler, *London, the Unique City* (London, 1937).
Rendall, Jane 'Bluestockings and Reviewers: Gender, Power and Culture in Britain, c. 1800–1830', *Nineteenth-Century Contexts* 26 (2004), 355–74.
—, '"Women that would plague me with rational conversation": Aspiring Women and Scottish Whigs c. 1790–1830', in *Women, Gender and Enlightenment*, ed. Sarah Knott and Barbara Taylor (Basingstoke, 2005), 326–47.
—, 'Gender, Philanthropy and Civic Identities in Edinburgh, 1795–1830', in *The Routledge History Handbook of Gender and the Urban Experience*, ed. Deborah Simonton (London, 2017), 213–14.

Riley, Margaret, 'The Club at the Temple Coffee House Revisited', *Archives of Natural History* 33, no. 1 (April 2006), 90–100.
Robelin, Roger de, *'Die Freimaurerei in Schweden im 18 Jahrhundert', Gold und Himmelblau. Die Freimaurerei, Zeitloses Ideal* (Abo, 1993).
Roper, Michael and John Tosh, 'Hegemonic Masculinity and the History of Gender', in *Masculinities in Politics and War: Gendering Modern History*, ed. S. Dudink, K. Hagemann and John Tosh (Manchester, 2004), 41–58.
Russell, Gillian, *Women, Sociability and Theatre in Georgian London* (Cambridge, 2007).
Russell, Gillian and Clara Tuite, eds., *Romantic Sociability: Social Networks and Literary Culture in Britain 1770–1840* (Cambridge, 2002).
Saul, Nigel, *For Honour and Fame: Chivalry in England, 1066–1500* (London, 2011).
Schellenberg, Betty, *Literary Coteries and the Making of Modern Print Culture, 1740–1790* (Cambridge, 2016).
Schmid, Susanne, *British Literary Salons of the Late Eighteenth and Early Nineteenth Centuries* (Basingstoke and New York, 2013).
Schneewind, J. B., *Essays on the History of Moral Philosophy* (Oxford, 2009).
Scrivener, Michael Henry, *Seditious Allegories: John Thelwall and Jacobin Writing* (University Park, PA, 2001).
Shepard, Alexandra, *Meanings of Manhood in Early Modern England* (Oxford, 2006).
Siegel, Jerrold, *The Idea of the Self. Thought and Experience in Western Europe since the Seventeenth Century* (Cambridge, 2005).
Simmel, Georg, *Soziologie* (Berlin, 1908).
——, 'The Sociology of Sociability', in *Simmel on Culture. Selected Writings*, ed. David Frisby and Mike Featherstone (London, 1997), 120–9.
Sirota, Brent S., *The Christian Monitors: The Church of England and the Age of Benevolence, 1680–1730* (New Haven, CT, 2014).
Smith, E. A., *Whig Principles and Party Politics: Earl Fitzwilliam and the Whig Party, 1748–1833* (Manchester, 1975).
Spacks, Patricia Meyer, *Gossip* (New York, 1985).
Spedding, Patrick, *A Bibliography of Eliza Haywood* (London, 2004).
Speier, Hans, 'Historical Development of Public Opinion', *American Journal of Sociology* 55, no. 4 (January 1950), 376–88.
Stephen, Leslie, *English Literature and Society in the Eighteenth Century* (London, 1904).
Stevenson, Christine, *The City and the King: Architecture and Politics in Restoration* (London and New Haven, 2013).
Stone, Lawrence, 'The Residential Development of the West End of London in the Seventeenth Century', in *After the Reformation*, ed. B. Malament (Manchester, 1980), 167–212.
Strohm, Reinhard, *Essays on Handel and Italian Opera* (Cambridge, 1985).
Strosetzki, Christoph and Bernard Bray, *Art de la lettre, art de la conversation à l'époque classique en France* (Paris, 1995).
Talmon, Jacob Laib, *The Origins of Totalitarian Democracy* (London, 1952).
Tapsell, Grant, ed., *The Later Stuart Church, 1660–1714* (Manchester, 2012).

Taylor, Brandon, *Art for the Nation: Exhibitions and the London Public 1741–2001* (New Brunswick, NJ, 1999).
Taylor, P. J., M. Hoyler and D. M. Evans, 'A Geohistorical Study of "The Rise of Modern Science": Mapping Scientific Practice through Urban Networks, 1500–1900', *Minerva* 46, no. 4 (2008), 391–410.
Thale, Mary, ed., *Selections from the Papers of the London Corresponding Society, 1792–1799* (Cambridge and New York, 1983).
Thomson, Ann, Simon Burrows and Edmond Dziembowski, eds., with Sophie Audidière, *Cultural Transfers: France and Britain in the Long Eighteenth Century* (Oxford, 2010).
Thompson, E. P., *The Making of the English Working Class* (Harmondsworth, 1980).
Thornton, Peter and Maurice Tomlin, *The Furnishing and Decoration of Ham House* (London, 1980).
Todd, Janet, *Mary Wollstonecraft: A Revolutionary Life* (London, 2000).
Trolander, Paul, *Literary Sociability in Early Modern England: The Epistolary Record* (Lanham, 2014).
Turberville, Arthur S., *Johnson's England, an Account of the Life and Manners of his Age*, 2 vols. (Oxford, 1933, 1965).
Turner, James Grantham, *Libertines and Radicals in Early Modern London: Sexuality, Politics and Literary Culture, 1630–1685* (Cambridge, 2002).
Van Damme, Stéphane, *Descartes. Essai d'histoire culturelle d'une grandeur philosophique (XVIIe–XXe siècle)* (Paris, 2002).
Vicinus, Martha, *Separate Spheres* (Bloomington, 1974).
Vickery, Amanda, *Behind Closed Doors: At Home in Georgian England* (New Haven, CT, 2009).
——, 'Golden Age to Separate Spheres? A Review of the Categories and Chronology of English Women's History', *Historical Journal* 36, no. 2 (June 1993), 383–414.
——, *The Gentleman's Daughter. Women's Lives in Georgian England* (New Haven, CT, 2003).
Vivian, Frances, *A Life of Frederick, Prince of Wales, 1707–1751*, ed. Roger White (Lewiston, 2006).
Wahrman, Dror, *The Making of the Modern Self. Identity and Culture in Eighteenth-Century England* (New Haven, CT and London, 2004).
Waith, Eugene M., *Ideas of Greatness: Heroic Drama in England* (London, 1971).
Walker, Matthew F., 'The Limits of Collaboration: Robert Hooke, Christopher Wren and the Designing of the Monument to the Great Fire of London', *Notes & Records of the Royal Society* 65 (2011), 121–43.
Walker, Sue, 'The Manners of the Page: Prescription and Practice in the Visual Organization of Correspondence', *Huntington Library Quarterly* 66, no. 3/4 (2003), 307–29.
Wall, Cynthia, *The Literary and Cultural Spaces of Restoration* (Cambridge, 1998).
Warner, Pamela J., 'Connoisseur vs Amateur: A Debate over Taste and Authority in Late Eighteenth-Century Paris', in *Penser l'art dans la seconde moitié du XVIIIe siècle: théorie, critique, philosophie, histoire*, ed. Carl Magnusson and Christian Michel (Paris, 2013), 177–200.

Weatherill, Lorna, *Consumer Behaviour and Material Culture in Britain, 1660–1760* (London, 1996).
Weinstein, Benjamin, 'Popular Constitutionalism and the London Corresponding Society', *Albion: A Quarterly Journal Concerned with British Studies* 34 (2002), 37–57.
Werkmeister, Lucyle, *The London Daily Press, 1772–1792* (Lincoln, NE, 1963).
Whyman, Susan, *The Pen and the People: English Letter Writers 1660–1800* (Oxford, 2009).
Withington, Phil, 'Company and Sociability in Early Modern England', *Social History* 32, no. 3 (2007), 291–307.
——, *Society in Early Modern England: The Vernacular Origins of Some Powerful Ideas* (Cambridge, 2010).
Zevi, Bruno, *Saper Vedere la Città* (Turin, 1960).

Index

Académie des Sciences, 114
Académie Royale de Peinture, 89, 91, 92, 93, 94, 107
Academies, 4, 89, 92–100, 103, 105–108, 146, 147, 151, 154, 191
Accomplishments, 56, 146, 272
Addison, Joseph, 1, 2, 23, 51, 52, 55, 56, 59, 73, 76, 77, 78, 127, 186, 187, 219
Alexander, William, 64, 101, 194
Alison, Archibald, 163, 167, 168, 171, 181
Amateurs, 91–107
America, 3, 13, 17, 109, 116, 140, 168, 172, 219, 257, 263, 273
Amsterdam, 70, 117, 118, 168, 201, 210
Anderson, Robert, 111, 140, 141, 173
Anne, Queen of Great Britain, 6, 22, 23, 45, 47, 52, 55, 66, 244
Ansbach, Caroline of, wife of George II of Great Britain, 15, 175, 210
Architecture, 5, 6, 10, 11, 13, 17, 20, 25–39, 43, 45, 46, 51, 52, 53, 65, 66, 77, 89, 116, 129, 131, 138, 139, 164–167, 176, 177, 207, 253, 256
Aronson, Nicole, 202
Assembly rooms, 17, 129, 131, 167, 170, 179
Aubrey, John, 45, 46

Bacon, Francis, 43
Badufle, Marjolaine, 240
Baillie, Joanna, 175, 179, 180, 216
Baillie, John, 207
Ballaster, Ros, 217
Balzac, Jean-Louis Guez de, 152, 154
Bannett, Eve Tavor, 145, 151, 158

Banquets, 105, 107, 108, 115, 120, 134
Barbauld, Anna, 172, 175, 180
Barclay, Craig, 225
Barrell, John, 220, 231, 253–258, 265
Barthe, Nicolas Thomas, 104
Barthes, Roland, 135
Bath (Somerset), 11, 12, 122, 127–31, 135, 138, 139, 142, 143, 158, 190
Beaconsfield (Buckinghamshire), 243
Beaumont, John, 104, 221, 234
Beaurepaire, Pierre-Yves, 109–124
Bedford House (London), 29
Bedford, Dukes of, 29, 30
Beguillet, Edme 109
Bellamy, John, 229
Bercé, Yves-Marie, 237, 238
Bergmann, Jörg, 81, 82
Berry, Mary, 181
Black Prince (Edward Plantagenet, Prince of Wales), 205, 206, 208
Black, David, 177
Blessington, Marguerite Gardiner, Countess of, 181
Bluestocking, 73, 74, 163, 164, 165, 167, 168, 170, 172–176, 181
Boileau, Nicolas, 202
Borsay, Peter, 10, 11, 46, 54
Boswell, James, 127, 183, 185–198, 240, 241
Boulogne (France), 115, 132, 133, 134
Bourdieu, Pierre, 57, 61
Boureau, Alain, 151, 153
Bourgeois public sphere, 10, 13, 14, 50, 59, 70, 73, 79, 80, 86, 219, 235, 243, 256

Bourke, Richard, 237, 247
Brady, Robert, 250
Brant, Clare, 151, 159, 200
Bray, Bernard, 151
Brenan, Beaumont, 104
Brest (France), 89, 118, 119, 120–123, 125
Brewer, John, 9, 10, 46, 54, 57, 62, 63, 131
Bristow, Robert, 58
British Empire, 67, 70, 76, 136, 237, 247, 273
Britishness, xv, 2, 4, 5, 6, 46, 59, 60, 64–67, 89, 90, 127, 128, 139, 141, 142, 143, 145, 154–158, 160, 162, 165, 184, 200, 247, 266, 271, 272, 273
Broadhead, Glenn J., 197
Bromwich, David, 241
Brooks's Club, 58, 242
Brown, Callum G., 176
Brown, George, 148, 168
Brown, Thomas, 80, 81
Brunton, Mary, 173, 178, 181
Bryson, Anna, 19
Burke, Edmund, 58, 184, 186, 187, 188, 194, 237–250
Burnet, Gilbert, 247
Burney, Frances, 158
Butler, Gerald J., 164, 175, 239, 248

Caine, Barbara, 209
Campbell, Bruce, 193
Campbell, Duncan, 75
Campbell, Thomas, 170, 173
Canton (China), 70
Capdeville, Valérie, 1–4, 5, 45–67, 186, 271–274
Cappe, Catherine, 179
Caribbean (The), 273
Carmontelle, Louis de, 104, 105, 106
Caroline, of Brandenburg-Ansbach, wife of George II of Great Britain, 210
Carr, Rosalind, 166, 167, 168
Carter, Philip, 56, 139
Caylus, Anne-Claude de Pestels, comte de, 94, 98, 99, 103

Censorship, 14, 47, 50, 86
Chancery Lane (London), 47
Charles II, King of England, Scotland and Ireland, 7, 13, 14, 18, 32, 46, 47
Charmois, Martin de, 93
Chartism, 273
Chesterfield, Earl of (see Stanhope), 57, 147
China, 69, 70, 71, 75, 76
Church of Scotland, 166, 167, 176, 177, 191
Cibber, Colley, 81
Cicero, 152, 153
Clans, 141, 243
Clark, John C. D., 7, 8, 16, 52, 135, 166, 176, 240, 242, 247
Clark, Peter, 46, 50, 51, 52, 107, 165, 220
Clayton, Antony, 219
Cleland, John, 130, 139
Club de l'Entresol, 110
Clubbability, 66, 186
Clubs, *see also under individual clubs*, xv, 1, 2, 4, 5, 6, 10, 13, 23, 45–67, 71, 77, 85, 107, 108, 110, 116, 165, 166, 167, 175, 176, 184, 186, 188, 189, 222, 226, 229, 230, 237, 240, 241, 242, 254, 256, 257, 259, 260, 264, 266, 271, 273
Cochin, Augustin, 94, 237, 238
Cockburn, Alison, 163, 167, 168, 181
Cocoa-Tree Chocolate-House/Club, 49
Coffee, 12, 14, 20, 29, 45–47, 49, 54, 62, 69, 70, 75, 77, 80, 165, 171, 219, 221, 231
Coffeehouses, *see also under individual coffeehouses*, 5, 10–14, 20, 23, 26, 28, 45, 46, 47, 49, 50, 51, 53, 54, 59, 62, 70, 75, 77, 79, 80, 86, 165, 219, 257, 260, 271
Cogan, Thomas, 221
Cohen, Michèle, xiii-xv, 18, 59, 60, 141, 271, 272
Col, Norbert, 184, 237–250
Coleridge, Samuel Taylor, 224, 235
Collège Royal (Paris), 113, 114
Colley, Linda, 18, 24, 49, 81, 273

Collins, Richard, 71, 72
Commerce, *see also Merchants*, 6, 11, 12, 13, 17, 18, 19, 35, 45, 46, 53, 56, 57, 62, 76, 86, 93, 100, 118, 131, 139, 142, 145, 148, 166, 169, 170, 248, 264
Company (notion), 6, 15, 16, 55, 57, 61–64, 66, 72, 73, 118, 135, 141, 146, 147, 158, 162, 183, 185–198, 210, 221, 223, 242, 250, 266
Conduct manuals, 4, 18, 19, 56, 61, 64, 74, 77, 84, 102, 132, 146, 177, 180
Cone, Carl B., 241, 242
Connoisseurs, 89, 91–108
Consumption, 6, 10–13, 16, 20, 45, 51, 54, 57, 69- 72, 74, 75, 77, 79, 84, 86, 131, 132, 135, 138, 227
Conversation, 2, 3, 6, 54, 55, 58, 59, 62, 63, 64, 69, 71–74, 76–80, 82, 84–87, 100, 102, 140, 142, 145, 146, 147, 151, 152, 169, 171, 172, 174, 183, 185–190, 194, 195, 197, 198, 226, 239, 260, 267, 271, 272
Copeland, Thomas W., 243
Cosh, Mary, 170
Cossic-Péricarpin, Annick, 12, 89, 127–144
Cottret, Bernard, 246, 247, 249
Covent Garden (London), 17, 29, 79, 159, 214
Cowan, Brian, 5, 7–24, 47, 51, 70, 219
Coypel, Antoine, 98, 99, 100
Coypel, Charles-Antoine, 98, 99, 100
Cromwell, Oliver, 250
Cruickshanks, Eveline, 246
Cullen, Robert, 194
Cumberland, William, Duke of, 216
Cunningham, Allan, 173
Cuper's Gardens (London), 158
Czennia, Bärbel, 239

Dachez, Hélène, 145, 162
Dant, Adam, 29
Dauphin, Cécile, 151, 153
Davenant, Charles, 39
Davison, Kate, 61
Day, Angel, 153, 154

De Luc, Jean-André, 113
Deane, Seamus, 247
Deffand, Marie de Vichy-Chamrond (or Champrond), marquise du Deffand, 174, 240
Defoe, Daniel, 22, 48, 52, 53, 239, 245
Delmé, Pierre, 58
Descartes, René, 109
Diderot, Denis, 103, 104, 106
Dignum, Charles, 222
Dingley, Robert, 58
Dissenters, 21, 22, 165, 255
Drury Lane (London), 17, 222
Dryden, John, 19, 152, 239
Dundas, Charles, 169, 194, 267, 268
Dundas, Henry, 169, 194, 267, 268
Duthille, Rémy, 184, 219, 226, 231, 251–268

East India Company, 70
Edgeworth, Maria, 172, 175, 180
Edinburgh Magazine (The), 163, 170, 173, 193
Edinburgh Review (The), 164, 170, 173, 174
Edinburgh, 61, 90, 153, 163–181, 191, 193, 194, 219, 265
Edward III, King of England, 205, 206
Edwards, Avery, 203
Effeminacy, 60, 64, 135, 137, 139
Elliot of Minto, Sir Gilbert, 166
Ellis, Markman, 6, 69–86, 165, 219
Enlightenment, 2, 3, 4, 11, 21, 90, 109, 119, 122, 127, 128, 142, 143, 158, 164–170, 172, 174, 175, 176, 248, 274
Epstein, James, 231, 258
Eriksson, Åke, 213

Fashion, 16, 29, 52, 54, 56, 84, 85, 104, 130, 132, 135, 147, 150, 153, 159, 171, 237, 239, 272
Fauquier, William, 58
Fawkes, Isaac, 79
Feltham, John, 225
Ferguson, Adam, 90, 137, 139, 141
Fielding, Thomas, 239, 245

Finn, Margot C., 273
Fletcher, Eliza, 90, 163, 167, 169–181
Foote, Samuel, 191
Fordyce, David, 150
Forster, Georg, 239
Fox, Charles James, 9, 169, 184, 226–232, 243, 244, 246
Francis, Philip, 17, 22, 30, 34, 43, 95, 96, 170, 171, 174, 243, 261, 269
Frederick the Great (Frederick II of Prussia), 239
Frederick, Prince of Wales, 200, 203–211, 213–217, 219, 249
Frederick-Maurice, Prince of Orange, 207, 208, 209
Freemasonry, 4, 109–125, 142, 166, 271
French Revolution, 7, 108, 169, 170, 184, 232, 238, 242, 244, 245, 246, 248, 250, 253, 255, 256, 259, 260, 265, 266, 267
'Friendly enemy', 183, 200–218
Friendship, 12, 54, 55, 64, 73, 78, 90, 93, 97, 98, 100, 102, 110, 113, 131, 140, 142, 148, 152, 153, 155–160, 162, 165, 167, 168, 170–173, 175, 185, 188, 189, 191–195, 197, 199–209, 211, 213–218, 224, 227–229, 242–246, 253, 255, 261, 265
Frost, John, 231, 258
Fry, Elizabeth, 180
Fuchs, Michel, 242, 247, 249
Fulwood, William, 147, 153
Furet, François, 237, 238

Garraway's Coffee-House, 53
Garrick, David, 58, 189, 205
Garside, Peter, 168
Gaskell, Philip, 149
Gender, xiv, 4, 6, 12, 58, 60, 63, 64, 66, 70, 78, 84, 86, 131, 158, 161, 163–181, 183, 185, 200, 202, 271
General Evening Post (The), 229, 230
Gentleman (ideal of), 6, 46, 53, 56, 57, 59, 60, 61, 64, 66, 79, 139, 141, 147, 151, 162, 195, 225
George III, King of Great Britain, 8, 46, 108, 258

Germany, 70, 112, 124, 125, 131, 164, 216
Gerrard, Christine, 203, 204, 210, 217
Gibbon, Edward, 58
Gibbons, Luke, 239, 247
Gignoux, John, 149
Gilmartin, Kevin, 227, 253, 256, 257, 266, 280
Gilpin, William, 90, 145, 160, 161, 162
Globe Tavern, 233
Glorious Revolution, 7, 13, 19, 21, 22, 45, 47, 48, 50, 66, 131, 184, 229, 237, 238, 239, 241, 243–250, 267
Glover, Katherine, 167
Gluckman, Max, 81
Godolphin, Sidney Godolphin, 1st Earl of, 244
Godwin, William, 165, 180
Goldsmith, Oliver, 18, 188, 241, 242, 246
Goodman, Dena, 3, 4, 14, 72, 73, 164
Gordon, Daniel, 3, 18, 30, 172, 219
Gossip, 69, 71, 73, 75, 77, 79, 80, 81–84, 85, 87, 171
Graham, Helen, 173, 174
Graham, Maria, 172
Grahame, James, 170
Grand Lodge of England, 111–114, 116, 119, 120, 121, 125
Grand Orient de France, 111–112, 119, 121
Grand Tour, 132
Grant, Anne, 20, 21, 70, 170–174, 178, 181
Gray, Faith, 179
Great Fire (of London), 25, 36, 37, 38, 40, 51
Green Ribbon Club, 47
Green, Georgina, 220, 231
Green, Lawrence D., 154
Greene, Jack P., 273
Gresham College, 35, 36
Grey Coat School, 179
Guevara, Antonio de, 155
Gwynn, John, 96

Habermas, Jürgen, 2, 13, 14, 50, 59, 70, 73, 74, 79, 80, 81, 86, 219, 226, 234, 235, 236, 255, 256, 260
Halley, Edmund, 42, 54
Hamilton of Bangour, William, 167
Hamilton, Elizabeth, 170–173, 175, 176, 178–181
Harrington, James, 46
Hartley, Robert, 173
Haslett, Moyra, 174, 175
Hawes, William, 221, 222, 224, 225
Hayman, Francis, 95, 96
Haymarket (London), 17, 79, 159
Hays, Mary, 158, 181
Heidegger, John James, 79
Helvetius, 115, 240
Highlands (Scotland), 163, 170
Highmore, Joseph, 97, 107
Hill, Aaron, 209, 210, 211, 214, 215
Hill, Brian W., 22
Hill, John, 148, 154, 156, 200
Hobbes, Thomas, 1
Hodgson, William, 231
Hogarth, William, 33, 63, 72, 107
Hogg, James, 169, 173
Homosocial culture, 4, 6, 58, 59, 64, 66, 90, 165, 166, 175
Hooke, Robert, 25, 37–41
Hornbeak, Katherine Gee, 146, 147, 154
Hospitals, *see also under individual hospitals*, 37, 105, 130, 224
Hume, David, 58, 136, 168
Hyde Park (London), 158
Hypochondria, 194

Illness, 70, 132, 135, 138, 210
Improvement, 1, 52, 54, 59, 63, 78, 82, 84, 130, 133, 147, 149, 154, 166, 179, 184
India, 70, 71, 172
Ingram, Allan, 21, 183, 185–198, 239, 240
Ireland, 2, 7, 17, 20, 165, 168, 179, 184, 239, 242, 247, 249
Irving, William, 153, 155
Italy, 19, 89, 95, 124, 127, 128, 131, 133–136, 139–143

Jacobin Club (Paris), 227, 254, 258, 259, 261, 265, 266
Jacobitism, 19, 24, 117, 204, 220, 247, 248, 249
Jacobs, Eva, 210, 211
Jeffrey, Francis, 170, 171, 172, 174
Johnson, Samuel, 51, 66, 80, 91, 92, 107, 127, 183, 185–191, 193–198, 237, 240, 241, 242
Jonathan's Coffee-House, 53, 62
Jones, Emrys D., 16, 54, 60, 127, 128, 129, 142, 143, 183, 199–218, 245

Kale, Steven, 164
Kant, Immanuel, 60, 183, 199, 200, 202, 203, 218
Kearsley, Catharine, 151
Keen, Maurice, 201
Keir, Elizabeth, 168
Kenyon, John P., 249
Kerhervé, Alain, 1–4, 90, 145–162
Killigrew, Thomas, 84
Kimber, Edward, 157, 158
Kit-Cat Club, 55
Klein, Lawrence E., 17, 18, 23, 55, 56, 57, 205
Knox, Vicesimus, 154
Kramnick, Isaac, 242, 243

L'Estrange, Roger (Sir), 15, 23, 47, 48
La Calprenède, Gautier de Costes, seigneur de, 202
Lalande, Jérôme, 113, 115, 122
Langford, Paul, 11, 245
Langton, Bennett, 188
Le Compte, Louis, 76
Le Goff, Jacques, 250
Leisure, 11, 12, 17, 45, 51, 54, 131, 161
Lennox, Charlotte, 202, 204
Lepan, Géraldine, 240
Letters and letter-writing, 3, 4, 14, 48, 49, 54, 55, 57, 73, 84, 90, 95, 122, 123, 127, 128, 129, 135, 136, 138, 140, 142, 143, 145–162, 163, 164, 170, 173, 174, 175, 179, 187–190, 207, 222, 229, 230, 238, 240, 242, 243, 244, 247, 268, 271

Levees, 171
Lieberman, Max, 201
Lilti, Antoine, 3, 16, 73, 164
Lincoln's Inn Fields (London), 79
Literary Club (or The Club), 107, 186, 188, 189, 237, 241
Lloyd's Coffee-House, 26, 53
Lloyd's Evening Post (The), 231
Lock, Frederick P., 85, 240, 242, 243
Locke, John, 1, 19, 21, 152, 248
Lockhart, John Gibson, 174
Loftis, John, 212
Lombard Street (London), 47, 53
London Corresponding Society (LCS), 184, 233, 251–269
London Gazette (The), 49, 52
London Season, 52, 140, 167
London Tavern, 13, 47, 184, 220–227, 233, 234, 256, 258
London, 2, 4, 5, 6, 7, 11, 12, 13, 16, 17, 18, 19, 23, 25, 27–33, 36, 38–41, 45–60, 65, 66, 69, 70, 71, 72, 77, 89, 91, 92, 96, 97, 105, 106, 107, 111–117, 119, 121, 124, 125, 131, 132, 133, 140, 143, 158, 164–168, 170, 171, 175, 177, 179, 180, 181, 184, 186, 188, 191, 192, 200, 219, 220–227, 231–234, 251–257, 261, 263, 264, 265
Louis XIV, King of France, 17, 93, 239
Loveday, Robert, 202
Lyotard, Jean-François, 234, 236

MacFaul, Tom, 200
MacGuire, Nancy Klein, 205
Mackenzie, Henry, 171
Macky, John, 49
Maclaurin, John, Lord Dreghorn, 194
Maitland, Elizabeth, Duchess of Lauderdale, 71, 194
Mandeville, Bernard de, 57, 199
Manogue, Ralph A., 227
Mansfield, Harvey C., Jr., 128, 249
Marienstras, Élise, 273
Marishall, Jean, 168
Marlborough, John Churchill, 1st Duke of Marlborough, 244

Martichou, Elisabeth, 91–108
Martinet, Marie-Madeleine, 25–44
Masculinity, 18, 58, 63, 64, 66, 70, 90, 141, 161, 162, 163, 165, 170, 200, 202, 271, 272
Masquerades, 17, 79
McCalman, Iain, 220, 257, 258, 259
McElroy, Davis D., 166
McGirr, Elaine, 204, 205
Medicine, 138, 224, 232, 234
Mee, Jon, 2, 229, 231, 255, 257, 260, 263, 264
Merchants, 53, 56, 57, 58, 62, 118, 122
Milton, Andrew Fletcher, Lord, 167
Mist, Nathaniel, 84
Mitchell, Leslie G., 193, 242, 243
Montagu, Elizabeth, 73, 181
Montesquieu, Charles-Louis de Secondat de, 240, 272
Montgomery, Richard, 193, 194
Montpellier (France), 89, 134, 135, 138
Monument (The) (London), 37, 38, 109
Moran, Mary Catherine, 166
Morning Chronicle (The), 231
Morning Post and Gazetteer (The), 231
Motteux, Peter-Antony (Pierre-Antoine), 75, 76
Muralt, Béat-Louis de, 272
Murray, Alexander, 194
Murrray, John, 170

Naples (Italy), 51, 111
Napoleonic Wars, 232, 245
National character, 4, 18, 32, 60, 66, 89, 100, 109, 110, 112, 115, 123, 128, 135, 136, 138, 139, 141, 143, 159, 164, 165, 167, 168, 171, 173, 174, 184, 223, 224, 232, 247, 253, 254, 264, 265, 267, 271, 272, 273
Networks, 2, 5, 17, 25–29, 31, 37, 38, 39, 41, 42, 43, 49, 53, 58, 66, 89, 90, 140, 165, 167, 171, 172, 175, 179, 181, 253, 254, 256–259, 271, 273
Newbery, John, 152, 156
Newman, Aubrey N., 203
Newman, David, 256

Newman, Gerald, 18
Newman, Ian, 184, 219–236, 258, 264
Newspapers/periodicals, *see also
    under individual names*, 4, 17, 22,
    51, 56, 74, 76–79, 87, 110, 149, 150,
    152, 163, 169, 170, 180, 194, 196,
    211, 219, 221, 223–227, 231, 234,
    235, 243, 266
Nice (France), 89, 129, 131, 133, 135, 140
Norfolk, Charles Howard, 11th Duke of,
    220, 222, 231

O'Brien, Conor Cruise, 242
O'Gorman, Frank, 224, 225, 234
October Club, 48
Optics, 37, 39, 40, 105
Orford, Earl of (*see Walpole, Horace*),
    244
Ovington, John, 74, 75
Owen, Robert, 180
Oxford, 37
Ozinda's Coffee-House, 49

Paine, Thomas, 184, 226, 228, 229, 233,
    246, 251, 252, 266
Panmure, Margaret, Countess of, 167
Paris (France), 3, 11, 51, 73, 89, 91, 92,
    99, 109–112, 114–118, 123, 124, 163,
    164, 191, 209, 240, 254
Parker, Graham F., 198
Pasquin, Anthony (*see Williams, John*),
    105, 106
Paterson, William, 214, 215, 216
Pearson, Roger, 210
Peddie, James, 177
Pepys, Samuel, 40, 46, 51
Perkins, Pam, 168, 172, 173
Pernety, Antoine-Joseph, 91, 92
Petty, William, 39, 46
Piggott, Charles, 231
Piles, Roger de, 94, 95, 98, 100, 101, 102
Pincus, Steven, 7, 14, 18, 45, 47
Pindar, Peter (*see Wolcot, John*), 105,
    106
Piozzi, Hester (*see Thrale, Hester*), 188,
    190, 242, 243

Pitt, William, the Younger, 8, 224, 228,
    232, 254, 266, 267, 268
Plassart, Anna, 169, 170
Playfair, John, 171
Pleasure gardens, 5, 10, 11, 13, 23, 110,
    131, 133, 158
Pliny, the Younger, 152, 153
Plumb, John H., 10, 23, 24, 54, 131
Pocock, John G. A., 55, 56, 240, 242,
    248, 250
Politeness, 3, 6, 10, 11, 17–20, 23, 46,
    55, 56, 57, 61, 62, 63, 66, 69–73, 76,
    78, 79, 84, 85, 134, 139, 142, 146–150,
    152, 153, 163–167, 169, 171, 173, 175,
    177, 179, 181, 205, 224, 258, 272
Politics, 1, 3–17, 20–24, 30, 39, 45–51,
    53, 55, 56, 58, 64, 65, 66, 70, 73, 80,
    86, 87, 107, 108, 110, 111, 122, 131,
    136, 137, 138, 142, 143, 164, 165, 167–
    170, 173, 174, 175, 179, 181, 183, 184,
    200, 201, 203, 204, 207, 209–215,
    217, 219, 220, 225–230, 232, 233, 235,
    237, 238, 239, 241–269, 273
Pont, Charles-Jean-François de, 242
Poor relief, 29, 132, 176, 178
Pope, Alexander, 85, 152
Porter, Roy, 8
Prendergast, Amy, 165
Price, Richard (Dr.), 50, 242, 247, 250
Prisoner, 204–209, 212, 217
Privacy, 2, 4, 10, 23, 30, 50, 58, 59, 60,
    64, 69, 70, 71, 73, 78, 80, 86, 96–99,
    137, 142, 151, 174, 175, 183, 185,
    196, 204, 223, 224, 225, 230, 231,
    233–236, 242, 243, 244, 256, 258
Processions, 31, 32, 35, 47, 222
Public opinion, 13, 14, 15, 45, 47, 49, 50,
    59, 65, 70, 74, 85, 86, 219, 226, 235,
    251
Publicity (public sphere), 3, 13, 14, 17,
    20, 45, 50, 59, 69, 70, 71, 73, 74, 79,
    80, 83, 86, 106, 221, 235, 256, 258,
    260, 268
Puget de la Serre, Jean, 153, 154
Pump rooms, 11, 129, 130

302 Index

Queen Street Academy, 95, 101

Radicalism, 16, 107, 124, 165, 184, 219, 220, 223, 226, 227, 231, 232, 233, 251, 255–258, 260, 261, 269, 273
Ramsay, Allan, 167
Ramsay, Andrew, 117
Ramsay, George, 8th Earl of Dalhousie, 191
Ramsay, William, 56
Rancière, Jacques, 250
Ranelagh (London), 131, 157, 222
Rasmussen, S. R., 27, 28
Religion, 8, 9, 16, 20, 21, 22, 24, 47, 74, 86, 134, 135, 148, 149, 176, 180, 190, 192, 201, 212, 213, 239, 245–248, 257, 259
Rendall, Jane, 90, 163–180
Restoration, 4–15, 17–27, 29–33, 35–41, 43, 45, 46, 47, 50, 51, 52, 55, 66, 71, 74
Reynolds, Joshua (Sir), 58, 63, 65, 100, 102, 106, 107, 186, 188, 191, 195
Rich, John, 79
Richardson, Jonathan, 92, 100, 101, 102, 106, 107
Richardson, Mary, 171, 173, 174, 175, 177, 180
Richardson, Samuel, 145, 155, 156, 159, 162
Ridgway, James, 227
Rituals, 58, 72, 89, 105, 119, 121, 129, 141, 142, 184, 201, 206, 220, 223, 224, 225, 228, 230, 234, 251, 257, 268
Robert, Adair, 229
Roberts, James, 78
Robertson, William, 3, 154
Romanticism, 2, 8, 17, 135, 164, 165, 173, 175, 208, 231, 235, 253, 256, 257, 258, 273, 274
Rota Club, 46
Rousseau, George, 200
Rousseau, Jean-Jacques, 239, 240, 248
Royal Academy Club, 108
Royal Academy of Arts, 91, 95, 97, 105, 106, 107
Royal Exchange, 36, 53

Royal Humane Society, 184, 220, 221, 224, 225, 234
Royal Society Club (Club of Royal Philosophers), 54, 58
Royal Society, 39, 41, 42, 54, 113, 114, 116, 122
Rozier, François, 113
Russell family, 2, 17, 29, 30, 86, 165, 175, 231, 258, 280
Russell Gillian, 2, 17, 86, 165, 175, 231, 258, 274

Salons, 2, 3, 13, 73, 74, 90, 103, 104, 107, 116, 164, 165, 167, 168, 174, 181, 184, 237, 240
Saul, Nigel, 201
Schmid, Susanne, 74
Schneewind, Jerome B., 199
Science, 25, 26, 39, 41, 42, 43, 54, 55, 92, 100, 116, 152, 170, 195
Scotland, 7, 89, 90, 111, 114, 117, 127, 142, 143, 166, 167, 168, 171–174, 176, 177, 179, 180, 186, 187, 191, 196, 219, 265, 271
Scott, Walter, 2, 163, 167, 171, 172, 173
Scudéry, Madeleine de, 202
Selfishness, xiii, 1, 202, 203
Sensibility, 274
Seven Years' War, 128, 158
Shackleton, Mary, 243
Shaftesbury, Anthony Ashley Cooper, Earl of, 17, 19, 47, 55, 56, 199
Shakespeare, William, 198, 200, 217
Sheridan, Richard Brinsley, 58
Siegel, Jerrold, 60, 61
Simmel, Georg, 2, 16, 63, 128
Sloane, Hans, 54
Smith, Adam, 61, 199
Smith, Ernest A., 229
Smith, Nigel, 219
Smith, Thomas, 16
Smollett, Tobias, 89, 90, 127–143, 239, 245
Smyrna Coffee-House, 49
Snow, John (Dr.), 132
Social contract, 1, 237, 239

Society for the Recovery of Persons Apparently Drowned, 221
Society of Dilettanti, 63, 65, 95, 107
Somers, John, 1st Baron Somers, 244
Spas, *see Watering places*, 11, 12, 13, 130
Spectator (The), xiii, 2, 23, 51, 52, 55, 56, 59, 62, 70, 73, 76, 77, 78, 79, 80
Spelman, Sir Henry, 249, 250
Spence, Elizabeth Isabella, 163, 257, 264
St Andrew St John, 230
St Guy's hospital, 224
St James's Coffee-House, 49
St James's Park/Square/Street, 48, 49, 52, 53, 79, 116, 158, 163, 192
St Thomas's hospital, 224
Stanhope, Philip Dormer, Earl of Chesterfield, 57, 147
Star (The), 222, 227
Steele, Richard, 23, 51, 56, 71, 73, 76, 77, 78, 181, 194
Sterne, Laurence, 141
Stewart, Dugald, 172, 175
Stewart, Helen, 172
Strange, Robert, 95
Strohm, Reinhard, 214
Strosetzki, Christoph, 151
Stuart, Margaret, 188
Stuarts, 7, 9–14, 16–23, 50, 164, 249
Sultan Saladin, 201, 204
Sun (The), 226, 227, 228, 229, 230
Sunderland, Robert Spencer, 2nd Earl of, 55, 244
Swift, Jonathan, 22, 48, 49, 152

Talmon, Jacob Laib, 238
Taste, 71, 72, 79, 92, 94, 96, 100–103, 106, 132, 153, 159, 169
Tate, Nahum, 72, 75, 76
Tatler (The), 51, 52, 56, 71
Tavernier, John, 146
Taverns, *see also under individual taverns*, 11, 13, 23, 45, 48, 50, 59, 107, 116, 184, 186, 219, 222–225, 227, 228, 252, 256, 257, 259, 260, 263, 264, 266, 268, 269, 271

Tea (drink, utensils, service, equipage), 6, 10, 69–87, 110, 167, 170, 171, 188, 192, 271
Tea-table, xv, 6, 10, 69–87, 271
Temple Bar, 33
Temple Coffee-House Botanical Club, 54
Thatched House Tavern, 116
Theatre Royal (Edinburgh), 167
Theatres, 5, 10, 11, 12, 17, 23, 37, 79, 81, 86, 110, 115, 167, 170, 204, 210, 211, 214, 258
Thelwall, John, 184, 220, 221, 223, 224, 231–235, 258, 259, 263, 266
Thicknesse, Philip, 143
Thompson, Edward P., 16, 224, 252–256, 258, 263, 267
Thompson, Judith, 224, 273
Thomson, James, 212, 213, 214, 216
Thrale, Hester (*see Piozzi*), 188, 190, 242, 243
Tiberias, Hugh, Count of, 201
Times (The), 55, 212, 222–227, 231, 259
Toasting, 55, 58, 184, 219–222, 224, 226, 230–235, 257, 258, 264, 266, 268
Tocqueville, Alexis de, 238
Todd, Janet, 223
Tone, Matilda, 173, 175
Toryism, 9, 19, 20, 22, 23, 24, 48, 49, 60, 146, 170, 173, 174, 190, 210, 241, 245, 248
Toulon (France), 134
Townshend, Charles, 146, 148, 149
True Briton (The), 222, 226, 231
Tuite, Clara, 2, 17, 165, 175, 231, 258, 280
Tunbridge Wells, 11, 12, 158
Turk's Head Coffee-House/Tavern, 46, 107, 186

Universities, 3, 12, 28, 35, 36, 43, 54, 77, 113, 119, 123, 146, 154, 162, 166, 171, 172, 176, 225, 253, 256, 258, 263, 265
'Unsociable sociability', 60, 183, 199–218
Urban renaissance, 11, 13, 17, 20, 51
Utrecht (Treaty of), 52

Van Aken, Joseph, 72
Van Hulst, Henri 94
Vauxhall (London), 13, 131, 157, 158, 222
Verkoje, Nicolaes, 72
Versailles (Treaty of), 94, 109
Vesey, Elizabeth, 74, 165
Virtuosi of St Luke, 95, 107
Vivian, Frances, 203
Voltaire, 116, 127, 209, 210, 211, 240
Voluntary associations, 50, 90, 165, 176
Voyer de Paulmy, René-Louis de, 2ème marquis d'Argenson, 110

Waith, Eugene M., 201
Walker, Sue, 39, 149
Wallace, James, 146, 148, 149, 176
Walpole, Horace (*see Orford*), 58, 95, 105
Walpole, Robert, 8, 23, 24, 203, 204, 207, 210, 212, 249
Warsaw (Poland), 111
Watelet, Claude-Henri, 94, 103
Watering places, *see Spas*, 11, 12, 13, 129, 130, 131, 135, 157, 158
Werkmeister, Lucyle, 227
West End, 29, 52, 53, 54

West, Gilbert, 29, 33, 45, 52, 53, 54, 133, 205, 206, 207, 208, 216
Westminster (London), 12, 48, 52, 139, 263
Wharton, Philip, Duke of, 47, 244
Whig Club, 226–230, 242
Whiggism, 19, 22, 23, 47, 49, 55, 170, 173, 174, 184, 226–230, 241, 242, 244, 245
White's Club/Chocolate-House, 58
Whyman, Susan, 150
Wilkes, John, 190, 192, 193, 194, 226
William III, King of England, Scotland and Ireland, 32
William of Orange, 7, 207, 208, 209, 244, 247
Williams, Harold, 49
Williams, John (*pseud. Anthony Pasquin*), 105, 108
Wilson, John, 14, 24, 75, 163, 173
Withington, Phil, 15, 16, 62, 66
Wolcot, John (*alias. Peter Pindar*), 105, 108
Wollstonecraft, Mary, 158, 223
Wordsworth, William, 224, 227, 235
Wren, Christopher, 25, 37, 39, 40

York Female Friendly Society, 179

www.ingramcontent.com/pod-product-compliance
Lightning Source LLC
Chambersburg PA
CBHW051600230426
43668CB00013B/1927